EUROPEANISATION OF ACCESS TO JUSTICE IN ENVIRONMENTAL MATTERS

This book analyses the ways in which Article 9 of the Aarhus Convention enables environmental access to justice in the Balkans, a region at the epicentre of extreme climate change events.

Adopting a law-in-context approach, the chapters explore national cultures and driving forces shaping the implementation of Aarhus standards in Albania, Croatia, North Macedonia, Romania, Slovenia and Serbia, paving the way for their comparative assessment.

The book combines EU law and the case law of the European Court of Human Rights with the bottom-up Europeanisation brought about by rising environmental protests and the activism of civil society organisations in the region. In doing so, it explores the extent to which these Balkan countries comply with requirements stemming from Article 9 of the Aarhus Convention, and whether, despite national differences, it is possible to talk about Europeanisation of access to justice in environmental matters.

The interdisciplinary approach and geographical scope of the book make it an important read for academics and practitioners, as well as for the civil society sector and policy makers grappling with the normative and practical challenges around environmental access to justice – both in and beyond Europe.

Europeanisation of Access to Justice in Environmental Matters

The Aarhus Convention in the Balkans

Edited by
Bojana Todorović
and
Roberto Caranta

• HART •
OXFORD • LONDON • NEW YORK • NEW DELHI • SYDNEY

HART PUBLISHING

Bloomsbury Publishing Plc

Kemp House, Chawley Park, Cumnor Hill, Oxford, OX2 9PH, UK

1385 Broadway, New York, NY 10018, USA

Bloomsbury Publishing Ireland Limited, 29 Earlsfort Terrace, Dublin 2, D02 AY28, Ireland

HART PUBLISHING, the Hart/Stag logo, BLOOMSBURY and the Diana logo are trademarks of Bloomsbury Publishing Plc

First published in Great Britain 2025

A catalogue record for this book is available from the British Library.

A catalogue record for this book is available from the Library of Congress.

Library of Congress Control Number: 2025930948

ISBN: HB: 978-1-50997-962-2
ePDF: 978-1-50997-964-6
ePub: 978-1-50997-963-9

Typeset by Compuscript Ltd, Shannon

For product safety related questions contact productsafety@bloomsbury.com

To find out more about our authors and books visit www.hartpublishing.co.uk. Here you will find extracts, author information, details of forthcoming events and the option to sign up for our newsletters.

This book is dedicated to all those brave individuals and organisations – in the Balkans and beyond – who persevere in the battle to preserve and improve access to justice in environmental matters even under unfavourable conditions.

FOREWORD

Environmental law, an area which is densely regulated by the EU, has been for quite some time a rewarding subject of 'EU comparative lawyering', a methodology that combines the study of EU law with a comparative law approach. In a context where EU environmental law is in several respects dependent on national legislative, administrative and judicial institutions, comparative research helps us to understand the impact of EU environmental law on national law and how EU environmental operates in domestic legal orders. In turn, the results of this type of research often reveal problems and gaps that exist in that law and, as such, the research may assist the EU institutions in developing appropriate answers to the problems and lacunae. This method serves well the development of environmental law in the EU and its Member States.

Like in other areas of EU law, the combination of EU and comparative law research and exchange of information in environmental law often takes place in the framework of –informal or institutionalised – academic working groups or fora set up by legal practitioners. An example of the former is the Avosetta Group (www.avosetta.oer2.rw.fau.de). As to the latter, the 'EU Forum of Judges for the Environment' (EUFJE) (www.eufje.org) can be mentioned. Important comparative law material is often made available through publications, usually on the respective websites.

The present volume is also the result of a joint project of a number of authors gathering and writing together under the umbrella 'Implementation of Article 9 of the Aarhus Convention in the Balkans'.

The Aarhus Convention, adopted within the framework of the UN Economic Commission for Europe, is based on the idea that every person has the right to live in an environment adequate to their health and well-being. Moreover, these persons have the duty –individually and in association with others – to protect and improve the environment for the benefit of both present and future generations. The implementation of the Aarhus Convention's objective rests on three pillars which are interconnected: in environmental matters citizens must (i) have access to information, (ii) be entitled to participate in decision-making, and (iii) have access to justice. Article 9 of the Convention is the central provision of the third pillar.

The EU is party to the Aarhus Convention and, as such, the Convention is part of EU law. Furthermore, the EU has adopted implementing measures both regarding the EU institutions and bodies (the Aarhus Regulation) and regarding the Member States (two directives, inserting inter alia new provisions into already existing directives). In various judgments, the Court of Justice of the European

Union has interpreted and applied Article 9 of the Convention either directly or through implementing EU legislation. In particular, outstanding judgments concern the standing of environmental non-governmental organisations (NGOs). In the Austro-German legal tradition, for instance, the standing of NGOs was extremely limited due to the requirement that the rule allegedly violated should protect individual rights of the person concerned. Therefore NGOs, which litigate in the interest of the general public, were denied standing. However, such rules are incompatible with Article 9 of the Convention, which requires wide access to justice. In brief, the Court's case law on Article 9 has considerably facilitated the access to the courts of environmental organisations.

The present volume fits into the EU comparative law tradition briefly indicated above. However, it broadens the perspective in various respects. In the first place, it does not focus only on law and legal analysis; it also addresses broader historical, cultural, societal and political context in which the law has to operate. This approach contributes greatly to a better understanding of the failures, success and challenges in meeting the Aarhus standards of access to justice in the Balkans.

Second, the volume goes beyond the EU comparative law approach concerning the EU and (some) Member States. While the first chapter examines how the provisions on access to justice laid down in Article 9 of the Aarhus Convention have been interpreted at the Convention level (by the Aarhus Convention Compliance Committee and in the Aarhus Convention Implementation Guide) and at the EU level, the second chapter turns to the Council of Europe and, in particular, to the case law of the European Court of Human Rights (ECtHR). It addresses, inter alia, the question in how far the case law of the ECtHR concerning the protection of the environment takes on board Article 9 of the Aarhus Convention in order to determine the scope of the right of access to justice in environmental matters. In fact, these chapters analyse the intricate interaction of EU law, the Aarhus Convention and its interpretation by the Aarhus Convention Compliance Committee (ACCC), and the case law of the ECtHR. It is mainly through these three channels that influence is exerted on the environmental access to justice in the countries of the Balkans. Some of these are EU Member States, while some other countries are still at a pre-accession stage and from a normative point of view are bound by the European Convention on Human Rights and the Aarhus Convention. However, as far as the latter countries are concerned, the pre-accession strategy has considerable effects for activities by civil society. The Aarhus standards have boosted their actions and gave an important impetus to 'environmental activism' by the civil society.

Six chapters in this volume concern three EU Member States and three candidates. The chapters contain a wealth of material on the normative and practical realities of the access to justice in environmental matters in these countries, making it patently clear that compliance at the normative level is one thing, but effective implementation in practice is another.

It is mainly on the basis of these 'national' chapters that the final contribution of this volume draws the lines together in a comparative analysis, pointing at clear progress and achievements on the one hand, but at the existing problems and weaknesses on the other hand. This last chapter is preceded by another comparative assessment, dealing with the question of administrative review as a mechanism to implement Article 9 of the Aarhus Convention. In that context, this penultimate chapter addresses the recent amendments of the Aarhus Regulation. This amendment aims at meeting the criticism of the ACCC regarding the limited standing of organisations or individuals in environmental matters under the Treaty on the Functioning of the European Union.

This book draws on a wide range of material, bringing together various perspectives in a fresh and innovative combination. The Aarhus Convention being a crucial factor in sustainable development and the fight against climate change, this study is timely, important and inspiring.

Sacha Prechal
Professor of European Law, Utrecht University

ACKNOWLEDGEMENTS

Preparing this book has been a wonderful and enriching experience, for which we are extremely grateful. None of it would have been possible without the contributions of our authors, whom we thank wholeheartedly for embarking on this journey with us, as well as for their enthusiasm and professionalism that made our jobs as editors all the more enjoyable. To Sacha Prechal, we extend our sincere appreciation for having accepted to write the Foreword to this book.

We would also like to express our gratitude to Hart Publishing for putting their trust in this project, and especially Roberta Bassi, Verity Stuart and Jon Lloyd for their support throughout the entire process of preparing the book, their professionalism and their pleasant communication.

Our special thanks go to Miriam Abdulahi for her help and support in organising the 'Implementation of Article 9 of the Aarhus Convention in the Balkans' workshop, which took place on 30 June 2023 at Turin University and was invaluable for crystallising the structure of the book. We are also very grateful to Ezgi Uysal at Turin University for inspiring conversations, her continual support and meticulous help with formatting some of the chapters of the book, as well as Benedetta Biancardi for believing in us, offering a fruitful exchange of ideas and motivation.

Finally, we express our gratitude for the research grant (*assegno di ricerca*) from the Italian Ministry of Education, University and Research (MIUR Dipartimenti di Eccellenza 2018–2022 – per il Dipartimento di Giurisprudenza) that kick-started the idea for this book, as well as Turin University for enabling Bojana to conduct research activities on the project *Environmental Democracy in the Balkans*, for a period of one year (23 November 2022–22 November 2023), together with Roberto.

Bojana Todorović
Roberto Caranta

CONTENTS

CONTRIBUTORS

Frosina Antonovska Joskoska is an environmental legal expert and researcher with extensive experience in the governmental and civil society sector. She is also a climate and energy policy coordinator for the Western Balkans at Climate Action Network Europe.

Konstantin Bitrakov is a teaching assistant in administrative law and public administration at the Faculty of Law 'Iustinianus Primus', Ss Cyril and Methodius University in Skopje (North Macedonia) and a PhD candidate at the Faculty of Law in Belgrade (Serbia). His research focuses primarily on public integrity, institutional design, anti-corruption, but also other issues in the field of administrative law.

Roberto Caranta is Professor in Administrative Law at the University of Turin (Italy) and works mainly on comparative administrative law and public procurement. He is also coordinator of the H2020 – MSCA ITN Sustainability and Procurement in International, European, and National Systems (SAPIENS) programme.

Dacian C Dragos is Jean Monnet Professor of Administrative and European Law at Babeş-Bolyai University (Romania) and co-director of the Center for Good Governance Studies. Since 2020, he has served as a World Bank ST Expert in Public Procurement and President of the National Research Ethics Committee. A former Marie Curie Fellow at Michigan State University, he was Scientific Coordinator for Romania's Administrative Procedure Code and has worked on administrative reform in Albania and Turkey.

Mirjana Drenovak-Ivanović is Full Professor in Environmental and Climate Change Law, Jean Monnet Chair in European Environmental and Climate Change Law, and founder of the Environmental Legal Clinic at the University of Belgrade Faculty of Law (Serbia). A former Chevening (PhD) and Fulbright (postdoctoral) scholar, in 2023 she received the Person of the Year award for outstanding contribution to consolidation of human rights and improving environmental protection from the OSCE Mission to Serbia. She specialises in environmental law with a particular emphasis on access to environmental justice.

Mariolina Eliantonio is Professor of European and Comparative Administrative Law and Procedure at Maastricht University (the Netherlands). Her research focuses on access to justice in environmental matters, as well as administrative cooperation, soft law and technical standardization in EU governance.

Giacomo Gattinara holds a PhD in international public law and EU law from the 'Sapienza' University of Rome (Italy) and is an affiliated member of the Institute for European Law of the Katholieke Universiteit Leuven (Belgium). He is also a member of the Legal Service of the European Commission and focuses on public procurement and international trade.

Gheorghe-Sorin Lodoabă-Cordon is a joint PhD candidate in law at Babeş-Bolyai University of Cluj-Napoca (Romania) and the University of Turin (Italy). He is Associate Lecturer at the Faculty of Law, and Faculty of Political, Administrative, and Communication Sciences, Babeş-Bolyai University (Romania), as well as a practising lawyer. His primary focus is on administrative law and the impact of digitalisation on law and administrative procedure development.

Bogdana Neamţu is Associate Professor and Head of the Department of Public Administration and Management at Babeş-Bolyai University (Romania). She obtained her PhD in 2008, with a thesis in urban growth management, after which she continued working on sustainability and good governance topics. She co-directs, together with Professor Dacian Dragos, the Center for Good Governance Studies, a small research unit dealing with free access to documents and information, alternative dispute resolution in public law, public procurement and corruption studies.

Lana Ofak is Full Professor and Chair of the Administrative Law Department at the University of Zagreb Faculty of Law (Croatia). Her research focuses on administrative procedure, judicial review and environmental law.

Carmen Plaza is Professor of Administrative and European Law and Director of the Institute of European Law and Regional Integration at the Faculty of Law of the Complutense University, Madrid (Spain). She was formerly a Legal Secretary at the Spanish Constitutional Court and Director General of Equal Opportunities of the Spanish government. Her research focuses on environmental law, human rights law, and European law and its impact on national public law.

Justine Richelle is a joint PhD candidate at Hasselt University (Belgium) and Maastricht University (the Netherlands). Her main research interests are public participation and access to justice in environmental matters in the EU.

Katja Štemberger Brizani is Assistant Professor of Administrative Law at the Faculty of Law, University of Ljubljana (Slovenia). Her academic and research work focus on public procurement and concession law and related legal institutions, such as administrative contracts, public services, alternative dispute resolution in administrative matters, and limitations on property rights for public benefit.

Franc Terihati is the Executive Director of the Centre for Legal Empowerment (Albania) and has over 14 years of experience working in the legal sector, with a focus on human rights, access to justice, environmental protection, the rule of law and elections. He is also the Managing Partner of Terihati Law & Tax and his areas of expertise are focused on data protection, contract law, commercial law, labour law, energy law and sports law.

Bojana Todorović holds a PhD in administrative law from the University of Belgrade Faculty of Law (Serbia) where she is a lecturer at the Public Law Department. Her academic and research work focus on public contracts in a comparative perspective, alternative dispute resolution and third-party enforcement mechanisms in public law.

Marko Turudić is Associate Professor in Administrative Law at the University of Zagreb Faculty of Law (Croatia). His academic and research work focus on administrative procedure and dispute, public procurement and regulatory agencies.

Introduction

BOJANA TODOROVIĆ AND ROBERTO CARANTA

I. Setting the Scene: Europeanisation of Access to Justice in Environmental Matters Through the Influence of EU Law and the Jurisprudence of the European Court of Human Rights on National Law and Practice

Access to justice in environmental matters, one of the pillars of the United Nations Economic Commission for Europe (UNECE) Convention on Access to Information, Public Participation in Decision-making and Access to Justice in Environmental Matters (hereinafter 'the *Aarhus Convention*'), is an essential component of sustainable development and the fight against climate change.[1] Given the transboundary nature of the fight against climate change and environmental protection, exchange of good practices and the need for international cooperation among the judiciary have been highlighted as one of the key preconditions for the attainment of United Nations (UN) Sustainable Development Goals (SDGs) – in particular SDG 13: Climate Action and SDG 16: Peace, Justice and Strong Institutions.[2]

Apart from the activities of the Aarhus Convention Compliance Committee (ACCC) in interpreting the provisions of the Aarhus Convention, the efforts of the European Union (EU) and the Council of Europe (CoE) to establish clear(er) standards of access to justice in environmental matters have been particularly relevant on this field. It is well established that both the EU, through its legislative activity and the jurisprudence of the Court of Justice of the European Union (CJEU), and the European Court of Human Rights (ECtHR) have been important

[1] Economic Commission for Europe, Meeting of the Parties to the Convention on Access to Information, Public Participation in Decision-Making and Access to Justice in Environmental Matters, Working Group of the Parties, Twenty-seventh meeting, Item 4 (c) of the provisional agenda, Substantive issues: access to justice, 'Report of the Task Force on Access to Justice on its fifteenth meeting' (Report of the Task Force on Access to Justice) ECE/MP.PP/WG.1/2023/4 (Geneva, 26–28 June 2023), https://unece.org/environment/documents/2023/06/working-documents/item-4-c-report-task-force-access-justice-its, 16.

[2] ibid 2 and 11.

promoters of Aarhus standards.[3] This is also reflected in the conclusions of the Judicial Colloquium that was held alongside the fifteenth meeting of the Aarhus Convention's Task Force on Access to Justice Report, in which it is stated that 'the ECtHR and CJEU continued to play a pivotal role for national courts in clarifying the definitions, legal norms and standards of judicial proceedings'.[4]

A corollary of this interplay between the norms of the Aarhus Convention as interpreted by the ACCC, international human rights law as warranted by the European Convention on Human Rights (ECHR) and EU law, has been the creation of a specific 'Aarhus space', 'in which many of the barriers between international … EU law … and national law have been removed and where individuals and groups can move freely between these bodies of law in order to protect the environment'.[5] Thus, the implementation of the requirements stemming from Article 9 of the Aarhus Convention by national institutions in EU Member States (that are, at the same time, parties to the ECHR) is greatly influenced by these European fora. In addition to potential benefits such as 'multiplying' the chances to bring environmental violations to the attention of judicial instances, the often divergent approach of European courts to adjudicating environmental procedural rights also runs the risk of making it more difficult for national authorities to comply with the Aarhus standards, which calls for further academic scrutiny.[6]

Moreover, the observed influence of various layers of European standards ie, the *Europeanisation* of (environmental) access to justice, goes beyond EU borders. Namely, the EU is a party to the Aarhus Convention,[7] rendering this international instrument an intrinsic part of EU law. Stemming from the EU's obligation to 'actively promote the Convention in its international relations', the Aarhus Convention 'has the potential to be one of the weapons in the arsenal of the European Union as a major force in the development of progressive environmental policies at the global level'.[8] This is well illustrated in the context of EU enlargement, seeing how countries aspiring towards EU membership are obliged to align their national legislation with the EU environmental *acquis*, which includes

[3] V Karageorgou, 'Access to Justice in Environmental Matters: Recent Developments at International and Regional Level and the Repercussions at the National Level' in J May and E Daly (eds), *Human Rights and the Environment: Legality, Indivisibility, Dignity and Geography* (Cheltenham, Edward Elgar, 2019) 155, 160.

[4] Report of the Task Force on Access to Justice (n 1) 17.

[5] E Hey, 'The Interaction between Human Rights and the Environment in the European "Aarhus Space"' in A Grear and LJ Kotze (eds), *Research Handbook on Human Rights and the Environment* (Cheltenham, Edward Elgar, 2015) 353, 376.

[6] J Richelle, 'Environmental Procedural Rights before European Courts: Still Searching for a Common Script or Multiplying Avenues of Protection?' (REALaw.blog, 2022) https://realaw.blog/2022/02/25/environmental-procedural-rights-before-european-courts-still-searching-for-a-common-script-or-multiplying-avenues-of-protection-by-justine-richelle.

[7] unece.org/environment-policy/public-participation/aarhus-convention/content#:~:text=The%20European%20Union%20(which%20as,Party%20since%2018%20May%20200.

[8] S Stec, 'EU Enlargement, Neighbourhood Policy and Environmental Democracy' in M Pallemaerts (ed), *The Aarhus Convention at Ten: Interactions and Tensions between Conventional International Law and EU Environmental Law* (Groningen, Europa Law Publishing, 2011) 35, 44–45.

relevant directives implementing the Aarhus Convention, as well as standards and principles shaped by the CJEU in its interpretation of the Convention.

The Balkan countries represent a particularly interesting case in point for exploring the described phenomenon for a number of reasons.

First of all, the Balkan Peninsula is highly vulnerable to the effects of climate change. Yearly heatwaves and wildfires, devastating floods, water shortages and poor air quality that place cities such as Belgrade and Skopje at the top of the list of the most polluted cities in the world are but a few examples of this problem. The environmental vulnerability of the Balkan Peninsula is a result of a 'critical combination of the socialist legacy (large industrial sites placed very near the residential areas, outdated technology and lack of care for the environment) and the negative effects of transition, economic recession and war'.[9] Given that the majority of countries in the Balkans are either EU Member States or (potential) candidate countries, their efforts in mitigating the adverse effects of this state of environmental emergency are embedded in the wider European framework, embodied in the European Green Deal,[10] as well as regional initiatives such as the Green Agenda for the Western Balkans,[11] or the Energy[12] and Transport Communities.[13]

Furthermore, the majority of countries in the Balkan region are parties to the Aarhus Convention, which means that standards related to ensuring access to justice in environmental matters and empowering members of the civil society sector to take a more active role in that process, are 'imposed' via two avenues – the Aarhus Convention itself and through the prism of EU law. However, recent literature indicates that the alignment with the EU environmental *acquis*, including the standards of the Aarhus Convention, has been one of the biggest stumbling blocks of both EU Member States from the Central and Eastern Europe (CEE) 'bloc' and aspiring members.[14] The alignment with the EU and Aarhus standards is often limited to compliance at the normative level, falling short of effective implementation in practice. Weak institutional capacity, overall lack of transparency of the public sector and corruption have been identified as some of the main contributors to the status quo. Focusing on the Serbian contemporary context (which holds

[9] J Vukelić and I Petrović, 'Social Capital as a Basis for Collective Action: The Case of Environmental Activism in Two Towns in Serbia' in P Cvetičanin and A Birešev (eds), *Social and Cultural Capital in Western Balkan Societies* (Niš, Center for Empirical Cultural Studies of South-East Europe and Institute for Philosophy and Social Theory of the University of Belgrade, 2012) 75, 81.

[10] For more on the European Green Deal, see https://commission.europa.eu/strategy-and-policy/priorities-2019-2024/european-green-deal_en.

[11] Commission, 'Guidelines for the Implementation of the Green Agenda for the Western Balkans Accompanying the Communication from the Commission to the European Parliament, the Council, the European Economic and Social Committee and the Committee of the Regions An Economic and Investment Plan for the Western Balkans', (Staff Working Document) COM (2020) 641 final.

[12] www.energy-community.org/aboutus/whoweare.html.

[13] www.transport-community.org/about-us.

[14] S Bogojević and M Drenovak-Ivanović, 'Environmental Protection through the Prism of Enlargement: Time for Reflection' (2019) 56 *Common Market Law Review* 949, 964–67.

true, more or less, for most of the countries of the so-called Western Balkans),[15] Bogojević finds that '[t]he corrosive effects on the rule of law … is particularly visible against an environmental backdrop',[16] manifested 'through attempts to withhold information, limit public participation and restrict access to the judiciary in areas relating to environmental protection'.[17] She concludes that '[p]opulism, the rule of law and environmental protection thus operate within a kind of Venn diagram that shows their interconnectedness',[18] which is a direct violation of both the Aarhus Convention and EU law.

Simultaneously, the past decade has seen a surge in various forms of bottom-up environmental activism, from instances of local 'social disobedience', through regular citizen-led street protests, to regional alliances of non-governmental organisations (NGOs) and citizen associations. In addition to being 'fuelled by concerns over the region's ecological heritage and the impact of human activity on natural resources',[19] these instances of environmental activism were also closely linked to broader, societal concerns and discontent with the institutions and the erosion of the rule of law. Moreover, civil society actors in the region often appear to be more empowered to institute court proceedings against acts and omissions of public authorities that have a significant impact on human health and the environment, as illustrated by the first climate lawsuit in Romania initiated by the Declic Association[20] or the lawsuit filed by the Renewables and Environmental Regulatory Institute (RERI), which resulted in a landmark ruling by the Higher Court in Belgrade ordering the Serbian state-owned power company to reduce its harmful sulphur dioxide emissions from thermal power plants.[21]

Against this background, this book examines the implementation of the third pillar of the Aarhus Convention in the Balkans, with a view to exploring the phenomenon of Europeanisation of access to justice in environmental matters as a result of the influence exerted by two relevant European systems – one established within the framework of the EU and the other under the auspices of the CoE – as well as the impetus brought about by the growing environmental activism in the region.

[15] A geopolitical term that covers countries that are aspiring towards EU membership, out of which the majority were part of the former Yugoslavia, European External Action Service: www.eeas.europa.eu/eeas/western-balkans_en.

[16] S Bogojević, 'The Erosion of the Rule of Law: How Populism Threatens Environmental Protection' (2019) 31 *Journal of Environmental Law* 1, 3.

[17] ibid 1–2.

[18] ibid 2.

[19] R Besliu, 'Protecting Nature, Empowering People: Environmental Protests in the Balkans' (*Green European Journal*, 5 June 2023), www.greeneuropeanjournal.eu/protecting-nature-empowering-people-environmental-protests-in-the-balkans.

[20] R Dumitrescu, 'Romania's First Climate Lawsuit Underway as NGOs Push for More Ambitious Goals' (*Romania Insider*, 19 April 2023), www.romania-insider.com/romania-first-climate-lawsuit-underway-april-2023.

[21] 'Historic Ruling: Serbia's State Energy Supplier Must Slash Toxic Plant Emissions Nationwide' (*RERI*, 25 November 2022), https://reri.org.rs/en/historic-ruling-serbias-state-energy-supplier-must-slash-toxic-plant-emissions-nationwide.

II. The Research Question and Our Methodology

The aim of the book is to *understand* and *explain* how the interplay of *internal* and *external* factors shape the extent to which selected Balkan countries comply with requirements stemming from Article 9 of the Aarhus Convention, to *detect* the normative, institutional or other challenges that may be hampering successful implementation in practice, and to *explore* whether despite national differences in the observed region it is possible to talk about the Europeanisation of access to justice in environmental matters.[22]

Regarding external factors, the focus of the book is on the influence of the EU's normative, judicial and policy instruments, as well as the ECtHR's case law on the implementation of Article 9 of the Aarhus Convention. While the interpretation of the Aarhus Convention by the ACCC, the CJEU and the ECtHR, as well as the interplay between the national and supranational Aarhus standards, have been analysed in the scholarly literature, this book intends to go further. The critical assessment of the interactions between provisions of the Aarhus Convention on access to justice in environmental matters as interpreted by the ACCC, the CJEU and the ECtHR will include EU environmental policy instruments in the enlargement process. Moreover, the book investigates the (lack of) success of selected countries in implementing Article 9 of the Aarhus Convention against the backdrop of such European influences, especially seeing how all of them are parties to the ECtHR and only some of them members of the EU as well.

With respect to internal factors, emphasis is placed on specific national contexts, the rising impetus of civil society and their importance for strengthening environmental democracy and the rule of law. In order to grasp the current trends in environmental litigation and the importance of the Aarhus Convention in bridging the gap between citizens and the civil society on the one hand, and public authorities on the other, it is necessary to go beyond a simple legal analysis and delve into broader historical and socio-political factors that have shaped environmental democracy in practice. Thus, a *law in context* approach combined with comparative analysis forms the methodological cornerstone of this book.

Understanding the success and challenges the observed countries experience in the process of implementing Aarhus standards, as well as the reasons behind the recent uptake of environmental activism in the region, is achieved through a number of steps.

First, in addition to the outline of the main *historical reasons* behind the present-day legal and environmental cultures in the selected Balkan countries given in section III below, the national chapters in this book 'open' with a *background* explaining the institutional set-up of access to justice in environmental matters, as well as specific political and/or societal factors that pave the way to

[22] For more on how the notion of Europeanisation is understood in the context of this book, see section V below.

understanding their success and/or struggles in the implementation of environmental access to justice standards, as well as how and to what extent the European integration process affected the normative and practical reality in this field.

Second, interdisciplinarity was also warranted by relying on methods such as *semi-structured dialogues with relevant national NGOs*, some of which have been actively involved in organising environmental protests, instigating administrative and judicial procedures, and contributing to legislative changes.

Third, we consider that the *diversity of our authors' backgrounds* contributes to securing interdisciplinarity of the book. Apart from academics, some of whom have had previous experience working as judges, in the NGO sector and/or the public administration, the pool of contributors includes a member of the Legal Services of the European Commission and an attorney at law with abundant experience with environmental litigation. Their experience and broadened perspectives inevitably contribute to painting a more nuanced picture of both transversal and national chapters.

Finally, and fourth, chapter three of this book relies on the synergy of sources in the fields of law, sociology and political science, including their proposed theoretical models on the legal mobilisation of environmental law, social (including environmental) movements and political and legal opportunity structures.

Given the common framework provided by the Aarhus Convention, by the ECHR and by the EU – even if only prospectively for candidates countries – the comparative analysis is guided by the assumption that the law and practice in the relevant jurisdictions are bound to answer to the same social function, thus meeting the requirement of the identity of both the social problem and its solution across jurisdictions.[23] Moreover, the traditional 'functionalist' method provides the required flexibility as – unlike in other sciences – it is 'non-technical and non-exact', 'flexible and elastic' and may be defined as 'heuristic'.[24]

The comparative analysis is enabled by the *questionnaire methodology* used for national chapters. The comparative analysis entails looking at 'implementation' in the substantive sense – not only the *enactment* of necessary legislative instruments, but also their *effective enforcement* in practice – *practical hurdles* (high court fees, restrictive locus standi rules, judicial workload stalling effective justice, corruption etc), the *role played by the EU* integration process (whether it enabled access to justice in environmental matters or made it more difficult) and *civic activity* (eg, environmental protests and lawsuits filed by NGOs). In other words, the comparative lens through which national experiences will be assessed is not focused only on 'formal' compliance with environmental access to justice standards, but also encompasses their 'practical' implementation, viewed as a 'process in which rules are

[23] J Husa, 'Traditional Methods' in M Siems and PJ Yap (eds), *The Cambridge Handbook of Comparative Law* (Cambridge, Cambridge University Press, 2024) 15, 18.

[24] ibid 23 f.

enforced and applied by the relevant administrative actors and target groups – not through intentions "on paper", but through activities "in action"'.[25]

III. The Balkans: *E Pluribus Unum*?

In this book, the term 'Balkans' is to be considered in a 'culturally neutral territorial or geographical sense'[26] that encompasses six countries, which are located in the Balkan Peninsula – Albania, Croatia, North Macedonia, Romania, Serbia and Slovenia. Thus, as already indicated, it includes both EU and non-EU Balkan countries.

This methodological choice has been made for at least three reasons: first, in order to be able to explore whether there is a difference in the approach (and success) of implementing requirements stemming from Article 9 of the Aarhus Convention depending on whether a particular country is an EU Member State or not; second, historical circumstances have prompted legal, economic, political and cultural similarities which enable a sound comparative exercise;[27] and, third and last, due to comparable trends in environmental democracy in the past decade.

While the described approach is justified not only by the geographical location of the relevant countries but also, inter alia, by seemingly shared experiences of communist rule in their recent past, the pursuit of EU accession as their foremost foreign political goal and the recent surge of civil society environmental activism – disregarding the differences among these countries and assuming that they all came out of a single 'Balkan mould' with a distinct mentality, cultural pattern etc would lead to overly simplistic and generalised conclusions.[28] Thus, any research focused on this complex and at times paradoxical region should be mindful of the *similarities* as well as the *differences* of the countries in the region, since both are crucial for fully grasping their present-day realities, including the state of environmental democracy.[29]

Apart from the obvious diversity in language(s), religion and divide along the lines of Ottoman or Austro-Hungarian influence and heritage,[30] one notable

[25] A Zhelyazkova and E Thomann, '"I Did it My Way": Customisation and Practical Compliance with EU Policies' (2022) 29(3) *Journal of European Public Policy* 427, 431; M Stanković, 'To Implement, or Not to Implement, That is the Question: The Role of Non-state Actors in Environmental Policy Implementation in Serbia' (Master's thesis, University of Gothenburg, 2021), 5.

[26] R Bideleux and I Jeffries, *The Balkans: A Post-communist History* (London, Routledge, 2007) 1.

[27] Husa (n 23) 18 ff.

[28] For criticism of such an approach, see Bideleux and Jeffries (n 27) 1–21.

[29] M Siems and PJ Yap, 'Introduction: A New Handbook for Comparative Law in a Global Context' in M Siems and PJ Yap (eds), *The Cambridge Handbook of Comparative Law* (Cambridge, Cambridge University Press, 2024) 1, 2 ff; the relevance of culture is highlighted by Q Xiangyang, 'Culture and Comparative Law Methodology' in M Siems and PJ Yap (eds), *The Cambridge Handbook of Comparative Law* (Cambridge, Cambridge University Press, 2024) 72.

[30] See G della Cananea, A Ferrari Zumbini and O Pfersmann (eds), *The Austrian Codification of Administrative Procedure. Diffusion and Oblivion (1920–1970)* (Oxford, Oxford University Press, 2023);

difference is that with the exception of Albania and Romania, the remaining countries (Croatia, North Macedonia, Serbia and Slovenia) were all part of one country that emerged in the aftermath of the First World War and – after having undergone several waves of ideological transformation, changes in political systems, forms of governance and even name[31] – existed as the Socialist Federal Republic of Yugoslavia (SFRY or 'Yugoslavia') from the end of the Second World War until its disintegration in the early 1990s.[32]

This is an important factor to consider in the analysis of the communist legacy in the recent 'political and legal history' of the analysed countries.[33] While a detailed account of this question would go well beyond the scope and aim of this introduction, we consider it important to highlight that while certain similarities do exist, the communist ideology that permeated the political, economic and social strata in the countries of the region in the period following the end of the Second World War – and, consequently, its imprint on the development of the civil society space and process of Europeanisation – was by no means identical. The Soviet-style communism dominant in countries of the Eastern Bloc (including Romania), firmly grounded in 'strongly 'vertical' power relations and power structures',[34] was characterised by a strong state, highly centralist decision-making and planned economy.[35] This environment was not fertile soil for organised and active civil engagement independent of the state,[36] making civil society 'almost non-existent', save for associations/gatherings that were considered 'benign' and enjoyed only formal autonomy, such as 'traditional craftsmen, philately groups, sport clubs, or associations for people with disabilities' or the Writers' Union.[37]

Z Kmieciak (ed), *Administrative Proceedings in the Habsburg Succession Countries* (Warsaw, Kluwer Polska, 2021).

[31] Bideleux and Jeffries (n 27); D Jović, 'Communist Yugoslavia and its "Others"' in J Lampe and M Mazower (eds), *Ideologies and National Identities* (Budapest, Central European University Press, 2006), available at: https://books.openedition.org/ceup/2438, 8.

[32] S Lilić and M Milenković, 'Administrative Procedure in Former Yugoslavia and the Austrian Administrative Procedure Act' in Z Kmieciak (ed), *Administrative Proceedings in the Habsburg Succession Countries* (Warsaw, Kluwer Polska, 2021) 119, 125.

[33] S Bogojević, '"Europeanisation" of the Judiciary in Southeast Europe' in S Rodin and T Perišin (eds), *Judicial Application of International Law in Southeast Europe* (Berlin, Springer-Verlag, 2015) 65, 65–66.

[34] Bideleux and Jeffries (n 27) 16.

[35] J Carmin and A Fagan, 'Environmental Mobilisation and Organisations in Post-Socialist Europe and the Former Soviet Union' (2010) 19(5) *Environmental Politics* 689.

[36] S Cibian, 'Observatorium 64 – Civil Society in Romania: Mapping the Vulnerabilities of a Consolidating Sector', www.maecenata.eu/2022/12/12/observatorium-64-civil-society-in-romania-mapping-the-vulnerabilities-of-a-consolidating-sector/#_ftnref6; see also B Neamtu and DC Dragos, 'Mimicking Environmental Transparency: The Implementation of the Aarhus Convention in Romania' in R Caranta, A Gerbrandy and B Müller (eds), *The Making of a New European Legal Culture: the Aarhus Convention* (Groningen, Europa Law Publishing, 2018) 205, 233 f.

[37] MI Tatar, *Importing Democracy from Abroad: International Assistance for Civil Society in Romania* (Oradea, University of Oradea Press, 2006), available at: https://nbn-resolving.org/urn:nbn:de:0168-ssoar-454561, 34.

Similarly, the communist rule in Albania, with its distinct features that included 'total isolation from the east and the west',[38] as well as incrimination of 'formal institutionalized group association' in the public and private spheres, created an increasingly hostile environment for the inception of civil society.[39] Still, Kovaci finds that 'some form of civil society activity continued to barely survive in the private sphere … through literature, culture, and hidden religion'.[40]

On the other hand, the Yugoslav version of socialism based on the tenets of a 'self-regulated society of class-conscious working people', the 'radical decentralisation of the state', non-alignment in its foreign relations and the concept of 'confederalized federalism' as opposed to unitarism,[41] was (at least nominally) premised on decentralisation seen by some authors as 'a step towards direct economic as well as political democracy'.[42] As Merdzanovic notes, 'the contours of Yugoslavia's political, economic, and social system allowed different degrees of citizen involvement'.[43] While these different forms of citizen involvement through 'enterprises, local councils and associations'[44] cannot be equated with the civic activity present in the Western type of liberal democracies, especially since their activities were often institutionalised, the civil society terrain was not completely 'barren'[45] and it cultivated 'environmental, feminist, peace, human rights, and counter-culture movement-like activities in the major urban centres' which, according to some authors, 'fostered a more diversified, bottom-up, and hence authentic building of socialist civil society in the 1980s, one which did not shy away from criticizing the political system'.[46]

Apart from the transparency culture (or lack thereof), a more or less prevalent centralisation and (in)activity of citizens in the public sphere, Bogojević identifies another pervasive repercussion of the political and legal histories of the countries in the region – and, we would add, even more of an oftentimes painful transition process – namely the 'similar attitudes towards law and the legal profession', in the sense of a strict adherence to legislative solutions and a strong hierarchy.[47] This rather technical or bureaucratic approach to the legal profession is closely tied

[38] A Krasniqi, 'Civil Society: The Most Detained Element of Albanian Transition', www.grin.com/document/266562?lang=en.

[39] K Kovaci, 'Democracy in Albania: Shortcomings of Civil Society in Democratization due to the Communist Regime's Legacy' (2014) 2(1) *Undergraduate Journal of Global Citizenship* 1, 7; Krasniqi (n 39).

[40] Kovaci (n 40) 7.

[41] Jović (n 32) 8.

[42] ibid 19.

[43] A Merdzanovic 'Liberalism in Yugoslavia: Before and after the Disintegration' in O Anastasakis et al (eds), *The Legacy of Yugoslavia: Politics, Economics and Society in the Modern Balkans* (London, IB Tauris/Bloomsbury Publishing, 2022) 15, 21.

[44] ibid 23.

[45] I Sokolić, D Kostovicova and A Fagan, 'Civil Society in Post-Yugoslav Space: The Test of Discontinuity and Democratization' in Anastasakis et al (n 44) 39, 42.

[46] B Baća, 'Three Stages of Civil Society Development in the Global East: Lessons from Montenegro, 1989–2020' (2024) 109 *Political Geography* 2.

[47] Bogojević (n 34) 66.

to a certain 'passivity' in the approach to the application of law which has been identified among judges and the judiciary.[48] By considering themselves as mere 'adjudicators', judges in the region often fail to take a more active role in the public sphere as 'carriers of societal change'.[49] This is a big stumbling block in the implementation of international law and standards, seeing how 'the role of the court is ultimately to activate a series of actors, including governments or businesses, to take measures to make international law both effective and possible'.[50] In addition, Bogojević points towards a particularly important role of national courts in the EU legal order for 'making EU law effective', which is why she considers that 'the Europeanisation of laws in Southeast Europe depends, and will depend once all Southeast European states become EU members, on the national judiciaries'.[51]

This leads us to another point of divergence between the observed countries, which concerns varying degrees of their EU integration. Whereas Slovenia, Romania and Croatia became EU Member States in 2004, 2007 and 2013 respectively, the remaining countries analysed in this book have the status of candidates for accession. However, they are currently at different stages of the accession process.[52] Among the candidate countries analysed in this book, with 22 negotiating chapters opened and two provisionally closed, Serbia 'has long been considered a frontrunner in the integration process'.[53] Still, its 'accession path has been stuck in an impasse from which it seems to be increasingly difficult to break out',[54] especially bearing in mind that the county's accession negotiations have been formally launched back in 2014.[55] Negotiations with Albania and North Macedonia have been officially launched in July 2022 (eight and 17 years after obtaining candidate status respectively) and are still in their early phases.[56] However, the accession paths of the two countries have been 'decoupled' recently, with Albania's prospects

[48] See especially D Popović, 'Mesto jugoslovenskog socijalističkog prava u uporednom pravu' (A Comparative Overview of Yugoslav Socialist Law) in D Popović, B Begović and Z Mirković (eds), *Socijalističko pravo u Jugoslaviji 1945–1990* (*Socialist Law in Yugoslavia 1945–1990*), vol 1 (Belgrade, University of Belgrade Faculty of Law, 2024) 99, 130–33.

[49] V Dabetić, 'Izazovi konsolidacije sudstva kao nezavisne grane vlasti u Srbiji na početku 21. veka' (Challenges of the Consolidation of Judiciary as an Independent Branch of Authority in Serbia at the Beginning of the 21st Century) (Doctoral dissertation, University of Belgrade Faculty of Law, 2023), 166.

[50] Bogojević (n 34) 65 and 67.

[51] ibid.

[52] On experiences in the EU accession process of individual countries, see especially Terihati, ch 4 in this volume, section III; Antonovska Joskoska and Bitrakov, ch 6 in this volume, section II; Lodoabă-Cordon, Dragos and Neamtu, ch 7 in this volume, section III; Drenovak-Ivanović, ch 8 in this volume, section II; and Štemberger Brizani, ch 9 in this volume, section II.

[53] S Epis, 'Regional Policy in Serbia's EU Accession Process' (*OBCT*, 30 October 2023), www.balcani-caucaso.org/eng/Areas/Serbia/Regional-policy-in-Serbia-s-EU-accession-process-227824; https://neighbourhood-enlargement.ec.europa.eu/enlargement-policy/serbia_en.

[54] ibid.

[55] M Dabrowski and L Léry Moffat, 'The Changing Dynamics of the Western Balkans on the Road to European Union Membership: An Update' (*Bruegel*, 22 July 2024), www.bruegel.org/policy-brief/changing-dynamics-western-balkans-road-european-union-membership-update#footnote4_f7b13kg.

[56] ibid.

of opening the first negotiating clusters being more 'palpable'.[57] Whether and, if so, to what extent the different levels and pace of EU integration have affected the environmental legal frameworks and the intake of Aarhus standards, as well as the possibility of civil society mobilisation in the environmental arena, is further explored in the individual contributions to this book.[58]

IV. On the Notion of Europeanisation Used in this Book

Even a cursory review of literature in the spheres of law,[59] sociology[60] and political science[61] indicates different conceptualisations of the term 'Europeanisation'. The complexity of the term that implies a 'dynamic, multifaceted, and malleable' content, enabling it to permeate different disciplines and methodological frameworks, is well captured by Anastasakis:

> Europeanization is an influential and fashionable term in social scientific terminology, as well as in the commonplace discourse on Europe. Its meaning can be specific and, at the same time, elusive and all-encompassing … It signifies a certain political, socio-economic, and cultural reality, but it is also an ideology, a symbol, and a myth. It has universal value by virtue of its historical, holistic, and globalizing nature. At the same time, its impact has internal consequences for Europe and an external significance for the rest of the world.[62]

Aware of the different 'faces'[63] of Europeanisation and the multitude of approaches[64] taken to explain and map out the meaning, scope and direction[65] of this phenomenon, here we limit ourselves to clarifying what is understood by the

[57] A Taylor-Braçe and G Gotev, 'Albania's EU Path Decoupled from North Macedonia While Skopje Remains in Limbo' (*Euractiv*, 26 September 2024), www.euractiv.com/section/politics/news/albanias-eu-path-decoupled-from-north-macedonia-while-skopje-remains-in-limbo.

[58] See especially Todorović, ch 3 in this volume, sections II and III; Terihati, ch 4 in this volume, section III; F Antonovska Joskoska and Bitrakov, ch 6 in this volume, section II; Lodoabă-Cordon, Dragos and Neamtu, ch 7 in this volume, sections II, III and V; Drenovak-Ivanović, ch 8 in this volume, section II; and Štemberger Brizani, ch 9 in this volume, sections II, III.A and IV.

[59] F Snyder (ed), *The Europeanisation of Law: The Legal Effects of European Integration*, (Oxford, Hart Publishing, 2000).

[60] See, eg, SM Büttner, M Eigmüller and S Worschech (eds), *Sociology of Europeanization* (Berlin, De Gruyter Oldenbourg, 2022).

[61] S Dosenrode, 'Europeanization' (*Oxford Research Encyclopedia*, 2000), https://doi.org/10.1093/acrefore/9780190228637.013.1477.

[62] O Anastasakis, 'The Europeanization of the Balkans' (2005) 12(1) *Brown Journal of World Affairs* 77, 77–78 and 80.

[63] See J Olsen, 'The Many Faces of Europeanization' (2002) 40(5) *Journal of Common Market Studies* 921; G Bandov and N Herceg Kolman, 'Research on Europeanization in Literature: From the Top-down Approach to Europeanization as a Multi-directional Process' (2018) 3(5) *Cadmus* 134, 143.

[64] See instead K Featherstone and CM Radaelli (eds) *The Politics of Europeanization* (Oxford, Oxford University Press, 2003).

[65] Bandov and Herceg Kolman (n 64) 134.

term in the context of this book – namely, the lens through which Europeanisation is viewed in the contributions is broad, both in *scope* and *direction*. On the one hand, it entails the 'top-down' influence of the EU (through its legislative and policy instruments, as well as the case law of the CJEU) – including the Aarhus Convention, which forms part thereof – and the CoE system epitomised but not limited to the jurisprudence of the ECtHR on the legal, institutional and policy levels of the countries analysed in this book.[66] On the other hand, it also encompasses the 'bottom-up' impact of environmental activism on selected Balkan countries with respect to access to justice in environmental matters. This book thus continues and widens the research on to what extent the Aarhus Convention is contributing to the rising of a common European legal culture in a wider sense, encompassing 'more than professors and judges'.[67]

V. Structure of the Book

The book is divided into three parts. Part I, entitled 'Access to Justice in Environmental Matters at the European Level: Instruments of Europeanisation', relies on the hitherto broadly construed notion of Europeanisation and takes a closer look at its various instrumentations in the EU and Strasbourg, and paves the way for the second and third parts. This part comprises three transversal chapters. Chapter 1, written by Mariolina Eliantonio and Justine Richelle, examines the interpretation of Article 9 of the Aarhus Convention in the Aarhus Convention Implementation Guide and by the ACCC, as well as by the CJEU, thus serving as a benchmark to show, first, the extent to which the legal systems examined in the book comply with Article 9 of the Convention and, second, whether an 'EU effect' linked to the membership to the EU may be identified when it comes to access to justice in environmental matters. Chapter 2 by Carmen Plaza analyses the different approaches to the protection of the environment through human rights in the case law of the ECtHR and some important intersections between human rights and environmental treaties, in particular between Article 9 of the Aarhus Convention and several articles of the ECHR, and explores the impact of the recent debates on establishing 'the right to a clean, healthy and sustainable environment' as a human right, on the role of the ECtHR. Finally, Chapter 3, written by Bojana Todorović, investigates two driving forces behind the Europeanisation of environmental democracy in the Balkans – the EU's enlargement policy in the environmental arena (*top-down Europeanisation*) and the growing environmental

[66] JB Auby, 'About Europeanization of Domestic Judicial Review' (2014) 7(2) *Review of European Administrative Law* 19, 19.

[67] R Caranta, A Gerbrandy and B Müller, 'Introduction' in R Caranta, A Gerbrandy and B Müller (eds), *The Making of a New European Legal Culture: The Aarhus Convention* (Groningen, Europa Law Publishing, 2018) 1, 8.

activism of civil society (*bottom-up Europeanisation*) – in order to provide a comprehensive and more nuanced overview of the specific Balkan context and the relationship between the EU, the Aarhus Convention and the role of civil society actors in the field of environmental protection, thus setting the scene for a better understanding of the national perspectives in this book.

The latter are grouped in Part II of the book, which is entitled 'National Perspectives: Access to Justice in Environmental Matters in Selected Balkan Countries' and contains six chapters by national experts from Albania (Chapter 4), Croatia (Chapter 5), North Macedonia (Chapter 6), Romania (Chapter 7), Serbia (Chapter 8) and Slovenia (Chapter 9).

Insights into the normative and practical realities of access to justice in environmental matters in the six observed Balkan countries enabled the comparative analysis, which is found in the third and final part of the book entitled 'Comparative Assessment'. This part comprises two self-standing chapters. Chapter 10 by Giacomo Gattinara deals with the administrative review mechanism as a tool to enforce Article 9 of the Aarhus Convention and attempts to understand and map out the extent to which administrative remedies for infringements of environmental law, available in the national legal systems considered here, match the requirements provided for in the Aarhus Convention. Finally, Chapter 11, written by Roberto Caranta and Bojana Todorović, the co-editors of this book, provides a comparative perspective on environmental access to justice in the Balkans and concludes on the effect of various sources of Europeanisation on bridging the gap between national differences and shaping standards and good practices in the observed field, in order to draw valuable comparative lessons for strengthening environmental democracy and the rule of law in the environmental context.

VI. The Balkans as an Example of ((Un)Successful) Europeanisation of Access to Justice in Environmental Matters?

Being the bastion of environmental democracy, the Aarhus Convention not only signifies a 'new chapter' in international (environmental) law, but also illustrates the desire to transpose the so-called 'Western democratic values' to the 'East' after the fall of communism in Europe.[68] In a way, the Aarhus Convention was *addressed* to CEE countries that had been nurturing a different attitude towards the environment, as well as a set of values underpinning the relationship between the state and its citizens (and their various forms of association).[69] Observed through this lens,

[68] L Vanhala, 'Shaping the Structure of Legal Opportunities: Environmental NGOs Bringing International Environmental Procedural Rights Back Home' (2018) 40(1) *Law & Policy* 110, 117.

[69] As Vanhala points out, the Aarhus Convention 'was adopted … as part of the "Environment for Europe" process', which 'was established in 1991 in part to help countries in Eastern Europe,

it is understandable why some authors refer to the Aarhus Convention as an illustrative example of a 'litmus test' of the application of EU law in Southeast Europe, which includes the Balkan region.[70]

The fact that representatives of the civil society and environmental NGOs (ENGOs) actively participated in its drafting demonstrates that the Aarhus Convention promoted 'bottom-up democracy' from the outset.[71] Furthermore, Article 3(8) of the Aarhus Convention requires parties to provide protection to individuals and their organisations that exercise their rights 'in conformity with the provisions of the Convention' from being 'penalized, persecuted or harassed in any way for their involvement'.[72] Since such harmful activity aimed at silencing and/or punishing environmental activists often comes from public authorities, the Meeting of the Parties (MOP) passed a decision in 2021 establishing the Rapid Response Mechanism for the protection of environmental defenders, thus providing an international platform for legal redress/protection in such cases.[73] This is especially relevant not only for ensuring the proper implementation of the Aarhus Convention, but also for giving impetus to environmental movements, especially in their nascent phase, such as those in the Balkans.

Taking into account instances of both good and questionable practices in selected countries, research into how Article 9 of the Aarhus Convention, under the influence of EU and ECHR law, enables environmental activism and democracy in the Balkans is a rich source of valuable lessons for ensuring effective access to justice in order to overcome the detected challenges that we hope would serve as a point of reference to EU and national stakeholders involved in the EU integration process, as well as other European and non-European parties of the Aarhus Convention.

the Caucasus and Central Asia improve their environmental standards after the fall of the iron curtain': ibid.

[70] S Rodin and T Perišin, 'Application of International Law as a Litmus Test for the Application of EU Law in Southeast Europe' in S Rodin and T Perišin (eds), *Judicial Application of International Law in Southeast Europe* (Berlin, Springer Verlag, 2015) 3. See also Todorović, ch 3 in this volume, section II.B.

[71] R Caranta, 'Environmental NGOs (eNGOs) or: Filling the Gap between the State and the Individual under the Aarhus Convention' in R Caranta, A Gerbrandy and B Müller (eds), *The Making of a New European Legal Culture: the Aarhus Convention, At the Crossroad of Comparative Law and EU Law* (Groningen, Europa Law Publishing 2017) 401, 404.

[72] https://unece.org/climate-change/press/rapid-response-mechanism-protect-environmental-defenders-established-under.

[73] T Weber, 'Are Climate Activists Protected by the Aarhus Convention? A Note on Article 3(8) Aarhus Convention and the New Rapid Response Mechanism for Environmental Defenders' (2023) 32(1) *Review of European, Comparative & International Environmental Law* 67.

PART I

Access to Justice in Environmental Matters at the European Level: Instruments of Europeanisation

1

Article 9 of the Aarhus Convention, its Transposition in the EU and its Interpretation by the Aarhus Convention Compliance Committee and the Court of Justice of the European Union

In Search of an 'EU Effect'?

MARIOLINA ELIANTONIO AND JUSTINE RICHELLE

I. Introduction

The Aarhus Convention is an international instrument codifying the environmental procedural rights of access to information, public participation in decision-making and access to justice, to which both the EU and its Member States are parties. In 2023, the Convention celebrated its twenty-fifth birthday. Still, there are shortcomings in the implementation of the procedural rights contained in the Convention. Indeed, the increasing body of findings of non-compliance made by the Aarhus Convention Compliance Committee (hereinafter ACCC or 'the Committee') and the growing case law of the Court of Justice of the European Union (CJEU) prove that the implementation of the environmental procedural rights is not without any hurdles.

This chapter focuses on the third pillar of the Convention: access to justice. This right is guaranteed under Article 9 of the Convention. Article 9 is further subdivided into different limbs: Article 9(1) requires access to review procedures relating to information requests made under Article 4 of the Convention; Article 9(2) concerns access to review procedures relating to decisions, acts or omissions subject to Article 6 (on public participation) and other relevant provisions of the Convention; Article 9(3) contains the more general obligation of access to review procedures for the public of acts and omissions of private persons and public authorities concerning national law relating to the environment; and, finally, Article 9(4) sets general minimum standards applying to all relevant review procedures, decisions and remedies.[1] The first two paragraphs of Article 9 therefore cover the application of the Aarhus Convention itself, while Article 9(3) is aimed at regulating the public's access to justice for violations of environmental law at large.[2] Article 9(5) on procedures facilitating access to justice is beyond the scope of this chapter.

The access to justice pillar is described by Jendrośka as the 'most underdeveloped in terms of the clarity and precision of the legal scheme envisaged in the Convention'.[3] Indeed, this provision contains relatively vague terms and leaves discretion to the parties when implementing certain rules. According to Jendrośka, the structure of Article 9 is quite clear, but, because the Convention results from international negotiations, certain terms and concepts included therein do 'not always convey a clear legal norm'.[4] This observation is corroborated by Ryall, who concludes that 'the general nature of the language used in Article 9 … creates problems for implementation and enforcement'.[5]

Against this background, Article 9 is subject to interpretation. At the Aarhus level, various tools have been set up in order to interpret and check the implementation of the Convention's rights and obligations, including Article 9. Indeed, when it comes to access to justice, a special Task Force has been created by the Meeting of the parties (MoP) in 2002, with the purpose of supporting the implementation of the access to justice pillar by exchanging information, sharing good practices and discussing measures to remove barriers to effective access to justice.[6] The mandate of the Task Force has subsequently been renewed and extended on multiple occasions, through decisions of the MoP.[7]

Furthermore, the Aarhus Convention Implementation Guide provides guidance, insights and examples on how to interpret the Convention in practice.[8] The Implementation Guide is not binding; however, it provides considerable

[1] For an overview of the provisions, obligations and implementation elements of the Access to Justice pillar of the Aarhus Convention, see J Ebbesson et al, *The Aarhus Convention: An Implementation Guide*, 2nd edn (New York, United Nations Publications, 2014) 190.

[2] European Parliament, 'Implementing the Aarhus Convention – Access to Justice in Environmental Matters' [2017] Briefing, 3.

[3] J Jendrośka, 'Access to Justice in the Aarhus Convention: Genesis, Legislative History and Overview of the Main Interpretation Dilemmas', (2020) 17(4) *Journal for European Environmental & Planning Law* 372, 373.

[4] ibid 372.

[5] Á Ryall, 'The Aarhus Convention: Standards for Access to Justice in Environmental Matters' in SJ Turner et al (eds), *Environmental Rights: The Development of Standards* (Cambridge, Cambridge University Press, 2019) 116, 131.

[6] The list on the UNECE website summarises the tasks of the Task Force: see www.unece.org/env/pp/tfaj-mandate.

[7] For an overview of the Decisions of the Meeting of the Parties, see especially www.unece.org/env/pp/tfaj-mandate.

[8] Ebbesson et al (n 1).

information on the drafting process of the Convention and the intentions of the Convention's authors, and gathers the key decisions of the Compliance Committee. Furthermore, the Guide has previously been referred to by the CJEU and the European Commission, thereby highlighting its relevance in interpreting the Convention.[9] Yet, it must be noted that the latest edition of the Guide dates back to 2014 and thus does not include developments that have arisen since then.

In addition, the decisions rendered by the ACCC contain key elements for the interpretation of the Aarhus provisions.[10] The compliance mechanism provided under the Aarhus Convention is often described in the literature as peculiar, or unusual, for various reasons.[11] Indeed, the Committee presents distinctive features, which are not found in other international environmental instruments.[12] First, the Committee is nominated by the parties to the Convention and environmental non-governmental organisations (ENGOs), and elected by the MoP.[13] This procedure underlines the role of ENGOs in securing the application of the Convention. The members of the Committee are independent experts. Second, the enforcement mechanism can be triggered in five different ways, including by communications from the public.[14] Based on the submissions, the Committee 'may examine compliance issues and make recommendations if and as appropriate'.[15] Third, the Committee is not a court, but its opinions represent

[9] In Case C-182/10 *Solvay v Région wallonne* ECLI:EU:C:2012:82, the CJEU described the Implementation Guide as 'an explanatory document', which can be taken into account to interpret the Aarhus Convention, although it clarified that the contents of the Guide 'have no binding force and do not have the normative effect of the provisions of the Aarhus Convention' (para 27). With regard to the European Commission, the Guide is mentioned in the Commission 'Notice on access to justice in environmental matters' C/2017/2616 [2017] OJ C275/1.

[10] Article 15 of the Aarhus Convention mandates the MoP to establish 'optional arrangements of a non-confrontational, non-judicial and consultative nature' to review compliance of parties with the Convention's provisions. This is the legal basis for the establishment of the Compliance Committee.

[11] See, eg, V Koester, 'Review of Compliance under the Aarhus Convention: A Rather Unique Compliance Mechanism', (2005) 2(1) *Journal for European Environmental & Planning Law* 31; J Darpö, 'Principle 10 and Access to Justice' in L Krämer and E Orlando (eds), *Elgar Encyclopedia of Environmental Law: Principles of Environmental Law*, vol VI (Cheltenham, Edward Elgar, 2018) 379; E Fasoli and A McGlone, 'The Non-compliance Mechanism under the Aarhus Convention as "Soft" Enforcement of International Environmental Law: Not So Soft After All!' (2018) 65 *Netherlands International Law Review* 27; and G Samvel, 'Non-Judicial, Advisory, Yet Impactful? The Aarhus Convention Compliance Committee as a Gateway to Environmental Justice' (2020) 9(2) *Transnational Environmental Law* 211.

[12] J Jendrośka, 'Aarhus Convention Compliance Committee: Origins, Status and Activities' (2011) 8(4) *Journal for European Environmental & Planning Law* 301.

[13] Darpö (n 11) 385.

[14] According to the Guide to the Aarhus Compliance Committee, 'a review of a specific Party's compliance may be triggered in five ways: (a) A Party may make a submission about compliance by another Party; (b) A Party may make a submission concerning its own compliance; (c) The secretariat may make a referral to the Committee; (d) Members of the public may make communications concerning a Party's compliance with the Convention; (e) The Meeting of the Parties may request the Committee to examine a Party's compliance with the Convention'. See Ebbesson et al (n 1) 6.

[15] Annex to Decision I/7, para 14 of the Meeting of Parties to the Aarhus Convention, cited in UNECE, 'Guide to the Aarhus Convention Compliance Committee', 2nd edn, May 2019, 8.

the authoritative interpretation of the Aarhus Convention.[16] The findings drafted by the Compliance Committee are not binding. Still, these decisions carry great importance: on the one hand, they can contribute to the development of international environmental procedural rights; and, on the other hand, the compliance mechanism is growingly moving towards enforcement with legal effect – and away from soft measures.[17] The ACCC findings become final when endorsed by the MoP. During that stage, the MoP is responsible for deciding on 'appropriate measures to bring about full compliance with the Convention'.[18] The findings of the ACCC are therefore paramount when discussing the interpretation and application of the Convention. Moreover, data show that the cases of non-compliance with Article 9 of the Convention represent the majority of the findings of the ACCC.[19] When assessing compliance with Article 9, the ACCC takes into consideration the general picture of access to justice in the party concerned, in light of the Convention's Preamble, which states that 'effective judicial mechanisms should be accessible to the public, including organisations, so that its legitimate interests are protected and the law is enforced'.[20]

Finally, since the EU is a party to the Convention, the CJEU has been called upon to rule on the interpretation of numerous provisions thereof, including Article 9. This chapter therefore considers the interpretation of Article 9 of the Convention in the Implementation Guide, by the ACCC and in the case law of the CJEU. The examination of Article 9 in these different fora serves a twofold aim. First, this chapter presents the rules in place and their interpretation so as to shed light on the limitations placed on the room for implementation by the Member States. Second, this chapter paves the way for the comparative analysis conducted in the following chapters in this book. Ultimately, by examining the access to justice obligations and showing how they have been interpreted by the Implementation Guide and by the ACCC, as well as by the CJEU, this chapter serves as a benchmark to show, first, the extent to which the legal systems examined in the book comply with Article 9 of the Convention and, second, whether an 'EU effect' linked to the membership to the EU can be identified when it comes to access to justice in environmental matters. For that purpose, the present chapter identifies, for each limb of Article 9, the corresponding procedural obligations. Indeed, there are four notions that fall under the umbrella of the concept of 'access to justice', namely: standing, costs of proceedings, scope and intensity of review, and remedies. This chapter looks at these four facets of access to justice

[16] Jendrośka (n 12) 301.
[17] Darpö (n 11) 385; Fasoli and McGlone (n 11) 52.
[18] Ebbesson et al (n 1) 9.
[19] UNECE, Findings and recommendations under the Aarhus Convention, as of October 2021. See: www.unece.org/environment/press/after-25-years-aarhus-convention-states-compliance-environmental-rights.
[20] See: ACCC/C/2008/31 Germany (ECE/MP.PP/C.1/2014/8), para 64. The 'general picture' approach was also used in the findings on communications ACCC/C/2006/18 Denmark (ECE.MP.PP/2008/5/Add.4) and ACCC/C/2011/58 Bulgaria (ECE/MP.PP/2014/13).

and how they are regulated and interpreted in the Aarhus Convention and the implementing EU legislation. In other words, for each obligation, it considers the relevant explanations from the Implementation Guide, the interpretation by the ACCC, the transposition at the EU level (in as far as the national legislation of the Member States is concerned),[21] and the interpretation of the Convention and the relevant EU legislation by the CJEU.[22]

II. Article 9 of the Aarhus Convention, the Explanations of the Implementation Guide and the Interpretation by the ACCC

A. Article 9(1)

Article 9(1) of the Aarhus Convention requires access to review procedures relating to information requests made under Article 4 of the Convention. Accordingly, the review procedures must be available to 'any person' that has requested information, and considers that 'his or her request for information under article 4 has been ignored, wrongfully refused, whether in part or in full, inadequately answered, or otherwise not dealt with in accordance with the provisions of that article'. This notion of 'any person' relates to any member of the public, natural or legal persons, associations, organisations or groups. According to the ACCC, denying standing to a non-governmental organisation (NGO) that made an information request and wishes to challenge the public authorities' response to that request would breach the Convention.[23] This decision confirms that the personal scope of Article 9(1) extends to NGOs. To have standing, the members of the public must have made a prior request for information and must claim this request was refused or wrongfully handled. Also, the review procedures must be carried out by a judicial or 'other independent and impartial body'.[24] This wording means that Article 9(1) paves the way for both court and court-like bodies. As an example of such quasi-judicial body, the ACCC held that the procedure before the Norwegian Parliamentary Ombudsman constitutes a review procedure within the meaning of Article 9(1) of the Convention.[25] The Convention requires parties in which courts have jurisdiction over such matters to also provide for an alternative 'expeditious' and 'inexpensive' review procedure. According to the Implementation Guide, such a requirement is justified by the fact that alternative procedures may be quicker and

[21] The transposition of the Convention for the EU institutions and the interpretation by the CJEU of Regulation No 1367/2006 therefore falls outside the scope of the chapter.
[22] The chapter reflects the state of the (case) law as it stands on 30 January 2024.
[23] ACCC/C/2004/1 Kazakhstan (ECE/MP.PP/C.1/2005/2/Add.1). See also Ebbesson et al (n 1) 191.
[24] Article 9(1) of the Aarhus Convention. See Ryall (n 5) 128.
[25] ACCC/C/2013/93 Norway (ECE/MP.PP/C.1/2017/16).

less costly.[26] Article 9(1) insists that the procedure must be expeditious and free of charge or inexpensive. The Implementation Guide confirms that expeditious means 'efficient and speedy'.[27] The Compliance Committee agrees that a lengthy review procedure breaches the requirement of expedition.[28] The Committee also pointed out that the time limits set out in Article 4(2) and (7) of the Convention are indicative of what is considered 'expeditious' and 'timely'.[29]

When it comes to the concept of an 'inexpensive' procedure, it is acknowledged that any member of the public must be able to afford it. The final decisions resulting from the procedure under Article 9(1) must be binding on the public authorities holding the requested information. Non-compliance in that respect was found by the ACCC in a case against Moldova, where the public authority failed to fully execute the final decision of the local Court of Appeal, thereby not complying with Article 9(1) of the Convention.[30] Finally, parties are encouraged to establish a general rule that the reasons for decisions be in writing and are required to provide a duty to state reasons at least where access requests are rejected.

B. Article 9(2)

Access to justice in the context of decision-making for projects covered by the public participation requirements under the Convention takes place via Article 9(2). This Article also mentions that the review procedures can relate to 'other relevant provisions' of the Convention, which means that parties can extend the procedure foreseen for Article 9(2) to other provisions of the Convention, such as Articles 3, 5, 7 and 8. In the event that parties do extend the procedure to these provisions, they must be careful: while Article 9(2) provides rights to the 'public concerned', this terminology is not used in the above-mentioned provisions.[31] Indeed, Articles 3, 5, 7 and 8 of the Convention instead refer to the 'public'. Parties must therefore decide how to determine the scope of the 'public concerned' when applying Article 9(2) to these provisions.[32] The 'public concerned' is defined in Article 2(5) of the Convention as 'the public affected or likely to be affected by, or having an interest in, the environmental decision-making; for the purposes of this definition, non-governmental organisations promoting environmental protection and meeting any requirements under national law shall be deemed to

[26] Ebbesson et al (n 1) 192.

[27] ibid.

[28] See, eg, ACCC/C/2004/1 Kazakhstan (n 23). The Committee also found a breach of the 'expeditious' requirement under art 9(1) of the Aarhus Convention in ACCC/C/2015/134 Belgium (ECE/MP.PP/C.1/2021/24), para 154.

[29] ACCC/C/2013/93 Norway (n 25) para 90.

[30] ACCC/C/2008/30 Republic of Moldova (ECE/MP.PP/C.1/2009/6/Add.3).

[31] Ebbesson et al (n 1) 193.

[32] ibid.

have an interest'.[33] Article 9(2) nevertheless leaves some room for discretion to the parties when it comes to standing. Indeed, according to that provision, standing requirements are determined in accordance with national law, but on the condition that members of the 'public concerned' who can show that they have a sufficient interest or prove the impairment of a right, must be granted standing.

Furthermore, the Convention has emphasised that standing rules must deliver the objective of 'wide' access to justice. In this context, for example, the Implementation Guide suggests that, while it is consistent with the objectives of the Convention to hold that actual participation in a decision-making procedure would indicate that the member of the public has the status of a member of the 'public concerned', it might be too restrictive to require that only persons who participate in the decision-making procedure would be granted access under Article 9(2).[34] This requirement is described by Ryall as 'an important benchmark which limits Parties' discretion to set restrictive standing rules'.[35] In this regard, the question of ENGOs' standing is central, and the findings and recommendations of the ACCC produced a shift towards inclusion of ENGOs in review procedures.[36] Indeed, the ACCC emphasised that standing rules must be 'in accordance with the spirit and principles of the Convention', and drafted 'with the objective of giving the public concerned wide access to justice under Article 9(2)'.[37] Particularly for ENGOs, standing requirements should be 'clearly defined, should not cause excessive burden on environmental NGOs and should not be applied in a manner that significantly restricts access to justice for such NGOs'.[38] As to criteria that could restrict access to justice to NGOs, the Committee found that barring NGOs from accessing justice because they do not have open membership with full voting rights for members was a breach of Article 9(2) of the Convention.[39] The ACCC therefore clearly links the objective of wide access to justice and the right of ENGOs' to access courts under the Convention. The inclusion of ENGOs under the 'public concerned' having access to the review procedure under Article 9(2) also showcases how important ENGOs are in terms of enforcement of the rights enshrined in the Convention.[40]

Review under Article 9(2) of the Aarhus Convention, as under Article 9(1), does not need to take place before a court of law.[41] The triggers and scope of review under Article 9(2) can be related to both substantive and procedural legality.

[33] Article 2(5) of the Aarhus Convention.
[34] Ebbesson et al (n 1) 195.
[35] Ryall (n 5) 129.
[36] ACCC/C/2005/11 Belgium (ECE/MP.PP/C.1/2006/4/Add.2), 28 July 2006.
[37] ACCC/C/2008/31 Germany (ECE/MP.PP/C.1/2014/8) para 71.
[38] ibid.
[39] ACCC/C/2016/137 Germany (ECE/MP.PP/C.1/2021/25) para 117.
[40] Ryall (n 5) 129.
[41] For an example of a decision concerning review that was not, according to the ACCC, carried out before an independent and impartial body established by law, see ACCC/C/2016/143 Czech Republic (ECE/MP.PP/C.1/2021/28).

An example of a flaw linked to the substantive legality of a decision was found by the Committee in a case against the Czech Republic, as Czech law did not allow members of the public concerned to have access to a review procedure to challenge the legality of the outcome of the environmental impact assessment (EIA) screening process.[42] In a case against the EU, the ACCC tackled an example of inadequate procedural legality, as the Directive at stake in this case did not provide access to justice opportunities in permitting procedures before the start of the construction of a project.[43]

Moreover, Article 9(2) opens up the possibility for preliminary administrative review procedure, which means that parties may require plaintiffs to exhaust administrative remedies before going to court, although on condition that these procedures are timely.

C. Article 9(3)

Article 9(3) of the Aarhus Convention concerns review procedures for acts and omissions of private persons and public authorities concerning national law relating to the environment. The material scope thereof is therefore quite broad.[44] This provision is described in the literature as the 'enforcement provision'.[45]

In terms of standing, Article 9(3) provides that the criteria for accessing the procedure, if any, are to be laid down in national law. The ACCC noted that these criteria should not be too strict.[46] This provision nevertheless leaves much discretion to parties in defining the admissibility of claims. Indeed, Article 9(3) grants access to the members of the 'public', defined in Article 2(4) of the Convention as 'one or more natural or legal persons, and, in accordance with national legislation or practice, their associations, organisations or groups'. The 'public' is therefore a wider category than the 'public concerned' referred to in Article 9(2). However, Article 9(3) enables parties to define, in national law, who precisely falls into the category of the 'public'. This focus on the national legislation criteria can be logically explained by the fact that the implementation of access to justice provisions is influenced by existing national rules.[47] Still, this leeway leads to a situation of diversity of approaches across the legal systems of the parties to the Convention,

[42] ACCC/C/2010/50 Czech Republic (ECE/MP.PP/C.1/2012/11). See especially para 82 of ECE/MP.PP/C.1/2012/11.

[43] ACCC/C/2006/17 European Community (ECE/MP.PP/2008/5/Add.10).

[44] The Implementation Guide confirms that Article 9(3) is 'applicable to a far broader range of acts and omissions than paragraphs 1 and 2'. See Ebbesson et al (n 1) 197.

[45] Z Mikosa, 'Implementation of the Aarhus Convention through *Actio Popularis*: Article 9(3) of the Aarhus Convention and *Actio Popularis*' in J Jendroska and M Bar (eds), *Procedural Environmental Rights: Principle X in Theory and Practice* (Cambridge, Intersentia, 2017), 263, citing M Hedemann-Robinson, *Enforcement of European Union Environmental Law*, 2nd edn (Abingdon, Routledge, 2015) 373.

[46] ACCC/C/2005/11 Belgium (n 36).

[47] Ryall (n 5) 130.

and to a certain lack of clarity in terms of identification by the parties of who falls under the category of the 'public'.[48] Compared to Article 9(2), which, together with Article 2(5), provides for a presumed interest and standing of ENGOs, the general wording of Article 9(3) enables parties to impose stricter standing conditions.[49] Nevertheless, although in theory the text of the Convention provides that only Article 9(2) is to be read in conjunction with Article 2(5), in practice Article 9(3) is also combined with Article 2(5) when dealing with standing requirements.[50] Such a construction in fact allows broader standing for ENGOs, which coincides with the Convention's objective of ensuring wide access to justice.[51] This is also in line with the ACCC's findings and recommendations, which advocate for the promotion of broad standing rules, including for NGOs.[52] The ACCC furthermore clarified that, although parties are not obliged to establish a system of *actio popularis*, Article 9(3) may not be used to effectively bar almost all members of the public from challenging acts and omissions.[53] Parties' discretion in respect to standing should be exercised in light of the Convention's general objective of ensuring wide access to justice.[54]

Unlike what is permitted under Article 9(1) and 9(2), the review under Article 9(3) must be performed by a court or an administrative authority.[55] In terms of *what* can be reviewed under this provision, the ACCC allows members of the public to allege a breach of environmental law, without the need for the breach to be established prima facie.[56] Also, the scope of the law relating to the environment as understood under Article 9(3) is not confined to procedural rights and must include both the procedural and substantive legality of a decision.[57] The Compliance Committee held that the reference to 'national law relating to the environment' also includes EU law applicable in the EU Member States.[58]

[48] ibid; F Passarini, 'Legal Standing of Individuals and NGOs in Environmental Matters under Article 9(3) of the Aarhus Convention' (2023) 3(2) *Italian Review of International and Comparative Law* 283, 286.

[49] A Danthinne, M Eliantonio and M Peeters, 'Justifying a Presumed Standing for Environmental NGOs: A Legal Assessment of Article 9(3) of the Aarhus Convention' (2022) 31(3) *Review of European, Comparative & International Environmental Law* 411, 412.

[50] ibid.

[51] ibid.

[52] ACCC/C/2006/18 Denmark and ACCC/C/2011/58 Bulgaria (n 20).

[53] See ACCC/C/2005/11 Belgium (n 36) para 35 and ACCC/C/2008/32 European Union (ECE/MP.PP/C.1/2011/4/Add.1).

[54] I Hadijyianni, 'Multi-level Governance in Action: Access to Justice in National Courts in Light of the Aarhus Convention' (2020) 26(4) *European Public Law* 889, 894.

[55] The Implementation Guide states: 'Paragraph 3 creates a further class of cases where members of the public can appeal to administrative or judicial bodies.' See Ebbesson et al (n 1) 197.

[56] ACCC/C/2006/18 Denmark (n 20).

[57] Ebbesson et al (n 1) 197: 'national laws relating to the environment are neither limited to the information or public participation rights guaranteed by the Convention, nor to legislation where the environment is mentioned in the title or heading. Rather, the decisive issue is if the provision in question somehow relates to the environment.' See also ACCC/C/2005/11 Belgium (n 36) and ACCC/C/2011/58 Bulgaria (n 20). See also Ebbesson et al (n 1) 199.

[58] Ebbesson et al (n 1) 198, citing ACCC/C/2006/19 Denmark (n 20).

Article 9(3) applies to procedures to challenge 'acts' by private persons and public authorities. The question of what falls under the notion of 'acts' under 9(3) was addressed by the ACCC, for instance, in a case against the EU, where it was found that state aid decisions qualify as acts as understood by Article 9(3) of the Convention.[59] This decision confirms the broad material scope of Article 9(3).

D. Article 9(4)

Article 9(4) of the Convention sets general minimum standards that apply to all relevant review procedures, decisions and remedies. Article 9(4) itself does not use the wording of 'general minimum standards'; however, this understanding comes from Article 3(5) of the Convention, which reads: 'The provisions of this Convention shall not affect the right of a Party to maintain or introduce measures providing for broader access to information, more extensive public participation in decision-making and access to justice in environmental matters.'[60] It can therefore be derived from this Article that the requirements set in Article 9(4) are minimum requirements, which can be broadened by the parties.[61]

There is no distinction among the instances to which the standards of Article 9(4) apply, and appeals are included, as confirmed by the ACCC: if a natural or legal person loses in first instance against a public authority, appeals the decision and loses again, the related costs imposed on the appellant are not in compliance with Article 9(4) of the Convention.[62] Under Article 9(4), the remedies must be adequate and effective. Adequacy is understood as encompassing various means of remedies, such as compensation of past damage, prevention of future damage, and restoration. The requirement that remedies must be effective relates to real and efficient enforcement.

The Convention also mentions that remedies may include 'injunctive relief as appropriate', which refers to relief designed to prevent or remedy injury by requesting the addressee either to stop an activity or cease a violation, or to take certain measures.[63] Such relief can be interim or final.

The question of remedies has already been heavily discussed by the ACCC. Indeed, in a case against Belgium, the Committee discussed the review procedures for town planning permits and area plans developed before the entry into force of the Convention in Belgium, and concluded that these procedures did not ensure access to justice and thus failed to provide an effective remedy.[64] Later, in findings

[59] ACCC/C/2015/128 European Union (ECE/MP.PP/C.1/2021/21), 14.

[60] Article 3(5) of the Aarhus Convention.

[61] On the minimum standards in art 9(4) and how to interpret them, see for instance O Kelleher, 'Systemic Climate Change Litigation, Standing Rules and the Aarhus Convention: A Purposive Approach' (2022) 34 *Journal of Environmental Law* 107, 113.

[62] ACCC/C/2008/24 Spain (ECE/MP.PP/C.1/2009/8/Add.1).

[63] Ebbesson et al (n 1) 200.

[64] ACCC/C/2005/11 Belgium (n 36).

against Spain, the Committee declared that a system where citizens cannot actually obtain injunctive relief – early or late in the procedure – indicates that, even if injunctive reliefs are theoretically available, the Convention is violated if they are actually not available in practice.[65] In another case, the Committee found that EU case law implied that there was no effective remedy when acts and omissions of EU institutions acting as public authorities were challenged, and, citing the *Plaumann* test, it declared that, when it is applied to environmental and health-related issues, 'no member of the public is ever able to challenge a decision or a regulation' before the CJEU.[66] On a more practical level, the Committee observed that in Bulgaria, instead of assessing all facts and arguments, the courts relied heavily on the conclusions contained in the environmental impact assessments and strategic environmental assessments decisions, despite the fact that the legality of these decisions was challenged in the main proceedings.[67] Such practice was deemed not compliant with Article 9(4) of the Aarhus Convention.

Article 9(4) also imposes the requirement that the procedures be fair. In this respect, allowing a court hearing to start without proper notification breaches this fairness requirement.[68] Also, the Committee has found that the fairness requirement of Article 9(4) is breached when a party calculates the time limit to bring judicial review 'from the date when the contested decision was taken, rather than from when the decision became known to the public'.[69] Fair and equitable procedures also mean that small ENGOs must be able to receive legal aid.[70]

In addition, the review procedure must not be prohibitively expensive. Breaches of this requirement have been established by the ACCC at different occasions.[71] Courts may, however, still assign 'reasonable costs'.[72] The notion of what constitutes reasonable costs has been addressed by the ACCC in various findings and is debated on a case-by-case basis.[73] Some general rules may nevertheless be derived from ACCC decisions: the Committee considers the cost system as a whole, in a systemic manner.[74] The review procedures must also be timely, meaning that the

[65] ACCC/C/2008/24 Spain (n 62).

[66] ACCC/C/2008/32 (Part I) European Union (ECE/MP.PP/C.1/2011/4/Add.1) paras 86–92.

[67] ACCC/C/2012/76 Bulgaria (ECE/MP.PP/C.1/2016/3).

[68] ACCC/C/2004/6 Kazakhstan.

[69] ACCC/C/2015/131 United Kingdom (ACCC/C/ECE/MP.PP/C.1/2021/23), para 132.

[70] See ACCC/C/2009/36 Spain, as described in Ebbesson et al (n 1) 202.

[71] See, for instance, ACCC/C/2011/57 Denmark, in which the Committee found that a fee of 3,000 Danish krone (approximately €400) for NGOs to appeal to the National Environmental Appeals Board did not comply with art 9(4) (ECE/MP.PP/C.1/2012/7, para 52). See also ACCC/C/2015/130 Italy, where filing fees at both first instance (€650) and second instance (€975) were declared prohibitively expensive by the Compliance Committee (para 77).

[72] This is confirmed in art 3(8) of the Convention, which reads: 'Each Party shall ensure that persons exercising their rights in conformity with the provisions of this Convention shall not be penalized, persecuted or harassed in any way for their involvement. This provision shall not affect the powers of national courts to award reasonable costs in judicial proceedings.'

[73] See, for instance, ACCC/C/2008/27 United Kingdom (ECE/MP.PP/C.1/2010/6/Add.2).

[74] ACCC/C/2008/33 United Kingdom (ECE/MP.PP/C.1/2010/6/Add.3), para 128.

Convention provides for a standard of timeliness of procedures.[75] Finally, parties should strive to make the decisions under the access to justice provisions of the Convention in writing and publicly accessible.

Having explained what Article 9 of the Convention entails, it may be observed that virtually all provisions discussed leave a large room for parties' discretion. From this point of departure, the next section explores how this Article has been transposed in the EU legal order for the legal systems of the Member States and how Article 9 and its transposing legislation has been interpreted by the CJEU.

III. Article 9 of the Aarhus Convention, the Transposition in EU Law and the Interpretation by the CJEU

A. The Access to Information Directive

Article 9(1) of the Aarhus Convention has been transposed through Directive 2003/4/EC, the so-called 'Access to Information Directive'.[76] The Directive contains an access to justice requirement in Article 6, which follows directly from the Aarhus Convention, although it offers even more protection than that mandated by the Convention. Indeed, it foresees both an administrative *and* a judicial review procedure for situations in which applicants claim that their request for information has been ignored, wrongfully refused, inadequately answered or otherwise not dealt with in accordance with the provisions of the Directive.[77] Standing to bring a claim under Directive 2003/4/EC, in line with Article 9(1), is granted to 'any person' submitting an information request, without the need to prove the existence of an affected interest or the impairment of a right.[78]

Equally in line with Article 9(1), Article 6 of the Access to Information Directive provides that final decisions concerning access requests shall be binding on the public authority holding the information and that reasons shall be stated in writing, at least where access to information is refused.

When it comes to the scope and intensity of review, in *East Sussex* the CJEU considered that, while it is for the legal systems of the Member States to determine the national rules on the matter, these need to comply with the principles

[75] Ebbesson et al (n 1) 201.

[76] Directive 2003/4/EC of the European Parliament and of the Council of 28 January 2003 on public access to environmental information and repealing Council Directive 90/313/EEC (Access to Environmental Information Directive) [2003] OJ L41/26.

[77] M Eliantonio, 'The Proceduralisation of EU Environmental Legislation: International Pressures, Some Victories and Some Way to Go' (2015) 8(1) *Review of European Administrative Law* 99, 103, 105.

[78] Case C-279/12 *Fish Legal and Emily Shirley v Information Commissioner and Others* ECLI:EU:C:2013:853, para 36.

of equivalence and effectiveness.[79] In the context of the Access to Information Directive, the Court declared that the requirement of effectiveness is fulfilled if a national court is at least able to 'apply effectively the relevant principles and rules of EU law when reviewing the lawfulness of the decision'.[80]

Finally, with respect to costs of proceedings, in line with Article 9(1), Article 6(1) of the Directive requires administrative remedies to be inexpensive or free of charge.

To conclude, it can be observed that the access to justice requirements provided by Article 9(1) have all been correctly transposed in Article 6 of the Access to Information Directive. In turn, this provision leaves room for manoeuvre to Member States when it comes to defining certain terms, such as an 'inexpensive' review procedure.[81] Yet, despite these remaining uncertainties, the provision has not generated much case law.[82]

B. The Public Participation Directive

i. Standing

With a view to aligning Member States' legislation with Article 9(2) and, partially, Article 9(4) of the Convention, the EU has enacted Directive 2003/35/EC (the 'Public Participation Directive'),[83] which amended the Environmental Impact Assessment (EIA) Directive[84] and the Industrial Emissions Directive (IED).[85]

[79] Case C-71/14 *East Sussex County Council v Information Commissioner and Others* ECLI:EU:C:2015:656. For more on this case and the question it raises, see M Eliantonio and F Grashof, 'C-71/14, *East Sussex County Council v Information Commissioner, Property Search Group, Local Government Association* (Judgment of 6 October 2015) – Case Note' (2016) 9(1) *Review of European Administrative Law* 35.

[80] *East Sussex County Council* (n 79) para 58. It has also been noted that the requirement that review procedures extend to whether an access request has been 'ignored, wrongfully refused or inadequately answered or otherwise not dealt with' in accordance with the provisions of the Directive itself covers both procedural and substantive errors in the handling of the access request, thus streamlining this procedural aspect with the requirements of the Public Participation Directive. See Eliantonio (n 77) 105.

[81] M Hedemann-Robinson, 'EU Implementation of the Aarhus Convention's Third Pillar: Back to the Future over Access to Environmental Justice? – Part 2' (2014) 23(4) *European Energy and Environmental Law Review* 151, 152; Á Ryall, 'Implementation of the Århus Convention through Community Environmental Law' (2005) 6(4) *Environmental Law Review* 274, 276.

[82] The Commission has noted in 2012 that, despite a generally good implementation record, certain shortcomings in the application of art 6 at the national level remain. See Report from the Commission to the Council and the European Parliament on the experience gained in the application of Directive 2003/4/EC on public access to environmental information COM(2012) 774 final.

[83] Directive 2003/35/EC of the European Parliament and of the Council of 26 May 2003 providing for public participation in respect of the drawing up of certain plans and programmes relating to the environment and amending with regard to public participation and access to justice Council Directives 85/337/EEC and 96/61/EC [2005] OJ L156/17.

[84] Directive 2011/92/EU of the European Parliament and of the Council of 13 December 2011 on the assessment of the effects of certain public and private projects on the environment (Environmental Impact Assessment Directive) [2012] OJ L26/1.

[85] Directive 2010/75/EU of the European Parliament and of the Council of 24 November 2010 on industrial emissions (integrated pollution prevention and control) [2010] OJ L334/17 (Industrial Emissions Directive).

With respect to standing rules, Article 11 of the EIA Directive and Article 25 of the IED closely transpose the wording of Article 9(2) of the Convention by providing that qualified members of 'the public concerned' must be able to have access to a court or another independent and impartial body established by law where they can maintain the impairment of a right or when they are able to show a sufficient interest. Like Article 9(2) of the Convention, the Public Participation Directive also proposes two models of access to justice; however, as is the case under the Convention, under the Directive, NGOs promoting environmental interests and meeting any requirements under national law must be deemed capable of showing sufficient interest or to have rights capable of being impaired in a legal system that has opted for a rights-based approach. These notions are also to be interpreted consistently with the objective of giving the public concerned wide access to justice.

These limitations to the freedom of Member States to set their own standing rules (especially with respect to claims brought by ENGOs) has been subject to an extensive body of preliminary questions sent to the CJEU. From the *Djurgården* case, it can be inferred that national law may require that an association be granted standing only if it has as its objective the protection of nature and the environment.[86] However, the number of members required for an NGO to be able to access the court cannot be fixed at such a level that it runs counter to the objective of facilitating access to justice.[87] In *Trianel*, the Court tackled the rights-based model foreseen by EU law and the Convention, and concluded that a procedural arrangement whereby NGOs are prevented to bring a claim where the rules relied on protect only the interests of the general public and not the rights or interests of individuals is not allowed under EU law.[88] Also the *Gruber* case confirms that, according to the CJEU, national rules concerning standing for the members of the 'public concerned' (*in casu*, a neighbour affected by a project falling within the scope of the EIA Directive) cannot be interpreted restrictively.[89] Furthermore, in the *Pigs in Danger* case, the CJEU considered the requirement of prior participation in the decision-making process as a requirement for later standing in judicial

[86] According to the Commission ('Notice on access to justice in environmental matters' (n 9) para 79), 'it appears permissible for a Member State to require that the protection of the environment constitutes a dominant or substantial objective of an NGO' for it to be able to gain standing, while it is more doubtful that the CJEU will condone a national rule whereby standing is granted to an NGO only if it can prove that it has as an *exclusive* object the environmental protection.

[87] Case C-263/08 *Djurgården-Lilla Värtans Miljöskyddsförening v Stockholms kommun genom dess marknämnd* ECLI:EU:C:2009:631. In the context of this case, the CJEU considered that a membership requirement of 2,000 members was not in line with the objectives of the EIA Directive.

[88] Case C-115/09 *Bund für Umwelt und Naturschutz Deutschland, Landesverband Nordrhein-Westfalen eV v Bezirksregierung Arnsberg* ECLI:EU:C:2011:289, [2011] ECR I-03673.

[89] Case C-570/13 *Karoline Gruber v Unabhängiger Verwaltungssenat für Kärnten and Others* ECLI:EU:C:2015:231, para 40. See also Case C-575/21 *WertInvest Hotelbetriebs GmbH v Magistrat der Stadt Wien* ECLI:EU:C:2023:425 concerning the limitation of access to a court for the members of the public concerned in respect of a decision determining that there is no need for an environmental impact assessment.

review procedures and concluded that it was in breach of the requirements of access to justice contained in EU law and the Aarhus Convention.[90]

Finally, it is noteworthy that, with the *LZ II* ruling, procedures which, strictly speaking, do not fall under the Public Participation Directive (*in casu* the appropriate assessment procedure foreseen by the Habitats Directive),[91] have also been considered as falling within the scope of application of Article 9(2).[92]

ii. Costs of Proceedings

In line with the requirements of Article 9(4), the Public Participation Directive sets some limits to the rules on costs applicable in the national legal systems by requiring that procedures not be 'prohibitively expensive'.[93] This requirement has in turn been interpreted by the CJEU on several occasions. This case law contributes to give flesh to the rather vague notion of 'not prohibitively expensive'.

In *Edwards*, the Court has held that this requirement should be taken to mean that 'the persons covered by [the provisions of the Public Participation Directive] should not be prevented from seeking, or pursuing a claim for, a review by the courts that falls within the scope of those articles by reason of the financial burden that might arise as a result'.[94] In the same ruling, the CJEU also specifically mentioned that a cost assessment by a national court should not be carried out solely on the basis of subjective elements such as the financial situation of the person concerned or the importance of the claim for the applicant or the environment, but must also be based on an objective analysis of the amount of the costs, particularly since members of the public and associations are naturally required to play an active role in defending the environment.[95]

[90] Case C-826/18 *LB and Others v College van burgemeester en wethouders van de gemeente Echt-Susteren* ECLI:EU:C:2021:7. It should be noted that the Commission submitted a proposal for the amendment of the EID which endorses this ruling. See art 70h of the 'Proposal for a Directive of the European Parliament and of the Council amending Directive 2010/75/EU of the European Parliament and of the Council of 24 November 2010 on industrial emissions (integrated pollution prevention and control) and Council Directive 1999/31/EC of 26 April 1999 on the landfill of waste' COM (2022) 156 final.

[91] Council Directive 92/43/EEC of 21 May 1992 on the conservation of natural habitats and of wild fauna and flora [1992] OJ L206/7 (Habitats Directive).

[92] Case C-243/15 *Lesoochranárske zoskupenie VLK v Obvodný úrad Trenčín* ECLI:EU:C:2016:838. This interpretation was confirmed in *Commission v Poland* concerning access to justice in claims against forest management plans, which have been regarded as falling within the scope of application of the Habitats Directive: Case C-432/21, *Commission v Poland* ECLI:EU:C:2023:139.

[93] It should be noted that this provision of the Public Participation Directive does not – in itself – have direct effect in lack of transposition by a Member State, but does set an obligation, on the part of the national courts, to interpret their national law, as far as possible, in line with the relevant provision of the Directive: Case-167/17 *Volkmar Klohn v An Bord Pleanála* ECLI:EU:C:2018:833.

[94] Case C-260/11 *The Queen, on the Application of David Edwards and Lilian Pallikaropoulos v Environment Agency and Others* ECLI:EU:C:2013:221, para 35.

[95] ibid paras 40–43. See for the same conclusion Case C-252/22 *Societatea Civilă Profesională de Avocaţi AB & CD* ECLI:EU:C:2024:13.

Therefore, in the opinion of the Court, the costs of proceedings must neither exceed the financial resources of the person concerned nor appear, in any event, to be objectively unreasonable.[96]

The CJEU has also held that this interpretation applies in the context of *all* the costs arising from participation in judicial proceedings, including legal representation costs, court fees, and the cost of evidence and experts' fees.[97] The CJEU has also clarified that the same requirements are applicable at all stages of proceedings, ie, not only at the stage of first instance proceedings, but also at the stages of an appeal or second appeal.[98]

The 'not prohibitively expensive' requirement does not prevent national courts, in the CJEU's view, from making cost orders addressed to unsuccessful litigants. However, a mere discretionary practice by the Irish courts aimed at reducing or at not imposing costs on litigants with insufficient means could not be considered as sufficient implementation of the Public Participation Directive.[99] Specifically in the context of interim relief proceedings, in *Commission v UK*, the Court also held that the discretionary practice of the UK courts to award protective cost orders contravened the requirements of the Public Participation Directive because it was not considered sufficiently clear.[100] Finally, the CJEU has indicated that, when reading Article 9(4) (and 9(5)) in the light of Article 47 of the Charter of Fundamental Rights of the EU 'a court called upon to make an order for costs against an unsuccessful party in an environmental dispute must take into account all the circumstances of the case, including that party's interest and the public interest in the protection of the environment'.[101]

iii. Scope and Intensity of Review

Pursuant to the Public Participation Directive, recalling Article 9(2) of the Convention, members of the public concerned must be able to challenge 'the substantive or procedural legality' of decisions that are subject to the participation requirements mandated by EIA and Industrial Emission Directives.[102]

With respect to the scope of judicial review (ie, on which grounds courts can adjudicate), the CJEU held in *Commission v Germany* that the possibility to challenge flaws of substantive or procedural nature in decisions under Article 9(2)

[96] Case C-530/11 *Commission v United Kingdom* ECLI:EU:C:2014:67, para 47.

[97] Case C-427/07 *Commission v Ireland* ECLI:EU:C:2009:457, [2009] ECR I-06277, para 92. This is also confirmed by Case C-470/16 *North East Pylon Pressure Campaign Limited and Maura Sheehy v An Bord Pleanála and Others* ECLI:EU:C:2018:185, concerning the costs of the proceedings brought to obtain 'leave' to bring a claim for judicial review.

[98] *Edwards and Pallikaropoulos* (n 94) paras 45 and 48.

[99] *Commission v. Ireland* (n 97) para 94. On the requirement of 'predictability' of costs, see also *Edwards and Pallikaropoulos* (n 94) para 58.

[100] *Commission v United Kingdom* (n 96).

[101] *Societatea Civilă Profesională de Avocaţi Plopeanu & Ionescu* (n 95) para 83.

[102] Although it should be noted that, in line with the *LZ II* ruling, the scope of art 9(2) is wider than that covered by the EIA and Industrial Emissions Directives.

of the Convention entails that it is not possible to restrict the 'scope of the review by the courts to the objections which have already been raised within the time-limit set during the administrative procedure which led to the adoption of the decision'.[103] In other words, rules on so-called 'preclusions' are in violation of EU law and the Convention. Furthermore, in the same case, the Court stated that a review confined to procedural legality would not be in compliance with the obligations stemming from Article 9(2) and the related EU secondary legislation.[104] In particular, the CJEU held that a Member State cannot limit the scope of a judicial review to the question of whether a decision not to carry out an environmental impact assessment was valid. Excluding judicial review in cases in which, having been carried out, an EIA is found to be vitiated by defects would render the provisions of the Public Participation Directive largely nugatory.[105] Conversely, in *Altrip*, the Court held that limiting access to court for challenges against procedural errors which conceivably has no influence on the final administrative decision is not in breach of the Convention, but national law cannot put on the applicant the burden of proof that a procedural defect did have an impact on the final decision.[106]

Specifically with respect to procedural legality, the CJEU has also contributed to explaining the extent to which it is allowed under national law to regularise procedural flaws in a decision. In *Križan*, when considering the scope for rectifying an error made by a public authority (specifically, a failure to make available certain information in a procedure to approve a landfill) at the stage of an administrative appeal from the decision of that authority, the CJEU concluded that regularisation was possible, provided all required options and solutions remained possible at the appeal stage.[107] Similarly, in the *Comune di Corridonia* ruling, the Court held that when an impact assessment should have been conducted, EU law does not preclude regularisation through the conducting of the procedure, after a project has been approved and concretely implemented, on condition, first, that national rules allowing for the regularisation do not provide an opportunity to circumvent the rules of EU law or to dispense with applying them, and, second, that the assessment carried out for regularisation purposes 'is not conducted solely in respect of the plant's future environmental impact, but must also take into account its environmental impact from the time of its completion'.[108]

[103] Case C-137/14 *Commission v Germany* ECLI:EU:C:2015:683, para 80.
[104] *Commission v Germany* (n 103).
[105] ibid para 48.
[106] Case C-72/12 *Gemeinde Altrip and Others v Land Rheinland-Pfalz* ECLI:EU:C:2013:712. In *IL and Others*, the court confirmed this stance and held that it is allowed to limit access to court to challenge those procedural defects in a decision, which are not such as to alter the content of that decision, to situations in which the defect actually deprived the claimants of their right to participate in the decision-making process. See Case C-535/18 *IL and Others v Land Nordrhein-Westfalen* ECLI:EU:C:2020:391.
[107] Case C-416/10 *Jozef Križan and Others v Slovenská inšpekcia životného prostredia* ECLI:EU:C:2013:8, paras 87–91.
[108] Joined Cases C-196/16 and C-197/16 *Comune di Corridonia and Others v Provincia di Macerata and Provincia di Macerata Settore 10 – Ambiente* ECLI:EU:C:2017:589.

When it comes to substantive legality and the intensity of review of the content of a decision, neither the Convention nor the Directive prescribes a specific type of control (eg, legality or merits, proportionality or unreasonableness). However, the CJEU has clarified when certain limitations to the control of the content of a decision might fall short of ensuring the review of 'substantive legality' required by Article 9(2) and the Public Participation Directive. For example, in *Gruber*, the Court established that an effective judicial review of a decision taken by an administration not to carry out an environmental impact assessment on a project must cover the legality of the reasons for the contested screening decision, including the question of whether the project is likely to have a significant effect on the environment.[109]

The analysis carried out above shows that Article 9(2) has been correctly transposed in the EU legal system through the Public Participation Directive. However, Article 9(2) itself and its EU implementation left significant room for diverse national implementations, some of which have been considered by the CJEU as insufficient under the Aarhus requirements. This case law has in turn contributed to cementing and specifying Member States obligations stemming from the EU provisions.

C. The Lack of Transposition of Article 9(3), the Soft Law Instruments and the Case Law of the CJEU

i. The Commission Notice and the Access to Justice Provisions in EU Secondary Law

While the access to justice requirements set out in Article 9(1) and (2) have found legislative transposition in the EU legal order, the third paragraph of Article 9 has had a very different trajectory. The Commission had originally presented a Proposal for a Directive of the European Parliament and of the Council on access to justice in environmental matters.[110] However, the Directive was never adopted (and was ultimately withdrawn in May 2014) owing to resistance by the Member States in Council.[111] Since 2012, however, the Commission has put the issue of the transposition of the third paragraph of Article 9 of the Aarhus Convention back on the legislative agenda and, for these purposes, commissioned some studies.[112] Despite the evidence pointing to the need for a general legislative transposition of Article 9(3), the Commission decided in 2017 to

[109] *Gruber* (n 89).

[110] 'Proposal for a Directive of the European Parliament and of the Council on access to justice in environmental matters' COM (2003) 624 final.

[111] Withdrawal of obsolete Commission proposals [2014] OJ C153/03.

[112] See https://environment.ec.europa.eu/law-and-governance/aarhus_en.

issue a soft law instrument, the Notice on access to justice in environmental matters.[113] This interpretative communication has the aim of bringing together the body of CJEU's case law on access to justice in environmental matters which had been issued up to that point and provided guidance to national courts on how to operationalise it.

Beyond the soft law guidance of the Commission, it should be noted that while Article 9(3) has not *in itself* been transposed in a way which is comparable to Article 9(1) and (2), ie, through a dedicated legislative instrument, it may be considered de facto transposed in those instruments of EU law which – by subject matter – fall within the scope of Article 9(3) and contain access to justice provisions. For instance, this is the case for the Environmental Liability Directive[114] and the Seveso III Directive.[115]

In particular, Article 12 of the Environmental Liability Directive provides private entities with the right, in certain circumstances, to request a competent authority to undertake action in relation to instances of environmental damage. Furthermore, Article 13 grants the same private entities the right to have 'access to a court or other independent and impartial public body competent to review the procedural and substantive legality of the decisions, acts or failure to act of the competent authority under the Directive itself'.

Both rights of request to the competent authorities and of access to court against the authorities' conduct are subject to a standing test which, for the most part, reproduces the one contained in the Public Participation Directive. Indeed, Article 12(1) of the Environmental Liability Directive (which is referred to by Article 13 and thus is also applicable to the right of access to court) provides that natural or legal persons have standing to file a request to the authorities or to bring a claim before a court only if they can show sufficient interest in environmental decision-making relating to the damage or maintain the impairment of a right, both to be interpreted, similarly to the Public Participation Directive, according to the domestic legal system of the Member States.

In the same way as the Public Participation Directive, the Environmental Liability Directive affords a preferential status to NGOs by stating that, when they meet the requirements set in national law, ENGOs are to be deemed as having sufficient interest or as having rights capable of being impaired. However, unlike the Public Participation Directive, the Environmental Liability Directive also affords standing in a third situation, namely to natural and legal persons who are

[113] Commission (n 9).

[114] Directive 2004/35/CE of the European Parliament and of the Council of 21 April 2004 on environmental liability with regard to the prevention and remedying of environmental damage (Environmental Liability Directive) [2004] OJ L143/56.

[115] Directive 2012/18/EU of the European Parliament and of the Council of 4 July 2012 on the control of major-accident hazards involving dangerous substances, amending and subsequently repealing Council Directive 96/82/EC (Seveso III Directive) [2012] OJ L197/1.

affected or likely to be affected by environmental damage, thereby setting a lower threshold for access to court than the Public Participation Directive.[116]

With respect instead to the Seveso III Directive, Article 23 provides that access to information requests under the Directive must be treated in accordance with the Access to Information Directive, while decisions subject to public participation under the Directive must be able to be challenged by the 'public concerned' through the review procedures set up by the EIA Directive (as amended by the Public Participation Directive).

Beyond these two instruments, no EU law provision has, for a long time, required Member States to transpose the requirements of Article 9(3). However, in a 2020 Communication, the Commission considered that, in order to ensure an effective implementation of the EU environmental *acquis* and in light of the hurdles faced by litigants in national courts, co-legislators should, as a matter of priority, 'include provisions on access to justice in EU legislative proposals made by the Commission for new or revised EU law concerning environmental matters'.[117] At the time of writing, the EU Regulation on Deforestation Products,[118] the recast Directive on Ambient Air Quality[119] and the recast Directive concerning Urban Wastewater Treatment[120] contain access to justice provisions mirroring the requirements of Article 9(3), and several proposals are pending to this effect, including in respect of soil monitoring[121] and the so-called 'green claims'.[122] The Nature Restoration Regulation, adopted by the Council in June 2024, does not contain any access to justice provision in relation to national restoration plans.[123]

[116] The Court has interpreted this provision in the *Folk* judgment in which it held that persons holding fishing rights must be granted standing under the Directive. See Case C-529/15 *Gert Folk* ECLI:EU:C:2017:419.

[117] Communication from the Commission to the European Parliament, the Council, the European Economic and Social Committee and the Committee of the Regions, 'Improving access to justice in environmental matters in the EU and its Member States' COM (2020) 643 final, para 33. It must be noted that the following sentence enumerates the proposals listed in the Commission's Communication, although there might be examples of inclusion of access to justice provisions in legislative proposals that are not explicitly mentioned in the Communication. Other measures are, for example: art 15 of Directive (EU) 2024/1203 of the European Parliament and of the Council of 11 April 2024 on the protection of the environment through criminal law and replacing Directives 2008/99/EC and 2009/123/EC [2024] OJ L1/28; and Article 26 of Directive (EU) 2024/1760 of the European Parliament and of the Council of 13 June 2024 on corporate sustainability due diligence and amending Directive (EU) 2019/1937 and Regulation (EU) 2023/2859 [2024] OJ L1/58.

[118] Article 32 of Regulation (EU) 2023/1115 of the European Parliament and of the Council of 31 May 2023 on the making available on the Union market and the export from the Union of certain commodities and products associated with deforestation and forest degradation and repealing Regulation (EU) No 995/2010 [2023] OJ L150, 9 June, 206–47.

[119] Article 27 Directive (EU) 2024/2881 of the European Parliament and of the Council of 23 October 2024 on ambient air quality and cleaner air for Europe (recast) [2024] OJ L, 20 November 2024, 2881.

[120] Article 25 of Directive (EU) 2024/3019 of the European Parliament and of the Council of 27 November 2024 concerning urban wastewater treatment (recast) [2024] OJ L, 12 December 2024, 3019.

[121] Article 22 in 'Proposal for a Directive on Soil Monitoring and Resilience (Soil Monitoring Law)' COM (2023) 416.

[122] Article 16 in 'Proposal for a Directive on substantiation and communication of explicit environmental claims (Green Claims Directive)' COM (2023) 166.

[123] Regulation of the European Parliament and of the Council on nature restoration and amending Regulation (EU) 2022/869, 2022/0195(COD).

ii. The Case Law of the CJEU

In the absence of transposition of Article 9(3), the CJEU has, over the course of the years, issued a number of important rulings clarifying the scope of application of this provision. The first step was taken in the *LZ I* case, in which the Court concluded that, while Article 9(3) cannot be relied directly by litigants before national courts, there is nevertheless a duty for these courts:

> [T]o interpret, to the fullest extent possible, the procedural rules relating to the conditions to be met in order to bring administrative or judicial proceedings in accordance with the objectives of Article 9(3) of that convention and the objective of effective judicial protection of the rights conferred by European Union law, in order to enable an environmental protection organisation … to challenge before a court a decision taken following administrative proceedings liable to be contrary to European Union environmental law.[124]

What has been heralded as the 'so as to enable formula' has been taken to require 'national courts to adopt a new understanding to … provisions on standing in order align them to the Aarhus Convention'.[125]

This case was followed by a number of rulings which all declared Article 9(3) as capable of granting standing to NGOs claiming the violation the Water Framework Directive,[126] requiring national authorities to amend action programmes aimed at reducing pollution from nitrates,[127] or challenging an administrative decision granting EC-type approval for vehicles.[128] In this line of case law, the Court has often linked Article 9(3) with Article 47 of the Charter on the right to an effective remedy, which, in combination, have been regarded as capable of creating obligations on Member States to ensure effective judicial protection of EU environmental law provisions.[129] Furthermore, as clarified by the Commission Notice discussed

[124] Case C-240/09 *Lesoochranárske zoskupenie VLK v Ministerstvo životného prostredia Slovenskej republiky* ECLI:EU:C:2011:125, para 51. For some thoughts on the extent of this duty of consistent interpretation, see J Darpö, 'Article 9.2 of the Aarhus Convention and EU Law: Some Remarks on CJEU's Case-Law on Access to Justice in Environmental Decision-Making' (2014) 11 *Journal for European Environmental & Planning Law* 367, 389.

[125] J Darpö, 'On the Bright Side (of the EU's Janus Face): The EU Commission's Notice on Access to Justice in Environmental Matters' (2017) 14 *Journal for European Environmental & Planning Law* 373, 377.

[126] Case C-664/15 *Protect Natur-, Arten- und Landschaftsschutz Umweltorganisation v Bezirkshauptmannschaft Gmünd* ECLI:EU:C:2017:987.

[127] Case C-197/18, *Proceedings Brought by Wasserleitungsverband Nördliches Burgenland and Others* ECLI:EU:C:2019:824. For more on the implication of this ruling as well as the *IL* ruling mentioned above in n 106, see V Karageorgou and K Pouikli, 'Access to Justice for Challenging the Decisions of the Competent Authorities for Alleged Violations of the EU Water Legislation before National Courts: Relevant Developments and Trends through the Lens of the CJEU Judgments in Cases C-197/18 and C-535/18' (2021) 30(4) *European Energy and Environmental Law Review* 128.

[128] Case C-873/19 *Deutsche Umwelthilfe eV v Bundesrepublik Deutschland* ECLI:EU:C:2022:857. See, however, the latest of these rulings, in which the Court held that enlarging the scope of art 9(3) does not require the absence of any standing limitations, and hence granting access only when applicants are able to show a 'private legitimate interest' as required by Romanian law does not breach the Convention. See *Societatea Civilă Profesională de Avocaţi Plopeanu & Ionescu* (n 95) para 63.

[129] For more on this, see M Eliantonio, 'The Relationship between EU Secondary Rules and the Principles of Effectiveness and Effective Judicial Protection in Environmental Matters: Towards a

above, the scope of review in proceedings under Article 9(3) should comprise both the procedural and substantive legality of a decision.[130] This notion has been implicitly interpreted in the *Craeyenest* ruling, in which the Court considered that a national court must be able to verify whether the sampling points to control air quality have been established in accordance with the criteria laid down in the relevant EU law provisions.[131]

This case law, which, as has been argued, 'has a strong purposive undertow',[132] is meant to compensate the lack of a legislative transposition of Article 9(3). Nevertheless, as has also been observed, the Court's intervention, albeit valuable, 'cannot conceal the pressing need for a more comprehensive regime',[133] which, however, seems currently to have been abandoned even by the Commission in favour of a sectorial approach.

D. The Partial Transposition of Article 9(4) and the Case Law of the CJEU

As mentioned above, Article 9(4) requires contracting parties to provide adequate and effective remedies, including injunctive relief as appropriate, and for those remedies to be fair, equitable, timely and not prohibitively expensive.

Insofar as procedures under Article 9(1) are concerned, there is nothing in the Access to Information Directive to transpose the provisions of Article 9(4). However, the requirements under Article 9(4) must certainly be considered applicable in the context of judicial proceedings under Article 9(1) of the Convention, as the preamble of the Access to Information Directive states that EU law provisions (therefore including the Directive itself) 'must be consistent with' the Convention.[134] However, at the time of writing, the Court has not ruled on the requirements of Article 9(4) in proceedings under Article 9(1) and, since the requirements of Article 9(4) are rather general in nature, it has been correctly observed that it would have been better if the Access to Information Directive had incorporated the requirements of Article 9(4) explicitly.[135]

New Dawn for the "Language of Rights"?' (2019) 12(2) *Review of European Administrative Law* 95; I Hadjiyianni, 'Judicial Protection and the Environment in the EU Legal Order: Missing Pieces for a Complete Puzzle of Legal Remedies' (2021) 58 *Common Market Law Review* 1; I Hadjiyianni, 'Multi-level governance in Action: Access to Justice in Light of the Aarhus Convention and its Implementation in the EU Legal Order' (2020) 26(4) *European Public Law* 889.

[130] Commission (n 9) para 128.

[131] Case C-723/17 *Lies Craeynest and Others v Brussels Hoofdstedelijk Gewest and Brussels Instituut voor Milieubeheer* ECLI:EU:C:2019:533.

[132] Kelleher (n 61) 116.

[133] C Poncelet, 'Access to Justice in Environmental Matters: Does the European Union Comply with its Obligations?' 24(2) (2012) *Journal of Environmental Law* 287, 295.

[134] Recital 5 of the preamble to the Access to Information Directive.

[135] Hedemann-Robinson (n 81) 152.

While the obligation to provide remedies which are fair, equitable, timely and not prohibitively expensive has been transposed in the Public Participation Directive discussed above insofar as Article 9(2) is concerned, the requirements of adequacy and effectiveness (and the possibility to foresee injunctive relief) cannot be found in the Public Participation Directive. Following the same line of reasoning as with respect to Article 9(1), the untransposed requirements of Article 9(4) should also be considered applicable in proceedings under Article 9(2) as, according to the case law of the CJEU, EU legislation implementing the Aarhus Convention must be interpreted in line with the latter.[136]

The CJEU has interpreted Article 9(4) on several occasions in the context of proceedings falling under the scope of Article 9(2). The case law linked to the costs of proceedings (ie, the prong of Article 9(4) which has found legislative transposition in the Public Participation Directive) has been discussed above in section III.B.ii.

When it comes instead to the notion of adequate and effective remedies, the CJEU interpreted this requirement in respect of proceedings falling under the scope of Article 9(2) in the *Križan* ruling. In this case, the CJEU stated that, despite the absence of transposition of this requirement in what is now the IED, members of the public concerned must be able to ask the reviewing court to order interim measures such as injunctive relief to suspend the application of a permit in order to prevent environmental damage.[137]

Finally, the CJEU has also had the opportunity to consider rules on time limits. While the Court did not do so explicitly, it is fair to subsume these rules under the requirement to provide adequate and effective remedies in the context of proceedings under Article 9(2). In the *Flausch* case, the Court held that if the notification of public participation procedure has been inadequate, the time limits laid down in national law (*in casu* 60 days) cannot be relied on against a member of the public concerned.[138]

With respect to proceedings falling under the scope of Article 9(3), it should be noted that neither the Environmental Liability Directive nor the Seveso III Directive contains explicit provisions on the matters covered by Article 9(4). In respect of the Environmental Liability Directive, it could be argued that Article 9(4) remains applicable because Article 13 states that the provisions of the Directive shall be without prejudice to 'any provisions of national law which regulate access to justice'. This should be taken to also include the Aarhus Convention itself, which is to be considered a 'component' of national law for the purposes of

[136] *Bund für Umwelt und Naturschutz Deutschland* (n 88) para 41.

[137] *Jozef Križan and Others v Slovenská inšpekcia životného prostredia* (n 107).

[138] Case C-280/18 *Alain Flausch and Others v Ypourgos Perivallontos kai Energeias and Others* ECLI:EU:C:2019:928. For critical remarks on this case and its implications, see V Karageorgou, 'The Interrelation between Public Participation and Access to Justice in the EIA Context in the Face of the Increasing Use of Digital Technologies: Comment on the CJEU Judgment in the A. Flausch et al Case (C-280/18)' (2021) 18 *Journal for European Environmental & Planning Law* 39.

this provision, since all Member States have signed and ratified the Convention.[139] However, as with the Access to Information Directive, it would have been better if the Environmental Liability Directive had also explicitly implemented the requirements under Article 9(4), which would have become binding for the Member States as a matter of EU law.

In respect of the Seveso III Directive, Article 9(4) ought to be considered applicable because of the reference made in Article 24 of the Directive to the relevant access to justice provision in the EIA Directive. What was therefore discussed above – both with respect to the transposition of Article 9(4) in the Public Participation Directive and the untransposed parts of this provision – also seems to be applicable in proceedings under the Seveso III Directive.

For all other areas falling within the scope of application of Article 9(3), as mentioned earlier, there is no legislative transposition. Yet, unlike with respect to Article 9(3) itself, the Court has not yet had the opportunity to rule on Article 9(4) when applied to proceedings under Article 9(3). Nonetheless, nothing seems to speak against extending the applicability of the case law concerning Article 9(4) in the context of proceedings covered by Article 9(2) to situations falling with the scope of the third limb of Article 9.

IV. Conclusions

This chapter has presented the rules on access to justice laid down in Article 9 of the Aarhus Convention, and how they have been interpreted and transposed at the EU level. The importance of the Aarhus Convention in promoting access to justice in environmental matters and the role of the Compliance Committee in interpreting the Convention and declaring non-compliance cannot be overstated. Similarly, the package of EU (hard and soft) measures designed to implement the Aarhus requirements in EU law insofar as the law of the Member States is concerned have doubtlessly made, together with the case law of the CJEU interpreting the Convention and these EU measures, a significant contribution towards guaranteeing access to justice before Member States' courts.

This chapter has shown that Article 9(1) and (2) has been fully and correctly transposed by the EU. While most of the provisions of the EU measures transposing the Convention leave significant room for manoeuvre to the Member States, the CJEU, adopting a purposive interpretation of the Convention, has shed light on several transpositions which fall short of ensuring a 'wide access to justice'. Nevertheless, given the discretion left for Member States to implement the EU requirements, some national divergences (and possibly inconsistencies with EU law) can certainly not be ruled out.

[139] Hedemann-Robinson (n 81) 161.

Article 9(4) has been subject to only partial legislation transposition, with possible remaining gaps of protection, which only the CJEU could fill if asked through a preliminary reference from a national court or infringement proceedings initiated by the Commission.

At the time of writing, a significant shortcoming seems to be the lack of a horizontal measure transposing the requirements of Article 9(3). In 2014, writing about the transposition of Article 9(3) in the EU, Hedemann-Robinson spoke about a 'fragmented delivery of safeguards and protections'.[140] Ten years later, a sectorial approach to the transposition of Article 9(3) seems to be the only feasible way forward. While this is certainly better than the status quo, the potential risks for fragmentation cannot be overlooked, with the ensuing difficulties for Member States to transpose this mosaic of similar – yet not completely overlapping – obligations.

This mosaic is further complicated, insofar as the courts of the EU Member States are concerned, by the presence of germane obligations for national courts, namely those stemming from Article 47 of the Charter and Article 19 of the Treaty on the European Union on the obligation to provide effective remedies and the *Rewe* principles of equivalence and effectiveness. This creates a 'layered' system of protection and a differentiated (and potentially stricter but also more confusing) set of obligations for the legal systems belonging to the EU.[141]

The next chapters in this collection will identify whether the presence of EU secondary rules transposing the Aarhus Convention as well as the interpretative intervention of the CJEU and the presence of additional EU guarantees of effective judicial protection have contributed to a system of access to justice which is more in line with the spirit of 'environmental democracy' which lies at the basis of the Convention.

[140] Hedemann-Robinson (n 81) 168.

[141] These pieces of the 'effective judicial protection' puzzle have not been discussed in this chapter. To understand more about what they entail for national courts, see, in general, M Bonelli, M Eliantonio and G Gentile (eds) *Article 47 of the EU Charter and Effective Judicial Protection, Volume 1: The Court of Justice's Perspective* (Oxford, Hart Publishing, 2022) and, specifically for environmental matters, Eliantonio (n 129) 95.

2

The Impact of the Right of Access to Justice under the Aarhus Convention on the Greening of the European Court of Human Rights

CARMEN PLAZA

I. Introduction: The Intersection of the Rome Convention and the Aarhus Convention on Access to Justice

Capellety and Garth wrote in 1978 that effective access to justice can be seen 'as the most basic requirement – the most basic "human right" – of a modern, egalitarian legal system which purports to guarantee, and not merely proclaim, the legal rights of all'.[1] As these authors also underlined, 'the words "access to justice" are admittedly not easily defined', and though its scope has varied over time and across jurisdictions, they serve to focus on two basic purposes of a legal system: 'First, the system must be equally accessible to all; second, it must lead to results that are individually and socially just.'[2]

In the realm of the European Convention on Human Rights (hereinafter ECHR or 'the Rome Convention')[3] the notion of 'access to justice' is enshrined in the right to a fair trial (Article 6) and the right to an effective remedy before a national authority for arguable violations of ECHR rights (Article 13). Under the Rome Convention, which is devoted to the protection of first-generation human rights, Member States must guarantee these rights following the standards set by the European Court of Human Rights (ECtHR) in the case law developed in its supervisory role. The Court plays a fundamental role in the European system of

[1] BG Garth and M Cappelleti, 'Access to Justice: The Newest Wave in the Worldwide Movement to Make Rights Effective' (1978) 27 *Buffalo Law Review* 181, 182.

[2] ibid.

[3] Rome, 4 November 1950.

human rights as the last guardian and the supreme interpreter of the rights set out in the Rome Convention when adjudicating, under Article 34 ECHR, 'applications from any person, non-governmental organisation or group of individuals claiming to be the victim of a violation by one of the High Contracting Parties of the rights set forth in the Convention or the Protocols thereto'.[4]

Most of the 46 ECHR Member States are also parties to the Convention on Access to Information, Public Participation in Decision-Making, and Access to Justice in Environmental Matters (hereinafter AC or 'the Aarhus Convention'),[5] adopted under the auspices of the United Nations Economic Commission for Europe (UNECE).[6] Therefore, there is a clear intersection between these two international treaties in relation to the right of access to justice of over 800 million people in Europe. However, under these two international treaties, access to justice pursues partially different goals and has a different scope and content.[7]

Access to justice under Article 9 AC is conceived as an instrument to strengthen environmental law enforcement through the protection of procedural and substantive environmental rights.[8] As already explained in Chapter 1,[9] it requires the parties to ensure adequate review procedures to safeguard the rights afforded in the other pillars of the Convention (the rights to access to information and public participation), as well as under national environmental law, following the guidelines and recommendations adopted by the Aarhus Convention Compliance Committee (ACCC).

This Convention provides wide access to justice to promote the actions of citizens and non-governmental organisations (NGOs) against regulatory and administrative action or inaction contrary to environmental law, making governments more accountable to people on environmental matters. Legal persons with the statutory goal of protecting the environment hold the rights to information, participation and access to justice on environmental issues. They benefit as members of the 'public' in general from the right of access to information enshrined in Article 4 AC and, according to Article 2.5 AC, they are considered as the 'public concerned' having an interest in the environmental decision-making under the terms of Article 6 AC. Article 9 provides access to justice for the

[4] See generally European Union Agency for Fundamental Rights & Council of Europe, *Handbook on European Law Relating to Access to Justice* (Luxembourg, Publication Office of the European Union, 2016) 17.

[5] Aarhus, 25 June 1998.

[6] Of the 46 Council of Europe Member States, only five (Andorra, Lichtenstein, Monaco, San Marino and Turkey) have not ratified the Aarhus Convention.

[7] See especially B Peters, 'Unpacking the Diversity of Procedural Environmental Rights: The European Convention on Human Rights and the Aarhus Convention' (2018) 1 *Journal of Environmental Law* 1; and Á Ryall, 'The Aarhus Convention: Standards for Access to Justice in Environmental Matters' in SJ Turner et al (eds), *Environmental Rights. The Development of Standards* (Cambridge, Cambridge University Press, 2019) 116, 123.

[8] See generally J Ebbesson et al, *The Aarhus Convention: An Implementation Guide*, 2nd edn (Geneva, United Nations Publication, 2014), 19, 187; Ryall (n 7) 123.

[9] See Eliantonio and Richelle, ch 1 in this volume, sections I and II.

beneficiaries of these two procedural rights (paragraphs 1 and 2 respectively) and it also requests the parties to ensure that, where they meet the criteria (if any) laid down in its national law, they have also access to administrative or judicial procedures to challenge acts and omissions by private persons and public authorities which contravene provisions of its national law relating to the environment (paragraph 3).[10] As to the role of environmental NGOs, the ACCC has underlined that these organisations, 'by bringing together expertise and resources, generally have greater ability to effectively exercise their rights under the Convention than individual members of the public'.[11] Given that the Achilles' heel of environmental law has, for decades, been weak and uneven implementation,[12] Article 9 AC emerges as a crucial instrument to enhance judicial scrutiny of infringements of environmental law and to address enforcement gaps.

In short, whereas Articles 6 and 13 ECHR attempt to protect first-generation individual human rights, access to justice under Article 9 AC attempts to protect broadly environmental rights and interests.

The links between the Aarhus Convention and the aims of the Council of Europe (CoE) were soon underlined by the Parliamentary Assembly of the CoE (PACE), which on 27 June 2003 recommended to the Member States of the CoE to 'safeguard the individual procedural rights to access to information, public participation in decision making and access to justice in environmental matters set out in the Aarhus Convention'.[13]

Yet, despite the intersection between both Conventions, the impact of Article 9 AC on the case law of ECtHR related to Articles 6 and 13 ECHR has been rather limited when compared with case law developed by the other European court – the Court of Justice of the European Union (CJEU) – on the implementation of the AC by the EU Member States. The same applies to Article 34 ECHR, establishing the 'Admissibility criteria' to access the ECtHR. The reasons for this disparate impact are evident: the EU is a party to the Aarhus Convention and therefore its provisions are integrated and have been implemented into secondary EU law, and are subject to interpretation by the CJEU;[14] on the contrary, the ECHR and the AC are two different international treaties that partially operate in different spheres, with different compliance organs and, as already mentioned, a notion of 'access to justice' that serves different purposes.

[10] ibid.

[11] ACCC/C/2004/05 (Turkmenistan).

[12] See, eg, JL Sax, *Defending the Environment: A Strategy for Citizen Action* (New York, Alfred, 1971); E Rehbinder and R Stewart, *Environmental Protection Policy* (Berlin, De Gruyter, 1988) vii; L Krämer, *Focus on European Environmental Law*, 2nd edn (London, Sweet & Maxwell, 1997) 1–25. More recently, see United Nations Environment Programme (UNEP), *Environmental Rule of Law: First Global Report* (Nairobi, UNEP, 2019) viii.

[13] Parliamentary Assembly of the Council of Europe Recommendation Rec(2003)1614 on environment and human rights, para 9.

[14] See Eliantonio and Richelle, ch 1 in this volume, section III.

The uneven but increasing influence of the Aarhus Convention on the scope of Articles 6, 13, and 34 ECHR is due to two factors: first, the greening of human rights through the ECtHR case law, as examined below; and, second, the instrumental use by the ECtHR of other international treaties to interpret and apply the ECHR.

As is well known, in defining the meaning of terms and notions in the text of the Convention, the Court 'can and must take into account elements of international law other than the Convention, the interpretation of such elements by competent organs, and the practice of European States reflecting their common values'.[15]

Thus, as most of the ECHR Member States also became members of the AC, in the case of *Taşkın and Others v Turkey*,[16] the Court declared the Aarhus Convention as a 'relevant international text' to interpret both Article 8 and Article 6(1) ECHR, and highlighted the increasing importance 'as acknowledged nationally, as well as at European and international level', of access to justice in environmental matters in its subsequent case law.[17]

However, in parallel to the development of an important 'environmental case law', the ECtHR has constantly recalled that '[t]here is no explicit right in the Convention to a clean … environment',[18] and, consequently, the Convention does not 'provide general protection of the environment as such'.[19] Furthermore, the Court has also consistently held that it is not bound by interpretations given to different international instruments by other bodies, 'having regard to possible differences in the content of the provisions of other international instruments and/or possible differences in the role of the Court and the other bodies'.[20] This is an approach that marks the limits to the impact of the Aarhus Convention in the interpretation of Articles 6 and 13 ECHR, and also of Article 34 ECHR, and puts into question the extent to which the individual rights and freedoms of the Convention can contribute to protecting the environment and, in particular, to combat global environmental crises such as climate change.

The following sections of this chapter first outline the different approaches developed at the global and European levels to protect the environment through the protection of human rights – and in particular through the protection of the right of access to justice – and the role played by the ECtHR case law in its development. Second, the chapter analyses to what extent the ECtHR has taken into account Article 9 AC to determine the scope of the right of access to justice in

[15] See *Demir and Baykara v Turkey* [GC] App No 34503/97 (ECtHR, 12 November 2008), para 85.

[16] See, eg, *Taşkın and Others v Turkey* App No 49517/99 (ECtHR, 10 November 2004), para 99.

[17] See, eg, *Lesoochranárske Zoskupenie VLK v Slovakia* App No 53246/08 (ECtHR, 2 October 2012), paras 55, 80. Though in this early case, the Court declared the complaint of an NGO inadmissible (at para 78).

[18] See, among others, *Hatton and Others v United Kingdom* [GC] App No 36022/97 (ECtHR 8 July 2003), para 96.

[19] *Kyrtatos v Greece* App No 41666/98 (ECtHR, 22 May 2003), para 52.

[20] *Caamaño Valle Spain* App No 43564/17 (ECtHR, 11 May 2021), paras 53–54.

environmental cases. Third, it examines the impact of the recent cases of climate change on the ECtHR's doctrine on access to justice. Finally, and looking ahead, it briefly considers the potential impact that the inclusion of a right to a clean, healthy and sustainable environment in a new protocol to the ECHR might have on the ECtHR's case law on access to justice to protect environment-based human rights.

II. Environmental Protection Through Human Rights: Four Overlapping Approaches and the Role of the ECtHR

The tight links between human rights and the environment have been progressively acknowledged over the last half a century.[21] There has been an increasing trend for human rights treaty bodies to explore these bounds, and the close connections between environmental protection and human rights are now beyond dispute.[22] Yet, the relationship between human rights and the environment remains intricate, multifaceted and in a state of constant evolution.

The interdependence between the environment and human rights was first highlighted at the global level in 1972 in the Stockholm Declaration adopted at the United Nations Conference on the Human Environment.[23] The preamble to this soft law instrument proclaimed that 'both aspects of man's environment, the natural and manmade, are essential to his well-being and to the enjoyment of basic human rights – even the right to life itself'. Furthermore, its first Principle states that 'man has the fundamental right to freedom, equality and adequate conditions of life, in an environment of a quality that permits a life of dignity and well-being'.[24]

The principles of the Stockholm Declaration, which laid down the foundations of modern environmental law, were reinforced two decades afterwards

[21] See especially A Boyle, 'Human Rights and the Environment: Where Next?' (2012) 23 *European Journal of International Law* 613, 642; JH Knox, 'The Past, Present, and Future of Human Rights and the Environment' (2018) 53 *Wake Forest Law Review* 649; F Francioni, 'International Law in an Environmental Horizon' (2010) 21 *European Journal of International Law* 41; JH Knox and D Boyd, 'Report of the Special Rapporteur on the Issue of Human Rights Obligations Relating to the Enjoyment of a Safe, Clean, Healthy and Sustainable Environment' (2018) United Nations General Assembly UN Doc. A/73/188; JH Knox and E Morgera, *Human Rights and the Environment: The Interdependence of Human Rights and a Healthy Environment in the Context of National Legislation on National Resources* (Rome, Food and Agriculture Organization of the United Nations, 2022); JH Knox and R Pajan, 'Introduction' in JH Knox and R Pajan (eds), *The Human Right to a Healthy Environment* (Cambridge, Cambridge University Press, 2018) 1.

[22] For an overview, see UNEP, *Environmental Rule of Law: Tracking Progress and Charting Future Directions* (Nairobi, United Nations Environmental Program, 2023) 103.

[23] 'Declaration on the Environment', UN Conference on the Environment, Stockholm, 5–16 June 1972, Principle 1.

[24] See in general LB Sohn 'The Stockholm Declaration on the Human Environment' (1973) 14 *Harvard International Law Journal* 423, 427, 439; Francioni (n 21) 44.

by the 1992 Rio Declaration, which introduced in its Principle 10 the bases for fundamental procedural rights for the protection of the environment: 'appropriate access to information concerning the environment that is held by public authorities'; 'the opportunity to participate in the decision-making process'; and 'access to administrative and judicial proceedings'. Thus, it established the basis for the three fundamental 'access rights' for individuals and environmental NGOs to 'best handle' environmental issues.

These founding principles, as enshrined in the Stockholm and Rio Declarations, have fostered four consecutive but overlapping approaches to the protection of the environment through human rights at the global and regional levels:

(i) First, in the early 1990s, the ECtHR triggered a process of 'greening' the first-generation human rights as protected in the Rome Convention by declaring that severe and persistent environmental degradation or risks could violate several fundamental rights of the ECHR.[25]
(ii) Second, in 1998 we witnessed the strengthening of the procedural rights of access to information, public participation and access to justice, as fundamental instruments for environmental protection and reinforcement of the effectiveness of substantive environmental law. Based on Principle 10 of the 1992 Rio Declaration, the Aarhus Convention expressly linked the protection of the environment to procedural human rights already enshrined in different instruments of international law such as the right to effective judicial protection.[26] Conversely, it also highlights the link between human rights and the environment, by affirming in its Preamble that 'adequate protection of the environment is essential to … the enjoyment of basic human rights'.
(iii) Third, the express acknowledgement of the link between human rights and climate change in the 2015 Paris Agreement, whose Preamble states that: 'Parties should, when taking action to address climate change, respect, promote and consider their respective obligations on human rights, the right to health, the rights of indigenous peoples, local communities, migrants, children, persons with disabilities and people in vulnerable situations and the right to development, as well as gender equality, empowerment of women and intergenerational equity.'[27]
(iv) Fourth, the proclamation of a human right to 'a clean, healthy and sustainable environment' by UN General Assembly Resolution 76/300 of 28th July 2022,[28]

[25] See section III below.

[26] See in general Boyle (n 21) 623; M Prieur, 'La participation d'Aarhus, instrument universel de la démocratie environnementale' (1999) *n. spécial Revue Juridique de l'Environnement* 9, 17; L Lavrysen, 'The Aarhus Convention: Between Environmental Protection and Human Rights' (2010) *Parcours des droits de l'homme* 647.

[27] See further L Rajamani, 'Human Rights in the Climate Change Regime: From Rio to Paris and Beyond' in Knox and Pejan (eds) (n 21) 236.

[28] A/76/L.75.

which also states that 'the right to a clean, healthy and sustainable environment is related to other rights and existing international law'.[29]

These four approaches currently co-exist, intersect and generate synergies towards the protection of the environment at the global and regional levels. Further, at the national level, another development following the Stockholm Declaration that should be taken into account is the introduction – from the 1970s onwards – of environmental clauses in national constitutions, shaped not only as a public obligation to protect the environment, but in some cases also as a right to a healthy or clean environment.[30] As the United Nations Environment Programme (UNEP) estimates, in 2023 over 160 countries recognised a right to a healthy environment at a regional, national or subnational level, and – according to the UN Special Rapporteur on the issue of human rights obligations relating to the enjoyment of a safe, clean, healthy and sustainable environment – over 100 countries have recognised the right to a healthy environment either explicitly or implicitly in their national constitution.[31]

In this framework, the ECtHR has played different roles in developing each of the four global or regional trends outlined above, which also affect the scope of access to justice under the Rome Convention.

As will be examined below, the ECtHR pioneered the first trend, whereas it has so far played a limited role concerning the second one, ie, promoting environmental protection through procedural access to justice, and Article 9 AC has had an uneven impact on the ECtHR case law on access to justice.[32] More recently, the role of the ECtHR in combating climate change through the protection of human rights has been put to the test through cases brought by youth groups and senior citizens. In a landmark ruling for protecting human rights against climate change, the ECtHR has developed new criteria for access to justice in climate litigation.[33] Finally, the international trend of recognising an autonomous human right to a clean, healthy and sustainable environment has reinvigorated the debate in the

[29] On this process, its challenges and achievements, see especially the reports of the UN Special Rapporteurs on Human Rights and the Environment, Professors JH Knox first (from 2012 to March 2018) and D Boyd (from March 2018 to April 2024): JH Knox, *Report of the Independent Expert on the Issue of Human Rights Obligations Relating to the Enjoyment of a Safe, Clean, Healthy and Sustainable Environment*, UN Doc A/HRC/22/43 (24 December 2012); Knox and Boyd (n 21); DR Boyd, *Recognition of the Right to a Healthy Environment in Constitutions, Legislation and Treaties: Eastern European Region*, UN Doc A/HRC/43/53, annex VI (2020). See also their academic works: D Boyd, 'Catalyst for Change: Evaluating Forty Years of Experience in Implementing the Right to a Healthy Environment' in Knox and Pejan (eds) (n 21) 17; JH Knox, *Introduction to Symposium on UN Recognition of the Human Right to a Healthy Environment* (published online by Cambridge University Press, 31 July 2023, https://doi:10.1017/aju.2023.25) 162–64.

[30] See UNEP (n 12) 2; C Plaza, 'Climate Governance: New Challenges to the So-Called "Environmental Democracy"' (2023) 35(1) *European Review of Public Law* 109, 116.

[31] UNEP (n 22) 92. See further the thorough analysis of JR May, 'The Case for Environmental Human Rights: Recognition, Implementation, and Outcomes' (2021) 42 *Cardozo Law Review* 983.

[32] See section III below.

[33] See section IV below.

CoE on the adoption of a new protocol to the ECHR enshrining the right to a clean, healthy and sustainable environment, which could in turn have a deep impact on the ECtHR case law and would therefore affect the scope of access to justice on environmental matters.[34]

III. The Greening of the Rome Convention and the (Limited) Impact of Article 9 of the Aarhus Convention on the ECtHR Case Law on Access to Justice

In contrast with other human rights regional treaties, the ECHR does not (yet) include any express reference to the environment.[35] At the time it was negotiated and signed – in the aftermath of the Second World War – the priority in Europe was to secure peace and justice, and the protection of human rights and fundamental freedoms was vital to this end.[36] In Western societies, a general concern for environmental degradation emerged only in the late 1960s and gained momentum on the global political agenda in the early 1970s.[37]

Following the conception of the Rome Convention as a 'a living instrument which … must be interpreted in the light of present-day conditions',[38] the ECtHR finally acknowledged the increasing importance of environmental protection in the early 1990s.[39] Since then, it has promoted the indirect protection of the environment by embedding environmental concerns in the interpretation and protection of several substantive human rights that can be undermined by severe environmental harm or risk.[40] This is the case, in particular, with the right to life (Article 2),[41] the right not to be subjected to inhuman or degrading treatment (Article 3),[42] the right to respect for private and family life as well as the home

[34] See section V below.

[35] See art 24 of the African Charter on Human and Peoples' Rights (27 July 1981, Nairobi); art 11 of the Additional Protocol to the American Convention on Human Rights in the Area of Economic, Social and Cultural Rights (17 November 1988, San Salvador).

[36] L Boisson de Chazournes, 'Environment – Human Rights and the Environment: An Evolving Relationship' in European Court of Human Rights, *Dialogue between Judges 2020, The European Convention on Human Rights: Living instrument at 70* (2020), 17, www.echr.coe.int/documents/d/echr/Dialogue_2020_ENG.

[37] See, eg, PH Sand, 'Origin and History' in L Rajamani and J Peel (eds), *The Oxford Handbook of International Environmental Law* (Oxford, Oxford University Press, 2021) 56; ZJB Plater, 'From the Beginning, a Fundamental Shift of Paradigms: Theory and Short History of Environmental Law' (1994) 27 *Loyola of Los Angeles Law Review* 981.

[38] See, eg, *Tyrer v United Kingdom* App No 5856/72 (ECtHR, 25 April 1978), para 31.

[39] See, eg, *Fredin v Sweden* App No 12033/86 (ECtHR, 18 February 1991), para 48.

[40] See generally Council of Europe, *Manual on Human Rights and the Environment* (Strasbourg, Council of Europe, 2022).

[41] See, eg, *Öneryıldız v Turkey* [GC] App No 48939/99 (ECtHR, 30 November 2004), para 71.

[42] See, eg, *Florea v Romania Balogh v Hungary* App No 37186/03 (ECtHR, 14 November 2010).

(Article 8),[43] and the right to the peaceful enjoyment of one's possessions (Article 1 of Protocol No 1)[44] – a trend that likewise extended to the interpretation of the procedural rights enshrined in Article 6 and, to a lesser extent, to 13 ECHR as well as Article 34 ECHR.[45] Since then, the Court's case law provides for indirect protection of the environment by sanctioning environmental violations that simultaneously result in an infringement of other human rights already recognised in the Convention.

The first Court's judgment on the right of access to justice in an environmental case also emerged in the early 1990s, before the signing of the Aarhus Convention. In the 1993 case *Zander v Sweden*, the ECtHR held unanimously that Article 6.1 ECHR had been violated in a case where the applicants – the owners of land adjacent to a waste tip that had polluted their drinking water – could not have the government's decisions upholding waste licensing reviewed by a court.[46] However, once the ECtHR established the connection between human rights and the environment, international and national environmental law standards became relevant when assessing the violation of the aforementioned human rights: the ECtHR interprets the states' obligations under the ECHR, taking into account elements of international law other than the Convention, or even of domestic law where such norms and principles apply in 'the majority of member states of the Council of Europe and show, in a precise area, that there is common ground in modern societies'.[47] Therefore, after most of the CoE Member States signed the Aarhus Convention, it was just a matter of time before the ECtHR considered it to be a relevant international standard in a case of alleged breaches of the right of access to justice in environmental matters, as it held in the case *Taşkın and Others v Turkey*.[48]

Taşkın is interesting for two additional reasons: first, the Court mentioned the Aarhus Convention as a relevant reference for deciding the case, even though Turkey was not yet a party. Second, although the right of access to justice is enshrined in Article 6 and Article 13 ECHR, the Court implicitly took into account the 'the access rights' of the Aarhus Convention to assess the violation of the 'procedural aspects' of Article 8 ECHR (respect for the private and family life). In this case, the applicants successfully alleged that the national authorities' decision to issue a permit to use a cyanidation operating process in a gold mine had given rise to a violation of their rights guaranteed under Article 8 and Article 6 ECHR. In its decision concerning the infringement of Article 8, the ECtHR recalled that in a case involving state decisions affecting environmental

[43] See, eg, *Powell and Rayner v United Kingdom* Series A No 172 (1990); *Lopez Ostra v Spain* Series A No 303 (1994).

[44] See, eg, *Fredin v Sweden* App No 18928/91 (ECtHR, 9 February 1991).

[45] See especially K Morrow, 'The ECHR, Environment-Based Human Rights Claims and Search for Standards' in SJ Turner et al (eds) *Environmental Rights: The Development of Standards* (Cambridge, Cambridge University Press, 2019) 41, 42–45.

[46] *Zander v Sweden* App No 14282/88 (ECtHR, 25 November 1993), para 29.

[47] *Demir and Baykara v Turkey* App No 34503/97 (ECtHR, 12 November 2008).

[48] *Taşkın and Others v Turkey* (n 16) para 99.

issues, there are two aspects to the inquiry which may be carried out by the Court: (i) the substantive merits of the national authorities' decision to ensure that it is compatible with Article 8; and (ii) the decision-making process followed by the national authorities 'to ensure that due weight has been accorded to the interests of the individuals affected'.[49] Thus, according to the Court's judgment, when a state must determine complex issues of environmental and economic policy, the decision-making process must grant public access to the studies and to information 'which would enable members of the public to assess the danger to which they are exposed'. Furthermore, the individuals concerned 'must also be able to appeal to the courts against any decision, act or omission where they consider that their interests or their comments have not been given sufficient weight in the decision-making process'.[50]

In relation to the violation of Article 6 ECHR in this case, the Court declared – with no express reference whatsoever to Article 9 AC – that notwithstanding the protection granted by the national courts to the applicants, the Turkish government deprived the judicial decisions of any useful effect due to the fact that the Council of Ministers authorised, once again, the continuation of production at the gold mine in an unpublished decision.[51]

When an applicant alleges the violation of both Articles 6 and 8 ECHR, the Court may decide to examine both provisions separately, as it did in *Taşkın*, while in other instances, it might consider it sufficient to examine the case, including due process issues, simply from the perspective of Article 8 – a matter that the ECtHR decides on a case-by-case basis, taking into account the circumstances of each a particular application.[52]

Since *Taşkın*, as will be explained below, the ECtHR has taken into account Article 9 AC in environmental cases concerning the violation of Article 6 ECHR only to a limited extent. In contrast, there has been no substantive reference to Article 9 AC in cases where the applicants have alleged a violation of Article 13 ECHR. Furthermore, the influence of Article 9 AC also seems to be rather limited concerning access to the ECtHR under Article 34 ECHR regarding individual or group applications in environmental cases.

A. The Right to a Fair Trial: The Impact of Article 9 AC on the ECtHR Case Law on Article 6 ECHR

According to Article 6.1 ECHR, '1. In the determination of his civil rights and obligations … everyone is entitled to a fair and public hearing within a reasonable time by an independent and impartial tribunal established by law'.

[49] ibid para 118.
[50] ibid para 119.
[51] ibid para 125.
[52] See *Verein KlimaSeniorinnen Schweiz and Others v Switzerland* App No 52600/20 (ECtHR 12 April 2024), para 294.

The right to a fair trial is conceived in the case law of the ECtHR as an instrumental human right to protect substantive or procedural rights – within the autonomous concept of 'civil rights' derived from the Convention – but not to directly protect the environment itself.

As the ECtHR recently recalled in the case of *Cangi and Others v Turkey*:[53]

> for Article 6§1 in its 'civil' limb to be applicable, there must be a dispute ('contestation' in the French text) over a 'civil right' which can be said, at least on arguable grounds, to be recognised under domestic law. The dispute must be genuine and serious; it may relate not only to the actual existence of a right but also to its scope and the manner of its exercise; and, finally, the result of the proceedings must be directly decisive for the right in question, mere tenuous connections or remote consequences not being sufficient to bring Article 6§1 into play.

The Court has recognised the existence of a civil right where the national law recognises a right to environmental protection and the rights to life, physical integrity and property are at stake.[54] The wording of Article 6(1) ECHR, as interpreted by the ECtHR, entails that such a provision does not apply to general interests for the protection of the environment. Public interest litigation through an *actio popularis* is not envisaged under the ECHR and applicants can only allege individual 'civil rights' in the terms interpreted by the ECtHR.[55] In other words, disputes relating exclusively to environmental protection as a public interest do not concern a 'civil right'. However, the fact that a proceeding aims at protecting the public interest in the environment does not necessarily rule out the possibility that the applicants might also have 'civil rights' affected.[56]

The individualistic conception of human rights in the ECHR collides with the role that the Aarhus Convention recognises for environmental NGOs as guardians of the general interest of environmental protection. As the ACCC has declared, 'the Convention is intended to allow a great deal of flexibility in defining which environmental organizations have access to justice'.[57] Consequently, even though the Aarhus Convention does not oblige the parties to establish a system of *actio popularis* in their national laws to allow anyone to challenge any decision, act or omission relating to the environment, the criteria for standing in the legal system of the member parties may not be so strict 'that they effectively bar all or almost all environmental organizations or other members of the public from challenging acts or omissions that contravene national law relating to the environment'.[58]

[53] *Cangi and Others v Turkey* App No 48173/18 (ECtHR, 14 November 2023), para 34 (quoting *Athanassoglou and Others v Switzerland* [GC] App No 27644/95, ECHR 2000-IV, para 43, as former authority in the context of environmental litigation).

[54] See, eg, *Zander v Sweden* (n 46) para 24; *Balmer-Schafroth and Others v Switzerland* [GC], App No 22110/93 (ECtHR, 26 August 1997), paras 33–34; and *Taşkın and Others* (n 16) para 132.

[55] *Ilhan v Turkey* [GC] App No 22277/93 (ECtHR, 27 June 2000), paras 52–53.

[56] See in general ECtHR, 'Guide to the Case-Law of the European Court of Human Rights – Environment', 31 August 2022, 19, https://ks.echr.coe.int/documents/d/echr-ks/guide_environment_eng.

[57] Communication ACCC/C/2005/11 (Belgium), ECE/MP.PP/C.1/2006/4/Add.2, para 35.

[58] See also Communication ACCC/C/2006/18 (Denmark) ECE/MP.PP/2008/5/Add.4, para 29.

The narrower role of environmental NGOs under the ECHR is evident in cases such as *Gorraiz Lizarraga and Others v Spain*[59] or *L'Erablière ASBL v Belgium*,[60] even if they can be considered as steps towards a more flexible approach to NGOs' applications in environmental cases.[61] In *Gorraiz Lizarraga*, five Spanish nationals and the 'Coordinadora de Itoiz' association relied on Article 6(1) ECHR alleging that they had not had a fair hearing in the judicial proceedings brought by them to halt the construction of the Itoiz dam. The ECtHR noted that the domestic proceedings were not related to any rights which the applicant association could claim on its behalf, but they had been geared to protecting 'civil rights' held by the association's members (who were also applicants before the ECtHR, but had not been parties to the domestic proceedings). However, the Court declared that the applicant association could allege a violation of Article 6(1) ECHR because it was set up for the specific purpose of defending its members' interests before the courts and those members were directly concerned by the dam project.[62]

In *L'Erablière ASBL*, the ECtHR concluded that the applicant association – which had lodged an action in the domestic courts to set aside the planning permission to expand a landfill site – had a sufficient connection with a right that it could claim on its behalf, as according to its statutes it has a geographically and materially limited aim, namely the protection of a local region and also all the founding members and administrators of the applicant association resided in the municipalities concerned and 'can therefore be regarded as local residents directly affected by the plans to expand the landfill site'.[63]

According to this case law, associations might, in principle, qualify for protection under Article 6(1) as long as the legal action cannot be regarded as an *actio popularis*, since they may seek the protection of the (individual) rights and interests of their members directly affected and/or claim a concrete and direct threat to the associations' possessions.

However, in cases involving the 'access rights' of the Aarhus Convention to information and public participation, the ECtHR has relaxed the Article 6(1) ECHR requirements.

Thus, in the admissibility decision of *Collectif national d'information et d'opposition à l'usine Melox – Collectif Stop Melox and Mox v France* (2006), the Court went a step further and declared that the classical criteria to acknowledge when Article 6(1) ECHR is infringed should be applied flexibly where an environmental NGO complains of a breach of that provision.[64] In this case, the three 'access rights' of the Aarhus Convention were at stake: the applicant association

[59] *Gorraiz Lizarraga and Others v Spain* App No 62543/00 (ECtHR, 27 April 2004), paras 45–48.
[60] *L'Erablière ASBL v Belgium* App No 49230/07 (ECtHR, 24 February 2009), paras 28–30.
[61] See Morrow (n 45) 52, with regard to *L'Erablière ASBL* (n 60).
[62] *Gorraiz Lizarraga and Others* (n 59) para 36.
[63] *L'Erablière ASBL* (n 60) para 28.
[64] *Collectif national d'information et d'opposition à l'usine Melox – Collectif stop Melox and Mox v France* App No 75218/01 (ECtHR, Admissibility Decision of 28 March 2006).

had asked the Conseil d'État for the annulment of a ministerial decree authorising the construction of an extension to the Melox plant to increase the manufacture of Mox-based nuclear fuels on the grounds that it had not been preceded by a public inquiry.[65] The French government contended that there was not a civil 'right' of which the applicant association could itself claim to be the holder. However, the ECtHR declared that such an approach would be 'at variance with the realities of today's civil society, where associations play an important role, in particular by defending certain causes before the domestic authorities or courts, especially in the field of environmental protection'.[66] It also pointed out that 'in a democratic society within the meaning of the Convention, the right to the proper administration of justice occupies such a prominent place that a restrictive interpretation of art 6.1 would not be consistent with the object and purpose of that provision'.[67]

Finally, the ECtHR also took the Aarhus Convention expressly into account to declare that organisations with legal personality, such as the applicant, undoubtedly form part of the 'public' and that under the Convention, 'the public has the right to be informed and to participate in the decision-making process'. The ECtHR concluded that the 'challenge' raised by the applicant association had a sufficient link with a 'right' that it could claim to have as a legal person. It also considered 'at least arguably' that such a 'right' was recognised under domestic law and that the 'challenge' was 'genuine and serious'.[68] In short, in the *Collectif Stop Melox* case, the ECtHR found Article 6(1) to be applicable as the rights to be informed and to participate in the decision-making process on environmental matters lay at the heart of the applicant association's claims, and associations are holders of these rights pursuant to the Aarhus Convention.

More recently, in *Association Burestop 55 and Others v France* in 2021,[69] the ECtHR confirmed the *Collectif Stop Melox* admissibility criteria, broadly recognising the locus standi of environmental NGOs before domestic courts to defend their rights of access to environmental information. The applicant, the environmental association MIRABEL-LNE, had challenged the authorisation of a project for radioactive waste, arguing that the information disseminated by the French nuclear agency was based on erroneous and fraudulent scientific and technical information. The French courts declared its claims inadmissible on the grounds that the object of its statutes was limited to the protection of the environment in general and did not expressly include nuclear hazards in particular.[70] As is well

[65] As required by art L 200-1 of the French Rural Code and the EU directives which provide for the right to information, consultation and participation of the 'public' in this area.

[66] *Collectif stop Melox* (n 64) para 4.

[67] ibid.

[68] ibid.

[69] *Association Burestop 55 and Others v France* App No 56176/18 (ECtHR, 1 July 2021).

[70] Unlike other claimant associations, whose appeals were admitted since their statutes specifically indicated that their mission was the fight against the environmental and health risks of the nuclear industry.

known, the right to access the courts is not absolute and may be limited on the basis of a legitimate interest, provided that it does not entail a disproportionate restriction of that right. In the case of French law, it required a connection between their statutory purpose and the collective interests they are intended to defend. The ECtHR rejected this strict distinction between protection against nuclear and environmental hazards, as it was clear to the Court that the former is fully linked to the latter. In this case, it concluded that:

> [T]he proceedings brought by the applicant associations, which sought to obtain compensation for the damage which the failure to recognise their right to information and to participate in the decision-making process in environmental matters had allegedly caused them, were directly decisive for that right.[71]

This conclusion follows from the principles arising from the Aarhus Convention regarding the right of access to justice of environmental NGOs.

Furthermore, as mentioned above, for an applicant to successfully invoke Article 6(1) ECHR, the dispute must be 'genuine and serious' and 'directly decisive' for the applicant's civil right, which entails that the outcome of the proceedings has to involve a straightforward benefit to its rights.[72] Thus, the Court has declared that the following cases did not fall within the scope of Article 6(1)ECHR: those in which the connection between the public authorities' decisions or omissions regarding licences of activities with an impact on the environment and the substantive rights invoked (such as the right to life, physical integrity or property) was 'too tenuous and remote'; those where the applicants failed to prove that they were 'exposed to a danger that was not only specific but above all imminent'; and those where the applicant just alleged a hypothetical environmental impact or damage.[73]

In *Cangı and Others v Türkiye* (2023), the ECtHR requested the applicant's proof of personal rights that were directly affected or in close vicinity to the activity concerned – again the extraction of gold using cyanide – even if their locus standi had been acknowledged by domestic courts under the *actio popularis* doctrine.[74]

The ECtHR seems to depart from the more flexible approach adopted in former cases, and in particular in *Okyay and Others v Turkey*, where it declared that the concept of a 'civil right' under Article 6 'cannot be construed as limiting an enforceable right in domestic law'.[75] In *Okyay* the applicants – who lived and worked in a city which was approximately 250 kilometres from the site of three thermal power plants that had been operating for years without any

[71] *Association Burestop 55 and Others v France* (n 69) para 59.
[72] On this standard, see generally Morrow (n 45) 48–53.
[73] On the lack of proven impact on the civil rights alleged by individuals living in the vicinity of nuclear power stations against the extension of the operating licence, see *Athanassoglou and Others v Switzerland* [GC] App No 27644/95 (ECHR 6 April 2000); *Balmer-Schafroth and Others v Switzerland* [GC] App No 22110/93 (ECtHR, 26 August 1997); *Sdružení Jihočeské Matky v Czech Republic* App No 19101/03 (10 July 2006).
[74] *Cangı and Others v Turkey* App No 48173/18 (ECtHR, 14 November 2023).
[75] *Okyay and Others v Turkey* App No 36220/97 (ECtHR, 12 July 2005), para 68.

permits – had locus standi under Turkish law, and successfully invoked Article 6(1) ECHR before the ECtHR when the national authorities failed to comply in practice and within a reasonable time with the judgments rendered by the Turkish administrative courts, as the ECtHR considered that the government deprived the right of Article 6(1) of any useful effect.

In *Cangi*, on the contrary, the ECtHR concluded that Article 6(1) ECHR was applicable only with respect to the applicants who lived or owned a property in close proximity to the goldmine causing pollution, as only in these cases the outcome of proceedings was 'directly decisive' for their right to live in a healthy environment. Accordingly, the public interest against the environmental impact of gold mines was declared insufficient to this end, even if the applicants had locus standi according to Turkish law in defence of their constitutional right to live in a healthy environment.

The Court justified the different outcomes with the following reasons: whereas in *Okyay* the Court relied on the fact that the applicants – though not living close to the thermal power plants – had nevertheless been affected by their emissions, as established during the domestic proceedings and the judicial rulings in their favour,[76] in *Cangi*, the Court argued that neither the fact that the applicants considered themselves to be 'public watchdogs' nor the informal movement they have created was sufficient for the Court to consider the proceedings to have been 'directly decisive for their civil rights and obligations'.[77] However, in *Cangi* the Court failed to explain why it construed the right of access to court in such a way that limited the scope that domestic law had granted it, as Turkey acknowledges the *actio popularis* in claims for a clean environment under its constitutional law.

This case law reflects the difference between the approach of the ECHR as interpreted by the ECtHR, and the AC as interpreted by the ACCC. Whereas the former focuses on the protection of access to justice as an individual human right, the latter is designed to broaden access to justice to protect the environment through legal action of the 'public' or the 'public concerned' widely conceived (as it includes environmental NGOs to promote their role as effective environmental defenders). Like Professor Boyle observed more than a decade ago, this is a significant difference, 'with important implications for any debate about an autonomous right to a decent or satisfactory environment', as NGOs 'tend to have high success rates in enforcement actions and public interest litigation'.[78]

In short, under Article 6(1) ECHR, as interpreted by the ECtHR, only those persons specifically affected in their substantial rights (health, private and family life, property etc) or in their procedural rights (access to information, participation and access to justice) by state activities or omission that cause severe

[76] ibid paras 66–67.
[77] ibid para 38.
[78] Boyle (n 21) 625–26, quoting the research of N Sadeleer, G Roller and M Dross, *Access to Justice in Environmental Matters*, Final Report, Doc ENVA.3/ ETU/2002/0030, pt I, s 3.

environmental damage or risk can invoke this provision. As far as environmental NGOs are concerned, they can request protection under Article 6(1) ECHR when they act in defence of the substantive and/or procedural 'civil rights' of their members and, under the Aarhus influence, they can also rely on Article 6(1) ECHR in disputes concerning their own 'civil' rights, as holders of procedural environmental rights.

B. The Right to an Effective Remedy: The Lack of Impact of Article 9 of the Aarhus Convention on the Application of Article 13 of the Rome Convention

The right to an effective remedy is an essential part of the right of access to justice, and therefore both the Rome Convention and the Aarhus Convention include express provision to protect it.

Under the Rome Convention, the right to an effective remedy is worded in Article 13 as follows:

> Everyone whose rights and freedoms as set forth in this Convention are violated shall have an effective remedy before a national authority notwithstanding that the violation has been committed by persons acting in an official capacity.

Consequently, the right to an effective remedy has no independent existence under the ECHR since, in order to invoke it, the applicant must also have an 'arguable claim' under another Convention provision.[79] Article 13 ECHR provides for effective remedies only against alleged violations of the human rights protected under the Convention, which is a substantial difference not only compared to Article 9 AC but also Article 6 ECHR, in the terms examined above.

As regards the Aarhus Convention, paragraph 4 of Article 9 requires that the procedures referred to in paragraphs 1, 2 and 3 of the same provision 'shall provide adequate and effective remedies, including injunctive relief as appropriate'.

In both cases, the states parties have a wide margin of discretion in the choice of legal remedies as long as they are effective. According to the *Aarhus Convention Implementation Guide*, effectiveness requires that the remedy provided by the administrative or judicial review procedure 'should be capable of real and efficient enforcement'.[80] As for the Rome Convention, Article 13 ECHR does not require any particular form of remedy to be offered (it does not even mention the option of injunctive relief). The discretion of the parties to the Convention is also subjected to the condition, which arises from the ECtHR case law, that the remedies are effective 'in practice as well as in law', which entails that they

[79] See *Hatton and Others* (n 18) para 138.
[80] Ebbesson et al (n 8) 200. See further, Ryall (n 7) 129.

are accessible and capable of providing redress with respect to the applicant's complaints.[81]

As stated by the *Guide to Case Law of the European Court of Human Rights – Environment*, the principles relating to the right to an effective remedy apply in a 'fairly standard manner' to environmental cases.[82] As a matter of fact, no express or implicit reference to Article 9 AC has been found in the ECtHR case law related to the infringement of Article 13 ECHR with an environmental background. This state of affairs can be observed in some of the most well-known cases in which the ECtHR has declared the infringement of Article 13 ECHR in environmental matters, such as *Hatton and Others v United Kingdom* (2003),[83] *Di Sarno and Others v Italy* (2012)[84] or, more recently, *Cordella and Others v Italy* (2019),[85] among others.[86]

In *Hatton and Others*, for example, the applicants alleged that government policy on night flights at Heathrow airport gave rise to a violation of their rights under Article 8 ECHR and that they were denied an effective domestic remedy for this complaint, in breach of Article 13 ECHR, as the remedy of judicial review was inadequate, the courts failed to examine the merits of the decisions by public authorities and it was 'prohibitively expensive to individuals'. Though the ECtHR concluded that there had not been a violation of Article 8 ECHR, as the national authorities had not overstepped their margin of appreciation, it found a violation of Article 13 ECHR as the scope of review by the domestic courts was considered to be limited to the classic English public law test of irrationality, unlawfulness and patent unreasonableness, but it did not allow for consideration of whether the increase in night flights represented a justifiable limitation on the right to respect for the private and family lives or the homes of those who lived in the vicinity of Heathrow Airport. In these circumstances, the ECtHR considered that the scope of review was not sufficient to comply with Article 13.

In *Di Sarno and Others*, the Italian authorities had failed for several years to adopt the measures necessary to solve serious problems of waste management in the Campania region and in the municipality of the applicant, who complained under Articles 8 and 13 ECHR. The ECtHR recalled that in the context of dangerous activities in particular, states must 'govern the licensing, setting-up, operation, security and supervision of the activity and must make it compulsory for all those concerned to take practical measures to ensure the

[81] *MSS v Belgium and Greece* [GC] App No. 30696/09 (ECtHR, 21 January 2011), para 288.
[82] ECtHR (n 56) 67–68.
[83] *Hatton and Others* (n 18).
[84] *Di Sarno and Others v Italy* App No 30765/08 (ECtHR, 10 January 2012).
[85] *Cordella and Others v Italy* App No 54414/13 (ECtHR, 24 January 2019).
[86] See, *Athanassoglou and Others v Switzerland* [GC] App No 27644/95 (ECtHR, 6 April 2000), paras 58–60; *VgT Verein gegen Tierfabriken v Switzerland* App No 24699/94 (ECtHR, 21 June 2001), paras 82–83; *Kolyadenko and Others v Russia* App No 17423/05 (ECtHR, 29 February 2012), paras 221–32.

effective protection of citizens whose lives might be endangered by the inherent risks'.[87] It declared in this case that despite the margin of appreciation left to the respondent state:

> [T]he protracted inability of the Italian authorities to ensure the proper functioning of the waste collection, treatment and disposal service adversely affected the applicants' right to respect for their homes and their private life, in violation of Article 8 of the Convention in its substantive aspect.[88]

In analysing whether the state had also breached the procedural aspect of Article 8, the Court recalled the importance of the right of access to information and quoted Article 5.1(c) of the AC on the scope of this right. However, the Court found no violation of the procedural aspects of Article 8 ECHR as the Italian administration had made public the information on the potential risks to which the people in general were exposed. Finally, the Court held – without any reference to the AC at this point – that the Italian government had also infringed Article 13 ECHR, as the applicants did not have access to effective remedies in the Italian legal system by which to obtain redress for the damage sustained to their rights to respect for private and family live and home.[89]

More recently, in *Cordella and Others*, 180 applicants had complained of the state's failure to adopt measures to protect their health and the environment from harmful emissions from a steelworks plant in Taranto. The Court held that the national authorities had failed to take all the necessary measures to provide effective protection of the applicants' right to respect for their private life and that the applicants had not had available an effective remedy to secure decontamination of the relevant areas affected by toxic emissions from the factory.

As already highlighted, and in contrast to the explicit references to the AC in the cases related to Article 6(1) ECHR examined above, the ECtHR has not made any express or implicit reference to the AC when applying Article 13 ECHR in these important judgments.

The different impact of Article 9 AC on Article 6(1) and 13 ECHR might be explained, at least in part, by the fact that Article 6(1) ECHR is *lex specialis* in relation to Article 13 and, therefore, in cases where the Court finds an infringement of Article 6(1), it normally does not consider it necessary to also examine the case in light of Article 13 ECHR as 'its requirements are less strict than, and are here absorbed by, those of Article 6 para 1'.[90] In addition, it could be interpreted as meaning that the Court considers its general case law on the scope of Article 13 ECHR to already provide sufficient protection and guidance for environmental cases.

[87] *Di Sarno and Others* (n 84) para 160.

[88] ibid.

[89] ibid para 112.

[90] See *Sporrong and Iönnroth v Sweden* App No 7151/75 (ECtHR, 23 September 1982), para 88; *Brualla Gómez de la Torre v Spain* App No 2673/95 (ECtHR, 19 December 1997), para 41; *Association Burestop 55 and Others v France* (n 69) para 64.

C. Access to the ECtHR under Article 34 ECHR: Individual Applications and the Limits for Environmental NGOs

According to Article 34 ECHR, any person, NGO or group of individuals may claim before the ECtHR to be the victim of a violation by one of the contracting parties of the rights set forth in the Convention.

The applicant must plausibly claim to be the direct or indirect victim of a violation of the Convention resulting from an act or omission attributable to the contracting state. In environmental cases, for an individual to have victim status, the applicant needs to show that his or her rights are impacted by environmental damage or risk, and the Court will consider issues such as the minimum level of severity of the harm in question, its duration and the existence of a sufficient link with the applicant, including the applicant's proximity to the alleged environmental harm.[91]

As to the environmental NGOs' standing, so far there have been significant limits on them in terms of accessing the ECtHR, which, once again, shows the different role that they play under the Rome Convention compared to the Aarhus Convention:

(i) First, under Article 34 ECHR, no one can lodge a claim only in the public or general interest. According to the ECtHR case law, environmental damage must adversely affect one of the rights safeguarded by the Convention and not simply harm the environment.[92] This implies a much narrower access to the ECtHR than the access to justice that Aarhus Convention parties should provide to individuals and NGOs under its Article 9, and a drastic reduction of the NGOs' role as environmental guardians. In the case of *Yusufeli İlçesini Güzelleştirme Yaşatma Kültür Varlıklarını Koruma Derneği v Turkey* (2021), the Court recalled once more that associations will only be granted victim status if they have been directly affected by the measure in question, as 'the sole fact that a non-governmental organisation considers itself as a guardian of the collective interests of its members does not suffice to make it a victim within the meaning of Article 34 of the Convention'.[93] It also recalled, once again, that the Convention 'does not envisage the bringing of an *actio popularis* for the interpretation of the rights set out therein or permit individuals to complain about a provision of national law simply because they consider, without having been directly affected by it, that it may contravene the Convention'.[94]

[91] *KlimaSeniorinnen* (n 52) para 472.

[92] *Di Sarno and Others* (n 84) paras 80–81.

[93] *Yusufeli İlçesini Güzelleştirme Yaşatma Kültür Varlıklarını Koruma Derneği v Turkey* App No 37857/14 (ECtHR, 7 December 2021), para 38.

[94] See also the case of *Aksu v Turkey* [GC] App Nos 4149/04 and 41029/04 (ECtHR, 27 July 2010); and *Burden v United Kingdom* [GC] App No 13378/05 (ECtHR, 29 April 2008), para 33.

(ii) Second, another barrier for NGOs to access the ECtHR has been the nature of the right at stake, as certain Convention rights, such as the right to life (Article 2) or the right to private and family life (Article 8), are not susceptible to being held by associations. Hence, NGOs can only act as representatives of their members or employees, but could not themselves claim to be the victim of their violation.[95]

Nevertheless, the Court has declared that Article 34 ECHR – like the other provisions of the Convention – must also be interpreted 'in an evolutive manner in the light of conditions in contemporary society' and, under the influence of the AC, it has partly acknowledged the important role that NGOs play, declaring that:

> [I]n modern-day societies, when citizens are confronted with particularly complex administrative decisions, recourse to collective bodies such as associations is one of the accessible means – sometimes the only means – available to them whereby they can defend their particular interests effectively. Moreover, the standing of associations to bring legal proceedings in defence of their members' interests is recognised by the legislation of most European countries.[96]

Consequently, the Court has found that there might be 'special considerations' for associations to lodge applications on behalf of the victims: under Article 34 ECHR, it has granted standing to associations in cases relating to Article 6(1) ECHR, as explained above, where the substance of the applicant association's claim before the domestic courts concerned its members' interests in respect of their private lives, families and homes, as well as – under the influence of the Aarhus Convention – when claiming their rights to information or to participate in the decision-making process.[97]

The Court has also clarified, in cases such as *Bursa Barosu Başkanlığı and Others v Turkey* (2018), that it does not regard NGOs' applications as constituting *actio popularis*, even when applicants defend an environmental general interest, if the 'dispute' raised by those applicants had a sufficient link with 'civil rights' of which their members could claim to be the holders.[98]

Binding it all together, despite the acknowledgement of the special role that environmental NGOs play in our society, the case law on access to the ECtHR under Article 34 ECHR is still far from allowing 'a great deal of flexibility in defining which environmental NGOs have access to justice' as required by Article 9 AC

[95] *Yusufeli İlçesini Güzelleştirme* (n 93) para 41.

[96] ibid para 39 (quoting *Gorraiz Lizarraga and Others* (n 59) para 38 and *Beizaras and Levickas v Lithuania* App No 41288/15 (ECtHR, 14 January 2020), para 81).

[97] See, in particular, *Gorraiz Lizarraga and Others* (n 59) paras 9–10, 32 and 36–39; *L'Erablière ASBL* (n 60) paras 28–29; and *Sailing Club of Chalkidiki 'I Kelyfos' v Greece* App Nos 6978/18 and 8547/18 (ECtHR, 21 November 2019), para 52.

[98] *Bursa Barosu Başkanlığı and Others v Turkey* App No 25680/05 (ECtHR, 19 June 2018). The Court finally declared that there had been a violation of art 6(1) ECHR as, by failing for several years to take the necessary measures to comply with several final and enforceable judicial decisions, the national authorities had deprived the applicant of effective judicial protection (at para 145).

and interpreted by the ACCC.[99] This is the current state of the ECtHR case law concerning the admissibility of individuals and NGO applications in environmental cases. However, as will be explained below, the Court has recently developed new and separate key criteria affecting the scope of access to the ECtHR in climate change cases: although the ECtHR builds the tests on its case law on human rights and the environment, it also establishes new requirements for ascertaining the victim status/standing of individual applicants, as well as for determining the locus standi of associations, with a deeper influence of Article 9 AC for the latter in climate change litigation.

IV. The Impact of the New Climate Change Cases on the ECtHR Doctrine on Access to Justice: A New Test for Access to Justice

Following the Paris Agreement's express acknowledgement of climate change and human rights links, we have witnessed a growing wave of rights-based climate litigation across Europe. The path blazed by *Urgenda v The Netherlands*[100] was soon followed by other national courts, such as the German Constitutional Court in the case of *Neubauer and Others v Germany*,[101] where violations of ECHR rights were central to the plaintiffs' arguments.[102] This wave reached the ECtHR with the applications of six young Portuguese nationals (*Duarte Agostinho and Others v Portugal and 32 Other States*),[103] of a Swiss NGO (*Verein KlimaSeniorinnen and Others v Switzerland*)[104] and of the former Mayor of the French town Grande-Synthe (*Careme v France*).[105]

The Grand Chamber of the ECtHR delivered its rulings on the first climate change cases on 9 April 2024. Despite the fact that the Court declared the cases of *Carême*[106]

[99] Communication ACCC/C/2005/11 (Belgium), ECE/MP.PP/C.1/2006/4/Add.2, para 35.

[100] *State of the Netherlands v Urgenda Foundation* (Supreme Court Judgment, 20 December 2019).

[101] *Neubauer et al v Germany*, BVerfG, Order of the First Senate, Case No 1 BvR 2656/18 (24 March 2021).

[102] There is also a growing literature analysing this phenomenon. See, eg, J Peel and HM Osofsky, 'A Right Turn in Climate Change Litigation?' (2018) 7 *Transnational Environmental Law* 37, 48; K Guruparan and H Moynihan, 'Climate Change and Human Rights-Based Strategic Litigation' (2021) Briefing Paper, Chatham House; A Savaresi and J Setzer, 'Rights-Based Litigation in the Climate Emergency: Mapping the Landscape and New Knowledge Frontiers' (2022) 13 *Journal of Human Rights and the Environment* 7.

[103] App No 39371/20.

[104] *KlimaSeniorinnen* (n 52).

[105] *Carême v France* App No 7189/21 (ECtHR, 9 April 2024).

[106] The case of *Carême v France* (ibid) was declared unanimously inadmissible, as the applicant, the former mayor of the Grande-Synthe municipality who alleged a violation of arts 2 and 8 by France's failure to take sufficient steps to prevent climate change, no longer had 'relevant links with Grande-Synthe and did not currently live in France'. Thus, he did not qualify as a 'victim' under art 34 ECHR, irrespective of the status he invoked, namely that of a citizen or former resident of Grande-Synthe.

and *Duarte Agostinho*[107] inadmissible on different procedural grounds, in its milestone ruling in the case of *KlimaSeniorinnen Schweiz and Others v Switzerland*, it stated that the Swiss Confederation had violated Article 8 (right to respect for private and family life) and Article 6(1) ECHR (access to court) of the NGO KlimaSeniorinnen, having failed to comply with the 1992 UN Framework Convention on Climate Change and the 2015 Paris Climate Agreement by not taking sufficient action to mitigate the effects of climate change and not effectively protecting the plaintiffs from the serious adverse effects of climate change on the lives, health, well-being and quality of life.[108]

This ruling addressed many essential issues, but this section is limited to a brief account of the main developments concerning the scope of access to justice and the impact of Article 9 AC on this new ECtHR case law.

First and foremost, it should be noted that the Court declared as a preliminary issue that the environmental case law to date was only of 'limited guidance' in climate change cases, as the latter 'raise unprecedented issues' and 'there are important differences between the legal questions raised by climate change and those addressed until now'.[109] Consequently, after identifying the key features that make climate change unlike any other environmental problem (highlighting, among other things, its global, polycentric and intergenerational dimensions), the ECtHR declared that 'it would be neither adequate nor appropriate to follow an approach consisting in directly transposing the existing environmental case-law to the context of climate change'.[110] Therefore, the Court announced the development of 'a more appropriate and tailored approach as regards the various Convention issues which may arise in the context of climate change', though without renouncing to draw 'some inspiration from the principles set out in the Court's existing case-law'.[111]

In fact, when examining the applicants' alleged violation of Article 2 (the right to life) and Article 8 (the right to private and family life), the ECtHR stated that 'one of the salient issues of the climate-change cases' which it considered was how to determine the victim status of the applicants to decide the admissibility of climate change cases. In that way, it departed from its former case law on environmental

[107] In *Duarte Agostinho and Others v Portugal and 32 Other States* App No 39371/20 (ECtHR, 9 April 2024) the application was also unanimously declared inadmissible. The case was addressed all together against 33 states. Although the ECtHR accepted that climate change was undoubtedly a global phenomenon, it noted that each state had its own share of responsibility to take measures to tackle climate change, and rejected the idea that, by way of judicial interpretation, the Court could extend the contracting parties' extraterritorial jurisdiction as requested by the applicants. Therefore, territorial jurisdiction was established only in respect of Portugal and the applicants' complaint against the other respondent states was declared inadmissible under art 35(3) and (4) ECHR. Finally, as the applicants had not pursued any legal avenue in Portugal concerning their complaints, the complaint against Portugal was also inadmissible due to the non-exhaustion of domestic remedies.

[108] *KlimaSeniorinnen* (n 52).

[109] ibid para 414.

[110] ibid para 422.

[111] ibid.

issues to elaborate new criteria on the victim status and locus standi in the climate change cases.[112]

The applicants were, on the one hand, the NGO KlimaSeniorinnen representing elderly women whose aim was to protect its members against the effects of climate change, and, on the other hand, four female members of the association. Before examining its claims on the merits, the Court established new criteria to determine the victim status and the standing before the Court, taking into account the special features of climate change conflicts, such as the indefinite number of persons affected by states' acts or omissions, and the climate change legal proceedings outcomes that go far beyond the rights of any particular individual or group. The ECtHR declared that the applicant association had locus standi and that Article 8 and Article 6 ECHR applied to its complaint.[113] On the contrary, it denied the victim status to the individual applicants and declared their complaints inadmissible under the criteria set in Article 34 ECHR.[114] This result was due to the new criteria for NGOs' locus standi that are, in fact, more aligned with the AC, whereas the threshold for individual applicants turned out to be more strict.

Regarding individual applications, on the one hand, the Court declared that for an individual applicant to claim victim status under Article 34 ECHR from alleged failures by the state to combat climate change, they need to show that he or she was 'personally and directly' affected by the impugned failures. This would require establishing the following circumstances concerning the applicant's situation: (a) the adverse effects of climate change due to governmental action or inaction affecting the applicant must be significant; and (b) there must be a 'pressing need to ensure the applicant's individual protection, owing to the absence or inadequacy of any reasonable measures to reduce harm'.[115] More importantly, the Court also warned that the threshold for fulfilling these criteria 'is especially high' and, given the exclusion of *actio popularis* under the Convention, whether an applicant meets that threshold will depend on a careful assessment of the concrete circumstances of the case, taking into account considerations relating to:

> [T]he nature and scope of the applicant's Convention complaint, the actuality/remoteness and/or probability of the adverse effects of climate change in time, the specific impact on the applicant's life, health or well-being, the magnitude and duration of the harmful effects, the scope of the risk (localised or general), and the nature of the applicant's vulnerability.[116]

This doctrine attempts to examine allegations of harm linked to state actions and/or omissions in the context of climate change affecting substantive individuals'

[112] ibid para 459.
[113] ibid para 526.
[114] ibid para 534.
[115] ibid para 487.
[116] ibid para 488.

Convention rights (such as the right to life or the right to respect for private and family life) 'without undermining the exclusion of *actio popularis* from the Convention system and without ignoring the nature of the Court's judicial function, which is by definition reactive rather than proactive'.[117]

On the other hand, the new criteria regarding NGOs' locus standi have become more open. After recalling that the AC emphasises the importance which NGOs play in the context of environmental protection, the Court also underlined 'the difference between the basic nature and purpose of the Aarhus Convention, which is designed to enhance public participation in environmental matters, and that of the Convention, which is designed to protect individuals' human rights'.[118] It further emphasised both: (a) the difference between climate change and 'the more linear and localised (traditional) environmental issues which the Aarhus Convention is designed to address'; and (b) the fact that the AC provides 'for a very broad standing of associations where the existence of an effect on the "public concerned" is assumed to exist (provided that the association is duly established under domestic law)', but that the ECHR system and the established ECtHR case law do not provide for an *actio popularis*.[119] Following these arguments, the Court identified the requirements for NGOs to have locus standi under Article 34 ECHR in climate change cases. According to this new test, the association must be:

(a) lawfully established in the jurisdiction concerned or have standing to act there;
(b) able to demonstrate that it pursues a dedicated purpose in accordance with its statutory objectives in the defence of the human rights of its members or other affected individuals within the jurisdiction concerned, whether limited to or including collective action for the protection of those rights against the threats arising from climate change; and
(c) able to demonstrate that it can be regarded as genuinely qualified and representative to act on behalf of members or other affected individuals within the jurisdiction who are subject to specific threats or adverse effects of climate change on their lives, health or well-being as protected under the Convention.[120]

Furthermore, the Court also clarified that, in assessing these requirements, it will have regard for other factors such as:

> [T]he purpose for which the association was established, that it is of non-profit character, the nature and extent of its activities within the relevant jurisdiction, its membership and representativeness, its principles and transparency of governance and whether on the whole, in the particular circumstances of a case, the grant of such standing is in the interests of the proper administration of justice.[121]

[117] ibid para 481.
[118] ibid para 501.
[119] ibid.
[120] ibid.
[121] ibid.

Finally, another important difference that the Court established with respect to environmental cases is that in climate change cases, the standing of an association to act on behalf of the members or other affected individuals within the jurisdiction concerned 'will not be subject to a separate requirement of showing that those on whose behalf the case has been brought would themselves have met the victim status requirements for individuals'.[122]

With regard to the infringement of the right of access to justice (Articles 6 and 13 ECHR) in *KlimaSeniorinnen*, the ECtHR noticed that the Swiss government denied the NGO locus standi and proceeded to examine the issue of the victim status of the NGO under Article 6 ECHR together with the applicability of that provision.

The Court confirmed that in this case there was a civil right involved within the meaning of Article 6 ECHR as the environmental 'rights of access' (to information, to participation and to justice) are 'widely acknowledged in international environmental law' (the Aarhus Convention) and recognised in domestic law.[123] After examining the various elements of the applicability of Article 6(1) ECHR, and in particular the notion of 'imminent harm or danger', the Court concluded that they could not be applied without properly taking into account the specific nature of climate change-related risks, 'including their potential for irreversible consequences and corollary severity of harm', and eventually declared that:

> Where future harms are not merely speculative but real and highly probable (or virtually certain) in the absence of adequate corrective action, the fact that the harm is not strictly imminent should not, on its own, lead to the conclusion that the outcome of the proceedings would not be decisive for its alleviation or reduction.[124]

This statement aims to prevent legal action initiated by NGOs against the most severe risks of climate change from being 'unduly' limited; as the ECtHR states, 'their legal actions must be seen in the light of their role as a means through which the Convention rights of those affected by climate change, including those at a distinct representational disadvantage, can be defended'.[125]

In this case, the Court stated that the applicant association *had* demonstrated an actual and sufficiently close connection to the matter complained of and to the individuals seeking protection against the adverse effects of climate change on their lives, health and quality of life. In other words, the association of elderly women sought to defend the specific civil rights of its members in relation to the adverse effects of climate change.[126] Finally, after examining the national legal proceedings, the ECtHR concluded that the Swiss courts did not address the issue

[122] ibid para 502.
[123] ibid para 610.
[124] ibid para 614.
[125] ibid.
[126] ibid para 621.

of the standing of the applicant association ('did not engage seriously or at all with the action brought by the applicant association'). Therefore, it declared that 'to the extent that the applicant association's claims fell within the scope of Article 6 § 1, its right of access to a court was restricted in such a way and to such an extent that the very essence of the right was impaired'.[127]

In conclusion, in *KlimaSeniorinnen* the Court acknowledged, under the influence of Article 9 of the AC, that recourse to collective bodies may be the only accessible or effective means to defend ECHR rights against climate change and, consequently, it has widened the scope of NGOs' access to justice to protect the ECHR human rights in this context. Ironically, although the ECtHR has been at pains to stress the differences between environmental cases on the one hand and climate change cases on the other, and has also identified the AC as an instrument for the defence of the environment, the fact is that there is arguably a greater reception of Article 9 AC in the ECtHR doctrine on the locus standi of NGOs in climate cases. It remains uncertain to what extent this case law will expand to protect human rights from the threats that the other two global environmental crises pose – massive pollution and exponential biodiversity loss – whenever contracting states of the Rome Convention infringe their international commitments in these areas.

As a final point, connected to the next and last section below, it should be noted that in *KlimaSeniorinnen*, the Court – which provides for a comprehensive and up-to-date review of the links between the environment and human rights and includes extensive references to the AC – also referred to the last step made towards the protection of the environment through human rights: the recognition of a human right to a clean, healthy and sustainable environment.

V. Access to Justice and the Right to a Clean, Healthy and Sustainable Environment: Looking Ahead

Upon the invitation of the Human Rights Council formulated in its Resolution 48/13 of 8 October 2021,[128] on 28 July 2022 the General Assembly of the United Nations adopted Resolution 76/300 on the human right to a clean, healthy and sustainable

[127] ibid para 638. It should be noted that the 'partly concurring partly dissenting Opinion' of Judge Eicke focused in particular on the infringement of procedural rights and argued that the Court 'would already have achieved much if it had focussed on a violation of Article 6 of the Convention and, at a push, a procedural violation of Article 8 relating in particular to (again) the right of access to court and of access to information necessary to enable effective public participation in the process of devising the necessary policies and regulations and to ensure proper compliance with and enforcement of those policies and regulations as well as those already undertaken under domestic law'. Therefore, there was consensus in the Court as to the violation of the right of access to justice.

[128] Human Rights Council Resolution 48/13, 'The Human Right to a Clean, Healthy and Sustainable Environment', A/HRC/RES/48/13 (18 October 2021).

environment.[129] The resolution was approved with 161 votes in favour (of the 169 Member States present), eight abstentions[130] and no votes against.[131] Further, as the ECtHR highlighted in *KlimaSeniorinnen*, 45 out of the 46 Member States of the Council of Europe voted in favour.[132]

The Declaration proclaims the right to a clean, healthy and sustainable environment as a human right that is important for the enjoyment of human rights. Further, it is particularly relevant that according to paragraph 3:

> [T]he promotion of the human right to a clean, healthy and sustainable environment requires the full implementation of the multilateral environmental agreements under the principles of international environmental law.

The United Nations' path towards recognising this right has been long and complex.[133] The difficulties found in this process are to some extent reflected in both the fact that it has finally been enshrined in a soft law instrument (ie, not legally binding) and in statements made by several states in the explanation of their favourable votes questioning, for example, the recognition of this right in a resolution without 'due regard for the usual formulation of international human rights law',[134] highlighting the lack of a 'common understanding' of what this right comprises,[135] or rejecting any legal relationship between the new right and existing international law as stated in paragraph 3 of the Resolution, as regards compliance with multilateral environmental agreements.[136]

While this Declaration undoubtedly represents a giant step towards shaping a global will to protect the environment more effectively, it is also undeniable that its implementation remains fraught with uncertainties. As Professor James R May states, the case for environmental human rights is 'complicated' and 'there is also spare demonstrable evidence that legal recognition of a right to a healthy environment improves environmental outcomes, suggesting a need for further interrogation'.[137] UNEP has also stated that 'while rights are an important tool for protecting humans and the environment, they are not a panacea', as the recognition of rights alone 'is not enough to ensure environmental sustainability'.[138] Therefore, though it is unquestionably a fundamental achievement, as Professor

[129] UN General Assembly Resolution, 'The Human Right to a Clean, Healthy and Sustainable Environment', A/RES/76/300 (28 July 2022).

[130] China, the Russian Federation, Belarus, Cambodia, Iran, Syria, Kyrgyzstan and Ethiopia.

[131] Official Records: A/76/PV.97.

[132] *KlimaSeniorinnen* (n 52) para 145.

[133] See n 29 above.

[134] See, eg, the statements of the UK in its 'explanation of vote', available at https://press.un.org/en/2022/ga12437.doc.htm.

[135] ibid.

[136] See, eg, the statement of the US in its 'explanation of vote' (ibid).

[137] May (n 31) 987. *cf* D Boyd (Special Rapporteur on the Human Right to a Clean, Healthy and Sustainable Environment), *The Right to a Healthy Environment: A User's Guide* (Geneva, United Nations, 2024) 10.

[138] UNEP (n 22) 90.

May warns: 'Recognising a right to a clean and healthy environment without judicial, legislative, regulatory, and other means to implement them is tantamount to Pyrrhic victory.'[139]

Therefore, the active implementation of the Declaration by national authorities and its application by national and international courts remain key for this right to strengthen the protection of the environment. Still, the mere declaration can be a useful guide not only for policy-makers but also for courts.[140]

In parallel to the UN work on the links between human rights and the environment, there has also been an ongoing debate in the Council of Europe on the adoption of a new protocol to the ECHR enshrining the right to a healthy environment. The Parliamentary Assembly of the Council of Europe (PACE) already called for 'drafting an additional protocol to the European Convention on Human Rights concerning the right to a healthy environment' in 2009, but this query was not followed up by the Committee of Ministers.[141] More recently, in 2021, it reiterated its recommendation that the Committee of Ministers should draw up a legally binding and enforceable instrument, such as an additional protocol to the Convention, as it 'would finally give the Court a non-disputable basis for rulings concerning human rights violations arising from adverse environment-related impacts on human health, dignity and life' and would make such a right enforceable in law in all countries which ratified it.[142] In September 2022, the Committee of Ministers of the CoE took a step further and adopted its Recommendation on human rights and the protection of the environment, where it requests its 46 Member States to consider recognising the right to a clean, healthy and sustainable environment as a human right at a national level.[143] After UN Resolution 76/300, the Council of Europe Heads of State and Government finally committed, in the Reykjavik Summit of 16–17 May 2023, to 'the political recognition of the right to a clean, healthy and sustainable environment as a human right, in line with United Nations General Assembly Resolution 76/300'[144] – in other words, to not go

[139] May (n 31) 1005.

[140] For a critical assessment, see also LJ Kotzé, 'The Right to a Healthy Environment and Law's Hidden Subjects', in *Symposium on UN Recognition of the Human Right to a Healthy Environment* (published online by Cambridge University Press, 31 July 2023, https://doi.org/10.1017/aju.2023.27) 198.

[141] Council of Europe's Parliamentary Assembly Recommendation 1885(2009) 'Drafting an Additional Protocol to the European Convention on Human Rights Concerning the Right to a Healthy Environment' (30 September 2009).

[142] PACE, Recommendation 2211 (2021) 'Anchoring the Right to a Healthy Environment: Need for Enhanced Action by the Council of Europe' (29 September 2021); see also PACE Resolution 2396 (2021) 'Anchoring the Right to a Healthy Environment: Need for Enhanced Action by the Council of Europe' (29 September 2021), which recommended that Member States should build and consolidate a legal framework – domestically and at the European level – to anchor the right to a safe, clean, healthy and sustainable environment, based on the United Nations guidance on this matter.

[143] Recommendation CM/Rec(2022)20 on Human Rights and the Protection of the Environment (27 September 2022).

[144] Reykjavík Declaration, 'United around Our Values', Appendix V, 'The Council of Europe and the Environment', adopted at the 4th Summit of Heads of State and Government, 16–17 May 2023 (Strasbourg, CoE, 2023) 21.

beyond a soft law instrument. The reaction of the Parliamentary Assembly of the CoE was, once again, to request a 'binding legal instrument as soon as possible'.[145]

There seems to be no end to this debate between the Parliamentary Assembly and the Council of Ministers. If the PACE's request is not successful, as Pedersen has stated:

> [I]t is evident that the European Court of Human Rights is willing and keen to make use of external sources and authorities. In the context of the potential of a possible right to a healthy environment in international law, it therefore seems uncontentious to argue that such a right might well provide further interpretive background for the Court.[146]

In fact, the ECtHR has occasionally referred to the 'right to live in a safe and healthy environment' in cases such as *Tătar* and *Di Sarno*, where it declared violations of the right of people concerned to respect for their homes and their private life (Article 8 ECHR).[147] This can be seen as a sign of 'the importance of protecting human health' that draws on the ECtHR's more general approach to environment-based claims.[148] This trend could be strengthened after the approval of UN Resolution 76/300. In *KlimaSeniorinnen*, the Court stated that although it is not for the Court 'to determine whether the general trends regarding the recognition of such a right give rise to a specific legal obligation', it also added that such a development 'forms part of the international-law context in which the Court assesses Convention issues before it … notably as regards the recognition by the Contracting Parties of a close link between the protection of the environment and human rights'.[149]

Still, if the CoE finally enshrined the right to a clean, healthy and sustainable environment in a binding instrument, it would have the deepest impact on the ECtHR's role as an environmental court and, in this new context, the scope of access to justice to protect this right would need to be widened to further align it with Article 9 AC. As the Parliamentary Assembly has argued, the recognition of a right to a clean, healthy and sustainable environment could not only be an incentive for stronger domestic environmental laws but would also strengthen the ECtHR's role in the protection of the environment, as it would make it easier for victims to lodge applications for remedies and would allow a violation to be found irrespective of whether another right had been breached, thus increasing the profile of this right.[150]

[145] PACE Recommendation 2272 (2024) on 'Mainstreaming the Human Right to a Safe, Clean, Healthy and Sustainable Environment with the Reykjavik Process'.
[146] OW Pedersen, 'The European Court of Human Rights and International Environmental Law: A Long Time Coming?' in Knox and Pejan (eds) (n 21) 93.
[147] *Tătar v Romanía* App No 67021/01 (ECtHR, 27 January 2009), para 107; *Di Sarno and Others* (n 84) para 110.
[148] Morrow (n 45) 57.
[149] *KlimaSeniorinnen* (n 52) para 448.
[150] PACE Resolution 2396 (2021) (n 142).

Ultimately, to echo the ideas of Capellety and Garth cited at the beginning of this chapter, access to justice can be regarded as the most basic human right to guarantee in the future – beyond the mere proclamation – the right to a clean, healthy and sustainable environment. Broad access to justice to protect it, as provided by Article 9 AC, will be essential 'to lead to results that are individually and socially just'.

3

Environmental Access to Justice in the Balkans Through the Lens of EU Enlargement

Between Top-down *and* Bottom-up *Europeanisation*

BOJANA TODOROVIĆ

I. Introduction

This chapter investigates two driving forces behind the Europeanisation of environmental democracy in the Balkans – the EU's enlargement policy in the environmental arena (*top-down Europeanisation*) and the growing environmental activism[1] of civil society (*bottom-up Europeanisation*). By going beyond a legal analysis and delving into the relevant and recent scholarly sources in the fields of sociology and political science, this chapter aims to provide a comprehensive and more nuanced overview of the Balkan context and at disentangling the intricate relationship between the EU, the Aarhus Convention and the role of civil society actors in the field of environmental protection, thus setting the scene for a better understanding of the national perspectives in this book.

A. Methodological Framework

In their assessment of environmental activism in post-socialist societies in Europe, Fagan and Buzogány identified four different approaches or 'waves' of scholarly research. The focus of the first one was on the inception of environmentalism as

[1] Environmental activism is understood here in a broad sense to include 'the activities of individuals and social movements aimed at protecting the environment': F Allen, 'Trends in Environmental Activism' (2023) 73(5) *International Political Science Abstracts* 673, 673.

part of the 'democratisation and national awakening processes in Central and Eastern Europe and the Soviet Union'. The second wave turned the scientific lens towards the rise of environmental non-governmental organisations (ENGOs) or, as the authors framed it, 'the influence of professionalisation and NGO-isation of environmentalism'. The third wave aligned with the EU accession process of the Central and Eastern European (CEE) countries and the role played by the 'EU's pre-accession conditionality and the "Europeanisation" not only of environmental and energy policies but also of state-society relations and civil society discourses'. The final, fourth wave goes beyond 'external drivers of transformation or the exogenous influences on protest forms' and instead 'places primary emphasis on the specificity of the domestic or "local" context', not neglecting the role of external factors either.[2] It is precisely this fourth – and most recent – wave of scholarly interest and literature that this chapter builds upon by bringing into play both the *external* influence – embodied in the EU and the Aarhus Convention – and the specific *internal* contexts in order to better grasp the practical realities in the observed Balkan countries.

The legal mobilisation theory provides useful insights as to *how*, *why* and *to what effect* different social categories and groups mobilise the law in order to achieve particular goals. As Vanhala points out: 'The mobilization of law to address environmental problems has become an important tactic in the repertoire of those confronting ever more complex and wide-ranging environmental challenges and related social problems.'[3] While the concept of legal mobilisation is not universally defined,[4] in its essence this term implies the reliance on available legal instruments and processes in order to attain a specific goal and/or influence the public discourse, 'policy and behaviour'.[5] This includes, but is not limited to, 'administrative procedures, quasi-judicial processes, and litigation'.[6] In fact, it is stated in the literature that: 'Litigation is the most important thing the environmental movement has done over the past fifteen years.'[7]

Different factors may affect the decision (not) to pursue the available legal mechanisms such as instigating litigation. They range from the (in)adequacy of the so-called *legal stock* or body of hard and sometimes soft law measures; *legal-opportunity structures* (LOS)[8] that are more or less favourable (stability of

[2] A Fagan and A Buzogány, 'Beyond Europeanization: Political Ecology and Environmentalism in Central and Eastern Europe' (2022) 31(7) *Environmental Politics* 1203, 1204.

[3] L Vanhala, 'Environmental Legal Mobilization' (2022) 18 *Annual Review of Law and Social Science* 101, 102.

[4] For example, see ibid 103–04.

[5] L Vanhala and J Kinghan, *Literature Review on the Use and Impact of Litigation* (London, Public Law Project, 2018), https://publiclawproject.org.uk/resources/literature-review-on-the-use-and-impactof-litigation, 5.

[6] For example, see Vanhala (n 3) 104.

[7] L Vanhala, 'Legal Opportunity Structures and the Paradox of Legal Mobilization by the Environmental Movement in the UK' (2012) 46(3) *Law & Society Review* 523, 524.

[8] Andersen sheds light on the links between *legal* opportunity structures (LOS) and the so-called *political* opportunity structures (POS), defining the latter as 'the institutional and sociocultural factors

institutions, especially courts; rules on standing; fees and other procedural hurdles etc); *access to resources* and questions related to the *knowledge*, *identity*, *culture* and overall *mentality* of civil society actors in a given context.[9] However, LOS scholars agree that 'procedural rules constraining or enhancing access to justice are a determining factor of legal opportunity'.[10] Bearing in mind the fact that the access to justice standards stemming from the Aarhus Convention precisely target such procedural rules that can *enable* or *disable* effective judicial protection in the environmental field, literature on legal mobilisation and LOS will be a valuable source of insight in order to better understand the implementation of this instrument in countries that are the focus of this book.

The analysis in this chapter is based on the hypothesis that the EU plays an ambivalent role in environmental access to justice in the Balkans. On the one hand, through its conditionality instruments in the accession process, it 'breathed life' into the civil society sector in the Balkan countries, which was crucial following the fall of socialist regimes and the period of democratic transition. Moreover, it is thanks to EU law and policy instruments that environmental issues have been placed higher up on the agenda in both current Member States and candidate countries. On the other hand, the accession process and the EU's *one-size-fits-all* approach towards empowering civil society in the region created a gap between professional organisations and other forms of individual and collective action (such as various grassroots movements), as well as the detachment of the former from the practical realities and the needs of local communities in their respective countries, which is particularly evident when it comes to environmental issues. Therefore, by being more receptive to local environmental activism, the EU has the potential to be the cohesive factor in bridging this gap and ensuring the effective implementation of Aarhus standards in the Balkans.

Building on the contextual background of the countries in the region painted in the Introduction to this book,[11] this chapter tests the above hypothesis in the following manner. First, it observes how national contexts are affected and shaped by the EU's environmental politics and policies in the accession process – a dynamic also known as *top-down Europeanisation* (section II). Second, the lens is turned towards the so-called *bottom-up Europeanisation*, epitomised in the instrumental role of relevant domestic actors and, more specifically, members of civil

that shape social movement options – by making some strategies more appealing and/or feasible than others'. She argues that with respect to: (1) access to formal institutional structures; (2) configuration of power; and (3) the existence of allies – POS and LOS are just two sides of the same coin. They differ with respect to the *frames* in which they operate; here, she singles out the legal stock or legislative framework that to a great extent shapes what kind of claims are even possible in a particular system, their legal basis, facts that are to be considered relevant etc. See EA Andersen, *Out of the Closets and into the Courts: Legal Opportunity Structure and Gay Rights Litigation* (Ann Arbor, University of Michigan Press, 2005), 6, 12–14.

[9] Vanhala (n 3) 105–08.

[10] Vanhala (n 7) 527.

[11] Todorović and Caranta, Introduction in this volume, section III.

society, which have been at the forefront of environmental access to justice in the recent years (section III). The final section of the chapter concludes on the interplay between these external and internal factors that have enabled or impeded compliance with the requirements stemming from Article 9 of the Aarhus Convention (section IV).

B. From Individuals to Professional (E)NGOs: Conceptualising the Civil Society Continuum

In order to assess the position of civil society players in the environmental access to justice arena within the Balkan context, we first need to identify *who* falls within the ambit of this concept. This is particularly relevant due to the different approaches of national legislators towards defining these categories of actors and granting them (procedural) legal rights.

Defining civil society is no easy academic endeavour, seeing how '[t]here is no universally accepted definition of civil society, and different authors construe the concept more or less broadly'.[12] As Caranta aptly notes, *civil society* is an 'elusive' concept which '[i]n most jurisdictions is not a term of [legal] art'.[13] In the most general sense, it is centred somewhere between the public and private spheres – at times positioned 'between the State and the market' and at others, between the state and the individual, although the latter may sometimes also be considered part of the definition of civil society.[14]

In its consultative document aimed at improving the 'culture of consultation and dialogue' at the level of EU governance,[15] the European Commission defines civil society organisations as the 'principal structures of society outside of government and public administration, including economic operators not generally considered to be "third sector" or NGOs [non-governmental organisations]'.[16] Therefore, it makes a distinction between NGOs and civil society organisations. In a more recent policy act aimed at strengthening the civil sector – especially in non-EU partner countries – the Commission encompasses 'a wide range of actors with multiple roles and mandates' within the domain of civil society organisations, including 'all non-State, not-for-profit independent and non-violent structures, through which people organise to pursue shared

[12] B Todorović, 'The Story of the Civil Supervisor: A Missed Opportunity to Strengthen Civil Control of Public Procurement in the Republic of Serbia' (2020) *Balkan Yearbook of European and International Law* 147, 150.

[13] R Caranta, 'Civil Society Organizations and Administrative Law' (2013) 36(1) *Hamline Law Review* 39, 39.

[14] ibid 47–48.

[15] Commission, 'Towards a reinforced culture of consultation and dialogue – General principles and minimum standards for consultation of interested parties by the Commission (Communication)' COM (2002) 704 final.

[16] ibid 6.

objectives and ideals, whether political, cultural, religious, environmental, social or economic or related to health'.[17]

An overview of the historical development of the Aarhus Convention and its standards on environmental access to justice leads us to the conclusion that the drafters of the Convention also had a broad concept of the non-state sector in mind. The definition of the 'public' from Article 2(4) illustrates this point well. By encompassing 'one or more natural or legal persons, and, in accordance with national legislation or practice, their associations, organizations or groups' under its umbrella, it aims to provide standing not only to formally established NGOs with legal personality, but also 'citizens' groups with less formal structures'.[18] Such an all-encompassing approach that provides protection to 'any form in which natural or legal persons may legally assemble in given legal framework, thus not necessarily requiring from NGOs to have legal personality'[19] accommodates the diversity of national legislative solutions.

This reading of the aforementioned provision is confirmed in *The Aarhus Convention Implementation Guide*, which stresses that the language of Article 2(4) is to be interpreted in such a way as to provide that 'associations, organizations or groups *without legal personality* may also be considered to be members of the public under the Convention'.[20] Moreover, reference to 'national legislation and practice' is called for. It is further stated that:

> [A]d hoc formations can only be considered to be members of the public where the requirements, if any, established by national legislation or practice are met. Such requirements, if any, must comply with the Convention's objective of securing broad access to its rights.[21]

Jendrośka points to the fact that while this had not been specifically debated, during the process of drafting the Aarhus Convention and its third pillar, 'the notion of 'NGOs' was broadly understood' so as to enable comprehensive standing:

> [N]ot only to the traditional well-established membership based large organizations but also to the groups of citizens organizing grassroots activities against a proposed project and to the associations of experts, whether the scientific experts assembled to deal with certain specific issue or legal experts providing environmental advocacy services.[22]

[17] Commission, 'Thematic Programme for Civil Society Organisations 2021–2027' [2021], 2. For more on the European Commission's Global Europe Civil Society Organisations programme, aimed at financial support civil society organisations outside of the EU, see https://ec.europa.eu/commission/presscorner/detail/en/ip_21_6792.

[18] J Jendrośka, 'Access to Justice in the Aarhus Convention: Genesis, Legislative History and Overview of the Main Interpretation Dilemmas' (2020) 17(4) *Journal for European Environmental & Planning Law* 372, 386.

[19] ibid 386.

[20] J Ebbesson et al, *The Aarhus Convention: An Implementation Guide*, 2nd edn (New York, United Nations Publication, 2014) 55.

[21] ibid.

[22] Jendrośka (n 18) 385.

Finally, in the explanatory *Note on Civil Society Space* prepared by the Aarhus Convention Secretariat, it is stated that 'the central tenets of facilitating a space in which civil society can strive and participate in decision-making are an "enabling" and "safe environment"' and one of the crucial elements thereof is an 'inclusive' (ie, broad) understanding of civil society, so as to ensure 'that no sectors of civil society are excluded from being heard or given the possibility to participate'.[23]

Any understanding of civil society and the various forms in which it is materialised in this chapter also needs to be coherent with the legislative framework and the practical reality of the countries which are the focus of this book. For complex historical reasons,[24] the nascence, development, role and impetus of the civil society sector has been in a constant state of flux. The result is a polymorphous landscape in which a number of different types of more or less formalised groups of citizens exist and pursue their activities in a rather ambivalent relationship with the state. Since the aim of this section is only to 'set the scene' for a better understanding of the national perspectives in this book, suffice it to say that while the organisational forms, registration requirements and other legal (procedural) specificities differ, all of the observed countries recognise and warrant freedom of association, in line with the standards stemming from the European Convention on Human Rights (ECHR), to which they are all parties.[25] Moreover, *associations* (both registered and not registered) and *foundations* are the most common types of formally recognised non-governmental and non-profit organisations.[26] On the other hand, various types of semi-institutionalised organisations and think-tanks, networks of local, national and even regional organisations and advocacy groups,[27] smaller community-based organisations and initiatives and the 'more radical' grassroots movements have also been recognised in the literature.[28]

Bearing the above in mind and without the intent of offering a universal definition of the term, this chapter relies on a broad understanding of civil society that includes *formal organisations* (ie, NGOs and other types of associations formally registered under national law) as well as various *configurations of informal groups* (such as citizens' initiatives, grassroots organisations, movements

[23] www.ohchr.org/sites/default/files/Documents/AboutUs/CivilSociety/Procedures/UN/UnitedNationsEconomicCommissionEurope.pdf, 1.

[24] Todorović and R Caranta, Introduction in this volume, sections I and III.

[25] D Rutzen, D Moore and M Durham, 'Reformist Leaders and Civil Society. The Legal Framework for Not-for-Profit Organizations in Central and Eastern Europe' (2009) 11(2) *International Journal of Not-for-Profit Law*, www.icnl.org/resources/research/ijnl/the-legal-framework-for-not-for-profit-organizations-in-central-and-eastern-europe#_ftnref64.

[26] ibid.

[27] In the Serbian context, see, for instance, Marš sa Drine, https://marssadrine.org.

[28] I Sokolić, D Kostovicova and A Fagan, 'Civil Society in Post-Yugoslav Space: The Test of Discontinuity and Democratization' in O Anastasakis et al (eds), *The Legacy of Yugoslavia: Politics, Economics and Society in the Modern Balkans* (London, IB Tauris/Bloomsbury Publishing, 2022) 39, 46–54.

of local communities, and campaigns), regardless of whether they have legal personality under national law, and of the strategies they employ – since both play an important role in spearheading environmental democracy in the Balkans. As Baća notes:

> Focusing solely on the institutionalized civic engagement and professionalized associational life prevents us from fully comprehending how these processes affected and were influenced by civil society as it materialized through protest politics, informal economy, everyday routines, kinship structures, online activism, and various other practices, both compliant and contentious, unfolding at the intersection of the state, the market, and the household sectors.[29]

II. EU Enlargement as an Instrument of *Top-down* Europeanisation of Environmental Access to Justice

The enlargement process is described in the literature as 'one of the EU's most powerful policy tools'.[30] The evolving 'essence' of this process is captured by Limante in the following way:

> Originally conceived as a procedure enabling third states to become Member States to the EU, the enlargement policy has evolved into a comprehensive system of rules and policies, whereby the aspirant states are to be reshaped into what the EU considers a "proper" Member State.[31]

The legal basis for the gradual opening up of the EU 'club' to new members is found in Article 49 of the Treaty on European Union (TEU), which paves the way for the possibility of 'any European state' that respects the values on which the EU is premised – ie, 'human dignity, freedom, democracy, equality, the rule of law and respect for human rights, including the rights of persons belonging to minorities' (Article 2 TEU) – to apply for membership.[32] In order to be successful in its application, the prospective candidate needs to comply with a series of general as well as country-specific criteria developed at the EU level – both of which have evolved and 'shape-shifted' over time, based, inter alia, on lessons learned with each enlargement wave.[33] It is important to note that this process is not merely technical, automatically resulting in accession as soon as the 'eligible' state fulfils the prescribed criteria, but also a 'political choice' of the EU, which inevitably

[29] B Baća, 'Three Stages of Civil Society Development in the Global East: Lessons from Montenegro, 1989–2020' (2024) 109 *Political Geography* 9.

[30] S Baker, 'EU Conditionality and Environmental Policy in Southeastern Europe' (2015) 63(3) *Südosteuropa* 372, 390.

[31] A Limante, 'The Western Balkans on the Way to the EU: Revisiting EU Conditionality' (2020) *Balkan Yearbook of European and International Law* 123, 132.

[32] ibid.

[33] ibid 133.

creates an asymmetrical dynamic between the EU and its Member States on the one hand, and aspirant members on the other.[34]

Due to the 'growing divergence between EU standards and the initial level of preparedness in candidate countries',[35] the focus of the EU accession process gradually shifted towards the rule of law and democracy requirements. These are epitomised in the so-called *Copenhagen criteria*[36] established at the European Council meeting in Copenhagen in 1993 that set 'detailed requirements related to EU *acquis*[37] compliance, reforms of public administration, judiciary, anti-corruption and market economy'.[38] After having been incorporated into the Treaty of Amsterdam and following the problematic experiences with the accession of Bulgaria and Romania where 'the absence of explicit rule of law conditionality caused much concern given high and persistent levels of corruption', these requirements were further translated into negotiating Chapters 23 (Judiciary and fundamental rights) and 24 (Justice, freedom and security) for the subsequent 'accession rounds'.[39]

The complex regional dynamic and the devastating effects of the violent dissolution of Yugoslavia made 'Europeanization even more of a challenge'[40] with respect to the countries that fall under the geopolitical umbrella of the Western Balkans (WB).[41] This left a mark on the accession process, which now needed to ensure 'substantial state building'[42] and to tackle issues relating to reconciliation and transitional justice, the rights of refugees and minorities, as well as certain country-specific, often politicised and thus highly sensitive problems.[43]

The accession paths of the WB countries build on the wider framework of the Stabilisation and Association Process for the WB, which entails a 'progressive

[34] Baker (n 30) 386.

[35] N Wunsch, *EU Enlargement and Civil Society in the Western Balkans: From Mobilisation to Empowerment* (London, Palgrave Macmillan, 2018) 22.

[36] These criteria concern: (1) stability of institutions guaranteeing democracy, the rule of law, human rights and respect for and protection of minorities; (2) a functioning market economy and the ability to cope with competitive pressure and market forces within the EU; (3) the ability to take on the obligations of membership, including the capacity to effectively implement the rules, standards and policies that make up the body of EU law (the 'acquis'); and (4) adherence to the aims of political, economic and monetary union. See https://eur-lex.europa.eu/legal-content/EN/TXT/?uri=LEGISSUM:accession_criteria_copenhague.

[37] The EU *acquis* comprises the 'accumulated legislation, legal acts and court decisions which constitute the body of European Union law. During the process of the enlargement of the European Union, the acquis is divided into 35 chapters for the purpose of negotiation between the EU and the Candidate Member States': A Hoxhaj, 'The EU Rule of Law Initiative towards the Western Balkans' (2021) 13 *Hague Journal on the Rule of Law* 143, 147 fn 11.

[38] Limante (n 31) 134.

[39] Wunsch (n 35) 22.

[40] T Börzel and A Fagan, 'Environmental Governance in South East Europe/Western Balkans: Reassessing the Transformative Power of Europe' (2015) 47 *Environment and Planning C: Government and Policy*, 5.

[41] Todorović and Caranta, Introduction in this volume, section III.

[42] Börzel and Fagan (n 40) 5.

[43] Limante (n 31) 137–38; Wunsch (n 35) 23–24.

partnership with a view of stabilising the region and establishing a free-trade area' with the aim of 'eventual EU membership'[44] and is implemented through the Stabilisation and Association Agreements (SAAs)[45] – the WB equivalent of Europe Agreements signed with CEE countries, including Romania and Slovenia.[46]

As a response to the 'enlargement fatigue' from which both sides (EU and prospective candidates) have been suffering and in order to make the process 'more credible', in 2020 the Commission revised the enlargement methodology for the WB countries. In a nutshell, the changes imply grouping negotiating chapters into six thematic clusters and an even stronger focus on the so-called *fundamentals* – ie, the rule of law, democratic institutions, public administration and the economy – since '[n]egotiations on the fundamentals will be open first and closed last and the progress on these will determine the overall pace of negotiations'.[47] Consequently, the conditions imposed on the WB countries – sometimes referred to in the literature as 'Copenhagen criteria +' – are considered to be 'the most complicated' with respect to breadth and typology compared to previous accession rounds.[48]

While the accession rounds preceding Croatia's accession were heavily top-down-oriented and mostly concerned the interaction between the EU and domestic institutions (mainly the executive), 'the European Commission gradually instituted a comprehensive consultation cycle with local civil society actors'.[49] The EU's approach towards a more comprehensive involvement of representatives of civil society in the accession process gradually evolved from consultations on drafting progress reports to more institutionalised forms of support through donations and regional initiatives such as the Civil Society Facility[50] or the Technical Assistance for Civil Society Organisations,[51] which aim at strengthening capacities

[44] https://neighbourhood-enlargement.ec.europa.eu/enlargement-policy/glossary/stabilisation-and-association-process_en.

[45] As Stec points out: 'the agreements provide a benchmarking mechanism for progress towards eventual European Union membership, employing financial assistance mechanisms, granting trade concessions and promoting regional cooperation'. S Stec, 'EU Enlargement, Neighbourhood Policy and Environmental Democracy' in M Pallemaerts (ed), *The Aarhus Convention at Ten: Interactions and Tensions between Conventional International Law and EU Environmental Law* (Amsterdam, Europa Law Publishing, 2011) 36, 39. For SAAs in individual WB countries, see, for example, Drenovak-Ivanović, ch 8 in this volume, section II.

[46] In drawing parallels between Europe agreements and SAAs, Mataija points out that the latter differ with respect to the preambles that do not explicitly mention accession, but rather pave the way for the *prospect* of membership, as well as the fact that they are based on more broadly construed *conditionality* instruments. In other 'operative aspects', the two types of agreements are quite similar, even in wording. See M Mataija, 'The Unfulfilled Potential of Stabilisation and Association Agreements before SEE Courts' in S Rodin and T Perišin (eds), *Judicial Application of International Law in Southeast Europe* (Berlin, Springer-Verlag, 2015) 11, 13–15.

[47] https://ec.europa.eu/commission/presscorner/detail/en/IP_20_181. See also Drenovak-Ivanović, ch 8 in this volume, section II.

[48] Limante (n 31) 144.

[49] Wunsch (n 35) 25.

[50] https://neighbourhood-enlargement.ec.europa.eu/enlargement-policy/policy-highlights/civil-society_en.

[51] www.tacso.eu/about-us/project-description.

of civil society organisations and providing them with financial support. Moreover, the Commission worked towards creating a more 'enabling environment' for civil society to be actively engaged in such a way that 'the dialogue between civil society actors and governments have thus become a horizontal policy measure that is evaluated separately in the annual progress reports'.[52]

Explaining the role of non-state actors in the EU accession process, Börzel and Buzogány point towards the – at least formally speaking – benefits of such a process in strengthening the civil sector in accession countries. Not only are non-state actors recognised as a *conditio sine qua non* partner for the effective implementation of the cumbersome EU *acquis*, but the EU itself also made the pace and success of accession conditional upon their empowerment and involvement. Moreover, states are now not only required (at times explicitly in certain pieces of EU legislation) to involve non-state actors in order to reach the set targets, but they are also motivated to do so in order to ensure the effective implementation of those policies in practice and to avoid potential negative consequences, such as litigation instigated by aggrieved non-state actors.[53]

A. Environmental Protection in the Accession Process: Between a Rock and a Hard Place

From the first legal basis for a common environmental policy introduced by the Single European Act in 1986, through the horizontal requirement of integrating environmental protection into all of EU's policies with a view to promoting sustainable development brought about by the Treaty of Amsterdam,[54] to granting the EU legal personality to conclude international agreements, environmental protection gradually occupied 'a central role in EU's external policy'.[55]

In a similar vein, environmental protection was not embedded in the enlargement process from the outset. Authors investigating the past half a century of EU enlargement reveal that up until the so-called 'Eastern Enlargement' in 2004 (and the enlargement waves thereafter), environmental protection played a marginal role in the accession process, which was mainly due to the focus on the creation of the European market, as well as the lack of adequate EU competences in that field.[56] It is only during the last three waves of accession that the EU's attitude towards

[52] Wunsch (n 35) 33–34.

[53] T Börzel and A Buzogány, 'Governing EU Accession in Transition Countries: The Role of Non-state Actors' (2010) 45 *Acta Politica* 158, 160–62.

[54] See in detail M Klamert, 'Article 11 TFEU' in M Kellerbauer, M Klamert and J Tomkin (eds), *The EU Treaties and the Charter of Fundamental Rights: A Commentary* (Oxford, Oxford University Press, 2019) 386–87.

[55] S Bogojević and M Drenovak-Ivanović, 'Environmental Protection through the Prism of Enlargement: Time for Reflection' (2019) 56 *Common Market Law Review* 949, 954.

[56] ibid 960–62.

environmental protection changed. This is reflected in the Europe Agreements/SAAs of the analysed Balkan countries, which contain a self-standing article dedicated to environmental matters and a general clause stating, mutatis mutandis, that:

> The Parties shall develop and strengthen their cooperation in the environmental field with the vital task of halting further degradation and start improving the environmental situation with the aim of sustainable development.[57]

Still, there is a visible discrepancy between the emphasis on environmental concerns as one of the 'core objectives' in the Treaties[58] and their position in the enlargement process. As Bogojević and Drenovak-Ivanović point out, environmental protection is not listed as one of the fundamental values on which the EU is based (Article 2 TEU), nor does it explicitly form part of the Copenhagen criteria, except with respect to the obligation of prospective candidates to align their national legislation with the abundant EU environmental *acquis*.[59] These authors conclude that the EU approaches environmental matters as a 'mere implementation checklist',[60] which is problematic given the fact that this policy field demands not only an adaptation of the legislative and institutional frameworks, but a continual mentality shift as well.

Moreover, the EU environmental *acquis* is considered to be the 'thorniest' part of the accession path of current and prospective members. This is due to the abundance of legal norms, entailing an entire palette of horizontal and sectoral pieces of legislation,[61] as well as case law, grouped under the umbrella of the negotiating Chapter 27 (Environment).[62] Moreover, their 'dynamic' and ever-evolving nature and an intimate link with 'questions concerning governance, and … the rule of law'[63] pose a serious financial and institutional challenge to prospective members,

[57] *cf* art 81 of the Romanian Europe agreement [1994] OJ L357, 31 December 1994 P 0002–0189, https://eur-lex.europa.eu/LexUriServ/LexUriServ.do?uri=CELEX:21994A1231%2820%29:EN:HTML; art 82 of the Slovenian Europe agreement [1999] OJ L51, 26 February 1999, 3–206, https://eur-lex.europa.eu/legal-content/EN/ALL/?uri=CELEX%3A21999A0226%2801%29; art 103 of the Croatian SAA [2005] OJ L26, 28 January 2005, 3–220, https://eur-lex.europa.eu/legal-content/EN/ALL/?uri=CELEX%3A22005A0128%2801%29; art 108 of the Albanian SAA [2009] OJ L107, 28 April 2009, 166–502, https://eur-lex.europa.eu/legal-content/EN/TXT/?uri=celex%3A22009A0428%2802%29; art 103 of the North Macedonian SAA [2004] OJ L84, 20 March 2004, 13–197, https://eur-lex.europa.eu/legal-content/EN/TXT/?uri=celex%3A22004A0320%2803%29 and art 111 of the Serbian SAA [2013] OJ L278, 18 October 2013, 16–473, https://eur-lex.europa.eu/legal-content/EN/TXT/?uri=celex%3A22013A1018%2801%29.

[58] Bogojević and Drenovak-Ivanović (n 55) 950 fn 5 and 954.

[59] ibid 953–57.

[60] ibid 957.

[61] Mainly in the form of directives, estimated at well above 200: https://neighbourhood-enlargement.ec.europa.eu/enlargement-policy/conditions-membership/chapters-acquis_en.

[62] https://neighbourhood-enlargement.ec.europa.eu/enlargement-policy/glossary/chapters-acquis-negotiating-chapters_en; Bogojević and Drenovak-Ivanović (n 55) 956. According to the new enlargement methodology, this now forms part of Cluster 4 – Green Agenda and Sustainable Connectivity: https://euneighbourseast.eu/news/publications/eu-accession-process-step-by-step.

[63] Bogojević and Drenovak-Ivanović (n 55) 952.

which is illustrated by the fact that none of the countries that acceded the EU since 2004 fully complied with the EU environmental *acquis* at the time of accession, and even more so by the number of transitional measures negotiated.[64]

Lastly, this policy field is also an arena in which the tensions between various and, often, conflicting interests are very palpable, resulting in serious political, societal and environmental challenges. Two examples of this phenomenon and the ambivalent role played by the EU in promoting the green transition in its immediate neighbourhood are given in the lines that follow.

The first one concerns the construction of small hydropower plants (SHPP) in mountainous rivers in Serbia. As a result of the requirement to reach the EU's ambitious renewable energy targets,[65] Serbia passed a series of legislative measures, which enabled the privatisation of natural resources (river water) and the status of 'privileged power producer' being granted to investors that embark on the construction of SHPPs. The financial incentives in the form of feed-in tariffs – including 'generous funds' from international lending institutions such as the European Bank for Reconstruction and Development (EBRD) or the European Investment Bank (EIB) – resulted in the popularity of this source of renewable energy and the mushrooming of SHPPs.[66]

However, instead of achieving greater renewable energy production (which was actually quite negligible), this approach led to flagrant violations of the administrative procedures for obtaining the necessary permits (at times bypassing them completely), the endangerment of the flora and fauna and livelihood of the local population – leading to mass protests that were encountered with a violent response from the police and the investors' private security.[67]

The described scenario in which a candidate country chooses to 'facilitate investments in renewable sources of energy at all costs', even to the detriment of the environment and the well-being of its citizens[68] – could have easily been set in another WB country. The obligations arising out of the membership in the Energy Community[69] and the race towards attaining renewable energy targets, coupled

[64] ibid 964–67.

[65] Which were, at the time, prescribed in the so-called Renewable Energy Directive, ie, Directive 2009/28/EC of the European Parliament and of the Council of 23 April 2009 on the promotion of the use of energy from renewable sources and amending and subsequently repealing Directives 2001/77/EC and 2003/30/EC. This piece of legislation has been repealed by Directive (EU) 2018/2001 of the European Parliament and of the Council of 11 December 2018 on the promotion of the use of energy from renewable sources (recast) [2018] OJ L328, 21 December 2018, 82–209.

[66] A Piletić, 'Renewable Energy and EU-Led Authoritarian Neoliberalization: Small Hydropower in Rakita, Serbia and the Upscaling of Environmental Struggles' (2024) 21(6) *Globalizations* 1092, 1097–98.

[67] ibid 1098–102; Bogojević and Drenovak-Ivanović (n 55) 974–76.

[68] Piletić (n 66) 1097.

[69] As stated on its website, the Energy Community is 'an international organisation which brings together the European Union and its neighbours' and aims at extending the EU internal energy market rules and principles to countries in Southeast Europe, the Black Sea region and beyond on the basis of a legally binding framework: www.energy-community.org/aboutus/whoweare.html.

with an abundance of water resources and lax conditions for granting concessions to investors, make this a regional environmental emergency.[70]

This example reveals the repercussions of requiring candidate countries to fully align with the EU *acquis* before accession, but without the additional 'layer of protection (that) exists for EU member states'.[71] The latter includes preventive tools such as the Environmental Implementation Review, which ensures the proper implementation of EU climate and environmental legislation whilst also 'raising public awareness about the importance of implementing environmental rules and main challenges' and enabling communication between national authorities and civil society on these issues.[72] Most importantly, this protection entails the possibility of 'intervention' of the European Commission and the European Court of Justice 'if national legal systems fail to uphold EU law'.[73]

The second example concerns the 'Jadar' lithium mining project in the western part of Serbia. In 2004 the British-Australian mining company 'Rio Tinto' conducted explorations of the Jadar river valley and discovered the presence of the mineral 'jadarite', found to be incredibly rich in lithium and boron.[74] Given that these raw materials are crucial for the burgeoning electric vehicles industry and as such 'central to both green and digital transitions',[75] Rio Tinto decided to embark on an investment that was to result in the biggest lithium mine and processing unit in Europe.[76] The project and the company itself received strong endorsement from the Serbian government, which enabled it to quickly obtain the approval of the spatial plan along with the necessary permits, in order to begin excavations.[77] However, these were forewarned by emerging scientific evidence of irreparable harm to the local ecosystem and the livelihood of local communities should the project be realised. Indications of grave illegality also resurfaced, among which the most striking had been intimidations of local residents into selling-out their land, failure to provide proof of environmental impact assessment and overall lack of transparency surrounding the project or the exclusion of the local communities and other relevant stakeholders from the

[70] For more on this issue across the region, see F Korançe, *Environmental Activism in the Western Balkans* (Prishtina, The Balkan Forum, 2022); B Pavlakovič et al, 'Small Hydropower Plants in Western Balkan countries: Status, Controversies and a Proposed Model for Decision Making' (2022) 12(9) *Energy, Sustainability and Society*, 1–13.

[71] Piletić (n 66) 1097.

[72] https://ec.europa.eu/commission/presscorner/detail/en/qanda_22_5328.

[73] ibid.

[74] C Stuehlen and F Anderl, 'Transnational Companies in Environmental Conflicts: Rio Tinto, Anti-mining Resistance in Serbia, and the Contradictions of Europeanization' (2024) *Z Friedens und Konflforsch*, https://doi.org/10.1007/s42597-024-00114-5, 6–7.

[75] https://joint-research-centre.ec.europa.eu/jrc-news-and-updates/5-ways-eu-scientists-are-making-batteries-better-safer-and-greener-2022-07-20_en.

[76] L Portal, 'Serbia and Jadar Lithium Mines: Will the Project Resume?' (*Blue Europe*, 15 June 2023), www.blue-europe.eu/analysis-en/country-analysis/serbia-and-jadar-lithium-mines-will-the-project-resume.

[77] Stuehlen and Anderl (n 74) 6.

consultation process.[78] Announced legislative measures that would pave the way for a 'smooth' continuation of project activities under the protective umbrella of 'national interest'[79] were the last drop, igniting mass protests throughout the country in 2022.[80]

As a response to public outrage (and just before the scheduled parliamentary elections), the government announced that the Jadar spatial plan will be annulled and all of the issued permits revoked, thereby officially (and ostensibly) cancelling the project. Nevertheless, it soon became clear that this had only been temporary and that 'Rio Tinto never stopped developing its project in Serbia'.[81] Moreover, since 2023 there have been indications of the project being 'revamped' due to its public endorsement by President Vučić and other public officials.[82] However, on 11 July 2024, the Constitutional Court of Serbia held a session in which it found the government decree that approved the Jadar spatial plan to be unconstitutional and illegal.[83] Consequently, the Serbian government passed a new decree in order to officially revive the project, which led to a new series of protests across the country.[84] While the fate of Rio Tinto's project is still unknown at the time of writing, grave violations of all three pillars of the Aarhus Convention are quite certain.[85]

Especially important from the standpoint of this chapter is the contradictory role of the EU in the lithium mining conundrum, and the links between the Jadar project and the accession process. A first peculiarity is the fact that the EU's public stance in this case has been timid and ambivalent. The European Commission's Progress Reports on Serbia send mixed messages: in 2021, it was considered that 'the government *committed to the highest environmental standards*, and to

[78] Z Kalmar, *Jadar Lithium Mine, Serbia: A Raw Deal ICT Metal Mining Case Study* (CEKOR, KORS and CEE Bankwatch Network, 2021) 7–9, https://bankwatch.org/publication/jadar-lithium-mine-serbia-a-raw-deal-ict-metal-mining-case-study.

[79] Stuehlen and Anderl (n 74) 8.

[80] M Petrović and J Pešić, 'Potentials and Obstacles for the Transnationalisation of Recent Environmental Struggles in Serbia' (2023) 61(2) *Sociologija i prostor* 397, 409.

[81] I Todorović, 'Vučić: Serbia to Reapprove Rio Tinto's Stalled Lithium Project with EU Guarantees' (*Balkan Green Watch*, 17 June 2024), https://balkangreenenergynews.com/vucic-serbia-to-reapprove-rio-tintos-stalled-lithium-project-with-eu-guarantees.

[82] ibid.

[83] I Todorović, 'Constitutional Court of Serbia Rules in Favor of Rio Tinto's Lithium Project' (*Balkan Green Watch*, 11 July 2024), https://balkangreenenergynews.com/constitutional-court-of-serbia-rules-in-favor-of-rio-tintos-lithium-project.

[84] I Todorović, 'Serbia Officially Revives Rio Tinto's Lithium Mining Project Jadar' (*Balkan Green Watch*, 16 July 2024), https://balkangreenenergynews.com/serbia-officially-revives-rio-tintos-lithium-mining-project-jadar.

[85] In addition to what has already been said, violation of the third pillar can also be discerned from the Constitutional Court's selective approach to access to justice. Unlike with respect to the above-mentioned case, in which it delivered a decision expediently, this institution still has not decided on the constitutional appeal submitted by a member of the civil society for more than a year. The appeal targeted the National Assembly's failure to consider the citizens' initiative to implement a mining moratorium. For more on this, see I Todorović, 'Constitutional Court of Serbia Rules in Favor of Rio Tinto's Lithium Project' (*Balkan Green Watch*, 11 July 2024), https://balkangreenenergynews.com/constitutional-court-of-serbia-rules-in-favor-of-rio-tintos-lithium-project.

carrying out a strategic evaluation of its environmental impact before changes to the spatial plan are made' (emphasis added);[86] in 2022 it was only stated that 'the Serbian government withdrew all permits for the Jadar lithium mine project in February 2022' as a result of the mass protests,[87] and in the 2023 Report there was no mention of the project,[88] even though it was one of the greatest sources of political and environmental contention.

Serious concerns that the EU is actively endorsing the project have been raised after the European Commission's spokesperson qualified the project as a 'very good opportunity for the socio-economic development of Serbia' amid nationwide protests,[89] as well as after the 'leakage' of documents asserting that representatives of Rio Tinto and the European Commission's DG Grow met on several occasions.[90] The signing of the Memorandum of Understanding for a 'strategic partnership on sustainable raw materials, battery value chains, and electric vehicles' between the EU and the Serbian government just days after the decision of the Constitutional Court emerged,[91] further chipped away at the already fragile support for and credibility of the accession process in the eyes of the public.[92] It also unearthed the 'EU's difficulty in reconciling its support for environmental struggles with its economic interests in the context of ecological transition',[93] placing Europeanisation in a 'negative context'.[94]

Both of these examples are telling of Baker's argument that in the accession process, the 'EU primarily acts as a regulatory agent, promoting stronger environmental management, while downplaying engagement with the transformative requirement embedded in the commitment to promote sustainable development'.[95]

[86] Commission, 'Serbia 2021 Report Accompanying the Document Communication from the Commission to the European Parliament, the Council, the European Economic and Social Committee and the Committee of the Regions, 2021 Communication on EU Enlargement Policy', SWD [2021] 288 final 114.

[87] Commission, 'Serbia 2022 Report Accompanying the Document Communication from the Commission to the European Parliament, the Council, the European Economic and Social Committee and the Committee of the Regions 2022 Communication on EU Enlargement Policy', SWD [2022] 338 final 123.

[88] In fact, lithium mining is mentioned only in the context of the lack of the Parliament's response to the citizens' legislative initiative to ban it. See Commission, 'Serbia 2023 Report Accompanying the Document Communication from the Commission to the European Parliament, the Council, the European Economic and Social Committee and the Committee of the Regions 2023 Communication on EU Enlargement Policy', SWD [2023] 695 final, 12.

[89] R Besliu, 'Protecting Nature, Empowering People: Environmental Protests in the Balkans' (*Green European Journal*, 5 June 2023), www.greeneuropeanjournal.eu/protecting-nature-empowering-people-environmental-protests-in-the-balkans.

[90] Stuehlen and Anderl (n 74) 19.

[91] https://ec.europa.eu/commission/presscorner/detail/en/ip_24_3922.

[92] Petrović and Pešić (n 80) 411.

[93] Besliu (n 89). In light of the social implications of the EU Green Deal, see K Arabadjieva and S Bogojević, 'The European Green Deal: Climate Action, Social Impacts and Just Transition Safeguards' (2024) *Yearbook of European Law* 1, 8–10.

[94] Petrović and Pešić (n 80) 411.

[95] Baker (n 30) 390.

B. The Aarhus Convention as Part of the EU Environmental *Acquis*: A 'Litmus Test' of the Application of EU Law in the Balkans?

The fact that the Aarhus Convention forms part of the EU environmental *acquis*, coupled with the commitments to promote and 'further strengthen the Aarhus principles' within the framework of the EU Green Deal in the global fight against climate change,[96] make the Convention an important 'policy tool in the hands of the European Union' aimed at tackling 'ecological challenges in its own territory, its immediate neighbourhood, and beyond'.[97]

The EU's leverage as a global 'Aarhus norm diffuser' is particularly relevant in the context of candidate countries in the accession process, where the EU and its conditionality instruments carry significant normative and political weight.[98] It is in this light that Rodin and Perišin consider the application of this international instrument – among others – as a 'litmus test' for the application of EU law in the acceding countries of South-East Europe.[99] Considering the Balkan countries' complex socio-political legacy that shaped the legal traditions and mentalities around transparency of the public sector (or the lack thereof), the involvement of citizens and their organisations in decision-making and litigation culture,[100] Stec argues that that 'for countries where there is not a historical interest in the Aarhus Convention EU candidacy can be a strongly positive factor'.[101]

A comparison of the dates of signature and/or ratification of the Aarhus Convention in countries that are analysed in this book, with the ones related to relevant milestones in the EU accession process, indicates that – in most cases[102] – these either coincide completely or are quite close.[103] Namely, Croatia signed the Aarhus Convention on 25 June 1998 and ratified it only on 27 March 2007, less than a year after it officially opened and provisionally closed the first negotiating chapter.[104] Romania ratified the Aarhus Convention on 11 July 2000, the year in which the negotiation process was officially launched,[105] and Slovenia signed the

[96] S Kingston et al, 'Empowering through Law: Environmental NGOs as Regulatory Intermediaries in EU Nature Governance' (2023) 12(3) *Transnational Environmental Law* 469, 471.

[97] Stec (n 45) 37.

[98] ibid 41–46.

[99] A reference to S Rodin and T Perišin, 'Application of International Law as a Litmus Test for the Application of EU Law in Southeast Europe' in S Rodin and T Perišin (eds), *Judicial Application of International Law in Southeast Europe* (Berlin, Springer-Verlag, 2015) 3, 5–6.

[100] Todorović and Caranta, Introduction in this volume, section III.

[101] Stec (n 45) 46.

[102] Only Albania's and North Macedonia's accession to the Aarhus Convention significantly pre-dates the EU accession process.

[103] https://unece.org/environment-policy/public-participation/aarhus-convention/status-ratification.

[104] https://neighbourhood-enlargement.ec.europa.eu/croatia_en#:~:text=Croatia%20applied%20for%20EU%20membership,country%20on%201%20July%202013. See also Ofak and Turudić, ch 5 in this volume, section II.

[105] https://ue.mae.ro/en/node/1455. See also Lodoabă-Cordon, Dragos and Neamtu, ch 7 in this volume, sections II and III.

Convention on 25 June 1998 and ratified it on 29 July 2004 – the year of its entry into the EU.[106] Finally, Serbia ratified the Aarhus Convention on 31 July 2009, the same year in which it formally applied for EU membership.[107]

While the *existence* and the *weight* of this seeming correlation between the EU accession process and the uptake of Aarhus standards needs to be confirmed based on insight provided by the national chapters in this book, there are at least three factors related to the structural deficits of the accession process, as well as the EU's internal challenges, that thwart its influence and credibility in prospective members.

First, the concept of environmental democracy, 'aimed at making up democratic deficits through empowerment of the public, and with particular reference to the role that environmental concern may play in such processes', is central to the Aarhus Convention.[108] The question arises as to whether its mechanisms of access to justice may very well be the missing democratic link in the aspiring EU members? If so, the EU should use this instrument wisely in order to steer its implementation in its immediate vicinity, in such a way as to enable more than a formal adherence to its democratic principles. Unfortunately, this does not seem to be the case. As Hoxhaj observes:

> The rule of law initiative so far has only served as a platform for dialogue between the Commission and members of the Western Balkans … it is very much a top-down approach, and has not fully engaged with environmental members of the civil society.[109]

Furthermore, the European Economic and Social Committee (EESC), in its *Contribution of civil society to the Green Agenda and sustainable development of the Western Balkans as part of the EU accession process* (own-initiative opinion), stressed that the civil sector has not been included in the green transition process in a satisfactory manner. Thus, not only is the accession process itself very much top-down-oriented, so is its environmental limb.[110] Therefore, the EESC pleaded for the reinforcement of 'the role of civil society in the monitoring of the governments' actions in fulfilling the necessary accession criteria, particularly as concerns the Fundamentals, as well as the cluster "Green agenda and sustainable connectivity"'.[111]

In assessing obstacles to civil society mobilisation in the accession process, Wunsch highlights the 'hurry up atmosphere' which pushes countries to adopt a bulk of legislation in order to align it with the EU *acquis* in urgency procedures,

[106] K Štemberger Brizani, ch 9 in this volume, sections II and III.B.

[107] https://neighbourhood-enlargement.ec.europa.eu/enlargement-policy/serbia_en. See also Drenovak-Ivanović, ch 8 in this volume, sections II and III.

[108] Stec (n 45) 41.

[109] Hoxhaj (n 37) 169.

[110] 'Contribution of Civil Society to the Green Agenda and Sustainable Development of the Western Balkans as Part of the EU Accession Process (Own-Initiative Opinion)', www.eesc.europa.eu/en/our-work/opinions-information-reports/opinions/contribution-civil-society-green-agenda-and-sustainable-development-western-balkans-part-eu-accession-process-own.

[111] ibid para 2.4.

thereby effectively excluding national civil society organisations from participating in public consultations. She also stresses the secrecy around the accession negotiations, thereby limiting access to relevant information.[112] These are in direct collision with the principles of transparency and public participation as warranted by the Aarhus Convention.

Second, the experience with CEE countries that are now EU Member States shows that 'Aarhus-related directives are transposed early when there is a combination of pressures from the accession process itself and domestic stakeholders'.[113] Given the weak institutional and democratic capacities of the (Western) Balkan countries and the lack of substantial 'public pressure' in the early phases of the accession process, the European Commission has been criticised for prioritising (through financial assistance and measuring progress made) directives related to infrastructure development over Aarhus-related legislation.[114] An additional problem in that context is the fact that many of the obligations stemming from the EU environmental *acquis* are not specific enough and leave plenty of room for discretion in their implementation.[115]

Third, and finally, unlike with respect to Article 9(1) and 9(2) of the Aarhus Convention that have been embodied by self-standing directives at the EU level, this is not the case with Article 9(3). In Chapter 1 of this volume, Eliantonio and Richelle stressed that the 'lack of a horizontal measure transposing the requirements of Article 9(3)' in combination with a multitude of sectoral solutions and general principles of EU law not only leaves room for divergences among Member States, but also creates a 'mosaic of similar – yet not completely overlapping – obligations' that could easily 'confuse' national courts and other authorities.[116] This problem is exacerbated with respect to candidate countries which, as we have seen in the previous section, cannot rely on EU institutional mechanisms in such cases. Moreover, the fragmentation of EU rules on environmental access to justice sends a weak and somewhat ambivalent political message, downplaying the importance of Aarhus standards.

III. *Bottom-up* Europeanisation of Environmental Access to Justice Through Environmental Activism

Enabling civil society actors to initiate legal proceedings or, in case of (overly) restrictive rules on standing, intervene in already commenced proceedings,[117]

112 Wunsch (n 35) 28.
113 Stec (n 45) 46.
114 ibid.
115 Bogojević and Drenovak-Ivanović (n 55)at 975.
116 Eliantonio and Richelle, ch 1 in this volume, section IV.
117 J Krommendijka and K van der Pasb, 'To Intervene or Not to Intervene: Intervention before the Court of Justice of the European Union in Environmental and Migration Law' (2022) 8(26) *International Journal of Human Rights* 1394, 1396.

has been widely recognised as an important 'third-party enforcement mechanism' of environmental law.[118]

Given that individuals are often 'ill-equipped' (with respect to expertise, time, financial and other material resources) to embark on expensive and unpredictable 'legal battles' in the name of defending the interests of amorphous concepts such as 'nature' or the 'environment', as well as 'future generations', ENGOs are seen as the crucial component in 'bridging the gap' between the individual and the state, ie, between private and public interests in the environmental field.[119]

Still, 'to go to court you need a reliable legal system'.[120] This implies the stability of institutions, the rule of law, transparency and the lack of existence of procedural hurdles that render the available legal mechanisms practically unattainable for (all or most) civil society actors. As we have already seen in section I.A of this chapter, a myriad of factors other than the stability of a legal system affect an individual's or organisation's decision whether to litigate.

In the context of environmental access to justice, the Aarhus Convention itself, as well as the EU legislation incorporating it, significantly contributes towards the 'international dimension of the legal opportunity structure',[121] expanding it through standards related to legal standing, costs and other procedural aspects.[122] The Aarhus Convention has therefore been invaluable in empowering ENGOs vis-a-vis public authorities or, as Caranta puts it, in being a 'major step from the descriptive to the prescriptive or normative approach to the role of NGOs in environmental law'.[123] Apart from granting them procedural rights, ie, 'privileged legal rights to … bring environmental judicial proceedings',[124] the provisions of the Aarhus Convention also create 'expectations' from states to design their legislative frameworks in such a way as to 'avoid creating unnecessary obstacles for those groups' with respect to the rules on their registration, but also 'support, such as tax benefits or even financial support'.[125]

Moreover, NGOs 'falling within the scope of article 10, paragraph 5, of the Convention and promoting environmental protection' have, along with the parties

[118] Vanhala (n 3) 102.

[119] R Caranta, 'Environmental NGOs (eNGOs) or: Filling the Gap between the State and the Individual under the Aarhus Convention' in R Caranta, A Gerbrandy and B Müller (eds), *The Making of a New European Legal Culture: The Aarhus Convention, At the Crossroad of Comparative Law and EU Law* (Groningen, Europa Law Publishing, 2017) 401, 401–03.

[120] L Chiodi and S Epis, 'Eastern Europe: Environment and Transnational Activism' (*OBCT*, 28 June 2022), www.balcanicaucaso.org/eng/Areas/Europe/Eastern-Europe-environment-and-transnational-activism-219056.

[121] Vanhala (n 7) 543.

[122] ibid 539–43.

[123] Caranta (n 119) 403.

[124] Kingston et al (n 97) 470.

[125] C Walek, 'Charity Law: The Aarhus Convention and its Practical Impact on NGOs Examples of CEE and NIS Countries' (2000) 3(1) *International Journal of Not-for-Profit Law*, www.icnl.org/resources/research/ijnl/the-aarhus-convention-and-its-practical-impact-on-ngos-examples-of-cee-and-nis-countries.

and signatories to the Aarhus Convention, the right to nominate candidates for the Aarhus Convention Compliance Committee.[126]

Finally, by enabling them to take part in the work of the Aarhus Convention 'bodies and mechanisms including the MOP, Task Forces and Working Groups', as well as to provide comments and feedback to progress reports on the implementation of the Convention produced by the states, ENGOs can 'exert influence' and actively 'engage with the implementation of the Convention's provisions'.[127]

Promoting such an active role of civil society actors and, in particular, ENGOs, the Aarhus Convention is a good case in point of Vanhala's argument that 'legal opportunity' is not a 'snapshot' of the existing legal and institutional framework imposed top-down, but rather a dynamic process in which citizens and their groups also contribute to 'making' more opportunities.[128]

The 'international dimension' of environmental protection is a direct result of the fact that: 'Environmental issues rarely remain local as they tend to transcend national borders, demanding international collaboration and management.'[129] Based on that premise, social movements literature explores the phenomenon of 'transnationalisation' of environmental activism and movements, understood in the broadest sense as the cross-border spill-over effect of national/local environmental 'battles'. This multifaceted phenomenon implies a variety of methods and processes, among which Pešić and Vukelić highlight the following:

(1) *diffusion* – the international circulation of ideas, tactics and repertoires of action;
(2) *domestication* – the internalisation of international goals, ideas and practices at the national level;
(3) *externalisation* – addressing international actors with the intention of influencing national governments; and
(4) *transnationalisation in a narrow sense* – meaning the transnational coordination of protests and other activities against international organisations and transnational corporations.[130]

These authors point out that in post-socialist countries of the (Western) Balkans – some of which are now EU Member States and others part of the accession process – the transnationalisation of environmental activism is 'strongly associated with processes of Europeanisation'.[131] In other words, the EU accession process is the background against which such transnationalisation occurs. Apart

[126] Ebbesson et al (n 20) 223; C Abbot and M Lee, 'NGOs Shaping Public Participation through Law: The Aarhus Convention and Legal Mobilisation' (2024) 36 *Journal of Environmental Law* 85, 90.
[127] Abbot and Lee (n 126) 97–99; Caranta (n 119) 405.
[128] For a detailed analysis, see Vanhala (n 7).
[129] J Pešić and J Vukelić, 'Europeanisation from Below at the Semi-periphery: The Movement against Small Hydropower Plants in Serbia' (2022) 64(1) *Sociologija* 5, 6.
[130] ibid.
[131] ibid 7.

from the *domestication* of the EU environmental *acquis* as the most obvious form of Europeanisation resulting from top-down pressures, they also identify other modalities 'initiated from below', such as the reliance of civil society actors on the new legal and political opportunity structures offered by the 'Brussels venue'[132] (*externalisation*) or the transborder networks formed between local and European organisations (*transnationalisation in a narrow sense*).[133]

It is through this theoretical lens that the genesis, characteristics and current trends of environmental activism in the Balkans will be observed in the remainder of this section, against the backdrop of its intimate and intricate relationship with the EU.

A. The Physiognomy of Environmental Activism in the Balkans

Contemporary social movements literature identifies certain features of environmental activism in post-socialist countries – including the countries of the (Western) Balkans – which distinguish them from their counterparts in developed countries of the 'Global North', as well as the developing ones in the so-called 'Global South'.[134]

First of all, the genesis of environmental activism took root at a later point in the European countries of the 'Global East' most of which formed part of the Soviet Union or fell under the Soviet influence. Pešić points out that while environmental issues gained momentum in Western Europe in the second half of the twentieth century, it was not until the late 1980s that environmental protests emerged in Eastern Europe, induced by environmental concerns as a result of the overexploitation of natural resources and intensive industrialisation in an effort 'to exit a difficult economic recession'.[135] The radicalisation of environmental movements in countries of the Eastern Bloc, including Romania, coincided with the fall of the communism.[136]

On the other hand, this development took a different trajectory in the countries of the (Western) Balkans and that are sometimes positioned at Europe's '(semi-) periphery' due to the 'geopolitical, economic and cultural' specificities.[137] Thus, the civil wars and the disintegration of the former Yugoslavia in the early 1990s pushed environmental issues aside due to more dire societal and economic problems. This prevented the civil society centred around environmental issues

[132] Wunsch (n 35) 57–59.
[133] Pešić and Vukelić (n 129) 8 and 22.
[134] ibid 9–10.
[135] J Petrović, *'Ekologija' na periferiji Evrope: stvaranje ekološkog pokreta u Srbiji ('Ecology' on the Periphery of Europe: The Creation of an Environmental Movement in Serbia)* (Belgrade, Službeni glasnik, 2020) 24–26.
[136] ibid.
[137] ibid 13.

from fully taking root in the new countries that emerged. However, environmental activism was not completely foreign to the countries that formed part of the former Yugoslavia. There are examples of legislation, organisations and even civic actions/movements in the environmental realm that could be traced back to the nineteenth century.[138] Instances of activism concerning nature conservation, development projects deemed harmful to the environment or even antinuclear movements could be traced, albeit these were mainly channelled through organisations that somehow formed part of the state/local institutional framework.[139] Hence, 'although activism was not very 'loud' during the Yugoslav period … it was active on issues of local relevance'.[140]

While the roots of civic activity in the environmental realm by far pre-dated the EU accession process, it was precisely the prospect of membership and EU's conditionality instruments that breathed life into the civil society sector and provided the impulse and financial resources, and steered the political course towards giving environmental issues a more significant place on the agenda – both in the CEE and the WB countries.[141] Environmental activism induced by the 'EU factor' was dominated by what is referred to in social movements literature as 'transactional activism', characterised by (semi-)professional ENGOs whose agenda is closely tied to the priorities of (mostly EU) donors and projects and that mainly employ 'soft' tactics including 'lobbying and advocacy'.[142]

Nevertheless, the (in)direct and undesired consequence of the EU's efforts to help build the civil society sector in these countries after the fall of socialism, along with the system of donor funding attributed to that end, led to the 'mushrooming' of such organisations that 'hijacked' environmental issues and their 'detachment' from the ordinary citizens and local communities.[143]

If the first wave of environmental activism in the Balkans was characterised by state patronage and a less overtly political approach, and the second wave by the burgeoning of professional ENGOs, the third wave brings about more diversity in *organisational forms* (local and grassroots initiatives, as well as professional ENGOs) and *political and legal instruments* employed (from mass protests to litigation), greater *ability to forge transnational ties* and readiness to *openly criticise*

[138] ibid 47–50.

[139] Z Oštrić, 'Ekološki pokreti u Jugoslaviji 1971–1991' (Environmental Movements in Yugoslavia 1971–1991) (1992) 1(1) *Socijalna ekologija* 83; Petrović (n 135) 24 and 48.

[140] R Rodela, A Udovč and M Boström, 'Developing Environmental NGO Power for Domestic Battles in a Multilevel Context: Lessons from a Slovenian Case' (2016) 27(3) *Environmental Policy and Governance* 244, 248.

[141] Petrović (n 135) 24–26.

[142] J Vukelić, M Petrović and A Kukuridi, 'Environmental Activism in Serbia: Challenges to Cooperation between Professional and Grassroots Organisations' (2021) 16(2) *Balkanologie: Revue d'études pluridisciplinaires*, para 5.

[143] On this phenomenon in the WB, see Wunsch (n 35) 33–34; A Fagan and F Ejdus, 'Lost at the Waterfront? Explaining the Absence of Green Organisations in the *Don't Let Belgrade D(r)own* Movement' (2020) 31(7) *Environmental Politics* 1289, 1292.

both domestic and EU institutions and policies.[144] The following subsection takes a closer look at this last and ongoing phase in the development of environmental democracy in the Balkans.

B. *Quo Vadis* Environmental Democracy in the Balkans?

Worsened living conditions as a result of climate change and investment projects relying on extractive activities, coupled with democratic backsliding[145] and frail institutional frameworks, are just some of the factors that brought environmental issues closer to ordinary citizens and paved the way towards the nascence of the new 'indigenous environmental movement' in the Balkans.[146] By being more rooted in the local context and causes, having looser organisational and decision-making structures, not being financial dependent on (a) particular donor(s) and by relying on 'bolder' strategies such as organising mass protests, blockades or litigation, these new forms of environmental activism are reminiscent of what is referred to in social movements literature as 'participatory activism'.[147]

Prominent examples include the Roșia Montană campaign in Romania that targeted the construction of a gold mine,[148] battles against the construction of hydropower plants across several WB countries, the fight against the construction of windmills in protected areas led by Slovenian ENGOs[149] or the already-mentioned efforts against the exploitation of lithium in western Serbia.[150]

Apart from managing to raise environmental awareness among the wider population, these instances of bottom-up activism reveal a link between environmental and broader societal issues, such as the fragility of the rule of law, and other systemic maladies of their respective countries. As Buzogány notes: 'The rule of law is very closely related to environmental policy and the use of natural resources … it is an umbrella many can identify with.'[151] This further strengthens the argument made in the literature and already highlighted in this chapter that progress in the environmental protection sphere in the accession process should be observed through the 'lens' of fundamental pillars – the observance of the rule of law and good governance.

[144] Pešić and Vukelić (n 129) 23; J Pešić and J Vukelić, *Environmental Initiatives in Serbia and Their European Perspective*, Policy Paper, 2023, www.balcanicaucaso.org/eng/Progetti/TraPoCo/Environmental-initiatives-in-Serbia-and-their-European-perspective, 6.

[145] In the case of Serbia, see S Bogojević, 'The Erosion of the Rule of Law: How Populism Threatens Environmental Protection' (2019) 31 *Journal of Environmental Law* 389, 389.

[146] Pešić and Vukelić (n 129) 22.

[147] Vukelić, Petrović and Kukuridi (n 142) para 5.

[148] S Soare and CD Tufiș, '"Roșia Montană, the Revolution of Our Generation": From Environmental to Total Activism' (2021) 22(2) *European Politics and Society* 259.

[149] Rodela, Udovč and Boström (n 140) 244.

[150] Besliu (n 89).

[151] Chiodi and Epis (n 120).

Another interesting characteristic of the extant environmental activism in the Balkans is its potential to forge regional and international ties in order to push for legislative and political changes and thus overcome the traditionally rooted pessimism towards their ability to 'influence decision-making', especially at the local levels.[152] For example, Piletić highlights that the 'European Water Movement – a continent-wide network of water movements fighting for water as a common good – offered support to the fight against SHPPs in Serbia … uniting environmental activists from the Balkans with those from other parts of Europe'.[153]

Furthermore, the impetus of this bottom-up Europeanisation in the environmental realm is also visible in the insistence of activists not only on the adherence to national legislation, but also to the rules and standards adopted at the EU level. Thus, experience from the already-mentioned movement against the 'Jadar' project demonstrates that while activists were highly critical of the EU institutions and environmental policies, they also advocated for the consistent application of 'the environmental regulations and frameworks set by EU legislation', since 'the EIA for the Jadar project should have had included public access to environmental information, environmental liability, public participation and access to justice', which was not the case.[154] Thus, paradoxically, the EU appears as what some authors refer to as a 'frenemy', since it is both the source of great contention and the 'main incentives for transnationalisation' of environmental movements in Serbia and the remaining WB countries.[155]

An especially illustrative example not only of the aforementioned trends in environmental democracy in the Balkans, but also of the importance of bottom-up pressures for the implementation of Aarhus standards, is the battle over preserving the Vjosa River in Albania.[156] In 1997, the Albanian government issued a concession for the construction the Kalivaç hydropower plant on the Vjosa River to an Italian investor. The construction officially commenced in 2007, albeit not in a continuous manner and with frequent halts.[157] Claiming that the public consultations that preceded the concession had not been conducted adequately and relying on deficiencies in the environmental impact assessment, a group of civil society actors challenged the contract before the Albanian Administrative Court in 2016, which became the first environmental lawsuit to be launched in that country. Finding the contested 'administrative acts and procedures … null and void … because they have been issued in contradiction of the procedures foreseen by law and the Concession Agreement',[158] the Administrative Court

[152] Pešić and Vukelić (n 129) 7.

[153] Piletić (n 66) 1101.

[154] Stuehlen and Anderl (n 74) 10.

[155] Pešić and Vukelić (n 129)23.

[156] See also Terihati, ch 4 in this volume, section V.D.i.

[157] 'HPP Kalivaç Revisited – Vjosa at Risk Once Again' (*RiverWatch*, 30 May 2017), https://riverwatch.eu/de/node/512.

[158] M Pravuljac and M Smoljak, *Are Balkan Countries Safeguarding Their Rivers? A Legal Analysis of Environmental Standards in Six Western Balkan Countries* (ClientEarth, EuroNatur and Riverwatch,

ruled in their favour. The competent ministry appealed the decision with the Tirana Court of Appeal, whose decision is still pending.[159]

In the meantime, the Albanian Ministry of Energy granted a concession to a consortium of Turkish and Albanian companies for the construction of the Poçem hydropower plant on the same river.[160] EcoAlbania – backed by an international civil society network – mobilised the scientific community in order to analyse the prepared environmental impact assessment, which resulted in the Ministry of Tourism's decision not to give the investor the green light in proceeding with the project. The investor filed a lawsuit against the negative decision of the Ministry to the Administrative Court. Relying on the tenets of national law and the Aarhus Convention, the Court enabled civil society actors to intervene in the proceedings, since they are 'entitled to be parties in this judgment, to be heard and to present their claims'.[161] On the merits, the Court found the decision of the Ministry to be legal and valid, and rejected the lawsuit.[162]

Looking at the structure of the involved civil society actors, we can see that they include both domestic and international/regional professional organisations, the scientific community/experts and local residents. More specifically, the Albanian ENGO (EcoAlbania) spearheaded the campaign, but was joined by two transnational organisations – Riverwatch and EuroNatur – as well as 38 residents of the affected area in filing the first lawsuit.[163]

The employed methods varied, ranging from conducting studies, organising mass protests and an international campaign, forging transborder networks to utilising available legal mechanisms, both domestic (before the Administrative Court) and those available under international instruments (eg, the complaints mechanism established by the Bern Convention).[164]

As for the results, these were successful on several fronts: first, in terms of favourable administrative judicial decisions; second, the European Parliament issued a recommendation to Albania to reconsider its policy of granting concessions for hydropower plants; finally, and most importantly, in 2023 the Vjosa River was granted the status of a protected area.[165]

Such pioneering instances of initiating court proceedings are reminiscent of a question Lisa Vanhala asked in a paper analysing the mobilisation of environmental

2024) 28, www.clientearth.org/latest/documents/are-balkan-countries-safeguarding-their-rivers-a-legal-analysis-of-environmental-standards-in-six-western-balkan-countries.

[159] ibid.

[160] ibid 29.

[161] ibid.

[162] ibid.

[163] ibid 28.

[164] ibid 29; E Mahmutaj, A Bujaroska and E Cerimagic, *From Aiming EU Accession Back to Albanian Participative Decision Making, Policy Analyses and Options to Improve Public Participation Practices in Environmental Decision Making* (Tirana, EDEN Center, 2017) 5.

[165] A Rama, 'In the Battle for the Environment, Activism is Not the Enemy: The Environmentalist Movement in the Balkans Continues to Grow and Adapt' (*Rosa Luxemburg Stiftung*, 24 September 2021), www.rosalux.de/en/news/id/45054/in-the-battle-for-the-environment-activism-is-not-the-enemy.

law by selected NGOs in the UK: why do ENGOs pursue legal cases despite facing what they claim is a relatively hostile legal opportunity structure?[166] She finds that '[i]t is only by regularly attempting to access justice that these groups credibly highlight the failings of the existing systems' and 'continually campaigning for environmental justice' that they can 'contribute to broader campaigns to enhance access to justice for others'.[167] While litigation in itself might not bring about the desired social change, and especially not in the short term, coupled with other methods (including political efforts), it can contribute to a shift in broadening and strengthening environmental access to justice.

IV. Concluding Remarks: The Aarhus Convention as the Missing Link between *Top-down* and *Bottom-up* Europeanisation of Environmental Access to Justice?

This chapter first highlighted and then disentangled the intricate and polycentric relationship between the EU and its (legal and policy) instruments in the accession process, the Aarhus Convention and the burgeoning activism of civil society actors in the Balkans. In our attempt to understand and map out the role of these three factors for the implementation of environmental access to justice in the selected Balkan countries, we relied on available legal sources, but also literature in the domains of political science and sociology and their proposed theoretical models related to the legal mobilisation of environmental law, social (including environmental) movements and legal/political opportunity structures. We were setting up a theoretical framework whilst constantly being aware of the subtleties of the region and even the differences between the countries of the region that require caution in drawing general conclusions.

The analysis has shown the immense role played by the EU and its conditionality instruments in both bringing environmental policies to the fore, making environmental issues an important aspect of the accession process, as well as empowering civil society actors and providing them with an additional platform to express their grievances and pursue their goals. It would not be an overstatement to say that the EU accession process revolutionised the role played by the civil society in acceding countries (some of which are currently Member States) and their relationship with the public authorities. The Aarhus Convention, being an integral part of the EU environmental *acquis* and providing an important impetus to civil society actors – especially ENGOs – and thus expanding the existing LOS, fits well into the picture painted above.

[166] Vanhala (n 7) 524.
[167] ibid 525.

In order to reap the benefits of its ambitious environmental standards and efforts in combating climate change, the EU needs to ensure that its policy 'at home' is synchronised with its policy in its vicinity – ie, the Balkan countries that are in the process of accession. The messages need to be consistent in order to strongly convey to the national authorities that are in charge of effectively implementing the *acquis*, that formal alignment that does not ensure 'behavioural compliance'.[168]

The European Commission places measures of improving access to justice in environmental matters in the context of the overall improvement of the functioning of the judiciary (eg, the EU Justice Scoreboard)[169] and securing the rule of law and fundamental rights in the Member States.[170] This, along with the horizontal nature of environmental law and policies adopted at the EU level, as well as the pursuit of sustainable development as one of the foremost political aspirations of the EU, brings us to the conclusions reached by Bogojević and Drenovak-Ivanović in the context of the accession process – namely, that the alignment with the EU environmental *acquis* and the progress made should be closely linked to the 'fundamentals' (ie, the rule of law). Actually, it takes it even further – civil society needs to be more actively involved. It is not enough to engage with the institutions, especially if it is recognised that they are weak and unresponsive to the needs of citizens.

At the same time, we are witnessing a growing dissatisfaction with the state of the environment and the policy choices made by both national and EU institutions that run counter to the stringent environmental standards imposed at the European and international levels. In the observed Balkan countries, this dissatisfaction translated into the rise of a new wave of environmental activism that contributes to bridging the gap between professional ENGOs on the one hand, and grassroots movements and other forms of looser citizen associations on the other. Through a synergy of more or less contentious methods that take place both within the institutional framework (litigation) and outside of it (mass protests), as well as the potential to forge alliances with initiatives and organisations in the region and beyond, these movements appear to be an even stronger factor pushing for the adoption and the enforcement of national and EU norms and values, including those stemming from the Aarhus Convention, than the conditionality instruments in the accession process. This is especially true in cases in which the EU is reluctant to provide unwavering support to local efforts aimed at combating the devastation of natural resources, the environment and the well-being of local communities due to its own (economic) interests being at play. Thus, compared to

[168] Börzel and Fagan (n 40) 10.

[169] https://commission.europa.eu/strategy-and-policy/policies/justice-and-fundamental-rights/upholding-rule-law/eu-justice-scoreboard_en.

[170] Commission, 'Notice on access to justice in environmental matters' C/2017/2616 [2017] OJ C275/1, para 14.

such instances of bottom-up environmental activism, top-down Europeanisation appears rather modest, meagre or only superfluous.

Moreover, the integration of the discourse on systemic societal problems, such as corruption and the decline of the rule of law with environmental concerns, further enhances environmental democracy and contributes to overcoming apathy, which is considered a chronic malady of post-socialist societies of the Balkans, stuck in transitional limbo on their way towards the EU – an ever-moving target.

PART II

National Perspectives: Access to Justice in Environmental Matters in Selected Balkan Countries

4

Environmental Justice Accessibility in Albania

FRANC TERIHATI

I. Introduction

Environmental justice is a concept that consists of balancing environmental advantages and burdens, identical participation in decision-making techniques and remediation of environmental damage. Environmental justice, at its core, addresses inequalities in environmental satisfaction and impacts on environmental dangers among communities, mainly vulnerable groups. This consists of ensuring that traditionally marginalised communities, frequently and disproportionately impacted by environmental pollution and degradation, have a voice in environmental decision-making and equitable access to sources and possibilities for environmental safety and enhancement. Attaining environmental justice requires not only legal and policy reforms to address systemic inequalities but also the development of inclusive governance structures that prioritise community engagement and empowerment. Furthermore, environmental justice intersects with other social justice problems, along with race, social rank and gender, highlighting the need for intersectional methods to cope with underlying root causes of environmental injustice. By promoting fairness, inclusivity and meaningful participation, environmental justice aims to create healthier, more sustainable communities for all individuals, regardless of their background or socioeconomic status.

In the past decade, Albania has developed comprehensive legislation relating to environmental protection. The legal system is based on the Albanian Constitution and includes various regulations such as general and special laws, bylaws of the Council of Ministers, ministerial orders, guidelines, norms and standards. Aligned with principles of EU environmental law, this legislation is largely harmonised with EU standards and has benefited from input coming from international experts, reflecting Albania's commitments as a signatory to relevant conventions.

Significant progress has been made in the case law on the implementation of the Aarhus Convention, enabling individuals, communities and non-profit organisations (NPOs) to bring claims regarding environmental degradation before courts. Successful outcomes in numerous cases have ensured the protection of the environment by preventing the operation of landfills without environmental permits, the construction of hydropower plants in protected areas, and the draining of water resources that harm the agricultural and farming activities of local communities and have stopped the development of commercial activities that damage the environment.

While important progress has been made, the training of judges and public officials, and the improvement of environmental legislation in Albania remains an ongoing endeavour. These efforts are directed towards tackling present-day environmental conservation issues, fostering sustainable growth and supporting Albania's journey towards EU integration.

II. The National Context and Background

In Albania, the judicial system consists of various court types, each with a specific jurisdiction and duties. After the recent judicial reorganisation, the judicial framework now includes a total of 13 Courts of First Instance of General Jurisdiction, two Administrative Courts of First Instance and one Administrative Court of Appeal, one court for organised crime and corruption, and the consolidation of the Courts of Appeal of General Jurisdiction into a single entity. However, there have been no alterations to the configuration of the Supreme Court and the Constitutional Court. In terms of their functions, the Administrative Courts handle disputes arising between individuals and public authorities, review decisions made by administrative bodies and address cases pertaining to administrative law, such as permits, licences and governmental actions. Conversely, the Courts of General Jurisdiction are responsible for resolving disputes within the private sector, including matters relating to property, family issues, contracts and similar concerns.

In environmental matters, jurisdiction typically lies with the administrative courts, given their specialisation in administrative law and competence in ensuring the correct enforcement of environmental legislation. These cases often concern conflicts between individuals and organisations vis-a-vis public authorities and private companies, regarding issues such as environmental regulations, permits or decisions affecting the environment.

With regard to administrative appeals, in certain cases, it is necessary to make an administrative request according to specific legal provisions. For example, Law number 10431/2011 "On the protection of the environment provides that:

> When there is a threat of pollution and damage to the environment, citizens enjoy the following rights:

(a) to request from the competent public authorities to take appropriate measures within specified deadlines and in accordance with the authority granted by the law;
(b) to bring a lawsuit in court against any public authority or private person, whether natural or legal, that has caused environmental damage or poses a risk thereof.

Competent institutions to hear administrative complaints[1] are established at the local and national levels. National institutions include agencies that are responsible for tourism, forestry, coastal and protected areas, and the Ministry of Tourism and Environment. Local institutions include the four Regional Environmental Agencies and the municipal police.

III. The EU Accession Process

According to the 'Albania 2023 Report' of the European Commission, the country still needs to intensify efforts to achieve full alignment and implementation in most areas of the EU environmental *acquis*. The implementation of the Directives on Environmental Impact Assessment (EIA) and strategic Environmental Assessment (SEA) requires significant improvement. The EIA quality and the relevant processes need to be improved, and recommendations from EIAs are rarely implemented; they should be enforced and monitored. Public participation and consultation in decision-making need to be improved, particularly at the local level.[2] Similar recommendations were previously highlighted in the 2021[3] and 2022[4] Reports of the European Commission.

These conclusions reflect the legal claims of the civil society, raised in judicial proceedings against the implementation of projects that damage the environment

[1] According to Albanian legislation, complaints and appeals are two different remedies. A complaint is a request to the public institution to address a violation, while an appeal is a request to object a decision of the public institution.

[2] For further details, see Commission, 'Albania 2023 Report accompanying the document Communication from the Commission to the European Parliament, the Council, the European Economic and Social Committee and the Committee of the Regions, 2023 Communication on EU Enlargement policy', SWD [2023] 690 final, 115, 119, 120, and 121, available at: https://neighbourhood-enlargement.ec.europa.eu/document/download/ea0a4b05-683f-4b9c-b7ff-4615a5fffd0b_en?filename=SWD_2023_690%20Albania%20report.pdf.

[3] Commission, 'Albania 2021 Report Accompanying the document Communication from the Commission to the European Parliament, the Council, the European Economic and Social Committee and the Committee of the Regions 2021 Communication on EU Enlargement Policy', SWD [2021] 289 final, 109, 111 and 112, available at: https://neighbourhood-enlargement.ec.europa.eu/system/files/2021-10/Albania-Report-2021.pdf.

[4] Commission, 'Albania 2022 Report Accompanying the document Communication from the Commission to the European Parliament, the Council, the European Economic and Social Committee and the Committee of the Regions 2022 Communication on EU Enlargement policy', SWD [2022] 332 final, 106, 109 and 110, available at: https://neighbourhood-enlargement.ec.europa.eu/document/download/dde85556-8061-41f3-ba0c-5e921158bc53_en?filename=Albania%20Report%202022.pdf.

and the adoption of legislation that reduces the surface of protected areas to favour economic development. The allegations that these activities were undertaken in the absence of consultation with the public, without taking into account the requests of the interested public in cases where the consultations were held and in the absence of the best techniques available within the framework of environmental protection – correspond to the findings in the European Commission's reports and have been upheld by the courts on numerous occasions.[5]

IV. Access to Information and Participation in Environmental Cases

Albania is among the early adopters of the Aarhus Convention, showcasing a strong commitment to its implementation. Since 1998, when the Republic of Albania initially signed the Convention, and particularly following its ratification by the Albanian Assembly in 2001, efforts towards its execution have expanded significantly. Serving as an international legal instrument, the Convention encompasses a framework of rights, obligations and prescribed procedures for its implementation by the signatory states. Its requirements, along with the rights and obligations it delineates, are centred on pivotal aspects of environmental relations. These are structured around three fundamental directions, each of which serves a distinct purpose regarding the right of the public to:

- request environmental information;
- engage in decision-making in environmental matters;
- have access to justice in environmental issues.

A. The Right to Environmental Information

Article 56 of the Constitution ensures the right to be informed about the state of the environment and its protection. While this article establishes the overarching principle that every individual has the right to access environmental information, the specific mechanisms for obtaining and providing such information, as well as the procedures to be followed, are outlined in laws and specialised bylaws. Public involvement in environmental decision-making is deemed to be crucial, sanctioned by both international and national regulations. The Aarhus Convention underscores this right as a cornerstone for environmental protection, which benefits from judicial remedies. Furthermore, Article 47 of Law

[5] For further information, see section V.D.iv below.

No 10431/09.06.2011 'On the protection of the environment' guarantees access to environmental information to all individuals and legal entities, without requiring a specific interest in the matter. This regulation is enforced alongside the legislation concerning the right to information,[6] which stipulates that any individual or legal entity, irrespective of their specific interest in the subject matter, has the right to request public information from public bodies. These bodies are required to provide the requested public information within a period of 10 days. Should the public authority fail to meet this deadline, the concerned party has the option to submit an appeal to the Commissioner for the Right of Information and Data Protection (hereinafter 'the Commissioner'). The appeal must be submitted within 30 days from either the notification by the public institution of its refusal to provide the information or from the expiration of the deadline by which the public institution should have provided the information. The Commissioner has 15 working days to examine the case. The Commissioner has the authority to compel the public institution to provide the requested information and may impose an administrative penalty for non-compliance. Public authorities are obliged to comply with the Commissioner's decision when ordered to provide the requested information, unless a court decides to suspend the implementation of the order.

The Commissioner operates as an independent public legal entity.[7] The Commissioner is appointed by the Parliament of Albania following the proposal of the Council of Ministers, for a five-year term, with the right to re-election. The Parliament determines the Commissioner's salary, the organisational structure, and the salary classifications for the staff of the Office of the Commissioner for the Right to Information and Protection of Personal Data.[8]

B. The Right to Participation in Environmental Decision-Making

Concerning participation, Articles 8 and 9 of Law No 10440/07.07.2011 'On environmental impact assessment' stipulates that before the granting of the relevant permit by the authority responsible for the development of the project, they must be subject to the preliminary assessment of the EIA or the in-depth procedure of the EIA. At the end of the preliminary EIA procedure, the National Environmental Agency makes a decision as to whether the project should or should not be subject to the in-depth procedure of EIA.

According to Article 12 Law No 10440/07.07.2011, at the end of the in-depth EIA procedure, the competent ministry issues an environmental declaration,

[6] Law No 119/2014 'On the right to information'.
[7] Article 29.2 of Law No 9887, dated 10 March 2008, 'On personal data protection'.
[8] Articles 33 and 37 of Law No 9887, dated 10 March 2008, 'On personal data protection'.

which may suggest to the authority responsible for the approval of development either to:

- approve the development permit, without any remarks from an environmental point of view;
- approve the development permit/licence, with the conditions that must fulfilled by the developer; or
- reject the development permit/licence request.

In Article 14, Law No 10440/07.07.2011 defines the actors participating in the EIA process, including public authorities, concerned individuals, communities and NPOs. Article 17 provides that the opinion and comments of the public and NPOs present at the meeting are recorded during the decision-making process of EIA. Should the opinion not be received according to the procedures defined in the law, the environmental declaration issued by the ministry at the end of the in-depth EIA procedure would be invalid.

According to Decision of the Council of Ministers No 247/2014, 'On determining the rules, requirements and procedures for informing and involving the public in environmental decision-making', the process of informing and involving the public during the preliminary EIA procedure includes the following stages:

(a) informing the public and obtaining their opinions through the National Environment Agency, along with providing clarifications about the procedure being implemented; and
(b) announcing and publishing the decision of the National Environment Agency on its website.[9]

The procedure for informing and involving the public during the in-depth EIA procedure includes the following stages:

(a) informing the public about the proposed project and obtaining its opinion when determining the issues to be addressed in the in-depth EIA report, accompanied by clarifications for the applicable procedure;
(b) informing the public about the communication that the National Environment Agency makes with the developer on issues that should be addressed in the in-depth EIA report;
(c) informing, raising awareness and consulting the public by the developer during the drafting of the in-depth EIA report;
(d) informing and involving the public of the organisation and realisation of the public hearing;
(e) informing the public and obtaining its opinion from the National Environment Agency in the review and approval phase of the Environmental Declaration; and

[9] Chapter 1, para 1 of the Decision of the Council of Ministers No 247/2014, 'On determining the rules, requirements and procedures for informing and involving the public in environmental decision-making'.

(f) informing the public during the monitoring of the environmental impacts of the project.

Every individual has the right to submit an appeal against the actions or inactions of public bodies regarding the development of public notification and consultation procedures. The competent body to hear such appeals is the relevant minister responsible for the environment. Despite legal provisions granting the public the right to participate in the consultation process, in most of the litigation cases such as *Vjosa, Thirra, Zall Gjocaj, Laknas and Protected Areas,*[10] the courts found that these provisions have not been respected by the public authorities in practice.

Article 6 of the Aarhus Convention emphasises that public notification regarding decision-making on a specific activity must occur promptly, at the outset of the process, and must be conducted appropriately, at the correct time, and in an effective manner. Public participation must be real and not just a formality. An EIA cannot be deemed comprehensive unless it includes a systematic consultation process with the public, detailing all aspects of the project to be undertaken and incorporating all feedback provided by the public.

V. Access to Justice in Environmental Cases

A. Administrative Appeal

In instances where the administrative decision-making process, such as the approval of a project, runs counter to community interests or causes significant environmental harm, all concerned parties have the right to initiate an administrative procedure by appealing to the superior administrative body overseeing the relevant decision-making process. This procedure is governed by Law No 44/2015 'Code of administrative procedures' and can be followed by judicial review. It is important to note that this rule applies only to those legal procedures where an administrative appeal is required by a specific law, as many administrative acts can be directly contested in court.

An administrative appeal can be lodged not only to challenge an administrative act but also to contest the inaction of a public body, which was obligated to act or issue an administrative act/decision within the legally defined time frame. According to Article 132, paragraph 1 of the Code of Administrative Procedures, the administrative appeal must be filed within 30 days from the date of notification of the administrative act or the objection to issue such an act. Failure to lodge the appeal within the time limits specified by law shall result in the expiration of the appeal period, even if the appeal could have been accepted.

[10] For more information, see section V.D below.

The United Colleges of the Supreme Court, in a decision in which all judges of the Supreme Court participated and is mandatory for all the courts, decided that:

> [U]tilising the administrative appeal to settle administrative disputes before resorting to court is obligatory only if the law governing legal relations and administrative activities in the relevant domain explicitly allows for an administrative appeal against the administrative act and specifies the particular administrative body or bodies to which the administrative appeal should be directed, according to the hierarchical order.[11]

According to Article 62/a, paragraph 8 of Law No 49/2012 'On the administrative courts and adjudication of administrative Disputes', as amended, the decision of the United Colleges of the Supreme Court is binding on courts in the trial of similar cases.

Article 14 of Law No 91/2013 'On strategic environmental assessment' provides that:

> [I]nterest groups, including the public, have the right to administrative appeal against the minister's statement and the ministry's position within 30 days from the announcement of the statement or position, in accordance with the provisions of the Code of Administrative Procedure.

Based on Article 16 of Law No 49/2012, it is provided that:

1. The lawsuit against the administrative action can be filed only after the exhaustion of the administrative appeal.
2. Excluded from this rule are the cases when:
   a) the law does not provide for a higher body for submitting an administrative appeal, or when the higher administrative body has not been constituted;
   b) the law expressly provides for the right to appeal against the administrative action directly to the court;
   c) the highest body in reviewing an administrative appeal has violated, with its decision, the rights or legitimate personal interests of a person who was not a party to the administrative proceeding.

In point a) of article 16 paragraph 2 of Law No 49/2012, it is determined that one of the exceptional cases of the general rule that the lawsuit against the administrative action can be filed only after the exhaustion of the administrative appeal, is when: 'the law does not provide for a higher body for the presentation of the administrative appeal'.

Article 25 paragraph 1 of Law No 10440/2011 'On environmental impact assessment', amended, provides that 'Every interested party, including the affected public, subject to this law, has the right to complain to the minister about the administrative acts issued by him and to the National Environment Agency about the administrative acts issued by it.'

Based on the legal provision mentioned above, no higher body has been determined for submitting an administrative appeal. According to this provision, the

[11] Decision 1, dated 26 November 2010.

party has the right to complain to the minister for the administrative acts issued by him and to the National Environment Agency for the administrative acts issued by him.

In this way, in Article 25/1 of Law No 10440/2011, it is not determined possible to submit an administrative appeal to a higher body, but it is determined possible to submit an administrative appeal to the same administrative body that approved the administrative act. This is not a case where a lawsuit against the administrative action can only be filed after exhausting the administrative appeal process, as the law does not establish a higher body for submitting such appeals.

Therefore, in situations where the law does not provide for a higher body to submit an administrative appeal, pursuant to point a) of Article 16, paragraph 2 of Law No 49/2012, a lawsuit against the administrative action may be filed without the requirement to exhaust the administrative appeal process.

B. Access to Court

Individuals, associations and interest groups have standing to bring lawsuits against an administrative act. When a lawsuit is initiated by an NPO, it is crucial that, along with the NPO's extract from the Registry of NPOs at the Tirana Judicial District Court, a copy of the Statute and the Act of the Foundation is also submitted to the Court. These documents serve to demonstrate that the activities of the NPOs are connected to the environment as a whole, or to specific elements or areas of the environment that are endangered by the project for which the contested administrative acts were approved (see also the cases discussed in section V.D below).

Additionally, it is necessary to verify the plaintiff's interest with the specific case, which applies to community members (natural persons). Various means of proof can be utilised for this purpose, including certificates of civil status, ownership certificates or any other relevant documents that establish the individual's connection to the area where the project is expected to be implemented.

Administrative acts may be challenged up to 45 days from the date of notification. In cases where the administrative act does not clearly indicate the right and the term of the claim, this term is extended to one year. The dispute will be heard in the Administrative First Instance Court, unless there is an objection to a normative bylaw, in which case the lawsuit must be brought before the Administrative Appeal Court. In this case, the Administrative Appeal Court will act as a first instance court.

Parties can submit a request for interim measures for the suspension of the implementation of the administrative act or any other appropriate measure. The interested party must prove to the court through written evidence that the implementation of the administrative act(s) could lead to significant, irreversible and immediate harm to the environment, and that the execution of the decision aimed at safeguarding the right in question may become either impossible or significantly difficult. Furthermore, it must be demonstrated that granting interim measures will not harm the public interest. This request must be examined by the court within five days.

The request for interim measure must fulfil the procedural conditions provided for in Articles 28 et seq of Law No 49/2012 'On administrative courts and adjudication of administrative disputes' as follows.

i. The Lawsuit is Supported by Documentary Evidence

a. The Lawsuit is Supported by Written Evidence (eg, an Environmental Expertise Act) Regarding the Possibility of the Right that is Requested to be Restored

It is not necessary to fully prove the existence of the right that is also the object of the judicial review, but only that there is the possibility of the right that is requested to be restored. It is thus sufficient for the court that the claim is supported by documentary evidence, which allows the court to establish a prima facie recognition of the claimed right that it has been violated.[12]

b. The Lawsuit is Supported by Written Evidence Relating to the Request for Interim Measures

The plaintiffs should not base their argument for interim measures based in facts or actions, as well as in their legal setting, which are related to the examination and resolution of the case in substance so as to avoid any kind of perception that the court is prejudiced resolving of the case on the merits or is not impartial in the trial.[13] In view of the evaluation of the request for taking the interim measures, the plaintiffs must submit written evidence which proves the serious, irreversible and immediate damage caused to them and which is not related to the review of the basis of the dispute.

ii. The Public Interest is not Seriously Harmed

The public interest should be understood as a balance, a relationship between individual and community well-being.[14] The constitutional concept of public interest, as it has already been developed in the constitutional case law, is quite broad and must be seen from the perspective of the concrete provision that is presented for control. It is difficult to list the cases of public interest or public reason leading to the limitation of a fundamental right in an exhaustive manner. They can only be

[12] Decision of the Supreme Court No 370/2010.

[13] Decision of the Supreme Court No 10/2004.

[14] Decision of the Administrative College of the Supreme Court No 52/2020; Decision of the Administrative College of the Supreme Court No 953/2020.

ranked negatively – that is, in terms of concrete limitation.[15] The court cannot grant interim measures if the public interest is seriously harmed.

iii. The Plaintiff Provides a Guarantee for the Damage that can be Caused

If it is deemed necessary by the court, the plaintiff must provide a guarantee, in the form and amount decided by the court, to cover any potential harm that may be caused to the defendant by the interim measures. The potential harm includes potential loss of third parties (eg, developers) by being stopped from starting their activities. The provision of a guarantee by the plaintiff is not a mandatory requirement in every case and it is requested by the court on a case-by-case basis if any damage may be caused to the defendant by the interim measures.

C. Duration of the Judicial Proceeding and Temporary Execution

The legislator has not defined a timeframe for concluding the first instance proceedings, while the Administrative Court of Appeal examines the case within 30 days from the date of receipt of the appeal from the court before which the appeal was filed. The Supreme Court reviews the case within 90 days from the date of receiving the appeal and associated documents from the court where the appeal was deposited. The examination of a case can only be expedited upon the request of the parties, based on the nature and specific category of the case, or for particularly serious and justified reasons, provided it does not conflict with the law. The presiding judge reviews the party's request for expediting the examination of the case no later than 30 days from the date of submission of the request.

Although the regulations do not explicitly state that cases concerning environmental protection constitute a valid reason to expedite the judicial process, parties advocating for environmental protection can petition the court for an expedited hearing due to the public interest and the significant number of affected citizens.

The Supreme Court is facing a backlog of nearly 23,000 cases.[16] A similar backlog has also affected the appellate courts and courts of first instance, where cases take an average of over six to seven years to be decided at both levels. As a result, this situation has infringed upon the right to a fair trial for communities or NPOs that may have obtained favourable rulings in the First Instance Court.

[15] Decision of the Constitutional Court No 10/2008; Decision of the Constitutional Court No 4/2011.

[16] Supreme Court of Albania, 'Prezantimi i Raportit Vjetor të Performancës së Gjykatës së Lartë 2023' (Presentation of the Performance of the High Court 2023), www.gjykataelarte.gov.al/sq/lajme/media/prezantimi-i-raportit-vjetor-te-perfomances-se-gjykates-se-larte-2023.

Due to the urgency or necessity of the right requested to be restored, Article 317 of the Civil Code has specified certain instances when the court's decision can be implemented with temporary execution. Additionally, in some other situations, it is up to the court's discretion to decide on temporary execution based on special circumstances that are not related to environmental litigation. A decision can also be issued with temporary execution in other instances where the plaintiff might suffer irreparable harm from delays in execution, or when executing the decision would become impossible or extremely difficult, including in environmental cases. In such cases, the court may require the plaintiff to provide a guarantee.

D. The Case Law on Access to Court of the Public and NPOs

In the interpretation of the standards outlined in the Aarhus Convention alongside Albanian legislation, the Supreme Court of Albania has recognised that the right to access courts for environmental issues differs from typical judicial disputes, where parties seek redress for infringed rights. Environmental matters exhibit a polycentric nature, diverging from the conventional adversarial framework of ordinary civil or administrative trials. Given the nature of the allegedly infringed rights in environmental cases, meeting one of the essential conditions for initiating legal proceedings – direct interest – poses challenges, as these cases often involve the protection of rights of a more general nature.[17] Through a systematic interpretation of the standards outlined in the Aarhus Convention, particularly Article 9, and the provisions of Article 15, letter d) of the legislation which regulates administrative disputes, it becomes apparent that granting access to courts for associations and interest groups concerned with environmental legislation merits special consideration. This ensures the procedural rights of these entities in matters concerning environmental protection. In summary, the Administrative College of the Supreme Court affirms that plaintiffs have active standing to bring lawsuits pertaining to environmental issues, provided they demonstrate a 'sufficient interest' in a specific case.

In Albania there have been several cases of *actio popularis* where the NPOs and affected communities have addressed the courts and succeed on environmental protection cases.

i. Annulment of the Construction of the Hydropower Plant in the Vjosa River

The Albanian government had approved the construction of hydropower plant in the Vjosa River, which is the last big wild river in Europe. For the first time,

[17] Decision No 1259, dated 30 July 2021, of the Administrative College of the Supreme Court (Residents of Laknas against the construction of a slaughterhouse in the forest developed by the residents).

members of the local community and an NPO brought an environmental case to the Administrative Court of First Instance in Tirana, which decided to annul the EIA. The grounds for the lawsuit in this judicial process were the inadequate EIA and lack of consultation with the affected community.[18]

ii. Annulment of the Licence for Producing Energy Through a Hydropower Plant in the Mat River

Two hydroelectric power plants were under construction on the Mat River, violating environmental laws and other regulations. A big part of the project was developed within the National Park 'Dea Lure', a protected area, and without consultation with the residents. Residents and two NPOs initiated a judicial review process requesting interim measures for the suspension of the construction works and the annulment of the project.

The Administrative Court of First Instance rejected the request for provisional measures. The decision was appealed to the Administrative Court of Appeal, which decided to reject the claims of the residents. The Administrative Court of First Instance also rejected the claims on the merits, despite accepting that there were several irregularities and infringements, but arguing that these cannot cause absolute invalidity of the procedure. The final decision of the Administrative Court of First Instance was appealed to the Administrative Court of Appeal. The residents initiated a new judicial process and, in January 2021, the Administrative Court of Tirana quashed the decision which licensed the company to produce energy with hydropower plants in a protected area. This decision was upheld by the Administrative Court of Appeal and by the Supreme Court.[19]

iii. Annulment of the Permission to Develop a Private Business in the Forest of 'Plepat E Brukes' in Laknas, Kamez

Forty residents of Laknas, Kamza challenged the construction of a slaughterhouse that would have completely and irreversibly damaged a communal forest that had been planted and managed over the past 50 years by the residents themselves by volunteering through their cooperative efforts. The Administrative Court of First Instance decided to suspend the construction of the slaughterhouse. The Administrative Court of Appeal overturned this interim decision, which was instead reinstated by the Supreme Court. Subsequently, the Tirana Administrative Court of First Instance decided on the merits to annul the decision that had

[18] 'The Court of Appeals Confirms the Verdict for the Cancellation of Poçem Hydropower Plant in Vjosa River' (*EcoAlbania*, 24 July 2024), https://ecoalbania.org/the-court-of-appeals-confirms-the-verdict-for-the-cancellation-of-pocem-hydropower-plant-in-vjosa-river/?lang=en.

[19] 'Zall-Gjocaj, MAT: The Supreme Court Decided to Revoke the Licence of the Concession Company for Energy Production in Zall – Gjocal HPP' (*Centre for Legal Empowerment*, 25 November 2022), https://cle.al/en/opposition-to-the-construction-of-zall-gjocaj-mat-hydropower-plant.

approved the construction of the slaughterhouse.[20] The court upheld the residents' claims that the project should have undergone a comprehensive EIA and that the land where the project was expected to being developed was, in fact, a forest rather than the 'grassland' indicated in the cadastral records.

iv. Prohibition of the Works for the Construction of a Hydropower Plant and of a Water Factory in Mirdite

A total of 166 residents and two NPOs challenged the construction of a hydropower plant and developing economic activities in the villages of Thirrë, Sang and Hebë, which would seriously damage the environment and the well-being of the residents of the area. The Administrative Court of First Instance of Tirana decided to annul the permit for the construction of the hydropower plant and one water factory in the village. Later on, the Administrative Court of Appeal accepted the request of the plaintiffs for the suspension of works in the implementation of the projects of the Thirre hydropower plant and of the water factory for the production of 'Bottle or container packaging'. The court stated that the public bodies did not guarantee an open decision-making process respecting the public consultation procedure and failed to identify, describe and evaluate negative impacts on the environment.[21]

v. Rehabilitation of the Landfill in Porto Romano, Spitallë, Durrës

Residents of a village near the landfill in Porto Romano, Durres, which was built without an environmental permit, addressed a complaint to the Municipality of Durres to close the landfill and to rehabilitate the territory. The Municipality did not adopt any decision, and the residents seized the Administrative Court of First Instance of Durres asking for an order to be addressed to the Municipality to close the landfill and to rehabilitate the territory. The plaintiffs submitted to the court the documents collected for the case, including an environmental expertise that confirmed the pollution of the air, land and water in Porto Romano.

While the residents were waiting for the Administrative Court of First Instance in Durres to set a date for the preliminary hearing, in September 2019,

[20] 'Opposition to the Construction of a Slaughterhouse in the Laknas Forest' (*Centre for Legal Empowerment*, 17 March 2022), https://cle.al/en/opposition-to-the-construction-of-a-slaughterhouse-in-the-laknas-forest.

[21] 'Victory for the Residents of Thirrë: The Administrative Court of the First Instance Decides to Cancel the Permit for the HEC and the Water Factory in the Village of Thirrë' (*Centre for Legal Empowerment*), https://cle.al/en/victory-for-the-residents-of-thirre-the-administrative-court-of-the-first-instance-decides-to-cancel-the-permit-for-the-hec-and-the-water-factory-in-the-village-of-thirre.

in response to a request for information, they were informed that the project for the rehabilitation of this landfill was approved and besides the rehabilitation of the area, it provided for the construction of an entertainment, sports and natural park.[22]

vi. Annulment of the Revision of the Protected Areas

Eleven Albanian environmental organisations have sued the Council of Ministers, requesting the annulment of two decisions assumed to violate the territorial geographical and socio-ecological integrity of protected areas.

These decisions reduce the surfaces, change the boundaries and decrease the status of protected areas. It is feared that this would remove precious habitats from specific enhanced protection, open the way for unsustainable developments in or near them, increase the negative impacts on the central parts of the protected areas, deplete habitats and species, and affect the biological diversity of these areas and all of Albania.

Through an intermediate decision, the Court of Appeal granted standing to the environmental organisations to continue the legal proceedings for opposing the revision of the protected areas.[23] The lawsuit was sent to the court on 26 January 2022, and the proceedings are still pending. The court has appointed a group of experts to determine the changes in the borders and surfaces of the protected areas and the evaluation of the environmental impacts on flora and fauna due to the contested decisions.

In addition to the cases specifically recalled above, there are also several cases pending regarding the protection of the environment from hydropower plants, landfills functioning without an environmental permit and reduction of the boundaries of the protected areas.

The main irregularities raised by the affected communities and NPOs before the courts have been:

(a) that the process of prior information and public hearings have not been conducted in accordance with the legal and regulatory provisions;
(b) that damage was inflicted upon biodiversity, flora, and fauna; and
(c) that damage to water resources resulted in economic losses due to harm inflicted upon agriculture and animal husbandry.

[22] 'Rehabilitation of the Landfill in Porto Romano, Spitalla, Durrës' (*Centre for Legal Empowerment*, 10 December 2019), https://cle.al/en/rehabilitation-of-the-landfill-in-porto-romano-spitalla-durres.

[23] 'Environmental and Legal Organizations Win the First Legal Battle, Gaining Legitimacy to Legally Challenge the Council of Ministers' Decisions That Reduced Areas of Value from Protected Areas, National Assets' (*AOS-Albanian Ornithological Society*, 20 September 2023), https://aos-alb.org/press-release-environmental-and-legal-organizations-win-the-first-legal-battle-gaining-legitimacy-to-legally-challenge-the-council-of-ministers-decisions-that-reduced-areas-of-value-from-protected.

VI. The Possibility of Resorting to Alternative Dispute Resolution

In Albania, the legal framework and the option of utilising Alternative Dispute Resolution (ADR) have been established by Law No 10385/2011 on 'Mediation in dispute settlement'. According to Article 2, point 2, mediation is applicable to resolving disputes across various domains, including civil, commercial, labour, family law, intellectual property, consumer rights, and conflicts between public administration entities and private entities.

In environmental cases, the utilisation of mediation can offer significant advantages, particularly in addressing intricate and multi-party disputes. These may involve issues such as pollution remediation, land use conflicts or natural resource management. Mediation serves as a valuable tool in fostering constructive dialogue and consensus-building among stakeholders, ultimately facilitating the development of more effective and sustainable solutions to environmental challenges.

In practice, there have not been any cases resolved through mediation between affected communities and/or NPOs against public institutions and/or private companies.

VII. Accessibility of the Enforcement Mechanism and Costs

In environmental cases, a variety of claims can be brought before a court depending on the specific circumstances and legal frameworks involved, such as the violation of environmental laws protecting endangered species or their habitats (based on Law No 9587/2006), water rights, ie, disputes over the use, allocation or pollution of water resources, including rivers, lakes, and groundwater (based on Law No 111/2012, 'On the integrated management of water resources'), improper waste disposal or inadequate pollution controls.

According to the Code of Civil Procedure and the Code of Administrative Procedures, administrative appeals can sometimes lead to quicker and less costly dispute resolution compared to judicial proceedings. This is due to administrative procedures being less formal and more streamlined, thus facilitating faster dispute resolution. Resolving disputes at the administrative level whenever feasible can also preserve judicial resources for cases where administrative remedies have been exhausted or are unavailable.

The costs relating to environmental cases typically include court fees, attorney fees and expertise fees. Court fees are determined by Law No 98/2017, which outlines the types of fees, their amounts, payment methods and cases of exemption from payment.[24]

[24] Law No 98/2017 'On court fees on the Republic of Albania'.

As per Joint Instruction No 33 issued on 29 December 2014, the fees are outlined as follows:[25]

Lawsuit: 3,000 ALL;[26]
Appeal: 200 ALL;
Lawsuits arising from causing damage or with a value above 100,000 ALL: 1% of the value.

Lawyers' fees are defined by the Joint Instruction Number 18/2020 of the Ministry of Justice and Ministry of Finance and are based on a minimum fee level, as stated below:[27]

Representation in the Court of First Instance 40,000 ALL;
Representation in the Court of Appeal 45,000 ALL;
Representation in the Supreme and Constitutional Court 60,000 ALL;
Preparation of appeal requests 15,000 ALL;
Appeals and requests in the Supreme and Constitutional Court 25,000 ALL;
Legal advice 500–1,500 ALL/hour.

Expenses incurred during legal proceedings in Albania, as outlined in Article 102 of the Code of Civil Procedure, encompass various categories, including taxes on legal acts, costs related to actions performed and other necessary expenditures. Taxes on legal acts are considered preliminary judicial expenses, while expenses for actions conducted during the trial and other essential trial costs constitute expenses incurred during the procedure itself. These expenses encompass a range of procedural activities conducted by the court, plaintiff, defendant, primary interveners and others involved in seeking a judgment. Such activities may include gathering witness testimony, obtaining expert opinions, examining evidence, conducting experiments and facilitating notifications via postal services, among others. According to Article 105 and 105/a of the Code of Civil Procedure, the party requesting such evidence is responsible for paying the associated expenses in advance. The court, taking into account the circumstances of the case and the financial situation of the parties, can charge costs to one or both parties, regardless of which of them requested the questioning of witnesses, the performance of expertise, the calling of an interpreter or the inspection. The loser pays principle applies.

However, payments to licensed experts for their expertise must not exceed 40,000 ALL. Due to the complex nature of environmental issues and the

[25] Joint Instruction No 33, dated 29 December 2014, 'On Determining the Service Fee for Actions and Services of the Judicial Administration of the Ministry of Justice, Procuracy and Notary'.

[26] Exchange rate 1 ALL = €0.00996185.

[27] Joint Instruction No 18/2011 'for the approval of the criteria for benefiting from payments and remuneration rates for lawyers who provide secondary legal assistance': www.drejtesia.gov.al/wp-content/uploads/2020/09/Udh%C3%ABzim-i-P%C3%ABrbashket-p%C3%ABr-miratimin-e-kritereve-t%C3%AB-p%C3%ABrfitimit-te-pagesave-dhe-tarifat-e-shp%C3%ABrblimit-t%C3%AB-avokatis%C3%AB-q%C3%AB-ofrojn%C3%AB-Ndihm%C3%AB-Juridike-Falas.pdf. The fees are based on a minimum level and every lawyer that is contracted has the right to ask for another fee.

necessity for comprehensive studies regarding biodiversity of flora and fauna, in practice costs of environmental expertise can range from 100,000 ALL to 200,000 ALL.

Access to justice represents an effective avenue for citizens to seek resolutions through judicial institutions. The enactment of the new Law No 111/2017, entitled 'On legal aid guaranteed by the state', has broadened the scope from a normative perspective compared to the previous legislation. This expansion includes widening the scope of free legal aid and extending the range of individuals eligible to benefit from this system. This law establishes a comprehensive system comprising primary legal aid, secondary legal aid and waiver of court fees, and court costs. Legal assistance aimed at familiarising individuals with legislation and resolving legal issues is referred to as primary legal assistance, while legal assistance aimed at accessing the court is referred to as secondary legal aid. The implementation of the law on legal aid is facilitated by various bylaws.

The provisions concerning secondary legal aid and exemptions from court costs and fees exhibit both partial identity and partial similarity, with variations on certain aspects. Secondary legal aid involves representation by attorneys listed and endorsed by the National Chamber of Advocates, following a request from an eligible individual as stipulated in Article 11 or 12 of this legislation. Initially, approval for secondary legal aid is granted by the court or relevant administrative body, after which an appointed lawyer, typically selected and replaced by the local chamber of advocates, assumes responsibility. However, in instances specified in Article 21, the administrative body, rather than the chamber of advocates, undertakes the appointment and substitution of the lawyer (Article 21/2).

Legal aid may be available to the following individuals (provided they meet other eligibility criteria): Albanian citizens residing in Albania; foreign citizens (or stateless persons) with temporary or permanent residence in Albania and a valid permit of stay, or those who enter Albania legally and benefit from international agreements ratified or based on reciprocity principles; and certain refugees or asylum-seekers.[28]

The law has established two categories of beneficiaries for legal aid: (a) individuals, irrespective of their income and wealth; and (b) individuals who prove to have insufficient income and properties to cover the expenses for legal services.

Affected communities are not categorised as a specific category eligible for free legal aid services. The legislation does not foresee the possibility to benefit from free legal aid for collective action. Members of communities can benefit from free legal aid only if they individually meet the criteria specified by law. In practice, communities or their members have not benefited from free legal aid under the state legal aid scheme. This is primarily due to the large number of participants involved in these types of cases and the requirement for specialised

[28] Law No 111/2017, art 10.

lawyers in environmental law to handle such cases. As a result, environmental issues are mainly addressed in court by lawyers and NPOs either pro bono or with donor support. Conversely, there have been many cases when residents have not addressed and followed environmental issues due to the inability to afford court costs, including legal representation and technical expertise.

VIII. Challenges of Access to Justice in Environmental Matters

Environmental laws can be intricate and difficult for the public to understand, leading to barriers in accessing justice. Ambiguities in regulations can also create uncertainty, making it challenging for individuals and communities to know their rights and obligations. Many individuals and communities affected by environmental issues lack access to legal aid or representation due to financial constraints. This limits their ability to navigate the legal system and seek remedies for environmental harm. Lack of precedent or established case law in environmental matters makes it challenging for litigants to predict legal outcomes and for courts to apply consistent standards. Judges and legal professionals may lack specialised knowledge and training in environmental law, impeding the effective adjudication of environmental cases. Environmental agencies and regulatory bodies may face resource constraints, including limited funding and staffing shortages, which hamper their ability to enforce environmental laws effectively. This can result in inadequate monitoring, enforcement and compliance measures. Insufficient opportunities for public participation in environmental decision-making processes can limit community engagement and accountability. Lack of transparency and consultation can erode trust in the legal system and hinder efforts to address environmental concerns collaboratively.

Addressing these challenges requires a multi-faceted approach, including legal reforms to simplify procedures and enhance access to justice, capacity-building initiatives to strengthen judicial expertise, and measures to promote transparency, accountability and public participation in environmental governance. Additionally, efforts to combat corruption and undue influence on regulatory bodies are essential to uphold the integrity of environmental enforcement mechanisms. Considering the current situation and Albania's efforts to join the EU, the country should focus on improving the drafting and implementation of environmental legislation as follows:

(1) improving the Code of Civil Procedure by including environmental protection decisions among the cases where the first instance courts can grant the decision with temporary execution;
(2) improving the legislation on free legal aid by including communities affected by environmental problems among the beneficiaries of free legal aid;

(3) making access to justice for individuals and communities affected from environmental issues effective by guaranteeing the right to judicial decision within a reasonable time by including environmental protection cases among those that are judged through an expedited court procedure;
(4) strengthening the initial and continuous training programs and activities by the School of Magistrates, the National Chamber of Advocacy and the Directorate of Free Legal Aid to enhance the capacity of judges, lawyers, and other legal professionals in environmental law and related fields; and
(5) foreseeing, promoting and incentivising the use of ADR mechanisms in the law 'For mediation on disputes resolution' to address and resolve environmental issues.

By implementing these measures and strengthening the legal framework for environmental protection, public institutions can enhance the effectiveness of enforcement mechanisms and better address environmental challenges for the benefit of present and future generations.

5

Implementation of Article 9 of the Aarhus Convention in Croatia

Is the Door Open or Shut? Examining Barriers to Access to Justice

LANA OFAK AND MARKO TURUDIĆ

I. Introductory Remarks on the Constitutional Right to a Healthy Environment

The narrative behind the Aarhus Convention highlights the crucial endeavour of equipping individuals and their associations with effective mechanisms to safeguard the right of every person of present and future generations to live in an environment suitable for his or her health and well-being. In this context, the year 2023 was marked by a significant decision of the Constitutional Court of the Republic of Croatia (CCRC),[1] which for the first time clearly held that the right to a healthy life and environment is a fundamental right of citizens protected by the Constitution of the Republic of Croatia (hereinafter 'the Constitution').[2] The case concerned the Decision on the Order and Dynamics of Landfill Closure[3] (hereinafter 'the Decision') adopted by the Minister competent for environmental protection under the then-valid Sustainable Waste Management Act. With this Decision, 27 non-hazardous waste disposal sites that did not meet legal requirements for health and environmental protection were closed, and their waste was diverted to landfills of local self-government units that harmonised the disposal of non-hazardous waste on their territory with legal requirements. This solution was intended to be a short-term measure until waste

[1] Decision and Ruling of the CCRC, No U-II-845/2019 and U-II-2160/2019 of 18 April 2023.

[2] The Constitution of the Republic of Croatia, Official Gazette (OG) 56/90, 135/97, 113/00, 28/01, 76/10 and 5/14.

[3] OG 3/19 and 17/19.

management centres became operational. However, these centres were not built within the stipulated period, and their construction is still far from realised. The consequence of this Decision was that certain local self-government units were obliged to receive unsorted and unused waste from other non-compliant units, leading to an enormously increased amount of waste they had to receive and dispose of. Given that the projects for most waste management centres are still being prepared or in the process of public procurement, the decision to divert waste from non-compliant landfills to compliant landfills has in practice become a permanent solution instead of a temporary one.

Based on the proposal of the City of Supetar and the company for the performance of communal activities founded by the City of Biograd na Moru, the CCRC decided to initiate the procedure for assessing the constitutionality and legality of the Minister's Decision because it determined that this was necessary for the protection of human rights and fundamental freedoms guaranteed by the Constitution and other highest values of the constitutional order established in Article 3 of the Constitution, including the preservation of nature and environmental protection. In this specific case, the CCRC also acted in light of the positive obligation of the state to create conditions for the effectiveness of the guarantee of a healthy life and environment, which is derived from Article 69 of the Constitution. The CCRC also examined the disputed Decision in light of Article 16 of the Constitution, which prescribes the obligation to respect the principle of proportionality when deviating from the fundamental rights guaranteed by the Constitution. The CCRC concluded that the measure of diverting waste from landfills that could not continue to operate due to non-compliance with the legal criteria to landfills that met the prescribed criteria undoubtedly represented a restriction of the fundamental right to a healthy life and environment. This limitation of the right to a healthy life and environment is especially emphasised for the citizens of those local self-government units that, based on the contested Decision, are obliged to accept diverted waste to their landfills.

The CCRC also found that the waste diversion measure does not meet the proportionality requirement prescribed in Article 16 of the Constitution. The contested measure of diverting waste without prior treatment represents an unconstitutional limitation of the fundamental right to a healthy life and environment.

Why is this decision of the CCRC significant? In 2001, Croatia took a step backwards when it no longer expressly provided citizens' constitutional right to a healthy environment but only the right to a healthy life. The Constitutional Amendment from 2001 changed the provision of Article 69, paragraph 2 of the Constitution from '[t]he state ensures the right of citizens to a healthy environment' to '[t]he state ensures the conditions for a healthy environment.' In other words, the state's duty to ensure citizens the right to a healthy environment was replaced with the duty to ensure the conditions for a healthy environment. Croatian legal scholars considered that, despite this Constitutional Amendment, the right to a healthy life is a special constitutional expression of the broader right to a healthy environment, and it should continue to be recognised as a constitutional right.[4] It took 22 years for the Constitutional Court to take this position and finally expressly state that the right to a healthy environment is constitutionally protected.

Interestingly, such an important decision for realising the constitutional right of citizens to a healthy environment was made without any mention of the Aarhus Convention, although no environmental impact assessment (EIA) and no public participation was carried out before the Minister's Decision was made. The procedure challenging the Decision was initiated on the basis of Article 40 of the Act on the Constitutional Court of the Republic of Croatia,[5] which enables anyone to submit a proposal to the CCRC to institute proceedings to review the constitutionality of the law or the constitutionality and legality of other regulations. Moreover, until today, there has not been a single decision of the CCRC in which the Aarhus Convention has been applied, although Croatia ratified it 17 years ago.[6]

The basic hypothesis of this chapter is that the application of the Aarhus Convention is neglected in practice, both by public authorities when they act in environmental matters and by administrative courts when they control the legality of administrative acts. The reason for this is poor (even incorrect) implementation of its provisions in the national legislation (sections II–V) and lack of knowledge or willingness of the competent public authorities and administrative courts to apply the Aarhus Convention (section VI). Due to space limitations, comprehensive coverage of all aspects of the implementation of Article 9 of the Aarhus Convention in Croatia was not possible. The chapter will primarily address the standing requirements and obstacles that hinder effective access to justice in environmental issues.

II. Croatia's Implementation of the Aarhus Convention

The Aarhus Convention came into force in Croatia on 25 June 2007.[7] It was implemented into the Croatian legal system mainly by the Environmental Protection

[4] L Ofak, 'The Approach of the Constitutional Court of the Republic of Croatia towards the Protection of the Right to a Healthy Environment' (2021) 16(31) *Journal of Agricultural and Environmental Law* 85, 85–98; F Staničić, 'Croatia: Constitutional Protection of the Right to a Healthy Life: Do We Need More in Order to Safeguard the Environment and Future Generations?' in JE Szilágyi (ed), *Constitutional Protection of the Environment and Future Generations Legislation and Practice in Certain Central European Countries* (Miskolc, CEA Publishing, 2022) 127.

[5] OG 99/99, 29/02 and 49/02 – consolidated text. The English version of the Act is available at: www.usud.hr/en/constitutional-act.

[6] Act on Ratification of the Convention on Access to Information, Public Participation in Decision-Making and Access to Justice in Environmental Matters, OG – International Treaties 1/07.

[7] OG – IT 1/07.

Act (EPA)[8] and subordinate legislation adopted on the basis thereof.[9] The EPA contains special provisions prescribed in Part IX (Articles 154–72) that regulate public information, participation of the public and public concerned, and access to justice in environmental matters. However, other general legislative acts apply as well. The most significant acts among these are:

- the Right of Access to Information Act;[10]
- the General Administrative Procedure Act[11] (GAPA); and
- the Administrative Disputes Act[12] (ADA).

A number of academic papers have been published discussing the issues surrounding the lack of compliance of Croatian legislation with the Aarhus Convention, particularly in Croatian journals and language.[13] These papers also delved into the challenges related to access to justice as they pertain to environmental issues. Several papers have also been published in English on this topic,[14] and the current chapter aims to contribute to the existing body of research from the Croatian perspective.

The European Commission has not yet taken any legal action against Croatia before the Court of Justice of the European Union (CJEU) for failing to meet its obligations under the Aarhus Convention. However, it has consistently

[8] Croatia adopted its initial comprehensive environmental legislation, the EPA, in 1994 (OG 82/94 and 128/99), which was replaced by the second EPA in 2007 (OG 110/07). The second EPA was revoked in 2013 following the introduction of the third EPA (OG No 80/13). This act is still in force and has been amended four times so far (OG 153/13, 78/15, 12/18, 118/18).

[9] The Decree on information and participation of the public and public concerned in environmental matters (OG 64/08) applies to issues concerning public participation (Article 6 of the Aarhus Convention). The government, pursuant to Art 268, para 3 of the EPA, was required to pass the new Decree within one year from the entry into force of the EPA in 2013. This has not been done yet. Until the new Decree enters into force, the previous one from 2008 remains in force. The 2008 Decree does not fully meet the requirements set out in Art 6 of the Aarhus Convention. Nevertheless, the constraints of space within this chapter prevent a thorough examination of this issue.

[10] OG 25/13, 85/15 and 69/22.

[11] OG 47/09 and 110/20.

[12] OG 20/10, 143/12, 152/14, 94/16, 29/17 and 110/21. On 14 March 2024, the Croatian Parliament adopted the new ADA, which entered into force on 1 July 2024.

[13] L Ofak, 'Harmonization of Croatian Legislation with EU Law in the Field of Water Protection with Special Emphasis on Public Participation and Access to Justice' (2018) 39(1) *Collected Papers of the Law Faculty of the University of Rijeka* 269; L Ofak, 'The Right of Associations to Participate and Their Access to Justice in Procedures of Natura 2000 Appropriate Assessments' (2019) 6567 *Informator* 18; L Ofak, 'Restriction of the Legal Position of the Parties in Special Administrative Procedures' (2014) 14(4) *Croatian and Comparative Public Administration* 987; E Ćerimagić, T Ćapeta and L Ofak, *Environmental Impact Assessment: How to Represent Environmental Protection in Court* (Pula, Zelena Istra, 2014), available at: www.zelena-istra.hr/media/filer_public/d6/a4/d6a4f397-858a-4cae-972c-4d22e06d3f50/kako_zastupati_zastitu_okolisa_na_sudu-prirucnik.pdf.

[14] L Ofak 'Application of the Aarhus Convention in Southeast Europe' in S Rodin and T Perišin (eds), *Judicial Application of International Law in Southeast Europe* (Berlin, Springer-Verlag, 2015) 43; L Ofak 'Access to Justice in Environmental Matters in Croatia' in V Tomoszková et al, *Implementation and Enforcement of EU Environmental Law in the Visegrad Countries* (Olomouc, Palacký University Faculty of Law, 2014) 306; L Ofak, Ž Leljak Gracin and D Radojčić, *Alternative Report on the Implementation of the Aarhus Convention in Croatia: Civil Dialogue for a Better Environment* (Pula, Zelena Istra, 2014), available at: www.zelena-istra.hr/media/filer_public/8d/f2/8df2cee9-5ac7-47b1-ad25-5cf893ada8aa/alternative_report_on_aarhus_convention_implementation_2011_2013.pdf.

highlighted deficiencies with access to justice in environmental matters. In the 2022 Environmental Implementation Review, the Commission emphasised the importance of improving public awareness of how individuals and environmental organisations can access review procedures in environmental issues.[15] Additionally, it highlighted restrictions in initiating administrative disputes before the court regarding challenging plans and programmes subject to strategic environmental assessment (SEA).[16] The Commission recommended that Croatia should enhance access to courts for the public concerned seeking to challenge administrative or regulatory decisions, especially in areas such as water, nature, and air quality planning. However, these priority actions were already pointed out to Croatia in 2019, and the Commission determined that there has been minimal or no improvement.[17]

In January 2023, the Commission issued Croatia with a letter of formal notice regarding the incorrect implementation of the Habitats Directive in relation to wind energy projects.[18] Although the case deals with the systematic failure to appropriately assess the impact of changes to wind farm projects on Natura 2000 sites, contrary to Articles 6(3) and 7 of Directive 92/43/EEC on the conservation of natural habitats and of wild fauna and flora, it also illustrates the difficulties that Croatian non-governmental organisations (NGOs) encountered in exercising their rights under the Aarhus Convention and initiating legal proceedings before the administrative court.[19]

Only one case from Croatia has been brought before the Aarhus Convention Compliance Committee, with two other cases deemed inadmissible. On 24 January 2012, the Croatian Association for Nature, Environment and Sustainable Development 'Sunce' (Sun) submitted a communication alleging Croatia's non-compliance with the Convention.[20] The Association claimed that waste management plans were adopted in several towns in Croatia without public participation. The Committee found that Croatia failed to comply with Article 7 of the Convention regarding public participation in preparing municipality waste management plans.[21]

Instances of Croatia being taken to the European Court of Human Rights (ECtHR) for environmental issues are also very rare. There have been only two

[15] Commission, 'Environmental Implementation Review 2022 Country Report – Croatia' SWD (2022) 258 final, 41.

[16] ibid 42.

[17] ibid.

[18] INFR (2020) 2204. See also 'January Infringements Package: Key Decisions' (26 January 2023), https://ec.europa.eu/commission/presscorner/detail/en/inf_23_142.

[19] Association Biom, 'Croatia Continues Violating EU Laws in the Case of Wind Farms' (10 February 2023), www.biom.hr/en/croatia-continues-violating-eu-laws-in-the-case-of-wind-farms. See section 6 of this chapter for an explanation of the case (Judgment of the High Administrative Court of the Republic of Croatia Usž-409/19-6 of 8 May 2020).

[20] Findings and recommendations with regard to communication ACCC/C/2012/66 concerning compliance by Croatia, https://unece.org/fileadmin/DAM/env/pp/compliance/CC-44/ECE_MP.PP_C.1_2014_4_ENG.pdf.

[21] ibid para 55.

relevant cases regarding noise pollution so far.[22] In *Udovičić v Croatia*, the ECtHR found that the applicant's right to respect for private and family life had been violated due to long exposure to excessive noise from business premises on the ground floor of the house where she lived. The ECtHR held that the authorities did not sufficiently address the multiple complaints made by the applicant over the course of 10 years, starting from when the bar and shop beneath her apartment opened until the proceedings began before the Court. In response to the ECtHR's judgment, Croatia adopted new rules to enhance protection from noise pollution. The new procedural provisions specifically pertain to sanitary inspectors when it comes to enforcing noise protection measures. The petitioner who points out violations of the regulations may be granted status of a party in the inspection procedure, allowing them to request expert examination in the field of noise to support their case. The costs of expertise are borne by the party for whom the outcome of the official expertise is unfavourable.[23]

Environmental cases against Croatian public authorities are brought before the CCRC more frequently than before the ECtHR. However, constitutional cases primarily focus on determining whether laws comply with the Croatian Constitution, with individual constitutional complaints being rare.[24] Compared to other European countries,[25] NGOs in Croatia have not fully adopted the practice of bringing cases to the CCRC to hold public authorities accountable for complying with environmental protection regulations. Continuing this chapter, we will focus on legal obstacles that make accessing justice in environmental matters difficult. Exploring the underlying social and other factors contributing to this phenomenon could be the focus of a separate research study.[26]

III. Access to Justice Relating to Environmental Information Requests

The Croatian Constitution guarantees the right to access information held by public authorities, which was explicitly established through the Amendment

[22] *Udovičić v Croatia* App No 27310/09 (ECtHR, 24 April 2014), www.coe.int/en/web/impact-convention-human-rights/-/new-powers-for-state-inspectors-after-woman-wins-noise-pollution-case; *Olujić v Croatia* App No 61260/08 (ECtHR, 20 May 2010).

[23] Expert examination at the request of the petitioner (Art 90 of the State Inspectorate Act, OG 115/18, 117/21, 67/23).

[24] Ofak (n 4); A Blagojević and M Majnarić, 'The "Green" Constitution of the Republic of Croatia and the Constitutional Court as a Protector of the Right to a Healthy Environment' (2023) 7 *EU and Comparative Law Issues and Challenges Series (ECLIC)* 33.

[25] For instance, Hoge Raad, 20 December 2019, 19/00135, https://uitspraken.rechtspraak.nl/details?id=ECLI:NL:HR:2019:2006; BVerfG, Beschluss des Ersten Senats vom 24 March 2021, 1 BvR 2656/18, Rn. 1-270, http://www.bverfg.de/e/rs20210324_1bvr265618.html; Verfassungsgerichtshof, G 123/2023-12, 27 June 2023, https://climatecasechart.com/wp-content/uploads/non-us-case-documents/2023/20230627_na_decision-6.pdf.

[26] See also Todorović, ch 3 in this volume, section III.

to the Constitution in 2010.[27] Even though Croatia has not signed the Council of Europe Convention on Access to Official Documents, the Right of Access to Information Act (RAIA) incorporates important international standards for effectively regulating access to information. International organisation 'ARTICLE 19' has published a set of principles setting out best practice standards on the right to information legislation.[28] The RAIA, in line with these international standards, includes principles of maximum disclosure, proactive obligation to publish and a high number of public authorities that are required to provide information. It also clearly prescribes a limited scope of exceptions subject to the proportionality and public interest test, ie, assessment if the interest against disclosure outweighs the public interest in favour of disclosure. The principles regarding facilitating access are incorporated by short deadlines for obtaining information[29] and by independent control of the Information Commissioner, who is appointed by the Croatian Parliament for a period of five years. The reimbursement of costs is restricted only to the actual costs of materials related to providing and delivering the requested information, as prescribed by pre-determined criteria.[30] The time spent by an employee of a public authority in collecting, preparing, and providing information to the applicant cannot be charged as a cost. The RAIA also supports the concept of public authorities holding open meetings and the promotion of open government.

If the request for information, including environmental information, has been ignored or wrongfully refused, the applicant may submit an appeal to the Information Commissioner. The second instance decision on the appeal must be rendered and served without delay, no more than 60 days from the appeal's submission date. Exceptionally, if the information has been classified by a degree of secrecy, under the act governing classified information, the Information Commissioner shall obtain the opinion of the Office of the National Security Council. In such cases involving classified information, the second instance decision must be rendered and served within 90 days after submitting the appeal.

[27] Article 38, para 4 of the Constitution states: 'The right to access to information held by any public authority shall be guaranteed. Restrictions on the right of access to information must be proportionate to the nature of the need for such restriction in each individual case and necessary in a free and democratic society, as stipulated by law.'

[28] T Mendel, *Freedom of Information: A Comparative Legal Survey*, 2nd edn (Paris, UNESCO, 2008), 30–40, https://law.yale.edu/sites/default/files/documents/pdf/Intellectual_Life/CL-OGI_Toby_Mendel_book_%28Eng%29.pdf.

[29] The public authority is obliged to enable the applicant to gain access to the information within no more than 15 days from the day the request is submitted. The time limits may be extended by up to 30 days insofar as: (1) the information must be sought outside the seat of the body of public authority; (2) a large number of different pieces of information are requested in one application; (3) it is necessary to ensure the completeness and accuracy of the information requested; and (4) the public authority is obliged to apply the proportionality and public interest test.

[30] Criteria for determining the amount of compensation for actual material costs and the costs of providing information, OG 12/14, 15/14 and 141/22.

The applicant may file a lawsuit against the second instance decision and institute an administrative dispute before the High Administrative Court of the Republic of Croatia (HAC). The lawsuit can be filed if the second instance body fails to render the decision within the prescribed time limits. The public authority that issued the first instance decision also has the right to initiate an administrative dispute against the decision of the Information Commissioner. The lawsuit has suspensive effect if the second instance decision granted access to information. The parties are exempted from paying court fees. The HAC must deliver a judgment within 90 days. The judgments rendered by the court in administrative disputes are binding.

Inspectors and other authorised officials of the Office of the Information Commissioner have the authority to supervise the implementation of the RAIA. Final decisions of the Commissioner that enable access to information and decisions that order the public authority to decide on the requests for access to information are binding and enforceable. The enforcement of the Commissioner's decision is implemented by imposing a sanction on the person responsible for the public authority. The sanction is executed by suspending the salary of the responsible person.

Although the EPA specifically regulates access to environmental information, when applicants are denied access, they invoke the provisions of the RAIA instead of the EPA. It is well-established case law of the Information Commissioner that appeals are resolved by applying the provisions of the RAIA, given the more favourable legal arrangement that benefits those seeking access to environmental information.[31]

Appeals regarding access to environmental information are not as common as one might expect. In 2022, only 23 cases were brought before the Information Commissioner. Of these appeals, 13 were lodged due to instances where requests for environmental information were ignored. Despite the relatively low number of environmental cases each year, the Commissioner's case law[32] is crucial in safeguarding the constitutional right of citizens to access information from public authorities, including environmental information.

IV. Access to Justice Relating to Public Participation in Decision-Making on Specific Activities

The right to a legal remedy in administrative matters, including environmental matters, is guaranteed by the Croatian Constitution, which provides the right to appeal against individual legal decisions made in first instance procedures before

[31] See summaries of the annual reports on the implementation of the RAIA available in English at: https://pristupinfo.hr/dokumenti-i-publikacije/izvjesca-o-provedbi-zppi/?lang=en.

[32] The case law is available online at: https://tom.pristupinfo.hr/pregledfilter1.php.

courts or other public authorities (Article 18). The right to appeal may only be excluded in cases specified by law if other legal venues for protection are available. This constitutional provision is further implemented in the GAPA, which prescribes the right to a legal remedy as one of the main principles of the administrative procedure (Article 12). A party has the right to an appeal against a first instance decision, as well as when an administrative body has not adjudicated on an administrative matter within a specific term unless provided otherwise by law. An administrative dispute can be initiated against a second instance decision or against a first instance decision against which an appeal is not allowed. The right to a legal remedy may be explained by the following example. An appeal shall not be permitted against the administrative decision issued by the Ministry of Economy and Sustainable Development in the EIA procedure. Still, an administrative dispute may be initiated before the administrative court. Against the administrative decision issued by the competent administrative body in the county or City of Zagreb, an appeal can be lodged with the Ministry of Economy and Sustainable Development.

The decisions can be challenged in the event of any law violations, including substantive and procedural violations. In procedures to which Article 9(2) of the Aarhus Convention applies, the claimant, under the ADA, may request the following:

- annulment of or declaring an individual decision null and void;
- issuing a decision which was not taken within the prescribed time limit;
- performance of an action which the respondent was obligated to perform in accordance with the rules and regulations or a decision.

The claimant may also request the court to adjudicate on the party's rights, obligations and legal interests. This means that administrative courts are empowered to render reformatory decisions, ie, to replace unlawful administrative acts which they annulled. However, they may not do that if the nature of things does not allow them, or where the public authority acted according to the discretion (*pouvoir discrétionnaire, freies Ermessen*) granted to it by the law. Still, in procedures where decisions are made on specific activities that may significantly impact the environment, the administrative courts regularly do not replace the administrative body's decision with their judgment. Instead, they annul the decision if it is found to be illegal and send the case back to the administrative body for a new decision.

According to the ADA, anyone who claims that his or her rights or legal interest have been violated has the right to initiate an administrative dispute. Legal interest can be an appropriate distance of the planned construction from his or her building, noise protection, possible negative impact on the stability of his or her building, fire safety, hygiene and health protection, environmental protection, etc. Prior participation in the administrative procedure is not required. The only condition is the mandatory use of an appeal in the administrative procedure, if such a possibility exists, as a prerequisite for initiating an administrative dispute. Put simply, if a party had the opportunity to file an appeal with the second instance public authority before initiating the administrative dispute in court, the lawsuit would not be admissible if the party did not utilise the appeal process.[33]

However, the EPA from 2007, as well as the new EPA from 2013, restricted the right to challenge the administrative decision only to those individuals who participated in the procedure as the public concerned and who can prove impairment of their right due to the location and/or nature and impact of the project (both conditions have to be fulfilled).[34] Therefore, the general rules of the ADA are more favourable than those of the EPA. This presents two problems.

First, it conflicts with the CJEU's ruling in the *Stichting Varkens in Nood* (*Pigs in Danger*) case.[35] Under Article 9(2) of the Aarhus Convention, Member States cannot restrict access to justice to the public concerned based on their participation in decision-making procedures. Although the case involved an NGO meeting the requirements,[36] the same applies to individuals who are part of the public concerned by the definition given in Article 2(5) of the Aarhus Convention.[37] As Wertheim explains, while the CJEU does not explicitly state this in its response, it appears that the same is also true for individuals who are part of the public concerned in general, not just NGOs.[38] In paragraph 36 of the judgment, the CJEU states that the aim of Article 9(2) of the Convention is to ensure that members belonging to the 'public concerned' have the right to bring an action.[39]

[33] The Aarhus Convention Implementation Guide also specifies that it is permissible to mandate the completion of administrative review procedures before pursuing further action: see J Ebbesson et al, *The Aarhus Convention: An Implementation Guide* (Geneva, United Nations, 2014), 196; RS Wertheim, 'C-826/18, *Stichting Varkens in Nood and Others v College van burgemeester en wethouders van de gemeente Echt-Susteren* (Judgment of 14 January 2021) – Case Note' (2021) 14(3) *Review of European Administrative Law* 47, 61.

[34] Articles 167(1) and 168(1) of the EPA.

[35] Case C-826/18 *Stichting Varkens in Nood and Others v College van burgemeester en wethouders van de gemeente Echt-Susteren* ECLI:EU:C:2021:7.

[36] 'Article 9(2) of the Convention on access to information, public participation in decision-making and access to justice in environmental matters, signed in Aarhus (Denmark) on 25 June 1998 and approved on behalf of the European Community by Decision 2005/370/EC must be interpreted as precluding the admissibility of the judicial proceedings to which it refers, brought by non-governmental organisations which are part of the "public concerned" referred to in Article 2(5) of that convention, from being made subject to the participation of those organisations in the procedure preparatory to the contested decision, even though that condition does not apply where such organisations cannot reasonably be criticised for not having participated in that procedure' (ibid).

[37] Under Art 2(5), the public concerned means the public affected or likely to be affected by, or having an interest in, the environmental decision-making.

[38] Wertheim (n 33).

[39] 'The purpose of Article 9(2) of the Aarhus Convention is therefore not to confer a right to bring an action against decisions and other acts which fall within the scope of Article 6 of that convention, relating to projects subject to public participation in the decision-making procedure, on the public in general, but to guarantee that right only to members of the "public concerned" who meet certain conditions': *Stichting Varkens in Nood and Others* (n 35) para 36.

Second, the requirements for bringing an action set forth by the EPA are stricter than those under the ADA. This goes against the principles of equivalence and effectiveness, according to which:

> [D]etailed procedural rules governing actions for safeguarding an individual's rights under EU law must be no less favourable than those governing similar domestic actions (principle of equivalence) and must not make it in practice impossible or excessively difficult to exercise rights conferred by EU law (principle of effectiveness).[40]

In the case of EPA's requirements, there appears to be a violation of the principle of equivalence, as the claimant is required to demonstrate impairment of his or her right in order to challenge decisions which fall within the scope of Article 6 of the Aarhus Convention. In other administrative disputes, the ADA only requires that individuals who claim their rights or legal interests have been infringed have the right to initiate an administrative dispute.

The criteria for NGOs (ie, associations) for initiating the administrative dispute are prescribed by Article 167(2) EPA:

- if they are registered in accordance with special regulations governing associations and if environmental protection, including protection of human health and protection or rational use of natural resources, is set out as a goal in their statute; and
- if they have been registered for at least two years before the initiation of the public authority's procedure (in relation to which it is expressing its legal interest) and can prove that in that period, they actively participated in activities related to environmental protection on the territory of the city or municipality where they have a registered seat in accordance with their statute.

Such associations shall have the right to appeal with the ministry competent for environmental and nature protection or to file a lawsuit before the competent court to challenge the procedural and/or substantive legality of decisions, actions or omissions. If an association does not meet these requirements, it is not assumed to belong to the public concerned. This does not prevent the association from proving its legal interest in a procedure; rather, such an interest must be proven since it is not automatically assumed.[41]

[40] Case C-240/09 *Lesoochranárske zoskupenie VLK v Ministerstvo životného prostredia Slovenskej republiky* ECLI:EU:C:2011:125, para 48; see also M Eliantonio, 'The Relationship between EU Secondary Rules and the Principles of Effectiveness and Effective Judicial Protection in Environmental Matters: Towards a New Dawn for the "Language of Rights"?' (2019) 12(2) *Review of European Administrative Law* 95.

[41] D Medvedović and L Ofak, 'The Legal Position of Associations in Environmental Protection Proceedings in the Republic of Croatia' (2011) 9(1) *Facta universitatis, Series: Law and Politics* 69, 81–82, http://facta.junis.ni.ac.rs/lap/lap201101/lap201101-05.pdf. An example may be a group of residents in a potentially affected area who come together to collectively address concerns about a project, despite not meeting the requirement of being registered for a minimum of two years.

V. Access to Justice Relating to Acts and Omissions which Contravene Provisions of National Law Relating to the Environment

A number of judicial actions provide members of the public with a form of legal redress in case of acts or omissions which contravene provisions of national law relating to the environment.[42] The main examples are as follows:

- initiating an administrative dispute (judicial review of administrative decisions or acts or failure to render a decision or act within the set period);
- action for breach of a civil duty (eg, protection against the nuisance, civil action requesting removal of the source of danger);
- private prosecution of misdemeanour; and
- private prosecution of criminal offences that are prosecuted through private lawsuits.

Indirect enforcement of environmental law is provided for by the constitutional right of an individual to submit petitions and complaints, to make proposals to the government and other public bodies and to receive answers from them (Article 46 of the Constitution). Individuals, as well as NGOs, are therefore entitled to submit complaints to competent authorities. In principle, the complaints are submitted to various inspectorates competent for different sectors (noise, water, waste, building etc). The problem arises in a situation in which members of the public are not satisfied with the actions of the competent authorities (inspectorates) since they are not granted the status of the party in inspection proceedings. The applicant who submitted the complaint is not a party to the inspection procedure in the sense of the EPA or other laws regulating other inspections. The only instance where this rule does not apply is when expert evidence is needed in relation to the implementation of noise protection measures. This provision was inserted into the State Inspectorate Act due to the need to enforce the judgment of the ECtHR in the *Udovičić v Croatia* case.[43] However, the Croatian legislator overlooked the importance of including the public concerned as a party in all other inspection procedures pertaining to monitoring acts and omissions that violate national environmental law.[44] In practice, because they do not have recognised party status, they cannot file a lawsuit in administrative courts – ie, their lawsuit would be dismissed.[45]

[42] Ofak, 'Access to Justice in Environmental Matters in Croatia' (n 14) 310–11.

[43] See section II above (nn 23 and 24).

[44] In Ofak, 'Restriction of the Legal Position of the Parties in Special Administrative Procedures' (n 13), the author discussed the restriction of party status and argued that this practice goes against both the Croatian Constitution and the European Convention for the Protection of Human Rights and Fundamental Freedoms.

[45] According to the case law of the CCRC (Decision No U-III/2446/2021 of 20 January 2022), living near a building that is the object of inspection does not in itself provide a legal basis for acquiring

In administrative procedures in which decisions about whether to allow certain activities that may have significant effects on the environment are made, public participation must be allowed during all the stages of decision-making on that activity rather than only in the EIA procedure.[46] Despite this, special legislative acts (eg, the Building Act, the Physical Planning Act, and other legislative acts with provisions concerning inspections) do not allow or significantly restrict the possibility for other members of the public concerned to participate in the procedure (except the party at whose request the procedure was initiated or against whom the procedure is conducted), even if the matter concerns their rights or legal interests. The consequence is that members of the public concerned are not allowed to challenge such decisions since special legislation does not recognise their right to participate.

To fulfil Croatia's obligations regarding Article 9(3) of the Aarhus Convention, the EPA introduced a new legal remedy for the re-examination of decisions, acts or omissions of public authorities and actions or omissions on the part of legal and natural persons (such as an operator, a company or a polluter) in environmental issues.[47] This remedy has never been used in practice by any member of the public. Several factors seriously impair its availability to the public concerned.

First, in order to be eligible for filing the action, the claimant has to prove a violation of his or her right due to the location of the project and/or the project's nature and/or impact. Moreover, Article 19(2) of the EPA, which regulates the principle of access to justice, stipulates that the violation has to be permanent. There are no other examples in Croatia where permanent violation, or even the proven violation of a right, is required for ius standi. In general, the claimant must only claim that his or her rights or legal interest have been violated;[48] he or she does not have to prove an actual violation. Why was this harsh requirement introduced in the EPA? One possible answer is that it resulted from an error in the translation of Directive 2003/35/EC from English to Croatian, which was then reflected in the EPA – namely, in the Croatian working (unofficial) version of Directive 2003/35/EC, the phrase 'maintaining the impairment of a right' has been translated as 'permanently violate rights'. It seems likely that this mistranslation was the basis for drafting the provisions on access to justice contained in the EPA of 2007. The legislator only partially corrected that error in the new EPA of 2013,

the status of a party in the inspection procedure. This particular case did not pertain to violations of environmental law, so it remains to be seen whether the Constitutional Court would render a similar decision in cases subject to the Aarhus Convention.

[46] See Aarhus Convention Compliance Committee decision in relation to the Czech Republic ACCC/C/2010/50.

[47] Article 169 in connection with Art 167(1) of the EPA.

[48] Legal interest in an administrative dispute is typically uncontested when the claimant was a participant in the administrative proceedings. 'Legal interest' means that the interest is based on law or is protected by law. Rights, obligations and legal interests derive from the regulations that govern specific administrative matters.

and the word 'permanent' in Article 167(1) was erased. However, a condition of permanent violation of the rights was retained in Article 19(2) of the EPA, which makes this provision contrary to the Aarhus Convention.[49]

Second, the time limits for instituting proceedings are very strict and arguably impossible to fulfil. The request for the re-examination of the procedural and material legality of the issued decision, act or omission in relation to environmental protection and contesting the legality of actions or omissions in environmental matters must be submitted before a competent court within 30 days from the date on which the contested decision was delivered to the parties or published on the website of the competent public authority, or, in the case of an act or omission, within 15 days from the date on which the deadline for performing the act or issuing the decision expired (Article 169(2) of the EPA). These time limits are contrary to the rules of Croatian administrative procedural law (ie, the GAPA and the ADA). Since, in most cases, members of the public concerned are not granted the status of the party to the proceedings, the decision will not be delivered to them, so they cannot fulfil the first requirement for filing an action within 30 days from the date on which the contested decision was delivered to the parties. Furthermore, the second requirement is excessively difficult to fulfil since it requires frequent searching of all the possible websites of all the possible public authorities that might be issuing and publishing decisions in environmental law. Moreover, a very small number of decisions in the field of environmental law are regularly published on the website (eg, EIA decisions, decisions on appropriate assessment and environmental permits), so there is very little chance that the members of the public will find them on the website of the competent public authority.

The third requirement, which applies in case of an omission, deviates from the approach taken by the GAPA and the ADA. In case of an omission, according to the general rules, an appeal or a lawsuit can only be premature if an applicant did not wait for the expiration of a prescribed time limit in which a public authority had to act. However, once this time has passed, an appeal or a lawsuit cannot be regarded as untimely if the failure to act or issue a decision still occurs.

Lastly, the requirement that violations of individual rights must be proven in order to be granted locus standi effectively bars almost all environmental NGOs from using this legal remedy. In conclusion, the legal remedy envisaged in Article 169 of the EPA will most likely never be used in practice.

In our view, this contradicts the principles of equivalence and effectiveness because procedural rules governing actions related to Article 9(3) of the Aarhus Convention are less favourable than those governed by the provisions of the ADA and make it in practice excessively difficult to exercise rights conferred by the Aarhus Convention. Additionally, this goes against the CJEU's rulings in cases that have addressed NGOs' right to access justice in environmental issues.[50]

[49] Ofak, Leljak Gracin and Radojčić (n 14) 4.

[50] See *Lesoochranárske zoskupenie VLK* (n 40) and Case C-664/15 *Protect Natur-, Arten- und Landschaftschutz Umweltorganisation* ECLI:EU:C:2017:987.

VI. Application of the Aarhus Convention by the Croatian Public Authorities and Administrative Courts

In examining instances of Croatian public authorities and administrative courts applying the Aarhus Convention, our research indicated that when the provisions of the Convention are relevant to the merits of the case, the public authorities and administrative courts will apply the norms of national legislation rather than the provisions of an international agreement. This phenomenon persists even when the applicant cites relevant provisions of the Aarhus Convention. For example, in one case, the Croatian Society for the Protection of Birds and Nature, an NGO, filed a lawsuit challenging the decision of the Ministry for Environmental and Nature Protection that there is no need for an EIA or an appropriate assessment under Article 6(3) of the Habitats Directive for the small hydroelectric power plant on the River Orljava. The NGO claimed that there was a breach of Article 6 of the Aarhus Convention. The alleged violation pertained to the failure of the public authority to notify the public concerned about changes made to the environmental protection report after its initial publication on the website, particularly since these changes significantly affected the report's content. The HAC rejected the appeal and confirmed the judgment of the first instance administrative court without any reference to the relevant provisions of the Aarhus Convention.[51] Although the HAC accepted, in principle, the applicant's complaint that the public concerned should have been informed about the amendments to the environmental protection report, it found that this violation did not affect the applicant's right to file a lawsuit and try to challenge the report in an administrative dispute. The Court considered the applicant's argument solely in terms of the ADA,[52] omitting any reference to the Aarhus Convention. It found that the public authority did not violate procedural rules (principles of access to information and public participation in relation to the amended report) in a manner that would render the challenged decision illegal. Put simply, the Court determined that there were shortcomings in the administrative procedure, but they were not significant enough to impact the validity of the public authority's decision. The Court did not take into account the perspective of Article 6(6) of the Aarhus Convention, which mandates public authorities to give the public all relevant information for decision-making. It is not uncommon for environmental reports and studies to undergo modifications during the course of a procedure. In accordance with Croatian regulations, public authorities are not required to provide disclosure to the public concerned

[51] Judgment of the HAC Usž-2546/17-2 of 15 February 2018.

[52] Pursuant to the ADA, the court will reject the claim if it finds that there were procedural errors leading up to the adoption of an individual decision, but these errors did not impact the outcome of the decision.

about such alterations. The public concerned is not given a chance to provide feedback on the revisions before a decision is made. These issues were not considered by the Court.

In another case, three NGOs (Biom, Sun, and Green Action) filed a joint lawsuit against the opinion of the Ministry for Environmental Protection and Energy that it was not necessary to carry out an EIA screening procedure for the changes to the existing project of the wind power plant Senj. The opinion was not publicly accessible, but it was provided to the NGOs upon their request submitted to the Ministry. In their lawsuit contesting the Ministry's decision, they alleged a breach of the right of the public concerned to access information and participate in the process. The application to alter the project was not disclosed to the public, nor was the Ministry's final opinion made public. Moreover, the Ministry did not inform the public about access to judicial review procedures as Article 9(5) of the Aarhus Convention required. The first instance administrative court dismissed their lawsuit, and the HAC rejected their appeal without addressing their claims of Aarhus Convention violations.[53]

Another crucial aspect to consider is that the Constitutional Court failed to consider the Aarhus Convention in a constitutional case initiated by an NGO, Green Action. The case involved their lawsuit against the decision of the Ministry of Environmental Protection and Nature to approve the EIA and grant an environmental permit for the Plomin Thermal Power Plant reconstruction project. This case highlighted the inability of the public concerned to challenge the project's compliance with spatial planning documentation, an issue that the CCRC disregarded.[54]

VII. Conclusion

To answer the question posed in the title of this chapter, the door to access to justice in environmental matters is partially open in Croatia, and barriers still exist. The main legislative and practical problems hampering access to justice in environmental matters concern the poor transposition of Article 9 of the Aarhus Convention into the EPA. The situation regarding the recognition of legal interest to claimants has led to the absurd situation that access to justice is easier according to the general provisions of the ADA relating to the initiation of an administrative dispute than according to the special provisions of the EPA. The EPA has made some progress in improving access to certain procedures for environmental NGOs, although not all procedures are accessible to them.

Furthermore, special laws (eg, the Building Act, the Spatial Planning Act and other legislative acts with provisions concerning inspections) do not permit or

[53] Judgment of the HAC Usž-409/19-6 of 8 May 2020.
[54] Decision of the CCRC U-II/5942/2013 of 18 June 2019.

excessively limit the involvement of the public concerned in decision-making, even when the issue directly affects their rights and legal interests. Members of the public concerned cannot dispute the decisions adopted on the basis of these special laws, as they are not granted the right to participate.

The first logical step in improving the legal framework regarding the implementation of Article 9 of the Aarhus Convention is to remove all the provisions from the EPA and the special laws that contravene it. Despite the authors' active participation in public consultations and their advocacy for alignment with the Aarhus Convention, the legislator has thus far ignored recommendations for improving the legal framework.

The failure of judges of the administrative courts to apply the Aarhus Convention points to the need to implement educational programmes as part of their continual professional development. These educational programmes should cover not only the Aarhus Convention but also other important topics within EU environmental law (eg, EIA, SEA and appropriate assessment). It is also essential not to overlook the ongoing training of civil servants responsible for making decisions in environmental issues, as the quality of their decisions can help prevent the initiation of administrative disputes. Moreover, it is imperative for the Republic of Croatia to carefully consider and address the critiques outlined by the European Commission in the Environmental Implementation Review Reports, particularly those pertaining to the implementation of the Aarhus Convention.

6

The Implementation of the Aarhus Convention in the Republic of North Macedonia

Limited Tools and Capacity for Environmental Justice

FROSINA ANTONOVSKA JOSKOSKA AND KONSTANTIN BITRAKOV

I. The National Context

The Republic of North Macedonia (hereinafter 'North Macedonia') has a diverse topography with rivers surrounded by high mountains and deep gorges, as well as big and small natural lakes, which makes it a biodiversity hotspot in Europe,[1] and the home of natural resources of regional and global importance.[2] Its climate differs greatly across specific areas.[3] With the processes of industrialisation and urbanisation, the rural areas were abandoned to a great extent, – ie, there was and still is a significant migration towards the cities.[4] Despite its relatively small territory, rich biodiversity and an abundance of sunny days (ie, solar energy potential),[5] the country finds decoupling growth from environmental

[1] Ministry of Environment and Physical Planning, 'Third National Climate Change Communication' [2014], 11.

[2] Ministry of Environment and Physical Planning, 'National Strategy for Nature Protection 2017–2027' [2018], 13.

[3] Ministry of Environment and Physical Planning, 'National Biodiversity Strategy and Action Plan for the Period 2018–2023', Skopje [2018], 19.

[4] Ministry of Environment and Physical Planning, 'Strategy for Environment and Climate Change 2014–2020' [2015], 8.

[5] 'North Macedonia Pioneering Energy Transition in the Western Balkans' (*Just Transition*, 19 January 2021), www.just-transition.info/north-macedonia-pioneering-energy-transition-in-the-western-balkans/#:~:text=share%3A,solar%20radiation%20per%20square%20metre.

degradation challenging. The biggest environmental concern remains air quality, with Skopje being the second most polluted capital city in Europe in 2022.[6]

Consequently, environmental awareness among citizens, as well as environmental action, is mainly related to cases of air pollution, particularly during winter, when urban areas face the highest concentrations of polluting substances.[7] The most significant mass air pollution demonstrations took place in the winter of 2019,[8] when citizens supported by around 30 civil society organisations (CSOs) marched for clean air. This was followed by protests against the import of waste during the same winter at the end of January.[9]

However, the increase in environmental awareness and activism on environmental issues of national or wider concern are mostly limited to the younger population, who follow the global trends and raise their voices. Thus, although North Macedonia is identified as a country that is particularly vulnerable to climate change and extreme climate events,[10] the most vocal public climate-related action was the one led by the students of the local branch of Fridays for Future.[11] More significantly, successful and massive mobilisation remains at a local level in cases of demonstrations against particular industrial operators,[12] small hydropower development[13] or plans for new mining activities.[14]

[6] Statista, www.statista.com/statistics/1220938/most-polluted-capital-cities-in-europe/#:~:text=Sarajevo%20was%20the%20most%20polluted,guidelines%20by%20roughly%20six%20times.

[7] State Air Quality Portal, https://air.moepp.gov.mk/?page_id=175.

[8] G Konev, 'Илјадници граѓани од цела Македонија го кренаа гласот за чист воздух на најголемиот еколошки протест досега' (Thousands of Citizens from Whole Macedonia Raised Their Voice for Clean Air at the Largest Ecological Demonstration Ever) (*Sakam da kazham*, 29 November 2019), https://sdk.mk/index.php/makedonija/iljadnitsi-gragani-od-tsela-makedonija-go-krenaa-glasot-za-chist-vozduh-na-najgolemiot-ekoloshki-protest-dosega.

[9] '[Фото] Граѓаните седнаа пред Собрание – бараат да се донесе забрана за увоз на отпад' ([Photo], Citizens Sat in Front of the Parliament – ~Requesting Ban for Waste Imports) (*Radio MOF*, 31 January 2020), www.radiomof.mk/foto-gragjanite-sednaa-pred-sobranie-baraat-da-se-donese-zakonot-za-uvoz-na-otpad/?fbclid=IwAR2X--6QbmX1hti-3UEb_yy9zrfAaZdlm3k_mSjWPAi-0SgXEbyuR-7JqRD0.

[10] Ministry of Environment and Physical Planning, '4th National Climate Change Communication', Skopje [2023], 14.

[11] 'Петоци за иднината Скопје: Ослободете ги средношколците два часа за да простестираат за својата иднина' (Fridays for Future Skopje: Release the High School Students for Two School Hours to Be Able to Demonstrate for Their Future) (*Fakulteti*, 19 September 2019), www.fakulteti.mk/news/19092019/petoci-za-idninata-skopje-oslobodete-gi-srednoshkolcite-dva-chasa-za-da-protestiraat-za-svojata-idnina.

[12] 'Во Кочани протест за загадување на воздухот од фабрика за хартија' (A Protest in Kochani Regarding the Air Pollution from Paper Factory) (*Kanal 5*, 12 August 2019), https://kanal5.com.mk/vo-kochani-protest-za-zagaduvanje-na-vozduhot-od-fabrika-za-hartija/a385391.

[13] S Naumovska, 'Протест против мали хидроцентрали на Кожуф: Ништо не знаевме додека не видовме багери' (Protest against Small Hydropower Plants in Kozhuf: We Didn't Know Anything Until We Saw the Machines) (*META*, 16 September 2023), https://meta.mk/protest-protiv-mali-hidrocentrali-na-kozhuf-nishto-ne-znaevme-dodeka-ne-vidovme-bageri.

[14] Z Dagzovska Spasovska, 'Струмичани на протест поради Иловица, како што го нарекоа, "рудникот на смртта"' (People from Strumica Protesting against Ilovica, as They Called it, 'the Mine of the Death') (*Slobodna Evropa*, 15 July 2023) www.slobodnaevropa.mk/a/strumichani-na-protest-poradi-kako-shto-go-narekoa-rudnikot-na-smrtta-/32504769.html.

The last Environmental Performance Review conducted by the United Nations Economic Commission for Europe (UNECE) assessed that the civil society lacks awareness of the availability of environmental information and procedures to access it, and that effective public participation procedures are largely underdeveloped and not aligned with the provisions of the Convention on Access to Information, Public Participation in Decision-Making and Access to Justice in Environmental Matters (hereinafter 'the Aarhus Convention').[15] It acknowledged that access to justice in environmental matters has been promoted in the past decade, but mostly as a project-based activity to develop the capacity of the judiciary and CSOs.[16] Human capacity, knowledge and expertise among the governmental authorities, the judiciary and independent review bodies as a prerequisite for effective access to justice in environmental matters to be achieved is still insufficient.[17]

A. The Judicial System and Administrative Disputes

The implementation of the Aarhus Convention in North Macedonia is predetermined by the specifics of the national context with regard to the regulations and institutional set-up, namely the organisation of the judiciary and the judicial review of administrative acts, as well as the relevant public (administrative) authorities in the field of environmental protection.

The judiciary is comprised of the following courts: 27 basic courts (which are courts of first instance) that deal with civil and criminal matters, four appellate courts which decide on appeals against the decisions of the basic courts, an Administrative Court that decides on administrative disputes, a Higher Administrative Court that decides on appeals against the decisions of the Administrative Court and, finally, a Supreme Court that decides primarily on extraordinary legal remedies. The judicial system is set up in accordance with Articles 98–105 of the Constitution and is further regulated by law.[18] North Macedonia also has its own Constitutional Court, although this is not considered part of the judicial system per se,[19] since it primarily decides on the constitutionality of laws and legality of bylaws. The Constitutional Court does so with a posteriori review of adopted laws and bylaws. The Constitutional Court is also competent to secure the enjoyment of human rights through the observance of the Constitution. However, the Constitution itself stipulates that the Constitutional

[15] United Nations Economic Commission for Europe, *Environmental Performance Reviews, North Macedonia, Third Review* (Geneva, United Nations, 2019) ECE/CEP/186, 104.

[16] ibid 108.

[17] ibid 129.

[18] Law on Courts, Official Gazette of the Republic of Macedonia No 58/06, 62/06, 35/08, 150/10, 83/18, 198/18 and Official Gazette of the Republic of North Macedonia No 96/19.

[19] M Risteska and E Shurkov, *The Transformative Role of the Macedonian Constitutional Court* (Sarajevo, Analitika – Center for Social Research, 2016) 8.

Court can only decide in cases relating to: freedom of belief, conscience, thought and public expression of thought, political association and activity, and equality (ie, prohibition of discrimination).[20]

Since North Macedonia has a specialised administrative judiciary which decides on administrative disputes against public (administrative) authorities, the respective courts (the Administrative Court and the Higher Administrative Court) have a vital role to play in the implementation of the Aarhus Convention. Judicial review is regulated by the Law on Administrative Disputes.[21] An individual or a legal person can file a lawsuit and initiate an administrative dispute against individual administrative acts and/or actions of the public authorities which affect his, her or its rights and legal interests. Administrative dispute can also be initiated for silence of the administration, ie, when a public authority has failed to comply with its obligation to adopt an individual administrative act within the legal deadline. In terms of standing, an administrative dispute can only be initiated if: (a) a public authority has adopted an individual administrative act or it has failed to do so in a timely manner;[22] and (b) this individual administrative act affects the party's rights and/or legal interests. However, the Law on Administrative Disputes allows organisations to file lawsuits when they need to protect the rights/interests of their members. This follows from the wording of Articles 20 and 21 of the Law on Administrative Disputes. Article 20, paragraph 1 defines the term 'plaintiff' in administrative disputes as follows:

> A plaintiff is a natural or legal person who believes that its right or legal interest has been violated by a final administrative act adopted in an administrative procedure, or in a misdemeanour procedure, as well as by the failure of the public body to act within the legally established deadline.

Article 21, paragraphs 2 and 3 provide that '[a] lawsuit for an administrative dispute can also be filed by a workers union organisation in the event that it considers that a certain administrative act is contrary to some right or direct interest of some of its members' and:

> In the event that a certain administrative act violates certain rights or interests of a natural person who is a member of an association which, according to its rules, is obliged to protect the rights and interests of its members, this association may, in coordination with that member and on their behalf initiate an administrative dispute against that administrative act.

Administrative disputes cannot be initiated against general legal acts (bylaws). Also, administrative disputes can be initiated primarily by persons who have been directly affected by the administrative act. Only exceptionally can administrative

[20] ibid 12.
[21] Official Gazette of the Republic of North Macedonia No 96/2019.
[22] This case is called 'silence of the administration'. If the party requests an individual administrative act from the public authority and the latter does not adopt it in a timely manner (within the deadlines set out by law), it is considered that the request has been denied. Therefore, the party may file a lawsuit.

disputes be initiated by a non-governmental organisation (NGO) as the plaintiff when the rights/interests of its members are infringed. The administrative dispute in North Macedonia is rights-based; if we refer to the distinction of objective and subjective administrative disputes, North Macedonia would fall into the group of countries which have the so-called subjective administrative dispute.[23] Yet, as is explained bellow, the rules for standing are more liberal for environmental matters.

Depending on the substantive laws and the types of individual administrative acts (decisions), in certain cases the party may be obliged to file an appeal and initiate the second instance administrative procedure before filing a lawsuit to the Administrative Court. Therefore, pre-trial review may or may not be mandatory. Article 14 of the Law on General Administrative Procedure[24] contains the following provisions:

- 'the party has the right to legal protection against every administrative action or real act[25] in accordance with law' (paragraph 1);
- 'against the first instance administrative acts the party has the right to appeal in cases established by law' (paragraph 2);
- 'against the administrative acts adopted in the second instance, as well as against the administrative acts adopted in first instance against which an appeal is not allowed, the party may initiate an administrative dispute' (paragraph 5).

Thus, two scenarios are possible: either the party can initiate an administrative dispute against a first instance administrative act (decision) or the party would first have to initiate a second instance administrative procedure by filing an appeal before the higher public (administrative) authority and only afterwards, if it is still not satisfied with the decision, would it be able to initiate an administrative dispute.

Once the administrative dispute starts, the Administrative Court has broad competences: it can review both procedural and substantive aspects, and it can also review whether the public authorities have determined the facts of the case correctly. In terms of its judgment, the Administrative Court can: (a) nullify the administrative act (decision) at hand and oblige the public (administrative) authority to adopt a new one, this time having in mind the Court's instructions; or (b) decide in *pleine jurisdiction*, meaning that its judgment will replace the

[23] For this distinction, see I Vezmar Barlek, 'Korelacija subjektivnog I objektivnog upravnog spora' (Correlation between Subjective and Objective Administrative Disputes) (2021) 42(2) *Zbornik radova Pravnog fakulteta Sveučilišta u Rijeci* (Proceedings of the Faculty of Law, University of Rijeka) 509.

[24] Official Gazette of the Republic of Macedonia No 124/2015.

[25] According to the definition in the Law on General Administrative Procedure of North Macedonia, a real act is an act or action of the public authority that is not an administrative act or an administrative agreement, which may have a legal effect on the rights, obligations or legal interests of a person, such as public information, receiving statements, keeping records, issuing certificates, enforcement actions and other factual actions.

administrative act (decision) and the Administrative Court shall decide on the merits of the case. The Administrative Court can also decide in *pleine juridiction* in cases of silence of the administration. In fact, as per the Macedonian Law on Administrative Disputes, the Administrative Court should always decide in *pleine juridiction* (Article 60, paragraph 1) with only one exception: the Administrative Court can reach cassation judgments (nullify the administrative acts) only in cases where the public (administrative) authority adopted a discretionary act or the nature of the case is such that deciding in *pleine juridiction* is not possible – that is, if the Administrative Court cannot fully determine the facts on the essential issues and the actual factual situation should be determined in the administrative procedure. In other words, the Administrative Court will reach cassation judgments only when deciding in *pleine jurisdiction* is not possible.

According to the Law on Administrative Disputes (Article 11), all administrative disputes must be resolved in a reasonable amount of time, no later than nine months from the delivery of the files (necessary to reach a judgment) or from the creation of conditions for decision-making after the lawsuit.

There is no specialisation in environmental matters. The Administrative Court does not have specialised departments for cases relating to the environment.

B. The Relevant Public (Administrative) Authorities in the Field of Environmental Protection at Various Levels

Several public (administrative) authorities play an essential role in the field of environmental protection. The Ministry of Environment and Physical Planning (MOEPP) is the key administrative authority for environmental protection. It monitors the environment, develops policies for the protection of the environment, water, soil, air etc, as well as for waste management and spatial planning. It also develops the legislation for the respective matters.

As a body within the MOEPP, the State Environmental Inspectorate carries out inspection supervision in the area of the environment (as per the Law on Environmental Inspection).[26] Inspection supervision in the area of environment is also carried out by municipal environmental inspectors (employees of the units of local self-government). The competences of the central and local inspectors are divided by the respective law; however, the law foresees the possibility for their cooperation in order to ensure coverage on the whole territory, as well as more effective control. At the same time, in order for the State Environmental Inspectorate to perform its tasks effectively, collaboration with the Ministry of Interior (police), the Customs Administration and the Public

[26] Official Gazette of the Republic of North Macedonia No 99/2022.

Prosecution, among other institutions, is necessary, bearing in mind the different competences.

The Environment Administration is also a body within the MOEPP. It performs technical expert tasks relating to the environment and the implementation of environmental legislation. For instance, it issues environmental permits, monitors the state of the environment, runs the Cadastre for Environment and the Register of Pollutants and Polluting Substances, conducts environmental impact assessment procedures and more.

Municipalities also have competences in policy planning, implementation and monitoring at the local level; however, they still rely heavily on the central capacity of the MOEPP. As stated earlier, they also have the obligation to assign their municipal environmental inspectors.

II. The EU Accession Process

North Macedonia has been an official candidate country for accession to the EU) since 2005.[27] Currently, North Macedonia is in the first phase of the negotiation process when the analytical review of the EU *acquis* by the Commission is conducted (screening process).[28] Clusters have not been opened yet.

In reference to the country's progress in the area of the Environment (Chapter 27), the latest report of the European Commission from October 2022 states:

> The country has some level of preparation in this area. Some progress was made in nature protection and in climate change, including by the preparation and adoption of the management plan for Galichica National Park. However, implementation remains a concern in all sectors. The country needs to considerably step-up ambitions regarding the green transition, notably in the context of the Green Agenda for the Western Balkans. In the coming year, North Macedonia should in particular: (a) accelerate efforts for the reduction of air pollution at the local and national level and the reduction of point and diffuse pollution of freshwater resources; (b) enforce measures to establish a regional waste management system, in particular in the East and Northeast regions; (c) implement the Paris Agreement, including by adopting a climate law, consistent with the EU 2030 framework.[29]

[27] www.consilium.europa.eu/en/policies/enlargement/republic-north-macedonia/#:~:text=North%20Macedonia%20applied%20for%20EU,North%20Macedonia%20in%20July%20202.

[28] European Commission, 'North Macedonia 2022 Report Accompanying the Document Communication from the Commission to the European Parliament, the Council, the European Economic and Social Committee and the Committee of the Regions, 2022 Communication on EU Enlargement policy', SWD (2022) 337 final, 3, available at: https://neighbourhood-enlargement.ec.europa.eu/document/download/48ba61f0-41ae-4cff-9517-29fac190f4bd_en?filename=North%20Macedonia%20Report%202022.pdf.

[29] ibid.

North Macedonia has continuously undertaken steps to align with the EU environmental *acquis*. Some of the main measures derive from the implementation of the National Programme for adoption of the Acquis Communautaire.[30] In this regard, the latest progress was achieved with the adoption of the Law on Air Quality amendments from 2021 which aligned the clean air legislation with Directive 2008/50/EC, widely known as the CAFE (Clean Air For Europe) Directive, the newly adopted waste management legislation (comprising six new laws transposing the EU waste legislation), the adopted amendments to the Law on Environment with regards to the identification and remediation of contaminated sites, and the adoption of the first specific Law on Environmental Inspection. Several pieces of legislation have been drafted and are currently undergoing the governmental legislative procedure, including the Draft Amendments to the Law on Waters, the Draft Law on Climate Action and the Draft Law on Industrial Emissions.[31]

Currently, the new Law on Nature Protection, Law on Cross-Border Trade of Endangered Species (implementing the Convention on International Trade in Endangered Species of Wild Fauna and Flora, known as CITES), as well as new Amendments to the Law on Environment with regard to the further alignment with the latest EU amendments on the EIA procedure are being drafted. The country also adopted numerous secondary legislative acts transposing different EU measures in the field of waters and waste management.

On the other hand, one of the high points in the environmental efforts in the past couple of years has been the aspiration towards and focus on nature conservation activities, which resulted in more sites achieving the status of protected natural areas.[32]

Most of the practical implementation of the obligations deriving from Chapter 27 is achieved through the Instrument for Pre-Accession Assistance[33] programme for environment, which mainly supports projects in the areas of waste-water treatment, waste management infrastructure and air-quality monitoring.

The key reform in order to address the prevention of environmental degradation and improve compliance with the environmental legislation was the increase of fines for environmental misdemeanours, leading to fines that were 20 times higher than those envisaged by the general misdemeanours fine policy.

[30] The National Programme for Adoption of the Acquis Communautaire (NPAA) is a comprehensive long-term document that defines the dynamic of the adoption of the Acquis Communautaire, strategic guidelines, policies, reforms, structures, resources and deadlines to be realised by the Republic of Macedonia to fulfil the requirements for European Union membership.

[31] Drafts available can be accessed at the governmental portal for public consultations (www.ener.gov.mk) or at the Ministry of Environment and Physical Planning website (www.moepp.gov.mk).

[32] Nature Department at the Ministry of Environment and Physical Planning, www.moepp.gov.mk/ministerstvo/organi-sostav/sektor-priroda.

[33] The means by which the EU has been supporting reforms in the enlargement region with financial and technical assistance since 2007.

III. Implementation of Article 9 of the Aarhus Convention

A. National Legislation and Ratification of the Aarhus Convention

The Aarhus Convention became part of national legislation with the adoption of the Law on Ratification of the Aarhus Convention in 1999.[34] North Macedonia accepts monism in terms of ratified international conventions, meaning that all international agreements ratified in accordance with the Constitution become a part of the internal legal order. Since they have to be ratified in accordance with the Constitution, they would have to be compliant with it. Once ratified, these international agreements cannot be amended by law, which means that they have supremacy over national laws and can be implemented directly by courts and public authorities. Further transposition of the obligations deriving from the Aarhus Convention is prescribed within the Law on Environment as well as in the Decree on the methods and procedure of providing access to environmental information.

With regard to the general environmental policy, the relevant provisions on environmental protection are contained in the Constitution, and the general and special laws:

- the right to a healthy environment is promulgated in the Constitution (Article 43);
- the Law on Environment is a general (framework) legislation for environmental protection.[35]

The special laws regulate the different environmental fields and media, such as air quality, nature protection, noise pollution, waste management and its waste streams.[36]

[34] Official Gazette of the Republic of Macedonia No 40/99.

[35] Official Gazette of the Republic of Macedonia Nos 53/05, 81/05, 24/07, 159/08, 83/09, 48/10, 124/10, 51/11, 123/12, 93/13, 187/13, 42/14, 44/15, 129/15, 192/15, 39/16 and Official Gazette of the Republic of North Macedonia Nos 89/22 and 171/22.

[36] Law on Ambient Air Quality (Official Gazette of the Republic of Macedonia Nos 67/2004, 92/2007, 35/2010, 47/2011, 59/2012, 163/2013, 10/2015, 146/2015 and Official Gazette of the Republic of North Macedonia No 151/2021), Law on Nature Protection (Official Gazette of the Republic of Macedonia Nos 67/2004, 14/2006, 84/2007, 35/2010, 47/2011, 148/2011, 59/2012, 13/2013, 163/2013, 27/2014, 41/2014, 146/2015, 39/2016, 63/2016, 113/2018 and Official Gazette of the Republic of North Macedonia Nos 151/2021 and 99/2022), Law on Noise Protection (Official Gazette of the Republic of Macedonia Nos 79/2007, 124/2010, 47/2011, 163/2013 and 146/2015 and Official Gazette of the Republic of North Macedonia No 151/2021) and other laws.

B. Access to Information, Public Participation and Access to Justice in Environmental Matters

i. Access to Information in Environmental Matters

The Aarhus Convention provisions on access to environmental information are transposed in the Law on Environment, specifically in Articles 51–55, while the provisions for dissemination are transposed in Articles 56–57. Accordingly, everyone has the right, without the need to prove his or her interest, to request validated data and information on environmental matters. If a request for access to information is denied, the party has both administrative and judicial protection guaranteed. In a wider context, the access to environmental information is also regulated with the open data laws, ie, the Law on Using Public Sector Data.[37] According to this law, institutions should publish the data they create in an open format (machine-readable format). This also covers environmental data.

ii. Public Participation in Environmental Matters

The Law on Environment contains several provisions related to the public participation in decisions on specific activities. The public has the right to participate in the preparation of plans (Article 61, Article 69), strategic assessments (Article 66-a), environmental impact assessment studies (Article 91) etc. Specific procedures to ensure public participation are in place, such as an obligation to make relevant documentation publicly available and accessible, compulsory organisation of public debates and minimum periods of time for the provision of relevant contributions. Sometimes the affected public[38] has additional participation rights:

- according to Article 91 of the Law on Environment, whenever a project in another country might have an impact in North Macedonia, the MOEPP shall communicate with the respective authorities from that country and shall inform the relevant Macedonian institutions as well as the affected public how to participate in the procedure for environmental impact assessment;
- according to Article 102 of the Law on Environment, if the MOEPP assesses that an installation in another country might negatively impact the environment in North Macedonia, it shall immediately notify the relevant authorities from the respective country of the intention to participate in the permit procedure, and shall also inform the affected public in North Macedonia how to participate in the permit procedure for that installation;

[37] Official Gazette of the Republic of Macedonia No 27/2014.
[38] For the meaning of the term 'affected public' and the difference between it and the more generic term 'public' see nn 47 and 48 below.

- according to Article 103 of the Law on Environment, the affected public may request the investor who seeks a type A integrated permit to organise a public discussion in relation to the integrated permit and the investor must oblige;
- according to Article 136, the affected public has the right to provide comments and opinion to the MOEPP or the municipality regarding applications for adjustment permits with adjustment plans.[39]

iii. Access to Justice in Environmental Matters against General Legal Acts before the Administrative Judiciary

Neither appeals nor lawsuits can be submitted against general legal acts or omissions to adopt such acts by the public (administrative) authorities. A specific court decision from a few years ago addresses this issue., In 2019, citizens from multiple municipalities, represented by an NGO called the Centre for Legal Research and Analysis, filed a special legal remedy to the Administrative Court – the Proposal for protection from illegal activities. The Proposal for protection from illegal activities was a legal remedy prescribed in the old Law on Administrative Disputes from 2006.[40] Basically, under the old law, citizens could file such a proposal if their rights or liberties guaranteed in the Constitution were infringed by an administrative action and there was no other legal protection. Citizens filed these proposals against the government, the MOEPP, and the State Environmental Inspectorate. In the proposals, they stated that their right to clean air had been infringed by an omission of the MOEPP and the government, since the MOEPP had not proposed and the government had not adopted a National Plan for Clean Air (a document that has to be adopted and enforced according to the air quality legislation). The Administrative Court dismissed these proposals,[41] stating that it can only decide in cases where rights/interests are affected by individual administrative acts or concrete actions by administrative servants. In the case at hand, according to the Administrative Court, the failure to adopt a National Plan for Clean Air is not a concrete administrative action, but rather a failure by the government to comply with its legal obligations and for this case the government is accountable only to the Parliament. A complaint against the decision of the Administrative Court was submitted to the Supreme Court. However, it was rejected. The Supreme Court found that the Administrative Court had interpreted the law properly.[42] Nowadays,

[39] Adjustment permits are obtained for installations existing prior to the applicable legislation, for the respective installations to be able to continue operating.

[40] Official Gazette of the Republic of Macedonia No 62/06, 27/08, 117/09, 150/10 and 171/10.

[41] Cases USPI-12/20, USPI-10/20, USPI-9/20, USPI 10/22, etc, all available at: http://www.vsrm.mk/wps/portal/central/sud/odluki/!ut/p/z1/04_Sj9CPykssy0xPLMnMz0vMAfIjo8zizdxNTAwsvA183ANCzQ0cfV0MPEIsvYwsjMz0C7IdFQH_rOQ-.

[42] Case USPIZH-8/23, available at: http://www.vsrm.mk/wps/portal/central/sud/odluki/!ut/p/z1/jY9BC4JAEIV_SwevzlC2WjchMMygQ6LNJTS21VhdWTf9-0l1CWppbm_43ns8IMiB2mKoRWFq1RZy0idiZxZ5HgY7TKJD6mO43-D2uIrnwZxB9gTwx4UI9I_fApA9PgOyVUQ-ewOWjBhISFW-5oZtuQgEkOZXrrl273p6V8Z0_dpBB8dxdIVSQnL3ohoHv1kq1RvIP0nomjTH21IOSTh7AJ01mvI!/

the legal remedy used – the proposal for protection from illegal activities – no longer exists. Therefore, one might conclude that citizens have no options to seek legal protection before the Administrative Court in cases such as this – ie, cases where public authorities fail to comply with their legal obligations (omissions to adopt general legal acts such as plans, rulebooks and programmes). This implies, in fact, that there is no judicial protection at all in cases where public authorities fail to comply with their legal obligations (in the environmental or any other area). This approach needs to be changed and the administrative judiciary should accept a different interpretation according to which the administrative judiciary can oblige public authorities to undertake actions to comply with their duties prescribed by law (for instance, to adopt plans when they have failed to do so or to implement certain measures for improvement of the air quality).[43] In fact, such interpretation would be in line with the latest Principled Position[44] of the Supreme Court from 8 October 2024.[45] Namely, the Supreme Court interpreted that: 'In exercising the right to a healthy environment, the provisions of the Law on Administrative Disputes are applied, which provide judicial protection from illegal acts and actions (or failed actions) that violate the constitutionally guaranteed rights and freedoms of man or citizen, when such specific judicial protection is not provided for by the Constitution or other laws.' Thus, the administrative judiciary should act upon lawsuits for failure to adopt bylaws which must be adopted in accordance to the law, as well as for all other actions of the public authorities which infringe the right to a healthy environment.

Discussing access to justice in environmental matters against general legal acts or omissions to adopt such acts by the authorities, the representative of the Centre for Legal Research and Analysis identified the general absence of will among the judiciary to deal with this topic as the main challenge.[46] This approach is inconsistent with the Aarhus Convention, specifically Article 9, paragraph 2. Alternatively, even if it is considered that Article 9, paragraph 2 is not applicable, paragraph 3 applies. Not adopting a bylaw which must be adopted is an omission by the public

p0/IZ7_6G4408K0LOHF70AUE15A8Q24D7=CZ6_6G4408K0LGPU70AMD0HT9J2826=LA0=Ejavax.portlet.action!searchAction==/#Z7_6G4408K0LOHF70AUE15A8Q24D7.

[43] For more arguments in this direction, see A Pavlovska Daneva and K Bitrakov '(Управно) судска заштита на правото на квалитетен амбиентален воздух' (Administrative Judicial Protection of the Right to Quality Ambient Air) (2021) 23 *Правен дијалог* (*Legal Dialogue*) 54, 64.

[44] A principled position is a type of an opinion adopted by the general session of the Supreme Court of North Macedonia (a session where all supreme justices participate) which clarifies how the Supreme Court should interpret laws in the future. As such, the principle positions are not *ex lege* obligatory for the lower courts, but it is prudent for them to respect them, since they might have their decisions annulled if they are not in line with the principle position of the Supreme Court.

[45] Principle Position from 8 October 2024, www.vsrm.mk/wps/wcm/connect/vsrm/3e0a123d-121c-4d36-8cab-4f9f08406926/%D0%9D%D0%90%D0%A7%D0%95%D0%9B%D0%95%D0%9D+%D0%A1%D0%A2%D0%90%D0%92++%D0%A1%D0%A3-03+%D0%B1%D1%80.+800-23+1.pdf?MOD=AJPERES&CACHEID=ROOTWORKSPACE.Z18_L8CC1J41L0B520APQFKICD0CU3-3e0a123d-121c-4d36-8cab-4f9f08406926-lpacrVh.

[46] Interview with Zharko Hadzi Zafirov, Centre for Legal Analysis (Skopje, North Macedonia, 19 December 2023).

authority. According to Article 9, paragraph 3, members of the public should have access to administrative or judicial procedures to challenge acts and omissions by private persons and public authorities which contravene provisions of the national law related to the environment. Since an administrative procedure does not exist – ie, citizens cannot initiate administrative procedure to review the omission of a ministry or the government to adopt a bylaw which must be adopted – there is no judicial protection.

Certainly, a general legal act may be disputed, once adopted, before the Constitutional Court if it is deemed unconstitutional. However, this does not help citizens in those cases where the general legal act is not unconstitutional, but merely one of low quality or altogether missing.

iv. Access to Justice in Environmental Matters against Individual Administrative Acts (Decisions) before the Administrative Judiciary

In reference to the access to justice in environmental matters against individual administrative acts (decisions), the rules for standing are a bit broader than the general rules from the Law on Administrative Disputes (Articles 20 and 21) presented above. Namely, as per the Law on Environment, the *public*[47] and the *affected public*[48] – which includes citizens' associations – have the right to file appeals against certain decisions (administrative acts). These appeals are filed with the State Commission for administrative proceedings and employment proceedings in the second instance. Clearly, even though this is not explicitly stipulated in the Law on Environment, the second instance decisions adopted by this State Commission on the appeals will be subject to judicial review in an administrative dispute. The decisions (administrative acts) against which the public and the affected public can file appeals are listed in several articles of the Law on Environment, for example:

- the public may file an appeal against the decision to implement or not to implement a strategic assessment on a planning document's impact on the environment and human health which is adopted by the authority preparing the respective planning document (Article 65, paragraphs 5, 6 and 11);
- the affected legal and natural persons, as well as NGOs founded to protect and advance the environment may file an appeal against the MOEPP's decision that

[47] According to the Law on Environment (art 5, para 1, item 25), the term 'public' means one and/or more legal and/or natural persons and organisations and associations of citizens established in accordance with the law.

[48] According to the Law on Environment (art 5, para 1, item 26), the term 'affected public' covers the public which is affected at the moment, or which may be affected in the future, or has an interest related to a certain environment related decision. The term 'affected public' also covers the NGOs founded for protection and advancement of the environment, as well as the natural persons who are likely to feel the consequences of a certain decision.

the investor of a certain project must perform a strategic assessment on the project's impact on the environment (Article 81);

- the affected legal and natural persons, as well as NGOs founded to protect and advance the environment, may file an appeal against the MOEPP's decision to give consent or reject the request for implementation of a project, which is adopted on the basis of the previous strategic assessment, the public debates and the received opinions in accordance with the law (Article 89, paragraph 1 in relation to Article 87);
- the affected legal and natural persons, as well as NGOs founded to protect and advance the environment, may file an appeal against the MOEPP's or the municipality's decision to issue an integrated permit (Article 108 for a type A integrated permit and Article 126 for a type B integrated permit)[49] etc.

Thus, in environmental matters, the rules on standing in administrative disputes are more liberal; in certain cases, the plaintiff does not need to prove the direct link between the decision (administrative act) and his or her rights/interests. Since the public and the NGOs have the right to appeal certain decisions, they also have to right to initiate an administrative dispute in cases when their appeals are rejected and/or dismissed. The NGOs do not need to prove that the persons affected by the appealed decision are their members.

The fee to file a lawsuit to the Administrative Court is less than €10.[50] Parties should not be discouraged to file lawsuits due to the fear that they will have to cover the other party's costs if they lose the case, since Article 15, paragraph 3 of the Law on Administrative Dispute provides: 'If the Court rejects or dismisses the lawsuit or the proceedings are stopped, each party shall bear its own costs in the proceedings.'

The Law on Free Legal Aid[51] is also quite liberal when it comes to primary legal aid (legal consultations) allowing NGOs, legal clinics at universities and the Ministry of Justice to provide it. The so-called secondary legal aid (being represented by an attorney) is only limited for persons in an unfavourable financial situation.

The appeals against the decisions (administrative acts) have suspensive effect, while lawsuits do not. This rule is applicable to all cases,[52] including environmental

[49] Both types of integrated permits are defined in the Law on Environmental Protection.

[50] For more information on judicial fees, see: http://www.vsrm.mk/wps/wcm/connect/usskopje/efde75ff-eda3-4f50-8a4b-e3e7829d5db5/%D0%98%D0%9D%D0%A4%D0%9E%D0%A0%D0%9C%D0%90%D0%A6%D0%98%D0%88%D0%90+%D0%92%D0%9E+%D0%92%D0%A0%D0%A1%D0%9A%D0%90+%D0%A1%D0%9E+%D0%A1%D0%A3%D0%94%D0%A1%D0%9A%D0%98%D0%A2%D0%95+%D0%A2%D0%90%D0%9A%D0%A1%D0%98.pdf?MOD=AJPERES&CACHEID=ROOTWORKSPACE.Z18_L8CC1J41L088F0A1K8MT8K06H7-efde75ff-eda3-4f50-8a4b-e3e7829d5db5-lnExqgx.

[51] Official Gazette of the Republic of North Macedonia No 101/2019.

[52] Lawsuits have suspensive effect only in misdemeanour cases, where fines or other sanctions have been imposed by a public (administrative) authority. If that decision is disputed before the Administrative Court, the lawsuit has suspensive effect.

cases. However, the Law on Administrative Disputes allows the plaintiff to submit a request for suspensive effect of the challenged act if the execution of the decision might result in damage which would be difficult to compensate and the suspension is not contrary to the public interest (Article 28).

The administrative courts have the possibility to review both procedural and substantive (il)legality in cases related to environmental matters. The decision can also be in *pleine juridiction*, but it is highly unlikely that such judgments will often be reached. The logic behind the courts' reluctance to decide in *pleine jurisdiction* is simple. As explained above, the administrative courts shall not decide in *pleine jurisdiction* if the nature of the case does not allow decision-making in full jurisdiction – that is, if the court cannot fully determine the facts on the essential issues and the actual factual situation should be determined in the administrative procedure. Since environmental cases are quite complex and the administrative courts do not have the necessary expertise, making it difficult to determine the facts of the case, it is reasonable to assume that the court would opt for a cassation judgment and send the case back to the public authorities. Of course, courts may use expert witnesses, but preparing expert testimonies would take a considerable amount of time, while the courts must decide in a reasonable amount of time (as per Article 11 of the Law on Administrative Disputes explained above), since the deadlines in administrative disputes are the same for all cases (ie, the deadlines are not longer in environmental cases).

v. Access to Justice in the Cases of Failure to Fulfil Obligations for Environmental Protection before the Regular Courts Deciding on Civil Matters

There are no significant cases before the regular courts (ordinary courts) deciding on civil matters that address the failure of the authorities to fulfil environmental obligations. Thus far, there have only been sporadic attempts by NGOs, which are also still developing their environmental capacities, to instigate strategic litigation cases. One example is the *case of BN and Macedonian Young Lawyers Association (MYLA) v Government of North Macedonia and Others*, a lawsuit claiming that the state's failure to fulfil its obligations regarding limiting the values of PM concentrations in the ambient air is a violation of human rights. The Skopje Basic Court rejected the lawsuit, highlighting that Article 9 of the Aarhus Convention guarantees access to justice with regard to the right to access public information or the right to public participation in the decision-making process, but not for the cases of violation of the right to health and other rights invoked in the claim.[53] The Skopje Appeal Court confirmed this ruling with an exception allowing the extraordinary remedy of a revision with the Supreme Court of North Macedonia, as it determined that the lawsuit raises legal questions important for ensuring

[53] Decision P4 No 578/19, 22.

a unified application of the law; however, the Supreme Court too rejected the plaintiffs' claim.[54]

In a similar claim submitted by AD and MYLA, the plaintiffs requested that the Basic Court in Struga determines that the existence and operation of the non-compliant municipal landfill in Struga violates the right to a healthy environment, and obliges the Ministry of Environment, local and communal authorities to take specific measures related to landfilling of waste at the current location and its remediation thereof. The court dismissed the claim stating that the plaintiffs did not ask for a determination of a specific right or legal relation, but instead requested a determination of facts, which was not within its authority.[55]

The key challenges identified by the above-mentioned CSO[56] with regard to their strategic litigation processes were the length of the proceedings, the lack of capacities within the judiciary in addressing environmental claims, as well as the costs and limited availability of experts and scientific institutions for expert testimonies. The missing explicit determination of competences in the judiciary on environmental matters (the unclear division between the civil and administrative courts), sustained by the general absence of will among the judiciary to deal with this topic, especially its substantial aspects, has emerged as a significant obstacle to access to justice.

vi. Alternative Dispute Resolution (ADR) in Environmental Matters

There are no ADR mechanisms in environmental matters, with the exception of the commission for dispute resolution envisaged in Article 144 of the Law on Environment. This commission was intended to address any disputes with regard to the negotiations and agreements between the operators and the authorities on the content and timeframe for the implementation of the operational plans of the installations before obtaining integrated environmental permits. As per the law, these operational plans expired by 2019 and this ADR mechanism can now only be triggered for the large combustion plants with a capacity over 50 MW, which have a possibility to obtain additional period of time for implementation of their operational plans, but no later than 2026.

IV. Conclusions

The overall lack of knowledge and capacity to address the enforcement of environmental legislation of the executive, but even more so the judiciary, has resulted in

[54] A Dangova Hug, 'Barriers to Access to Justice in North Macedonia for Violations of Human Rights in the Context of Air Pollution' (2024) 9(1) *Business and Human Rights Journal* 183.

[55] https://myla.org.mk/49488.

[56] Interview with Jasna Arangelovik, the Macedonian Young Lawyers Association (Skopje, North Macedonia, 19 December 2023).

a serious gap in the implementation of the responsibilities under Article 9 of the Aarhus Convention. The key challenges are: legal inconsistencies, lack of capacity within the judiciary in terms of addressing environmental claims, high costs and limited availability of experts and scientific institutions for expert testimonies in cases before the regular courts deciding in civil cases, missing explicit determination of competences in the judiciary on environmental matters, and, finally, a general absence of will among the judiciary to deal with this topic.

The impacts of the EU's actions, such as the support of the establishment of the Public Communications Office of the competent Ministry two decades ago or the aid provided to CSOs for their efforts to bring the Convention closer to the citizens, are limited.

Regardless of the slow progress, it is certain that actions like these are gradually opening the door towards enabling effective access to justice in environmental matters and provoking some individual interests within the judiciary. However, a systemic approach in establishing the necessary capacity building is still not foreseen and is far from being implemented.

7

The Aarhus Convention in Romania

Challenges Regarding Access to Justice and Actio Popularis

GHEORGHE-SORIN LODOABĂ-CORDON, DACIAN C DRAGOS AND BOGDANA NEAMȚU

I. National Context and Background

Within Central and Eastern Europe's former communist countries, Romania stands out for its notable legislative advancements in regulating openness and transparency within the public administration. However, despite initial state-of-the-art legislation, its practical implementation raises various challenges. These challenges are primarily manifested by weak administrative capacity and expertise, particularly at the local and rural levels, and a prevalent sense of citizen apathy. Consequently, the public exerts little significant pressure upon authorities to enhance transparency and openness. Compounding these inefficiencies creates a deep-rooted distrust in the justice system, leading to a limited number of legal challenges being pursued against illegitimate administrative decisions.

The Romanian judiciary system is structured into four levels: the district courts, the tribunals, the appeal courts, the High Court of Cassation and Justice, and a separate constitutional court. Starting with tribunals, each court has a specialised unit ('section') that deals with administrative law matters. The laws establishing procedural rules are the Administrative Code[1] and Law No 554/2004.[2] The competence of the courts is split in first instance between the tribunal and the appeal court. The tribunal rules over complaints regarding administrative acts issued by the local public administration and, in cases regarding taxes, contributions, customs duties and accessories to these taxes, up to three million RON.[3] The other issues, comprising administrative acts of the central public authorities and

[1] Emergency Ordinance No 57/2019, Official Journal of Romania (2019) DLV.
[2] Law on Administrative Judicial Review, No 554/2004, Official Journal of Romania (2004) MCLIV.
[3] €600,000 (€1 = ~ 5 RON).

taxes over three million RON, are heard by the specialised chambers of the appeal courts.

Most environmental cases are heard by tribunals as courts of first instance. The majority of applications are for the annulment of administrative acts. The number of cases involving environmental protection has been growing in the past five years, illustrating the enhanced involvement of non-governmental organisations (NGOs) and other groups in the administrative decision-making process. Nonetheless, the specific aspect of NGOs taking an active stance is more nuanced. For example, appeals in response to decisions following public information requests constitute only about seven per cent of all environmental case filings.[4] This suggests that while NGOs are increasingly involved in environmental matters, their direct engagement in litigation related to accessing information remains relatively limited.

At the administrative level, the main body governing and overseeing implementation is the Environment, Waters and Forests Ministry.[5] This establishes the national public policy on the environment, green economy, biodiversity, protected natural areas and climate change, and elaborates its implementation strategy and regulations. Several organisations function either in coordination with the Ministry or as its subordinates. The National Administration of Romanian Waters and the Environment Fund Administration coordinate with the Environment Ministry. Directly under the Ministry or under its authority operate the National Meteorology Administration, ROMSILVA,[6] the National Environment Protection Agency, the Danube Delta Biosphere Reserve Administration, the National Environment Guard and several local Forestry Guards. Most of these organisations have county-level offices.

II. The Aarhus Convention in the National Legislation

Romania signed the Aarhus Convention on 25 June 1998 and ratified it through Law No 86/2000,[7] which entered into force on 11 July 2000. According to Article 11(2) of the Constitution, international treaties ratified by Romania are part of the national legal order. Thus, at least in theory, the Aarhus Convention's

[4] https://lege5.ro/App/Search?Mode=2&Search_SectionTypeId=28&did=hazdinrs&pid=ga&Search_Term=Or donan%C5%A3a%20de%20urgen%C5%A3%C4%83%20nr.%20195%2F2005%20privind%20protec%C5%A3ia%20mediului&Page=1&Rec=10&CollapseFilters=0&LFT=544.

[5] Article 1 of Decision No 43/2020 establishing the Environment, Waters and Forests Ministry, Official Journal of Romania (2020) LV.

[6] The National Forestry Registry.

[7] Law for the ratification of the Aarhus Convention, regarding access to information, public participation in decision-making procedure and access to justice in environmental matters, Official Journal of Romania (2000) CCXXIV, https://legislatie.just.ro/Public/DetaliiDocumentAfis/22438.

provisions have been directly applicable since its ratification. The main transposition work was finalised in 2005, with a few amendments made in the following years.[8] Since its initial implementation, there have been no notable changes in the legislative framework, but some amendments have been introduced under the obligation to transpose EU Directives. Chapter IV of Governmental Decision (GD) No 878/2005,[9] which has not changed since its adoption, is the only special provision regarding access to justice in environmental matters. The only notable innovation was the adoption of Law No 179/2022 on open data and the reuse of information in the public sector.[10] This creates an obligation for the administrative bodies to make all documents and information more accessible and easier to obtain. While this is a commendable legislative effort, based on the administration's previous history, there are few indications that its implementation will be effective.

The specificity of the Romanian legislative process is to resort to government emergency ordinances (GEOs) instead of laws adopted by the Parliament. GEOs are acts issued by the government with the same force as laws, which later need to be approved by the Parliament.[11] After Romania acceded to the EU on 1 January 2007, EU directives were also often transposed through GEOs. The perceived advantage in swiftness is paramount – the legislation is adopted more quickly and changes are easier to make. However, this results in legislative instability and a high probability that the GEO will be amended in Parliament after a couple of months or even years. In some cases, this leads to errors – when a critical act is changed, it is difficult to amend all the subsequent legislation, so deficiencies occur in practice.

III. The Effect of the European Integration Process on National Environmental Matters

Romania started the process of accession to the EU on 1 February 1993 when it signed the European agreements. In the following years, aligning the national legislative, administrative, and judicial systems with European values resulted in several reforms.

[8] Governmental Emergency Ordinance for changing and completing some normative acts regarding non-fiscal taxes and tariffs, Official Journal of Romania (2009) CDXLIV https://legislatie.just.ro/Public/DetaliiDocumentAfis/108212.

[9] Governmental Decision No 878/2005, regarding public access to environmental information, Official Journal of Romania (2005) DCCLX.

[10] Law Regarding Open and Reusable Public Data, Official Journal of Romania (2022) DLXXVII https://legislatie.just.ro/Public/DetaliiDocumentAfis/256414.

[11] DC Dragoş and B Neamtu, 'Mimicking Environmental Transparency: The Implementation of the Aarhus Convention in Romania' in R Caranta, A Gerbrandy and B Müller (eds), *The Making of a New European Legal Culture: the Aarhus Convention: At the Crossroads of Comparative Law and EU Law* (Groningen, Europa Law Publishing, 2017) 205.

Regarding environmental matters, initiating the EU accession negotiations in 1999 kick-started the legislative reform, forcing the Romanian legislator to implement and transpose several pieces of European legislation into the national legal order. At the same time, the legislator understood that in order to rise to the European standard, several other harmonisation measures had to be introduced. During the EU accession procedure, several new governmental ordinances were adopted in environmental areas, such as genetically modified organisms (GMOs), waste disposal, ozone layer protection and water quality.[12] The first reference to the Aarhus Convention's implementation can be found in the National EU Accession Programme.[13] Even though Romania signed the Convention on 25 June 1998 and ratified it in July 2000, as mentioned in the previous section, the initial implementation was just a simple translation.

The framework for the application of the Aarhus Convention was put forward in 2005 when Romania had to finalise the process of harmonisation prior to the European Parliament's Assent procedure. Along with GD No 878/2005, there was a revamping of the Environmental Protection Law of 1995 through the Government Emergency Ordinance No 195/2005 regarding Environmental Protection.[14] It is important to note that even in the explanatory memorandum, it is pointed out that the changes were made pursuant to 'the need for enforcing the commitments made in the European Integration process'. Another important aspect is that this legislation did not follow any standard legislative process as it was adopted through a special fast-track procedure that denotes the national legislator's tardiness. The same trend can be observed in other environmental issues, such as pollution,[15] protected natural areas[16] and aquaculture,[17] as well as in other areas within the European *acquis*.

Most of the time, the Romanian legislator is complacent in transposing European legislation or international agreements, but only if they are long overdue.

[12] Governmental Ordinance No 98/1999 concerning the trade regime and the implementation of restrictions on the use of halogenated hydrocarbons that deplete the ozone layer, Official Journal of Romania (1999) CDXXIII; Governmental Ordinance No 155/1999 for the implementation of waste management records and the European Waste Catalogue, Official Journal of Romania (1999) CXVIII; Order of the Minister of Waters, Forests and Environmental Protection No 166/1999 regarding the establishment of the Water Registry, Official Journal of Romania (1999) LXXI. Governmental Ordinance No 49/2000 concerning the regime for the acquisition, testing, use, and commercialization of genetically modified organisms through modern biotechnology techniques, as well as the products derived from them, Official Journal of Romania (2000) XLVIII.

[13] National European Union Accession Programme, Vol I, May 2000, 234 (Chamber of Deputies – Romanian Parliament), www.cdep.ro/comisii/integrare/pdf/2001/rd_pn2000.pdf.

[14] Governmental Emergency Ordinance No 195/2005 regarding Environmental Protection, Official Journal of Romania (2005) CXCV.

[15] Governmental Emergency Ordinance No 152/2005 regarding the prevention and integrated control of pollution, Official Journal of Romania (2005) MLXXVIII.

[16] Governmental Emergency Ordinance No 47/2007 regarding the regime of protected natural areas, the conservation of natural habitats, flora, and fauna, Official Journal of Romania (2007) CDXLII.

[17] Emergency Ordinance No 23/2008 regarding fishing and aquaculture, Official Journal of Romania (2008) CLXXX.

In the case of GEO No 195/2005 on Environmental Protection, once transposed, further changes have been made through other equivalent procedures, including adjusting the national legislation to European principles and the commitments made by Romania.[18] Some of these changes were made following the European Commission's notices regarding directive transpositions and compliance. While this could count as proper implementation, we cannot but underline that the legislator failed to promote environmental values unless forced by EU legal obligations.

IV. Access to Justice

Regarding access to justice, a distinction must be made between Law No 544/2001, the Romanian Freedom of Information Act (FOIA),[19] and GD No 878/2005 on access to environmental public information.[20] The first is the general (primary) law establishing free access to public information, and the second is a *lex specialis* (secondary law), which applies only to access to environmental information. As we will show in this chapter, the existence of two distinct rules does not bring about clarity in environmental cases, with claimants and courts often unsure as to which law should be applicable.[21]

The Law on Administrative Judicial Review No 554/2004 governs the general administrative procedure, establishing the rules governing complaints and judicial review.[22] The general procedure requires a pre-trial administrative review in the form of an appeal before the administrative body that issued the act or failed to do so or before the hierarchically superior body within 30 days from the moment of the communication of the decision or the expiration of the legal deadline for answering a request (30 days from the moment of registration). After lodging the appeal, the administration has another 30 days to respond to the complaint. If it fails to do so or offers an inadequate answer, the individual may lodge a subsequent complaint before a court of law. It is important to note that the administrative appeal is mandatory, but does not limit the scope of the judicial review in any way, with the claimant having the possibility of introducing new grounds of complaint before the court.

[18] Romania's commitments included increasing funding for environmental agencies, enhancing institutional capacity, developing harmonized environmental legislation, improving water pollution management, and achieving broader European environmental standards. See n 13 above.

[19] Freedom of Information Act regarding public information no 544/2001, Official Journal of Romania (2001) DCLXIII.

[20] Governmental Decision No 878/2005 (n 9).

[21] Dragoş and Neamtu (n 11).

[22] Law on Administrative Judicial Review No 554/2004, Official Journal of Romania (2004) MCLIV.

A. FOIA and the Standard of Sufficient Legitimate Interest

When the judicial review regards the refusal of access to information, the special judicial review provisions of the FOIA Law No 544/2001 apply. The applicant can be an individual, a company, an NGO or any other legal person, as the provisions in Law No 544/2001 do not differentiate between the different types of applicants. The judicial action is not conditional upon the completion of an appeal procedure before the administrative body which issued the act or refused to answer the request for public information. The administrative appeal is optional and does not have a suspensive effect on the deadline for lodging a complaint before the court of law.[23] Not wishing to discourage applicants from going before a court of law with an alleged breach of their rights to public sector information, Law No 544/2001 exempts such action from any court fees and stipulates that the proceedings should be expeditious (Article 22).

It is also possible for applicants who are dissatisfied with the public body's answer regarding access to public information to lodge a petition with the Ombudsman (the People's Advocate in Romania). The Romanian Ombudsman is a hybrid Ombudsman.[24] It is an autonomous body that reports only to the Parliament, independent of any other authority. In 2022, according to the annual report of the Ombudsman, around one per cent of the total petitions were related to the right to a healthy environment (116 complaints) and eight per cent on the issue of free access to public information (906 complaints).[25] In Romania, the Ombudsman is perceived, at least by citizens, as a last resort instance (although not an effective one) that can be approached when other venues are exhausted or when the deadlines applicable for certain court proceedings have expired.[26]

Governmental Decision No 878/2005 sets out an additional set of rules regarding the interpretation and implementation of the Aarhus Convention whilst creating more stringent conditions for access. The rules governing access to justice refer back to those from the general Law on Administrative Judicial Review No 554/2004. However, FOIA should be the *lex generalis* that governs the

[23] Thirty days from the moment when the rejection was communicated or from the expiration of the legal deadline for answering a request, which amounts to 10 or 30 days, depending on the complexity of the information requested – ibid.

[24] DC Dragoş, B Neamţu and D Balica, 'The Romanian Ombudsman and its Interaction with the Courts: An Exploratory Research' (2010) *Transylvanian Review of Administrative Sciences*, available at: https://rtsa.ro/tras/index.php/tras/article/download/180/176; DC Dragoş, B Neamtu and R Hamlin, 'Law in Action: Case Studies in Good Governance' (2011) *Institute for Public Policy and Social Research, Michigan State University*, available at: https://papers.ssrn.com/sol3/papers.cfm?abstract_id=2487973.

[25] R Weber, 'Romanian People's Advocate Annual Report 2022' (2023), available at: https://avp.ro/index.php/activitatea-avp/rapoarte-anuale.

[26] L Hossu and R Carp, 'A Critical Assessment of the Role of the Romanian Ombudsman in Promoting Freedom of Information' (2011) 7 *Transylvanian Review of Administrative Sciences*, available at: https://rtsa.ro/tras/index.php/tras/article/view/285; Dragoş, Neamtu and Hamlin (n 24).

procedural rules of GD No 878/2005, as it both regulates access to information, so therein lies a conundrum.

The first difference between the two laws (FOIA and Law on Judicial Review) is the obligatory nature of the administrative appeal. Law No 554/2004 imposes a pre-trial administrative appeal, but Law No 544/2011 does not. Suppose the claimant chooses GD No 878/2005 as the basis for its complaint. In that case, it will mean that according to Article 7 of Law No 554/2004, a lack of administrative appeal renders the claim inadmissible.[27] The only situation in which the appeal is not mandatory is when it is introduced by the Ombudsman or the Public Ministry (the Prosecutor's Office). However, the administrative appeal is optional if FOIA is chosen as the procedural legal ground. Given the difference in procedures and the beneficial timeline provided by the FOIA, all cases regarding access to information in environmental matters have been grounded on Law No 544/2001. Moreover, under Article 22 of the Civil Procedural Code, the Romanian courts can and often do change the legal grounds the parties chose to fit their actual request. So far, the courts have decided that any request for information, regardless of its source, must be ruled by the provisions of the FOIA if the ultimate objective of the claimant is to obtain public information.[28]

Another difference in substantive law between these two acts is the requirements for the claimant's standing.[29] GD No 878/2005 fails to properly translate Article 2, paragraph 5 of the Aarhus Convention, leaving out the most crucial aspect regarding NGOs – the fact that the interest in obtaining the information is presumed. Because of this legislative gap, under the provisions of Article 17 of GD No 878/2005, the NGO (and any other claimant) must prove that the improper response to the information request has breached some personal rights. This is inconsistent with the provision of Article 5 of GEO No 195/2005, where it is expressly stated that the sole requirement for an NGO to obtain standing is to explicitly state in its charter that environmental protection is its core mission.

On the other hand, the rules established by the FOIA, as *lex generalis*, are even more stringent, requesting the claimant to prove actual damages that were incurred alongside the rights that have been breached, which comes into direct conflict with the rules provided by GEO No 195/2005, creating unclear and contradictory provisions.

This led to inconsistent rulings of the national courts, with some cases being dismissed following the reasoning that a private entity must prove an individual private interest[30] and not just a general one, being unable to act on behalf of others, while in other cases, this issue was not even debated.[31] A notable decision in this

[27] Dragoş and Neamtu (n 11).
[28] Decision No 10/2018 (Timişoara Appeal Court).
[29] Dragoş and Neamtu (n 11).
[30] Decision No 121/2019 (Piteşti Appeal Court).
[31] Decision No 2091/2019 (Bucharest Appeal Court).

matter is a recent ruling of the High Court of Justice, which sets a powerful precedent by limiting the right of access to justice in the case of NGOs even more:

> As social bodies [such as NGOs] are private persons; their right to plead in administrative matters based on public interest is directly linked with and contingent on defending a legitimate private interest, as the latter follows from the idea of the former. When discussing legitimate interests for social organisms, the legislative body does not refer exclusively to public interest … therefore, if the social body is interested, the interest can only be of itself.[32]

Furthermore, comparing judgments from Decision No 977/2021[33] and Decision No 121/2019,[34] we can see that the courts additionally stated that the claimant did not prove any damage that it might have incurred as a result of the rejection of the public administration to provide the required information. There is a risk of imposing a true *probatio diabolica* on NGOs and other private entities, where not only do they have to find a personal private interest alongside the general public one but they also have to prove that they, as an entity, suffered losses from the refusal of the administration.

The final blow recently came from the Court of Justice of the European Union (CJEU). In the judgment delivered in 2024 in *Societatea Civilă Profesională de Avocați AB & CD*[35] the CJEU provided some clarification on the concept of *actio popularis* as applied in Romania and regarding the possible costs of an environmental case. The CJEU seems to favour, in part, the view of the Romanian Constitutional Court,[36] according to which the interest of an organisation that has another aim than the protection of the environment needs to be linked to a private legitimate interest or, at least, connected to a legal situation which is directly related to the aim of the entity.[37] The Court acknowledges that Romanian law grants general standing in environmental cases *only* to environmental non-governmental organisations (ENGOs):

> In environmental matters, an exception to the latter rule is laid down in Article 20(6) of OUG No 195/2005 for non-governmental organisations promoting environmental protection. That provision allows them to rely primarily on a legitimate public interest without being required to demonstrate a legitimate private interest.
>
> In the present case, the parties agree that the law firm partnership AB & CD, the applicant in the main proceedings, cannot be treated as such an environmental protection organisation and that, consequently, under national law, it falls within the category of

[32] Decision No 8/2020 regarding the review in the interest of law of art 1, para (1), art 2, para (1), let a), r) and s) and art 8, para (11) of (12) of Law No 554/2004 (High Court of Cassation and Justice).

[33] Decision No 977/2021 (High Court of Justice).

[34] Decision No 121/2019 (n 30).

[35] Case C-252/22 *Societatea Civilă Profesională de Avocați AB & CD v Consiliul Județean Suceava and Others* ECLI:EU:C:2024:13.

[36] Decision No 461/2021 regarding the constitutionality of art 2, para (1), let a), r) and s), art 8, para (11) and art 15, para (3) of Law No 554/2004 (Constitutional Court).

[37] *Societatea Civilă Profesională de Avocați AB & CD* (n 35) paras 46–47.

> applicants who have standing to bring proceedings only where they establish a legitimate private interest.

Consequently, the Court concluded that:

> Article 9(3) of the Convention on access to information, public participation in decision-making and access to justice in environmental matters, signed in Aarhus on 25 June 1998 and approved on behalf of the European Community by Council Decision 2005/370/EC of 17 February 2005, must be interpreted as not precluding national legislation under which a legal entity, other than a non-governmental organisation for the protection of the environment, is recognised as having standing to bring proceedings against an administrative measure of which it is not the addressee only where it claims that there has been a failure to observe a legitimate private interest or an interest connected to a legal situation which is directly related to the object of that entity.

The dispute in *Societatea Civilă Profesională de Avocați AB & CD* related to the interpretation of Article 2(4) and Article 9(3)–(5) of the Aarhus Convention on access to information, public participation in decision-making and access to justice in environmental matters. This judgment also applies to claims involving information requests because the administrative procedural rules do not differentiate standing based on claim type.

Article 1 of the Law on Administrative Judicial Review which is used by some courts as *lex generalis* when applying the Aarhus Convention reads that 'any person whose right or legitimate interest has been breached' can file for judicial review. The courts then linked the public interest represented by the Aarhus Convention with the private one described by the Law on Administrative Judicial Review.[38] The same issue arose when parties grounded the claim on the FOIA, because Article 22 reads that a person can request judicial review 'if there was a breach of a private right or interest'.[39]

[38] Decision No 1175/2021 (Constanța Appeal Court).

[39] The Pitești Appeal Court, when analysing the case, decided that the trial court's decision was just, based on the parties' depositions and the applicable law. To arrive at this conclusion, it stated that the information requested was not useful for the claimant and could not protect its private interest and that the claimant failed to prove actual damages that it could incur as a result of the administrative bodies' denial: 'Through the claim registered on 09.03.2018, the claimant, requested the following public information … The legal issue that is under discussion in this case concerns the trial courts' interpretation of the legal provisions, specifically related to the justification of the plaintiff's personal interest in relation to the strictly technical nature of the data concerning the operating parameters of the Costești City Wastewater Treatment Plant … It is true that according to Art 6 para 1 FOIA "Any person has the right to request and obtain … public information" … However, according to Art 22 para 1 FOIA "If a person's rights are breached, he/she can request judicial review"' – Decision No 121/2019 (n 30).

The trial court stated that: 'According to Article 22, paragraph 1 of Law No. 544/2001, the condition of harm is essential to uphold the validity of an action brought under this legal provision. It cannot be admitted that the refusal of a public authority or institution to provide the requested information should be sanctioned if it is not detrimental to the rights granted to a person by the law on access to public interest information.

The same is reflected in the provisions of Article 8, paragraphs 1 and 1^1 of Law No. 554/2004 on administrative litigation, which state: "(1) A person harmed in a right recognized by law or in a

Moreover, the administrative *lex specialis* is completed by the Civil Procedural Code[40] and the rules on standing are the same in both situations (information requests claims and annulment procedures).[41]

Another important aspect is that some courts consider that the claimant must prove interest for requesting the public information when challenging the administrative refusal.[42] The administration often uses lack of interest and standing as a defence for both the information request and the subsequent litigation. Based on the current legislation and jurisprudence, as stated before, if the claimant cannot prove an interest in requesting the information than the case might be dismissed as founded by a person without interest. Thus, the substantial arguments from Case C-252/22 apply not only in cases of the annulment of an administrative act, when debating interest and standing, but also in any other environmental cases.

B. The Issue of Confidential Information

The administration's defence, grounded on the Law Regarding Classified Information No 182/2002,[43] is a significant obstacle to applying the FOIA and the Aarhus Convention. Some documents are classified on the basis of secondary law, such as mining and petrol exploitation files. In such cases, the complainant might only find out about the classified status of the documents during court proceedings.[44] In its decision, the court is limited strictly to the claims made by the party. The complainants often cannot modify their claim to include a request for annulment of the act protecting such documents, as it would entail a separate claim against a different administrative body. An important aspect to be highlighted is that in this situation,[45] the claimants challenged, in a separate legal

legitimate interest by a unilateral administrative act, dissatisfied with the response received to the prior complaint, or who has not received any response within the timeframe provided by Article 2, paragraph (1) letter h), may refer the competent administrative litigation court to request the annulment, in whole or in part, of the act, compensation for the damage caused, and possibly, reparation for moral damages.'"

It is true that, based on the legal grounds of the claim, the lack of procedural interest could not be invoked. However, the person who initiates an action based on Article 22, paragraph 1 of Law No. 544/2001 must aim to defend a legitimate private interest, the violation of which would lead them to consider themselves harmed in their rights under Law No. 544/2001' – Judgment No 746/2018 (Argeş Tribunal).

[40] Law No 134/2010, Official Journal of Romania (2015) CCXLVII.

[41] *Societatea Civilă Profesională de Avocați AB & CD* (n 35) paras 6–14.

[42] 'As a consequence, regarding the necessity of justifying an interest in the transmission of such information, the tribunal finds that, to file an action based on Law No. 544/2001, it is necessary to justify a practical benefit, as the legal provisions are established to protect the right to information of any citizen or public institution. In the present case, no harm to any right has been proven through the response provided by the public authorities obligated to disclose public information, nor has there been any proven interest in obtaining this information at present.' – Decision No 7945/2014 (Bucharest Tribunal).

[43] Law No 182/2002 regarding Classified Information, Official Journal of Romania (2002) CCXLVIII.

[44] Decision No 1019/2017 (High Court of Cassation and Justice).

[45] ibid.

case, the legality of Order No 202/2003 that offered exploitation information, any data related to the exploitation, as well as other documents and contracts related to the exploitation programme, and the status of confidential information. The Bucharest Appeal Court dismissed the request, finding that the order was lawful on the grounds of the hierarchy of legal acts, stating that the challenged order has to be in accordance with Law No 182/2002 regarding Classified Information[46] and therefore analysed only the overall legality of the order without checking if it was adequate to the facts of the case.

On the other hand, if the confidentiality of the aforementioned information or documents is not provided in the secondary legislation, but is established by the administration for the first time, then the administration has the burden of proof regarding the decision to classify such information. If the administrative body fails to do so, the court will order it to provide the documents at issue.[47]

A middle-ground solution can be found in Decision No 2091/2019,[48] where it was concluded that the administration is obliged to provide the requested information, even though some might contain classified information, by removing personal and confidential information from the documents.

C. Continuous Uncertainty on *Actio Popularis*

Article 9, paragraph 3 of the Aarhus Convention confers upon members of the public the right to 'challenge acts and omissions by private persons and public authorities that contravene provisions of its national law relating to the environment'. The provision has been translated verbatim into national law through GEO No 195/2005, which introduced the *actio popularis* system in the environmental realm, thereby granting NGOs the capacity to initiate legal proceedings against public authorities for violations of environmental legislation. The provisions outlined in Article 5 of GEO No 195/2005 affirm the right of every individual to a healthy and ecologically balanced environment. To fulfil this objective, the government ensures the right of individuals to directly access environmental information, (alone or in association with an ecological protection organisation), participate in the decision-making process pertaining to formulating environmental policies and legislation or issuing implementing regulations, and drafting plans and programmes, complain, directly or through NGOs, to public authorities, and request damages for any injustice. Moreover, individuals can file administrative appeals, either directly or through environmental protection organisations, irrespective of whether any harm already occurred. Individuals have the right to seek compensation for the damage suffered. Under Article 5 of GEO No 195/2005, the sole requirement for an NGO to obtain standing is to

[46] Law No 182/2002 regarding Classified Information (n 43).
[47] Decision No 2586/2017 (Bucharest Tribunal).
[48] Decision No 2091/2019 (n 31).

explicitly state in its charter that environmental protection is its core mission, with the GEO No 195/2005 framework underscoring that NGOs act to represent natural persons' rights and legitimate interests.

The admissibility of *actio popularis* seems to be possible based on the general Law on Administrative Judicial Review 554/2004. Starting from the definition of the concepts 'public' and 'interested public' in GEO No 195/2005 regarding environmental protection and GD No 878/2005, as well as the Law on Administrative Judicial Review 554/2004, the terms 'public' or 'person' seem to be broadly construed. Article 2 of the Law on Administrative Judicial Review 554/2004 defines the *injured person* as:

> [A]ny person whose right or legitimate interest was breached by a public administration through an administrative act or lack of response to the request for access to environmental information … in regard to this law, groups of natural persons that reclaim subjective rights or legitimate private interest, not constituted into a legal person, as well as social organisms that claim breach of either public interest or rights and legitimate interest of other determined natural persons are assimilated in the definition of injured person.

When analysing the relevant case law, it can be observed that in the initial stages of implementation, the national courts were eager to apply the Aarhus Convention directly and to provide NGOs and other bodies with a full right of standing, creating an environment that seemed to favour *actio popularis*. The courts stated that as long as the subject matter of the case coincides with the NGO's registered objective laid out in its statute, it also had an interest as a claimant.[49] This followed the logic that NGOs have as their primary purpose the protection of citizens in different areas and, therefore, can function as mediators between the state and its citizens based on the public legitimate interests or rights. Moreover, some courts ruled that environmental administrative judicial review pertains directly to protecting public interests; therefore, NGOs do not need to prove the existence of any private interest.[50]

In 2017, another judicial trend arose, stating that the claimant must prove, in all cases, the existence of a private interest and damage associated with the alleged breach of law to be able to bring the claim.[51] The latter reasoning was, unfortunately, consolidated by Decision No 8/2020.[52]

The reasoning for the early years of the Aarhus implementation was brought back through some decisions in late 2020 and 2021, meaning that the claimants' interest could be a general, public one. Some progressive courts decided to interpret the High Court Decision in a permissive manner, allowing standing if the ENGO had litigation as one of the objectives included in its charter.

[49] Decision No 390/2016 (Bistrița Năsăud Tribunal).
[50] Decision No 738/2017 (Cluj-Napoca Appeal Court).
[51] Decision No 315/2017 (Bucharest Tribunal).
[52] Decision No 8/2020, above n 32.

A decision from 2021[53] stated that the private interest stems from the statute and purpose of the NGO, and as long as one of the goals of the organisation is expressly formulated to include resorting to legal actions as a means to protect the environment, then the criteria of sufficient private interest are satisfied. The same conclusion was reached when the claimant, aware of Decision No 8/2020 of the High Court of Cassation and Justice, sought to argue that the interest protected was private.[54]

The conclusion was that at that time, most courts required that there has to be a breach of private interest, not just a public one,[55] justified by a direct infringement of the ENGOs' rights, with the distinction that from late 2020, some progressive courts have linked the idea of private interest to the ENGOs' statute, thus allowing more ENGOs to prove standing.

In this context, at a national level, the main trend is to ban *actio popularis* in administrative law, including environmental law, with only a few progressive courts accepting that the private interest can stem from the objectives set out in the ENGOs' charter. This statement is also grounded on the recent judgment of the Constitutional Court, which stated[56] that 'through the adoption of the challenged article,[57] the legislative body aimed at ruling out the so-called *actio popularis* and found the provisions to be in accordance with the Constitution'.

D. Scope of Review by the Courts

The review by courts is limited to procedural aspects; they seldom go into the case's merits[58] and, for instance, analyse the quality of the response given by the public bodies. The intensity of the review of discretionary decisions is weak. Complex factual decisions exceed the knowledge of the judges who rule on these cases. In most cases, the court's reasoning is, at most, one or two pages long and argues mainly on the legal procedure without analysing proportionality. A few recent decisions lean more on the factual elements of the case,[59] though they seldom enter the technical realm. One reason for this can be attributed to the

[53] Decision No 529/2021 (Timişoara Appeal Court).

[54] Decision No 1873/2020 (Constanţa Tribunal).

[55] Decision No 977/2021 (above n 33).

[56] Decision No 461/2021 (above n 36).

[57] Art 2 para (1) a), r) and s), of art 8 para (11) and of art 15 para (3) from Law no 554/2004.

[58] 'The fact that the claimant is dissatisfied with the response they received does not mean there was an unjustified refusal to address the request. The High Court of Cassation and Justice consistently holds that a public authority response addressing all issues outlined in a submitted memorandum is not an unjustified refusal, even if it does not satisfy the petitioner. The authority retains the prerogative to determine the content of its response, but it must always adhere to legal requirements', Decision No 7088/2020 (Bucharest Tribunal); Decision No 121/2019 (Piteşti Appeal Court); Decision No 1391/2018 (Bucharest Tribunal); Decision No 7495/2014 (Bucharest Tribunal); Decision No 725/2011 (Bucharest Appeal Court).

[59] Decision No 390/2016, above n 38.

prohibitive costs of specialised external expertise and the reluctance of NGOs to pay for it in cases where there is a need for an external expert to oversee the technical part of the documentation.

Under Law No 544/2004, the court is empowered, first, to annul an administrative act partially or entirely and compel the administrative authority to issue administrative acts, certificates, permits etc. It is authorised to assess the legality of acts or administrative activities that form the basis of the administrative act under scrutiny.

Second, the court can grant compensatory damages, encompassing both material and moral aspects, upon the claimant's request. In cases where damages are sought, the claimant retains the right to act against the responsible public servant who failed to address their request or respond adequately. If the action is admitted, the public servant and potentially their hierarchical superior can be held jointly liable for the awarded damages alongside the public authority. The time limit for requesting damages through a separate action is one year from the date that the complainant quantified the damage suffered. This is not the best solution, as it leaves the complainant with the decision as to when the deadline will start.

One important aspect is that if the complainant brings an action before the court based on a breach of public interest, the only remedies that can be obtained are the annulment of the act or the order to the public authority to issue an administrative act or to undertake a specific administrative action, under the sanction of penalties for delays or fine. Regarding damages, in the past, NGOs requested the symbolic amount of €0.20 (1 RON). Even in these situations, the courts have been reluctant to grant damages.

Under Law No 554/2004 (Articles 14 and 15), in well-justified circumstances and to prevent imminent damage from occurring, it is possible to request as an injunctive relief the suspension of the execution of the administrative act whose annulment is requested by the claimant. The claimant can lodge a complaint with the court either together with the administrative appeal (the pre-trial procedure) or alongside the court action in the annulment of the administrative act. Additionally, while pending litigation, the claimant can approach the court with a separate action requesting the granting of an injunction.

The problem with injunctive relief is that its effectiveness depends upon how quickly the courts decide on the request for the suspension of the execution of the administrative act. Even though, in theory, such cases are to be dealt with expeditiously, this rarely happens in practice. For example, there are cases when the court needed one or two years to rule on a request for injunctive relief.[60] To prevent any abuses from public authorities, the law states that if the public authorities issue a new administrative act similar in content to the one challenged, the new act is automatically suspended. In this case, the administrative appeal to the issuing authority is no longer mandatory.

[60] Decision No 117/2020 (Constanța Appeal Court); Decision No 1080/2021 (Bucharest Appeal Court).

The judgment of the first instance court can be challenged before the Appellate Court, whose ruling is final. A critical issue is how court rulings are executed once they become final. Suppose the administrative authority is compelled to undertake actions such as annulment, replacement or modification of the administrative act or issuing certificates or other pertinent documents. In that case, it is obliged to fulfil these obligations within the timeframe stipulated in the ruling or, at the latest, within 30 days from the date on which the judgment became final. If the deadline for executing the ruling is not complied with, a fine can be applied in the amount of 20 per cent of the minimum gross salary per day of delay. The head of the public authority or the public servant found responsible is the one who must pay the damages. The complainant is also entitled to damages for delays, but only up to three months. The claimant must go to court and request damages and the application of the sanction. Provided that the public authority is still not executing the ruling after paying this fine (it has no more than 30 days after paying the fine to comply), criminal charges can be brought against the responsible civil servant(s) (jail time from six months to time years or a fine ranging from €500 to €2,000 (~ 2,500–10,000 RON)).

E. Costs and Effectiveness of Judicial Remedies

Generally, court proceedings are lengthy in Romania, even when the law mandates an expeditious procedure. There is no sanction for judges who invoke the workload in their defence. In many cases, the authorities' intention is not necessarily to win the case, but to drag out the court proceedings for as long as possible. Their reasons for doing so are twofold: in the first place, in some cases, a project gets executed in the meantime, and after its completion, a sanction such as the demolition of a building is perceived as excessive; and, second, public authorities hope that complainants will give up, discouraged by the lengthy proceedings.

In terms of costs, the fees for initiating a court action are low. However, environmental cases are expensive in terms of the technical expertise they can sometimes require and the legal expenses. According to Romanian law, the complainant, upon losing the case, will have to reimburse the other party for all the legal costs incurred during the court action. The mere prospect of an unfavourable outcome in the litigation presents a disheartening outlook for ENGOs, most of which are small entities nationwide and rely on limited financial resources derived from membership fees, donations and occasional grants. In some cases, the claimants needed to pay tens of thousands of euros in attorney fees.[61]

Limited financial resources are the predominant factors compelling both ENGOs and individuals to try to find procedural breaches of environmental

[61] Decision No 529/2021, above n 42; Decision No 263/2012 (Târgu Mureş Appeal Court); Decision No 977/2021, above n 33.

regulation. When an individual seeks to challenge the validity of an environmental report, the necessity for a counter-expertise arises, inevitably incurring substantial costs. Interviewed ENGOs also mentioned that there are few court-appointed experts in environmental matters.[62] Most of them collaborate closely with the tenderers from public procurement procedures, raising issues of impartiality and incompatibility when being called to provide impartial judicial professional expertise in specific cases.

Legal aid is available only for natural persons with limited financial means who reside in Romania or another EU Member State. Legal aid is available for all other types of proceedings except for criminal proceedings and it can go towards paying lawyers' fees, interpreters' fees, judiciary executors' fees etc. Legal aid is limited in amount: for one calendar year, one person cannot receive legal aid for any or all the items mentioned above accounting for more than 10 times the minimum national gross salary.[63] The reference year is the year when the request for legal aid was drafted – in 2023, for instance, the maximum amount was €6,000.

NGOs are not eligible for legal aid, which has significant implications, particularly in environmental judicial review. This is particularly noteworthy as many environmental NGOs express a solid willingness to actively participate in cases pertaining to environmental issues, despite grappling with limited financial resources. Consequently, the ability of NGOs to fully assert their legal standing becomes significantly eroded, as their financial constraints prevent them from effectively pursuing legal remedies.

In the recent Case C-252/22, already referred to above, the Court also assessed the issue of possibly prohibitive costs in the preliminary ruling. However, the Court failed to provide an accurate answer, simply stating that:

> Article 9(4) and (5) of the Convention on access to information, public participation in decision-making and access to justice in environmental matters, signed in Aarhus on 25 June 1998 and approved on behalf of the European Community by Council Decision 2005/370, read in the light of Article 47 of the Charter of Fundamental Rights of the European Union, must be interpreted as meaning that, in order to ensure compliance with the requirement that judicial proceedings not be prohibitively expensive, a court called upon to make an order for costs against an unsuccessful party in an environmental dispute must take into account all the circumstances of the case, including that party's interest and the public interest in the protection of the environment.[64]

This ruling leaves room for interpretation at the national level, as Romanian law only recognises the standing of environmental NGOs and not any other NGO or person. This means that in the case at issue, the interests of the NGO that could justify standing could be only those of the party, stemming from its statute or an

[62] More on ENGOs activity in environmental matters in the section below/following section.
[63] Government Emergency Ordinance concerning public legal aid in civil matters, Official Journal of Romania (2008) CCCXXVII.
[64] *Societatea Civilă Profesională de Avocați AB & CD* (n 35) para 83.

infringement of the NGOs' private interest, and not the (general) public interest. Furthermore, suppose the public interest is not recognised as the scope for standing to sue. In that case, the national judge cannot balance the public interest in litigation against the private interest in developing the project. In other words, the ruling leaves the party that initiated proceedings at the 'mercy' of the national judge and could give rise to prohibitive costs for the claimant.

Regarding costs for the claimant, the above decision of the CJEU is technically correct, but, again, leaves the interpretation of what 'prohibitively expensive costs' mean to the national courts. This is unfortunate because, in Romania, there are several instances where ENGOs have had to resort to public donations to cover litigation costs. An ENGO was even liquidated in one case because it could not bear the expenses.[65] This inequitable situation was brought to the attention of the Association for the Defence of Human Rights in Romania – the Helsinki Committee (APADOR-CH) – which made a formal request to the Ministry of Justice to rethink the current legislative framework in order to protect ENGOs from similar situations.[66]

V. ENGOs in Romania: Some Empirical Insights

In an attempt to provide some empirical evidence on the functioning of ENGOs in Romania, we identified (based on their legal status and involvement in environmental projects) 222 ENGOs registered between 2000 and 2024. Of these, only 48 were active, with multiple project engagements. Despite initial willingness, just 12 ENGOs responded to our questionnaire, supplemented by direct interviews with two organisations based in Bucharest and Cluj-Napoca.[67]

[65] In 2018, two ENGOs challenged the Environmental Agreement for the construction of a new commercial centre and its subsequent documentation in Cases 25248/3/2018 and 4858/3/2019. Their claim was dismissed, and the two ENGOs that initiated the procedure faced foreclosure due to prohibitively expensive litigation costs and had to resort to donations in order to bear the expense. However, one ENGO was unable to collect and pay the requested costs and was liquidated by the Court. More information is available at: www.agerpres.ro/justitie/2023/12/29/asociatia-salvati-bucurestiul-anunta-ca-a-strans-cu-ajutorul-donatiilor-banii-pentru-cheltuieli-de-judecata--1226048; www.clujust.ro/asociatia-salvati-bucurestiul-a-ajuns-la-dizolvare-din-cauza-cheltuielilor-de-judecata/; https://buletin.de/bucuresti/asociatia-salvati-bucurestiul-infiintata-de-nicusor-dan-dizolvata-de-instanta-pentru-12-000-de-euro-ong-ul-anunta-o-strangere-de-fonduri.

[66] 'APADOR-CH cere Ministerului Justiției modificarea legii care duce la dizolvarea ONG-urilor pentru neplata cheltuielilor judiciare' (APADOR-CH Requests the Ministry of Justice to Amend the Law That Leads to the Dissolution of NGOs for Non-payment of Judicial Costs), www.presshub.ro/apador-ch-cere-ministerului-justitiei-modificarea-legii-care-duce-la-dizolvarea-ong-urilor-pentru-neplata-cheltuielilor-judiciare-305245.

[67] Online questionnaire (19 January 2024). The questionnaire comprised questions about the type of the ENGO – operational/advocacy/mixed, its size and geographical scope. In the second part, the questions related to the types of activities pursued by the ENGO, such as conferences, workshops, public protests and their impact, and whether the ENGOs have made requests for public information or not. The third part included aspects regarding how public authorities respond to requests for information and clarity of the response, accompanied by a request for detailed information regarding such

Among these environmental NGOs, operational activities were the primary focus (such as project development, litigation and humanitarian aid).[68] Five were exclusively operational, four combined project management with advocacy (with a primary focus on protests, workshops and conferences, and other activities that can influence a country's policy-making process)[69] and only three were solely dedicated to advocacy. Active membership typically fell below 10 members, except for one ENGO, which had more than 50 members. Geographically, seven ENGOs operated nationally, while the remaining nine were confined to sectorial or local initiatives. Most environmental NGOs organised an average of three to four annual events, such as conferences and workshops. However, NGO representatives generally considered public engagement moderate at best.

Regarding the ENGOs' interaction with public authorities, a recurring answer was that they often received incomplete or delayed information. The ENGOs faced these operational challenges in their advocacy or mixed operational roles, leading them to adopt strategies such as direct communication with public bodies and initiating media campaigns to publicise their difficulties. Concerning adherence to the Aarhus Convention, the most common issues were non-responsiveness to information requests and improperly prepared documentation, which are particularly acute in matters related to forest administration. In cases where responses were provided, they often contained incomplete or irrelevant information; sometimes, the administrative body required the ENGOs' physical presence to access documents without providing copies.

We noticed differences in the quality and promptness of responses, with national public bodies providing more precise and timely information than local ones. However, there was no significant variation in responsiveness to general versus environmental information requests. Geographical differences were also evident, with responses from authorities in Transylvania being of notably higher quality than those from Bucharest or southern Romania. It is believed that the Transylvanian administration performed better due to its Austro-Hungarian heritage.

cases (if applicable). We also inquired about possible differences between local/regional and national authorities. The fourth part related to the usage of administrative appeal and its success. The fifth part related to the judicial process, the number of overturned decisions and the existence of guidelines designed explicitly for ENGOs regarding access to justice. We requested information regarding the average length of a case, the (proper) execution of the courts' decisions and cases where the public body chose to ignore such decisions. The sixth part regarded the policies the ENGOs implemented to raise awareness and obtain favourable decisions in environmental cases. The interviews were conducted by Lodoabă Gheorghe-Sorin: interview with Bankwatch Romania (10 August 2023); interview with Roxana Mândruțiu, lawyer, Declic (12 January 2024).

[68] P Willets, 'What is a Non-governmental Organisation? Paperwork Produced from Research Project on Civil Society Networks in Global Governance' (City University, 2002), available at: www.gdrc.org/ngo/peter-willets.html.

[69] NZ Abiddin, I Ibrahim and SA Abdul Aziz, 'Non-governmental Organisations (NGOs) and Their Part towards Sustainable Community Development' (2022) 14(8) *Sustainability* 4386.

ENGOs stated that administrative judicial review typically extends beyond two years, often leading to a practical inapplicability of the rulings, as the projects in question were usually completed by the time of the judicial decision. Even in cases with favourable outcomes for ENGOs, public authorities often disregarded these rulings or re-issued the annulled administrative acts, hoping that the ENGOs would not file subsequent complaints. One ENGO also noted that after losing a court case and being obligated to comply with the court decision for annulment of the contract, the public authority re-initiated the same procedure with the same party. The ENGO had to start a new plea to repeal the new administrative act. The cost of environmental litigation varied, starting at around €500–1,000 for more straightforward cases and exceeding €4,000 when specialised expertise was required. These excessive costs frequently deterred ENGOs from pursuing legal action.

The primary challenge for ENGOs regarding access to justice is the prohibitive litigation costs coupled with a lack of financial resources for ENGOs earmarked for public interest litigation, the low probability of suspending administrative acts' effects, and the lack of specialised lawyers and courts. These challenges reflect ENGOs' operational difficulties in engaging effectively with public authorities and advocating for their causes.

VI. Conclusions: Strategic Reforms are Needed for Advancing Environmental Justice in Romania

Analysed through the lens of Article 9 of the Aarhus Convention, Romania's journey towards effective environmental justice reveals a landscape marked by legislative reforms, challenges and, unfortunately, stagnation.[70] The Romanian legal system, while theoretically comprehensive, faces practical difficulties in implementing the best practices due to administrative inefficiencies, procedural complexities and a lack of specialised knowledge of environmental law within the judiciary.

The challenges posed by the legal framework are multiple: contradicting provisions, a lack of coordination between different legal sources for environmental decision-making and judicial review procedures, and the inclination of courts to ban *actio popularis* or to interpret the law restrictively and not in line with international or European standards.

Notably, the participation of the Romanian legal system, while theoretically comprehensive, faces practical difficulties in implementing the best practices due to administrative inefficiencies, procedural complexities and a lack of specialised knowledge of environmental law within the judiciary. ENGOs in administrative

[70] Dragoş and Neamtu (n 11).

decision-making and the promotion of *actio popularis* are hindered by limited access to environmental information and constraints in standing in court in the public interest in environmental disputes.

There is a pressing need for specialised environmental legislation to create a robust governance framework, providing judges with clear guidelines. Establishing courts dedicated to ecological cases, trained in environmental law and equipped with necessary resources is recommended. The courts are reluctant to ask for technical expertise, as they rely on the expertise of the administration, which in many cases is actually the expertise of the private developer of the project.[71] These measures would ensure a comprehensive evaluation of environmental matters.

Improving access to information and public representation is crucial for transparency and accountability. Reforming the processes governing access to classified documents and making the justification for classifying documents compulsory would prevent obstructions in administrative proceedings. Additionally, explicit regulations for the declassification of information are essential.

Empowering NGOs in environmental litigation is vital for administrative compliance. Revising the criteria for standing in court and providing legal or financial support to ENGOs can facilitate greater participation. Implementing the Aarhus Convention's rules on standing is a starting point for adhering to international and European standards, contributing to Romania's sustainable and ecologically responsible future.

[71] D Dragoş and B Neamtu, 'The Habitats Directive in the Romanian Courts: Procedure vs Substance' in M Eliantonio, E Lees and T Paloniitty (eds), *EU Environmental Principles and Scientific Uncertainty before National Courts. The Case of the Habitats Directive* (Oxford, Hart Publishing, 2023).

8

The Greening of General and Special Administrative Procedures to Implement the Aarhus Convention

The Case of Serbia

MIRJANA DRENOVAK-IVANOVIĆ

I. The National Context

A. A General Overview of the Organisation of the Judiciary and the Judicial Review

The Republic of Serbia is a parliamentary democratic republic based on the rule of law. The supreme representative body and holder of constitutional and legislative authority is the National Assembly, while the Government of the Republic of Serbia is the holder of the executive power.[1] The judiciary system consists of courts, with general and special jurisdiction,[2] which are autonomous and independent in their work, adjudicating by the Constitution, laws and other general acts, generally accepted rules of international law, and ratified international treaties.[3] The Constitution and the Law on the Organisation of Courts establish the framework of the judicial system.[4]

The Law on Organisation of Courts established the courts of general jurisdiction (basic, high and appellate courts and the Supreme Court) and the Administrative Court, misdemeanour courts, the High Misdemeanour Court, commercial courts and the Commercial Appellate Court as courts of specialised jurisdiction. The Supreme Court is the highest court in the Republic of Serbia. The Law on Administrative Disputes (LAD) stipulates that cases in administrative matters are

[1] See Constitution of the Republic of Serbia, Official Gazette, No 98/2006 and 115/2021, art 98.
[2] ibid arts 142(1), 143(1) and 143(2).
[3] ibid art 142.
[4] Law on Organization of Courts, Official Gazette of the Republic of Serbia No 10/2023.

heard before the Administrative Court in a public hearing. An appeal cannot be made to the Court decision taken in administrative disputes. Only extraordinary legal remedies are allowed, which are heard before the Supreme Court.[5]

The Serbian Constitution establishes the Constitutional Court as an independent body to protect constitutionality, legality and human and minority rights and freedoms.[6]

B. Judicial Review of Administrative Acts and Omissions

An administrative act may be challenged by a regular administrative legal remedy – an administrative appeal – by extraordinary legal remedies in administrative procedure, and before the Administrative Court. As a party in decision-making in matters that have or may have an impact on the environment, one may recognise not only the administrative authorities but also the public. By involving the interested public in decision-making, the transparency of the procedure and reporting to the public on the state of the environment and planned interventions is ensured, and it provides an opportunity to consider the local and wider impacts of planned activities on the environment and human health. The new Law on General Administrative Procedure (LGAP) contains a provision for the interested public as a party to the procedure. Legal standing is entrusted not only to individuals but also to 'representatives of wider interests of the public authorised by a special law' and 'representatives of collective interests'.[7] Associations can have different forms of legal status that are not conditioned by limitations in terms of years of existence or conditions related to the quality of work. To obtain legal standing, associations, as representatives of the broader interests of the public, do not have an obligation to prove that the outcome of the administrative procedure affects the rights, obligations or legal interests of the association that requested the status, but that the outcome of the administrative procedure can affect the interest they represent – ie, the interest of environmental protection.

In an administrative procedure, representatives of the wider interests of the public have the right to present the facts that are important for deciding an environmental administrative matter in the procedure.[8] As a party to the proceedings, they have the right to comment on the offered evidence, to participate in its presentation and to propose it. They have the right to ask questions to other parties, experts and witnesses. The authority conducting the proceedings is obliged to

[5] Law on Administrative Disputes (LAD), Official Gazette of the Republic of Serbia No 111/2009, art 49.

[6] See Constitution of the Republic of Serbia, art 166(1).

[7] Law on General Administrative Procedure (LGAP), Official Gazette of the Republic of Serbia, No 18/16, 95/18, art 44, para 3. See V Cucić, 'Fino podešavanje Zakona o opštem upravnom postupku' (Fine-Tuning of the General Administrative Procedure Act) (2018) 66(2) *Annals of the Faculty of Law in Belgrade (Belgrade Law Review)* 139.

[8] LGAP (n 7) art 11.

decide on all requests and proposals of the representatives of the wider public interest of the party as a party to the proceedings.

Administrative Court proceedings may be initiated by challenging a final administrative act. Therefore, administrative appeals must be exhausted before the initiation of the Administrative Court procedure. The right to legal protection is guaranteed by the Constitution and by the legal acts that regulate the procedural legal position of the parties in a certain procedure.[9] If a natural or legal person or another legal entity believes that its right or legal interest has been violated by an administrative act, it may initiate an administrative dispute. A group of persons or an organisation that does not have the status of a legal entity also has the right to initiate an administrative dispute, eg, an environmental association or environmental non-governmental organisation (NGO), provided that it can be the holder of rights and obligations that were decided in the administrative procedure.[10] The public prosecutor can initiate an administrative dispute when he or she believes that the adopted administrative act violates the law, thereby infringing the public interest.[11]

The implementation of the principle of prevention in environmental law also relies on adequate legal protection that enables the removal of the source of the danger of damage even before damage occurs. The basis of the right to legal protection from a source of danger that threatens significant damage to an unspecified number of persons is found in the lawsuit for the elimination of the source of danger of damage, which, due to the elements related to the conditions for filing a lawsuit and the circle of persons who can be plaintiffs, is called an environmental lawsuit in the literature or *actio popularis*, which is regulated by the Law of Contract and Torts.[12]

C. The Relevant Public (Administrative) Authorities in the Field of Environmental Protection at Various Levels (Central/Local)

The Constitution of the Republic of Serbia stipulates that the Republic of Serbia shall establish and ensure the system of environmental protection and provide for sustainable development, protection and improvement of health and animal life, and management of hazardous and radioactive substances (Article 97,

[9] Constitution of the Republic of Serbia, art 36; P Dimitrijević and N Milenković, 'Svrha pravnih sredstava u upravnom sporu' (The Purpose of Legal Remedies in Administrative Disputes) (2020) 59(88) *Collection of Paper Faculty of Law Niš* 93.

[10] LAD (n 5) art 11, para 2.

[11] ibid para 3. For the legal position of representatives of collective interests in Serbian legal framework and case law, see M Drenovak-Ivanović, *Pravni položaj zaštitnika kolektivnih i širih interesa javnosti u zaštiti životne sredine* (*The Legal Position of Representatives of Collective Interests in Environmental Protection*) (Belgrade, University of Belgrade Faculty of Law, 2021) 29–56.

[12] Official Gazette, Nos 29/1978 et seq.

paragraph 1, item 9). Responsibility for environmental protection is divided between the Republic of Serbia, autonomous provinces (Article 74, paragraph 2) and local self-government units (Article 190 paragraph 1, item 6).

The basis of an administrative authority's work in environmental protection is found in constitutional standards. One of the competences of the Republic of Serbia is planning and ensuring sustainable development and the system of protection and improvement of the environment.[13] However, matters of provincial interest in the field of environmental protection are regulated by the Serbian Constitution.[14] The municipalities should also look after the state of the environment through their organs.[15]

The Ministry of Environmental Protection was created as an independent ministry in 2017. It has such a status in the current Law on Ministries.[16] Before that, its competences were attributed to other ministries (energy, science and spatial planning). The Environmental Protection Agency was founded in 2004 to develop a system for collecting and processing data in the field of environmental protection. The Agency has a significant role in establishing an information system on issues in the field of environmental protection, as well as in introducing an integrated environmental impact assessment. In reporting, the Agency cooperates with the European Environment Agency and the European Network for Information and Observation Network.

The Commissioner for Information of Public Importance was established to facilitate the exercise of rights of access to information of public importance held by public authorities and to monitor the compliance of public authorities with the duties provided for in the Law on Free Access to Information of Public Importance (LFAIPI).[17]

Established as an independent authority in 2005, the Protector of Citizens in the Republic of Serbia is in charge of protecting the rights of citizens and controlling the work of state administration authorities, authorities responsible for the legal protection of property rights and interests of the Republic of Serbia, as well as other bodies and organisations, companies and institutions entrusted with public powers.[18] To protect the individual and collective rights of citizens, the Protector of Citizens' work is aimed at preventing irregularities and illegalities, as well as (cases of) maladministration.[19] At the employee level of that institution, there is

[13] Constitution of the Republic of Serbia, art 97, para 1, item 9.

[14] ibid art 183, para 2, item 2.

[15] ibid art 190, para 1, item 6.

[16] Law on Ministries, Official Gazette of the Republic of Serbia, No 128/2020, 116/22, 92/23, art 2, para 1, item 4.

[17] Law on Free Access to Information of Public Importance (LFAIPI), Official Gazette of the Republic of Serbia, Nos 120/04, 54/07, 104/09, 36/10 and 105/21.

[18] Law on the Protector of Citizens, Official Gazette of the Republic of Serbia, No 105/2021, art 1, para 1; Constitution of the Republic of Serbia, art 138, para 1.

[19] M Davinić, *Nezavisna kontrolna tela u Republici Srbiji* (*Independent Control Bodies in the Republic of Serbia*) (Belgrade, Dosije studio, 2018) 117–18.

a specialisation for performing tasks in the field of protecting citizens' rights to a healthy environment. In the practice of the Protector of Citizens, one may find many examples in which opinions with recommendations were announced regarding the work of administrative bodies in the field of environmental protection.[20]

II. Harmonisation of EU Environmental Law and the EU Accession Process

In December 2009, Serbia applied for EU membership. In 2011 the European Parliament ratified the Stabilisation and Association Agreement (SAA) between the EU and Serbia. To identify potential challenges and assess the institutional and financial frameworks for the adaptation to the environmental *acquis*, one of the most important strategic documents in the process of approximation was adopted in December 2011: the National Environmental Approximation Strategy.[21] The approximation in the field of the environment and climate change has significant economic challenges.[22] The Negotiating Team for Accession Negotiations of Serbia to the EU was established in August 2015 with a view to taking part in the development of negotiating positions and it is responsible for conducting accession negotiations. The plan for the transposition of the environmental *acquis* is set out in the National Programme for the adoption of legal *acquis* for the period 2022–25.[23]

The new approach to EU enlargement, set out in the revised methodology on EU enlargement (2021), is based on the clustering of 35 chapters of the EU *acquis* in six negotiation clusters. The connection of the chapter on environment and climate change with the Chapters on energy, transport policy and the Trans-European networks, in Cluster IV, indicates the obligation of the candidate country to design public policies with careful weighing of the interests engaged in all areas of the cluster. Cluster IV (Green Agenda and sustainable connectivity) was opened for negotiations in December 2021. The EU's Common Position on Chapter 27 sets out eight closing benchmarks presented at the opening of Cluster IV in December 2021.[24]

[20] The Ombudsman's decisions and their influence on national authorities are presented in M Drenovak-Ivanović, *Ekološko pravo* (*Environmental Law*) (Belgrade, University of Belgrade Faculty of Law, 2021) 171–78.

[21] National Environmental Approximation Strategy for the Republic of Serbia, Official Gazette of the Republic of Serbia, No 80/2011.

[22] S Bogojević and M Drenovak-Ivanović, 'Environmental Protection through the Prism of Enlargement: Time for Reflection' (2019) 56(4) *Common Market Law Review* 949.

[23] www.mei.gov.rs/upload/documents/nacionalna_dokumenta/npaa/NPAA_2022-2025_EN.pdf.

[24] The European Union Common Position for Chapter 27 is available at: www.mei.gov.rs/upload/documents/pristupni_pregovori/pregovaracke_pozicije/27_eu_common_position.pdf.

In the field of horizontal environmental legislation, special attention is paid to the application of the standards of the Aarhus Convention (AC).[25] The gap between the transposition and implementation of the horizontal environmental *acquis* was pointed out in the reports of the European Commission on Serbia's progress in integration as early as 2012, and the Annual progress report of the European Commission for Serbia for 2021[26] pointed out a deep divergence and concrete, individual examples in which this may be especially noted (decision-making of air quality plans, irregularities in the involvement of the public in the wake of COVID-19 restriction measures, irregularities and lack of transparency in environmental impact assessment procedures related to Chinese investments etc).[27]

It is stressed in the closing benchmarks that Serbia should 'demonstrate that it will be fully prepared to ensure the effective implementation and enforcement of the horizontal Directives at the date of accession'.[28] According to other closing benchmarks, in the further transposition of the environmental *acquis*, attention should be paid to the: (1) full transposition of the revised Directive on the reduction of national emissions of certain atmospheric pollutants; (2) creation of systematic and strategical approach in the reduction of emissions; (3) establishment of a waste prevention programme with a waste management plan; and (4) more dynamic alignment with the *acquis*. The cornerstone for that is the development of administrative capacity following the Action Plan. Bearing in mind that the Serbian Negotiation Position accepts the *acquis* as in force on 1 June 2019, a transposition and an implementation plan for the environmental *acquis* that has been developing between June 2019 and the conclusion of the negotiations should be prepared.[29]

[25] A Hoxhaj, 'The EU Rule of Law Initiative towards the Western Balkans' (2021) 13(1) *Hague Journal on the Rule of Law* 143.

[26] Commission, 'Serbia 2021 Report Accompanying the Document Communication from the Commission to the European Parliament, the Council, the European Economic and Social Committee and the Committee of the Regions, 2021 Communication on EU Enlargement Policy' (hereinafter 'Serbia (Progress) Report'), SWD (2021) 288 final, 128–30. *cf* European Commission, 'Serbia 2012 Progress Report', SWD (2012) 333, 78; European Commission, 'Serbia 2014 Progress Report', SWD (2014) 302 final provisoire, 99; European Commission, 'Serbia 2015 Report', SWD (2015) 211 final, 78; European Commission, 'Serbia 2019 Report', SWD (2019) 219, 87; European Commission, 'Serbia 2020 Report', SWD (2020) 352, 115–16; European Commission, 'Serbia 2022 Report', SWD (2022) 338 final.

[27] M Drenovak-Ivanović, 'Zelena Agenda za Zapadni Balkan: Smernice za noveliranje ekološkog zakonodavstva' (Green Agenda for the Western Balkans: Guidelines for Amending Environmental Legislation) in S Lilić (ed), *Perspektive implementacije evropskih standarda u pravni sistem Srbije: Zbornik radova* (*Perspectives of Implementation of European Standards in Serbian Legal System – Collection of Papers*), vol 10 (Belgrade, University of Belgrade Faculty of Law, 2020) 133.

[28] European Union Common Position for Chapter 27 (n 24) 17.

[29] M Drenovak-Ivanović (ed) *Uticaj ekološkog acquis-ja na razvoj ekološkog prava u Srbiji, Zbornik radova* (Influence of the Environmental *Acquis* on the Development of Environmental Law in Serbia, Collection of Papers) (Belgrade, University of Belgrade Faculty of Law, 2022), available at: https://ius.

III. Implementation of Article 9 of the Aarhus Convention

A. The Legal Framework for Environmental Protection

In the Republic of Serbia, several special laws that regulate different aspects of environmental protection were adopted in the 1970s and 1980s. The first systematic law which regulated environmental protection in a comprehensive and unified manner and established basic standards of environmental protection in Serbia was adopted in 1991. The new approach to environmental protection became part of the legal framework in 2004, when the current Law on Environmental Protection, the Law on Environmental Impact Assessment, the Law on Integrated Pollution Prevention and Control, and the Law on Strategic Environmental Impact Assessment were adopted. In 2009, 16 special laws that regulate issues of importance for certain areas of environmental protection were adopted. In May 2009, the AC became a part of the Serbian legal system through the adoption of the Law on Ratification of the Convention on Access to Information, Public Participation in Decision Making, and Access to Justice in Environmental Matters.[30] After 2010, laws in the fields of water, air, forest, soil, biological diversity, nature protection, industrial risk management, integrated chemical management, waste management, climate change and sustainable use of natural resources contain provisions that harmonise domestic law with international regulations, EU and regional standards.

Further development of Serbian environmental law was determined by two initial elements: the institutional capacity for environmental protection policy, and the legislative reform and harmonisation of Serbian legislation with EU legal standards in the field of environmental protection. By signing the SAA in 2008, the Republic of Serbia assumed the responsibility of developing cooperation with the EU Member States in the fight against environmental degradation, and of undertaking continuous work to improve the current state of environmental protection to achieve sustainable development (Article 111 SAA).[31] The process of harmonisation of Serbian legislation with EU legal standards in the field of environmental protection was thus formally launched.

bg.ac.rs/publikacije/%d1%83%d1%82%d0%b8%d1%86%d0%b0%d1%98-%d0%b5%d0%ba%d0%be%d0%bb%d0%be%d1%88%d0%ba%d0%be%d0%b3-acquis-%d1%98%d0%b0-%d0%bd%d0%b0-%d1%80%d0%b0%d0%b7%d0%b2%d0%be%d1%98-%d0%b5%d0%ba%d0%be%d0%bb%d0%be%d1%88.

[30] Law on Ratification of the Convention on Access to Information, Public Participation in Decision Making and Access to Justice in Environmental Matters, Official Gazette of the Republic of Serbia, No 38/09.

[31] Stabilisation and Association Agreement between the Republic of Serbia, on one side, and European communities and their states in the other, Official Gazette of the Republic of Serbia, No 83/08.

B. Mechanism(s) Available for Access to Justice in Environmental Matters for the Enforcement of Article 9 AC

i. Legislative Provisions on the Implementation of Article 9(1)

The starting point of the protection in administrative procedure of the right to a healthy environment is the idea that, regardless of its content in a legal system, the protection is achieved if three pillars of the AC, as procedural requirements, are guaranteed and applied. As a minimum guarantee, it is determined that the parties to the AC (hereinafter 'PC') must establish a system in their national legislation to ensure that persons claiming that they were arbitrarily or unjustly denied access to environmental information and participation in environmental decision-making have a right to legal protection before a court or another independent and impartial body (the Commissioner for Information of Public Importance, the Ombudsman, a special environmental court etc), which is established by law. Thus, the first reason for establishing guarantees of legal protection is the initiation of a 'free of charge or inexpensive for reconsideration by the public authority' of a decision in an environmental administrative matter.[32] The procedure for exercising the right of free access to information of public importance is conducted on the basis of the LFAIPI, which, in this case, is the *lex specialis* and the Law on Environmental Protection (LEP). However, if not otherwise specified by the LFAIPI, the LGAP applies.

The Serbian Commissioner for Information of Public Importance, as an appellate authority in the procedure of exercising the right of access to information, has made an outstanding contribution to the understanding of the special status of environmental information, but has also contributed to the creation of new case law on matters such as the interpretation of exceptions to rights of access to environmental information. The Commissioner indicated on several occasions that the right of access to environmental information is guaranteed by the Constitution of the Republic of Serbia as a basic human right and, as such, by international treaties ratified by the Republic of Serbia, including the European Convention on Human Rights (Article 10).[33]

In the past two years, there have been an increasing number of cases where the public has expressed interest in access to information about the quality of groundwater in the area where geological research is carried out for the exploitation of mineral raw materials. In one such case, a citizens' association requested information from the competent authority on the amount of electricity produced on an

[32] AC, art 9(1). The special status of environmental information is reflected in the exemption from payment of fees for access to documents that contain this information. In that sense, environmental NGOs that request a copy of a document for the purpose of carrying on their registered activities, as well as all persons who request information regarding a threat to, or protection of, public health and environment, shall be exempted from the duty to reimburse costs: LFAIPI (n 17) art 17, para 4.

[33] Opinion of the Commissioner for Information of Public Importance and Personal Data Protection, No 011-00-731/2013-02, 15 November 2013.

annual basis in hydroelectric power plants.[34] Such a request was rejected based on the application of the rules on exclusion and restriction of free access,[35] with the explanation that it is information marked to be kept as a business secret. This is an exception to the right of access that is also prescribed by the AC. Ruling on the appeal, the Commissioner for Information of Public Importance took the view that the public authority was obliged to explain how access to the requested information could threaten the energy stability of the Republic of Serbia. Following a series of earlier decisions,[36] the Commissioner pointed out that information on the environment, and especially on the level of polluting substances and emissions, is par excellence information of public importance that the public has a 'greater interest in knowing'.

The Commissioner's views that public authorities are obliged to provide the requested information, even when they do not have the obligation to perform analyses and prepare reports in which such data are generated if such information is contained in documents at their disposal, have significant importance for the implementation of AC standards on access to environmental information.[37] The practice of the Commissioner shows that he has an important role to play in the application of international law. It may be noted that the Commissioner, when explaining his decisions, often refers to the sources of international law and the decisions of the European Court of Human Rights (ECtHR).

ii. Legislative Provisions on the Implementation of Article 9(2)

One of the possible preconditions for the initiation of judicial proceedings is a previous legal protection procedure before an administrative authority and the exhaustion of legal remedies in an administrative procedure.[38] Another prerequisite is the existence of legal standing to dispute the substantial and procedural legality of the decision in environmental matters, or any acts and omissions that interfere with the application of the provisions of the AC, ie, acts or omissions of natural persons and public authorities which are in conflict with the national environmental law provisions of the PC.[39] The rules determining if there is a legal standing in an administrative procedure are shaped by the national laws of the PC.

Aside from the Law on Environmental Impact Assessment, the Law on Strategic Environmental Impact Assessment and the Law on Integrated Pollution

[34] Opinion of the Commissioner for Information of Public Importance and Personal Data Protection, No 071-01-89/2021-03, 18 October 2021.

[35] LFAIP (n 17) art 9, para 5.

[36] Decision of the Commissioner for Information of Public Importance and Personal Data Protection, No 071-01-2478/2021-03, 6 September 2021.

[37] Decision of the Commissioner for Information of Public Importance and Personal Data Protection, No 071-01-1871/2020-03, 1 October 2020.

[38] AC, art 9, para 1, item 2; VG Ranganath, 'Access to Environmental Justice: Retrospect and Prospect' (2017) 7(3) *IUP Law Review* 28.

[39] See section IV.A below.

Prevention and Control, there are laws in Serbia that either do not regulate public participation in procedures potentially relevant for the environment or do so in a way that creates doubts as to whether the public concerned has or does not have the right to participate as a party to the proceedings. In such a regulatory environment, it remains uncertain whether administrative decisions can be made in fields with large environmental impact, such as chemical or waste management, mining and energy, without involving the public concerned.

One such law is the Law on Energy, whose provisions on issuing energy permits do not regulate public participation in the procedure.[40] One of the prerequisites for issuing an energy permit is related to environmental protection, which points to the potential and real environmental impact of an energy facility for which the permit is sought. If the LGAP does not stipulate a clear procedural presumption, it is unclear whether other parties may take part in this procedure, aside from/in addition to the investor seeking an energy permit, ie, whether this is a case of explicit one-party procedure, without the participation of the public concerned, or a procedure allowing provisions of the contradictory law without exception, where the associations dealing with environmental protection are allowed the status of a party with an opposing interest to the investor's. The involvement of such associations of citizens depends on whether they can acquire the status of a party to the proceedings only if they prove a violation of a superior legal interest in a particular case or, beyond, a violation of environmental protection interest they support as an association. In practice, this leads to an ad hoc approach of administrative authorities and uneven case law.[41]

Another example is found in the Law on Waste Management, which obliges the authority responsible for issuing permits for the treatment, storage, reuse or disposal of waste to inform the public upon receipt of a request for the issuance of such a licence, but not to involve the public concerned in decision-making.[42] Local authorities may collect the opinion from interested authorities and organisations only if it is necessary. On the other hand, the Law on Waste Management does not use the term 'public concerned' but NGOs and consumer organisations. In practice, this leads to denying the status of a party to the proceedings to informal groups that are threatened or may be threatened by issuing permits due to this special law.[43]

The Law on Chemicals[44] and the Law on Air Protection[45] also fail to provide solutions that undoubtedly grant the public concerned with the status of a party

[40] Law on Energy, Official Gazette of the Republic of Serbia, Nos 145/14, 95/18, 35/23 and 62/23.

[41] M Drenovak-Ivanović, 'On Current Issues Regarding Energy Permit and Assessment of Impacts of Hydropower Premises in the Environmental Law in Serbia' (2014) 51(1) *Collected Papers of the Law Faculty of the University of Split* 151.

[42] Law on Waste Management, Official Gazette of the Republic of Serbia, Nos 36/2009, 88/2010 and 95/2018.

[43] Drenovak-Ivanović (n 11) 48–50.

[44] Law on Chemicals, Official Gazette of the Republic of Serbia, Nos 36/2009, 88/2010, 92/2011 and 25/2015.

[45] Law on Air Protection, Official Gazette of the Republic of Serbia, Nos 36/2009 and 10/2013.

to the proceedings in environmental decision-making or legal standing to file an administrative appeal.

iii. Legislative Provisions on the Implementation of Article 9(4)

Parties to the AC have the obligation to ensure that the procedure for review of a decision in environmental matters is 'fair, equitable, timely and not prohibitively expensive'.[46] In the national legal framework, one may not identify any special rule for judicial expenses or costs related to the carrying out of the various evidence, or the participation of experts and witnesses during the consideration of a case relating to the environment. The LAD stipulates that the provisions of the law governing the litigation procedure shall be applied accordingly to the matters relating to administrative disputes if not regulated by the LAD.[47] The Civil Procedure Code stipulates that the court shall exempt a party from the liability of paying the costs of the proceedings where that party's material situation does not allow them to bear such costs. Exemption from the payment of the costs of proceedings includes exemption from the payment of fees and the deposit for the costs of witnesses, expert witnesses, on-site inspections and court notices. The court may also release a party from the liability of paying fees only, in accordance with a special law. Prior to the decision on exemption on cost of proceeding, the court shall carefully consider all the circumstances, in particular the value of the subject of litigation, the number of persons supported by a party as well as the earnings and property owned by the party and the party's family members.[48]

During the entire proceedings, the court shall accept the right of the party to free representation when the party is completely exempt from paying the costs of the proceedings if that is necessary for the protection of rights of the party or if that is provided by a special law. The court is obliged to decide on the right to a free representative within eight days after submission of request, ie, within eight days of delivery of complaint to the court of second instance.[49]

In the period 2016–18, the Environmental Law Clinic, established in 2015 at the Faculty of Law of the University of Belgrade, provided free legal aid to environmental associations and NGOs, supported by the Organization for Security and Co-operation in Europe (OSCE) and the United Nations Development Programme (UNDP).[50] As part of the Jean Monnet Chair in European Environmental and Climate Change Law, the Environmental Law Clinic organises a series of seminars to educate environmental organisations about access to environmental justice.[51]

[46] AC, art 9(4).

[47] LAD (n 5) art 74.

[48] Civil Procedure Code, Official Gazette of the Republic of Serbia, Nos 72/2011, 49/2013, 74/2013, 55/2014, 87/2018, 18/2020 and 10/2023, art 168.

[49] ibid art 170.

[50] Cultivating Serbia's Future Environmental Guardians: OSCE Mission's Lasting Impact through the Environmental Law Clinic, www.osce.org/mission-to-serbia/562842.

[51] Jean Monnet Chair in European Environmental and Climate Change Law, http://environment.ius.bg.ac.rs.

IV. Transformation of General Administrative Procedure as a Basis for Better Legal Protection in Environmental Matters

A. The Public Concerned and Authorities Empowered to Represent the Public Interest as Parties to the Proceedings

Serbian law and the practice of administrative authorities and the Administrative Court of Serbia indicate that the participants in environmental decision-making, as well as in procedures when acting on an administrative appeal or a suit in an administrative dispute, must prove the existence of a legal interest following special laws. This further influences the possibility of participation in an administrative dispute, bearing in mind that in order to become a party to the administrative dispute, it is previously required to participate in an administrative procedure. To establish general standards for the administrative procedure in environmental matters, the new LGAP introduces several provisions, entrusting the right of participation in decision-making in an administrative procedure to 'representatives of public interest empowered by a special law' and 'representatives of collective interests'.[52] This means that a general administrative procedure was transformed to provide:

> [R]epresentatives of public interest empowered by a special law, representatives of collective interests or representatives of broader public interest organised according to current regulations with the right to participate as parties to the administrative procedure in a case when an outcome of an administrative procedure possibly influences these interests.[53]

Legal standing is now granted to legal persons and associations of citizens dealing with the protection, improvement and promotion of environmental protection, as protectors of collective and broader public interests, assuming that they have a legal interest in participating in procedures concerning environmental protection.[54] The new LGAP, following the positions of the Court of Justice of the European Union (CJEU)[55] and assuming that environmental protection is a value of public interest, intended to introduce a rule allowing natural persons, informal groups or legal entities to simply prove that the outcome of a procedure may affect

[52] J Jerinić, 'U ime javnosti: legitimacija zastupnika kolektivnih interesa i širih interesa javnosti u upravnim stvarima' (In the Name of the Public: Representatives of Collective and Wider Interest of the Public in Administrative Matters in Serbia) (2020) 11(2) *Pravni zapisi* (*Union University Law School Review*) 504.

[53] LGAP (n 7) art 44, para 3.

[54] Z Tomić, *Komentar Zakona o opštem upravnom postupku sa sudskom praksom i registrom pojmova* (*Commentary of the Law on Administrative Disputes with Case Law and a Register of Terms*) (Belgrade, Official Gazette of the Republic of Serbia, 2022), 321.

[55] Case C-115/09 *Bund für Umwelt und Naturschutz Deutschland, Landesverband Nordrhein-Westfalen eV v. Bezirksregierung Arnsberg* ECLI:EU:C:2011:289, ECR I-03673.

interests that they represent in order to have their status of a party to the proceedings acknowledged. This will exempt these subjects from having to prove that their interests have been violated or that there is a threat to do so, which would have been the case when separate decisions related to the state and protection of the environment are made to acquire the status of party to the proceedings.

One of the first cases where an environmental association was recognised as a party in an administrative procedure, on the grounds of Article 44 paragraph 3 LGAP, is the Cable Car Construction case in Kalemegdan Park. An environmental NGO filed a lawsuit claiming that the permit for preparatory works was unlawfully issued and that public authority had authorised construction works without a decision on the Study on environmental impact assessment (EIA).[56] Under the Serbian Law on Environmental Impact Assessment (Article 3.3), EIA is mandatory for the projects planned in areas where underprotected natural resources are recognised by the law as areas of special value. The first question that arises is whether the environmental NGO has legal standing. Following the Serbian LAD, a natural, legal or other person may be the plaintiff in an administrative dispute if his or her right or legal interest was harmed by the administrative act (Article 11 paragraph 1 LAD). The environmental NGO claiming to have legal standing is an association established by the provisions of the Law on Associations.[57] According to its Statute, the association is established to promote and improve the right to a healthy environment and overall management of natural resources and renewable energy resources.

In that case, the Administrative Court pointed out that there is an inseparable connection between the protection of the environment and the protection of cultural heritage. The Law on Environmental Protection and the Law on Environmental Impact Assessment represent a legal framework that considers cultural heritage and historical heritage as part of the environment. The Administrative Court then concluded that the interested public who claims that there has been a violation of rights in the protection of cultural immovable property can be a party in an administrative dispute. In other words, the environmental NGO has legal standing based on the LAD to file a lawsuit for the annulment of the contested decision.[58] The Administrative Court concluded that construction works that were not supported by the Decision on EIA might cause irreversible damage to cultural heritage, as the area is of special value, and an irreversible damage to cultural heritage and environment that could hardly be repaired. For that reason, the Administrative Court decided to suspend all construction works until the final judgment on the legality of the construction permit.[59]

[56] Decision of Administrative Court, 7 U 6063/19, 12 February 2021.

[57] Law on Associations, Official Gazette of the Republic of Serbia, No 51/09.

[58] LAD (n 5) art 11 para 1.

[59] See M Drenovak-Ivanović, 'Recent Changes of Serbian Public Law and its Impact on Environmental Protection', International scientific conference Environmental impact of illegal construction, poor planning and design IMPEDE 2019, 419–27. Two environmental NGOs submitted a communication to the Aarhus Convention Compliance Committee on 27 January 2020. The communication alleged that the party concerned failed to comply with art 6(4) and (8) of the Convention with respect to the

In March 2023, the Supreme Court issued an opinion on the legal standing of environmental NGOs analysing more sophisticated legal issues.[60] In its judgment, the Supreme Court stated that environmental associations do not have an a priori right to be a party in an administrative dispute, but that the court must assess in each case whether such an association can have legal standing to file a lawsuit. This also applies to procedures conducted to determine the illegality in the EIA procedure. In the specific case, the Supreme Court pointed out that an environmental organisation can launch a lawsuit against a building permit when it comes to a project for which it was determined that there is an obligation to carry out an environmental impact assessment procedure, and that procedure was not carried out. Before making the decision, the Supreme Court assessed whether there is a legally relevant connection with the subject matter of the decision from the administrative act, whether the disputed construction permit violated the interest of environmental protection that the association deals with, as well as whether the infringed interest of environmental protection was based on the Law on Planning and Construction, bearing in mind that the building permit was adopted by the application of that law.

Such a legal understanding introduces the criteria based on which, in subsequent cases, it is determined whether there is legal standing. An illustrative example can be found in the judgment of the Supreme Court from August 2023.[61] Chronologically, the environmental association filed a lawsuit against the decision on the construction permit allowing an investor to build a wastewater treatment plant. The environmental association considered that it had legal standing to file a complaint with the Administrative Court and to initiate an administrative dispute. That was claimed bearing in mind the fact that a construction permit was issued for a facility for which an EIA study had been required, and in this case, no such consent was attached to the permit application. The association, relying on Article 9(3) AC, Article 44, paragraph 3 LGAP and Article 81(a) of the Law on Environmental Protection, considered neither the obligation nor the need to prove their right or interest based on the law because they were acting to protect the wider interest of the public. In January 2024, the Administrative Court concluded that the building permit did not affect the right of the environmental organisation or its legally based interest.[62] In addition, the Administrative Court found that the investor, according to Articles 135 and 148 of the Law on Planning and Construction and accompanying bylaws, can submit a study on EIA until the beginning of project implementation.[63] In its judgment, the Administrative Court

coal-fired thermal power plant project, and art 9(4) of the Convention regarding access to injunctive relief in general. Pending case ACCC/C/2020/179 Serbia.

[60] Supreme Court's opinion announced in Decision Uzp 132/2021, 17 March 2023.

[61] Judgment of the Supreme Court Uzp 41/2023, 8 August 2023.

[62] Decision of Administrative Court 3 U 28354/22, 25 January 2023.

[63] In the judgment of the Administrative Court (7 U 6063/19, 12 February 2021) that we analysed earlier, the lawsuit was accepted and the decision that allowed the execution of preparatory construction works was annulled, as it represented a different factual situation.

pointed out that legal standing should arise out of a legally significant connection with the essence of the case. The environmental organisation did not have legal standing in the administrative procedure in which the construction permit was decided, nor did it request the recognition of legal standing. Therefore, neither the right nor the obligation of that organisation was decided by the challenged decision.

Evaluating the legality of the challenged decision, the Supreme Court upheld the decision of the Administrative Court concluding that in analysing that specific administrative dispute, the environmental association did not have legal standing. A detailed analysis of the Supreme Court's decision regarding the case at hand points out its relevance in future cases in which the issues on environmental NGO's legal standing in administrative disputes would be raised. The Supreme Court first considered whether the EIA must be submitted during the procedure of issuing a construction permit or whether it may be provided in a later phase, for example, before the beginning of the construction works. If it is needed only in a later phase, then there is no legally relevant connection between the subject matter of the decision in the administrative procedure and the interest of the environmental protection environment. The Supreme Court then considered that participation in the EIA procedure as a right, but also as an obligation of the interested public. Based on that, it can be expected that in future cases, the participation of the complainant in the administrative proceedings that preceded the administrative dispute, without the possibility of direct participation in the administrative dispute, will be set as a criterion for determining active legitimation.

B. *Actio Popularis* in Recent Environmental Case Law

The criteria based on which it can be determined whether there is a legally relevant connection between the environmental association and the case being decided on, which provides a basis for legal standing, was also discussed in the practice of the Aarhus Convention Compliance Committee. They refer to elements that can indicate when the legal standing of an environmental NGO is closer to the *actio popularis* approach, and when there is sufficient interest that guarantees its right to participate in decision-making and legal protection.[64]

A new approach in the active identification of representatives of collective and wider interests of the public in administrative proceedings introduced by Article 44, paragraph 3 LGAP has also left a mark in civil proceedings. For the first time in Serbian case law, a decision was recently made on an *actio popularis* claim because of a need to review the role of protectors of collective and wider interests of the public and their status in access to environmental justice in the judicial

[64] See ACCC/C/2008/31 (Germany) ECE/MP.PP/C.1/2014/8, ACCC/C/2008/33 (UK) ECE/MP.PP/C.1/2010/6, ACCC/C/2014/99 (Spain) ECE/MP.PP/C.1/2017/17 and ACCC/C/2014/111 (Belgium) ECE/MP.PP/C.1/2017/20.

practice. Although the *actio popularis* claim, which is available for everyone to use when demanding the elimination of a source of danger threatening considerable damage, was already prescribed in the Law of Contract and Torts of Serbia in 1978, it was only 44 years later, in September 2022, that the Higher Court passed – for the first time – a judgment which allowed a claim and granted legal standing to an environmental NGO.[65] In this case, an environmental NGO was granted legal standing, and a claim was upheld to prohibit an energy company from emitting the polluting substance of sulphur dioxide (SO_2) in a concentration higher than its annual emission limit value.

In the case of legal protection against private parties, respect of the precautionary principle requires that there is a legal path that enables the elimination of a source of danger threatening considerable damage even before the damage occurs. The basis in Serbian law for such a legal path can be found in a claim for elimination of a source of danger threatening considerable damage, which, due to the elements regarding the provisions for filing a claim of plaintiffs, is called an environmental lawsuit or *actio popularis* in the relevant literature. Article 156 of the Law of Contract and Torts stipulates that:

> [E]veryone may demand from another that he/she eliminates a source of danger threatening considerable damage to him/her or to an unspecified number of persons, as well as to refrain from an activity causing a disturbance or danger of loss, should the ensuing disturbance or loss be impossible to prevent by adequate measures.

In this case, an environmental NGO filed a lawsuit to eliminate the risk of damage. The Higher Court upheld the claim and ordered the defendant to 'coordinate his operating activities with the normative framework and to operate his activities in a way that does not endanger lives and health of people'.[66]

In recent ECtHR case law, one may find a new approach to legal standing in cases related to climate change. In *Verein KlimaSeniorinnen Schweiz and Others v Switzerland*, the ECtHR recognised NGOs as 'a vehicle of collective recourse aimed at defending the rights and interests of individuals against the threats of climate change'.[67] To have legal standing as protectors of individuals against the adverse effects of climate change on human lives and health, NGOs should fulfil certain criteria. First, the NGO should be either legally established in the relevant jurisdiction or have standing as a party to the proceedings. Second, the NGO should prove that, in accordance with the statute, it was established to protect human rights

[65] Judgment of the Supreme Court, No 181/21 of September 22, 2022; the judgment became final in August 2023.

[66] The case and its influence are analysed in: M Drenovak-Ivanović, 'Analiza strazburških principa zaštite životne sredine u međunarodnom pravu ljudskih prava' (The Analysis of Strasbourg Principles of Environmental Protection in International Human Rights Law) in S Lilić (ed), *Perspektive implementacije evropskih standarda u pravni sistem Srbije: Zbornik radova* (*Perspectives of Implementation of European Standards in Serbian Legal System – Collection of Papers*), vol 13 (Belgrade, University of Belgrade Faculty of Law, 2023) 115.

[67] *Verein KlimaSeniorinnen Schweiz and Others v Switzerland* App No 53600/20 (ECtHR, 12 April 2024), para 523.

as a result of climate change. Third, the NGO should demonstrate that there are previous activities or circumstances on the basis of which it can be considered a qualified representative that can protect the wider collective interest of individuals affected by the adverse effects of climate change on their life, health or well-being, as a right which is protected by the European Convention of Human Rights.[68] Not only that it is the first ECtHR judgment of its kind establishing that mitigating climate change is an obligation that can fall under the umbrella of the protection of human rights, but it is also a judgment that expands the legal standing of associations. With the aforementioned criteria, the associations' legal standing has been expanded so that it provides the possibility of effective protection of the rights it guarantees, taking into account that the European Convention of Human Rights does not provide the possibility for the application of *actio popularis*.

What this brief account of approaches shows is that the question of who is a party to the proceedings demands a diverse range of legal responses, which tend to depart from traditional models of regulation.

V. Conclusion

Procedural requirements that guarantee that the right to a healthy environment of a quality set as an object of general interest in a country will be protected have become an almost universal legal instrument. It is accepted and exercised in comparative environmental law across the world and, as such, has become a general principle of law recognised by civilised nations. The adoption of the AC, the UNEP Bali Guidelines and the Escazú Agreement contributed to this goal. The failed attempt of the European Commission to draw up a proposal Directive that would develop new legal remedies in the EU Member States suggests that rights recognised at the national level have a dominant role in the development of procedural requirements.[69] Further development of access to environmental justice is conditioned by the transformation of procedures in national law so that, in line with the culture and tradition and with best practices, a legal framework is established that recognises new instruments of legal protection adapted to the specifics of environmental law.

The practice of protecting the right to a healthy environment in Serbia reveals that the support for the implementation of the pillars of access to environmental justice is found in the general administrative procedure. This is further reflected in the possibility of participation in the administrative dispute, bearing in mind that it is necessary for the party in an administrative dispute to have previously taken part in the administrative procedure. Therefore, this process underwent many transformations that led to a system in which the protection of the right to

[68] ibid para 502. For a detailed analysis of this case, see Plaza ch 2 in this volume, section IV.
[69] See Eliantonio and Richelle, ch 1 in this volume, section III.C.i.

a healthy environment has changed. The new case law on legal standing, taking as a fact that environmental protection is the value of public interest, introduces the rules requesting natural persons, informal groups or legal entities to prove that the outcome of the proceedings may have an impact on the interests they represent, in order to be recognised as a party to the proceedings. By doing so, they are exempt from the burden of proving the status of affected parties and a violation of their own interests that would occur with the adoption of individual decisions relating to the status and protection of the environment to acquire the status of a party to the proceedings. The likelihood of an outcome achieved by the involvement of the public concerned in administrative proceedings or administrative disputes is strengthened by the introduction of the principle of predictability. It obligates the competent administrative authority acting in administrative matters to take into account earlier decisions taken in the same or similar administrative matters. The challenge that remains in finding new legal mechanisms for protecting the right to a healthy environment is the consistent inclusion of authorities empowered to represent the public interest in the definition of entities that have a legal standing and providing courts with an opportunity to apply exemptions indicated in environmental *acquis* and the CJEU case law when deciding on legal costs in environmental matters.

9

Access to Justice in Environmental Matters from the Perspective of Slovenian Law

KATJA ŠTEMBERGER BRIZANI

I. The National Context

A. General Overview on the Organisation of the Judiciary and the Judicial Review of Acts/Omissions of the Administration

The unified judicial system of the Republic of Slovenia consists of general and specialised courts. The general courts operate at four levels of subject-matter jurisdiction, and the territorial jurisdiction is also determined by the system of local distribution of courts. In the first instance, district and regional courts adjudicate civil and criminal cases and other cases for which the law so provides, while in the second instance, higher courts act as courts of appeal. The Supreme Court of the Republic of Slovenia has the status of the highest court in the country and has an important role in ensuring uniform case law. As a rule, it adjudicates on regular legal remedies against the decisions of the courts of the second instance and extraordinary legal remedies against the final decisions of the courts.[1] In addition to the general courts, there are two specialised courts: labour and social courts (with the higher labour and social court acting as an appeal court) and the Administrative Court (with headquarters in Ljubljana and three external departments), which provides judicial protection in administrative matters (and other matters provided for by law) and has the status of a higher court, although it rules as the first court in the system of administrative supervision (Articles 97 et seq of the Courts Act).[2]

[1] B Žuber and R Laubscher, 'The Relationship between Constitutional and Administrative Judiciaries and Adjudication in the Slovenian and South African Legal Orders' in E Fourie et al (eds), *Universality of the Rule of Law: Slovenian and South African Perspectives* (Cape Town, African Sun Media, Sun Press, 2021) 29, 30.

[2] Official Gazette of the RS, Nos 94/07 et seq.

The Constitutional Court is the highest body of the judicial power for the protection of constitutionality, legality, human rights and fundamental freedoms. It is therefore not considered to be 'the last instance on legal remedies against the decisions of lower instances', but as judicial body *sui generis*.[3] It is autonomous and independent in relation to all other state authorities, including other courts (Article 1 of the Constitutional Court Act (CCA)).[4]

Control over acts of the administration is divided between the Constitutional Court and the Administrative Court. The Constitutional Court is competent to review the constitutionality and legality of general legal (administrative) acts: implementing regulations, local authorities' regulations and general acts issued for the exercise of public authority (hereinafter referred to also as 'implementing regulations'). It also decides on constitutional appeals alleging breaches of human rights and fundamental freedoms by individual acts of state and local authorities, and holders of public authority (Article 160(1) of the Constitution of the Republic of Slovenia, hereinafter 'the Constitution')[5] if all legal remedies have been exhausted beforehand.[6]

The Administrative Court decides on the legality of final (individual) administrative acts[7] that affect the legal position of the plaintiff (Article 2(1) of the Administrative Dispute Act (ADA-1)) and on the legality of other acts, if a (ADA-1 or special) law so provides.[8] On the other hand, the Administrative Court has no power to review the constitutionality and legality of implementing regulations with *erga omnes* effect. It does, however, have the power to disregard an unlawful (and unconstitutional) implementing regulation that it should have applied in its decision-making (*exceptio illegalis*) and to rule directly based on the law, but only with *inter partes* effect. The power to interfere with the validity of regulations belongs only to the Constitutional Court.[9] Furthermore, the Administrative Court has jurisdiction to rule on the legality of individual acts and actions by which the authorities interfere with the human rights and fundamental freedoms of individuals if no other judicial remedy is available (so-called quasi- or subsidiary administrative dispute)[10] (Article 157(2) of the Constitution and Article 4 of the

[3] C Ribičič, 'Constitutional Position and Functioning of the Constitutional Court of the Republic of Slovenia' in C Ribičič and I Kaučič, *Referendum and the Constitutional Court of Slovenia* (Regensburg, Universitätsverlag, 2016) 31, 37.

[4] Official Gazette of the RS, Nos 64/07 et seq.

[5] Official Gazette of the RS, Nos 33/91-I et seq.

[6] Žuber and Laubscher (n 1) 39–41.

[7] For the definition of an administrative act, see art 2(2) of the Administrative Dispute Act, Official Gazette of the RS, Nos 105/06 et seq, ADA-1.

[8] E Kerševan and V Androjna, *Upravno procesno pravo: upravni postopek in upravni spor* (*Administrative Procedural Law: Administrative Procedure and Administrative Dispute*) (Ljubljana, IUS Software, GV Založba, 2017).

[9] J Čebulj, 'Commentary on Art. 125 of the Constitution' in M Avbelj et al (eds), *Komentar Ustave Republike Slovenije* (*Commentary on the Constitution of the Republic of Slovenia*) (Nova Gorica, Nova univerza, Evropska pravna fakulteta) 641, 644.

[10] E Kerševan and R Sitar, 'Varstvo ustavnih pravic v upravnem sporu' (Protection of Constitutional Rights in Administrative Dispute) in M Kambič et al (eds) *Odsev dejstev v pravu: da mihi facta, dabo tibi ius: liber amicorum Janez Kranjc* (*Reflection of Facts in Law*) (Ljubljana, Pravna fakulteta, 2019) 231, 237.

ADA-1). Administrative court decisions are only exceptionally subject to appeal. They are decided by the Supreme Court as the appellate court (Articles 73 of the ADA-1 et seq). The latter also has jurisdiction to rule on review as an extraordinary remedy in an administrative dispute.

B. Relevant Public (Administrative) Authorities in the Field of Environmental Protection

Environmental protection is a shared responsibility of all three branches of power: the National Assembly (and the Council of State) is obliged to provide the appropriate legislative framework, while in the executive branch of power, the main role is given to the Ministry of Environment, Climate and Energy and the Ministry of Natural Resources and Spatial Planning as state administration bodies. They are responsible for adopting implementing regulations in the field of environmental protection (besides the government), individual legal acts (usually as an appellate body), carrying out material acts, development, monitoring tasks, and (state) public environmental protection services.[11] These tasks are carried out by the responsible ministry, either directly or through its constituent bodies (the Environment Agency and the Environment and Energy Inspectorate as constituent bodies within the Ministry of Environment, Climate and Energy, and the Surveying and Mapping Authority, the Slovenian Nuclear Safety Administration, the Slovenian Water Directorate and the Natural Resources and Spatial Planning Inspectorate as constituent bodies within the Ministry of Natural Resources and Spatial Planning) and other state administration authorities (administrative units). It is also possible to delegate (some of) these tasks to the private sector (through public authority and concession). In the field of nature protection, the Nature Conservation Institute is also involved. Since environmental protection according to the Aarhus Convention also includes access to environmentally relevant information, the Ministry of Public Administration should also be highlighted. The latter is responsible for regulating this area and carries out promotion and development tasks to ensure the transparent and open functioning of the authorities.

Judicial review of environmentally significant decisions and acts is primarily exercised by the Constitutional Court and the Administrative Court, but civil courts decide on compensation for damages in the context of environmental protection. Moreover, Article 231 of the Environmental Protection Act-2 (EPA-2) allows anyone, including a member of the concerned public (non-governmental

[11] Articles 8 et seq of the State Administration Act, Official Gazette of the RS, Nos 113/05 et seq. For more on the administrative tasks of the administration, see B Bugarič, 'Commentary on Arts 8–9 of the State Administration Act' 503 and 506; R Pirnat, 'Commentary on Arts 11–12 of the State Administration Act' 511–512; and S Pličanič, 'Commentary on Art 13 of the State Administration Act' 513, all in R Pirnat et al (eds), *Komentar zakonov s področja uprave* (*Commentary on Laws in the Administration Field*) (Ljubljana, Inštitut za javno upravo pri Pravni fakulteti, 2004).

organisations (NGOs)),[12] to request an injunction from civil courts against an activity that constitutes an interference (or a significant risk of interference) in the environment (*actio popularis*).[13] Criminal courts deciding on criminal liability for environmental crimes should also be mentioned. However, the latter two courts do not have the power to directly interfere with the legal validity of such a decision (as the basis for an environmental intervention)[14] and will therefore not be discussed further.[15] In addition to representatives of all branches of government, other state actors are also involved in environmental protection – eg, the Information Commissioner, the Human Rights Ombudsman and the Court of Auditors – as autonomous and independent state bodies.[16]

The interplay between the responsibilities of different bodies in the context of environmental protection is also characteristic at the municipal level. These are divided between the mayor, who is the proponent of municipal (including environmental) policies, and guardian of legality,[17] the municipal council as the highest decision-making body at the municipal level,[18] and the municipal administration. A separate body of municipal authorities is usually formed to perform environmental protection tasks.[19]

In addition to public authorities, NGOs acting in the public interest in one or more environmental-related fields (environmental protection, nature conservation or spatial planning),[20] governed (generally) by the Law on Non-Governmental Organisations (Law of NGOs),[21] and citizens' initiatives, both representing the concerned public within the meaning of the Aarhus Convention, also play an important role in the field of environmental protection. Their role in legal proceedings will be discussed further below.

II. The EU Accession Process

Slovenia applied for EU membership on 10 June 1996. The programme and timetable for adapting Slovenian environmental legislation with the requirements of

[12] See further section III below.

[13] This legal basis shall be distinguished from art 133 of the Obligations Code (Official Gazette of the RS, Nos 97/07 et seq) (as *lex generalis*), which does not allow for an injunctive claim against a generally useful activity, comprising all permitted economic activities (including for environmental interference).

[14] T Pucelj Vidović, 'Sodno varstvo pri odločanju o posegih v prostor v luči zahtev Aarhuške konvencije: doktorska disertacija' (Access to Justice Regarding Decisions on Land Use in Light of the Aarhus Convection: Doctoral Thesis) (Ljubljana, Univerza v Ljubljani, Pravna fakulteta, 2022) 50–52.

[15] Nor will legal protection in the inspection procedure be discussed.

[16] *cf* S Vrbica and N Videtič, *Pravna sredstva na področju varstva okolja: priročnik za nevladne organizacije in civilne iniciative* (*Remedies in the Field of Environmental Protection: A Handbook for NGOs and Civil Initiatives*) (Ljubljana, Pravno informacijski center nevladnih organizacij – PIC, Ministrstvo za okolje in prostor, 2010).

[17] Article 33 of the Local Self-Government Act, Official Gazette of the RS, Nos 94/07 et seq, LSGA.

[18] ibid art 29(2).

[19] ibid art 49.

[20] Art 6 of the Law of the NGOs.

[21] Official Gazette of the RS, No 21/18.

EU law were set out in Slovenia's Environmental Accession Strategy. In it, the fundamental challenges in the accession process were identified concerning water quality, waste management, and air and soil pollution, gaps in sectoral and implementing legislation (especially about waste management, chemical substances and noise emissions), the absence of adequate (financial, administrative) mechanisms to bring legislation into line with EU law, and the supervision of its implementation.[22] Given the above, full transposition of the environmental *acquis* was expected in the medium term, while effective harmonisation of laws was only expected in the longer term. The fundamental challenges to Slovenia's EU membership in the environmental field can thus be divided into institutional, legislative, implementation and financial.[23]

By 1998, Slovenia had made some progress in adopting environmental framework legislation, but this was not significant. It still had difficulties in enforcing the legislation at the operational level and did not yet provide sufficient financial and other (administrative) resources. In 2003, Slovenia managed to meet a substantial part of the requirements, but continued to struggle with problems in the areas of air and water quality, waste management, nature protection, industrial pollution, genetically modified organisms, noise and nuclear safety. However, the Commission assessed that Slovenia will be able to implement the EU *acquis* in all areas of environmental policy by the time of its expected accession to the EU.[24]

On 31 March 2004, the National Assembly adopted the new Environmental Protection Act (EPA-1)[25] (which entered into force on 7 May 2004), which, together with the Nature Conservation Act,[26] the Forest Act,[27] the Water Act[28] and the Access to Public Information Act (APIA),[29] transposed most of the EU environmental legislation,[30] except the following, for which a transitional period had been agreed in the accession negotiations: in the field of municipal wastewater (until the end of 2015), packaging and packaging waste management (until the end of 2007) and integrated prevention and control of industrial pollution (until the end of September 2011). Slovenia has thus (at least formally) fulfilled the

[22] Z Kus, 'Okoljska pristopna strategija Slovenije za vključitev v EU' (Slovenia's Environmental Accession Strategy for EU Accession)' in V Ogorelc Wagner (ed), *Evropska unija, Slovenija in trajnostni razvoj* (*European Union, Slovenia and Sustainable Development*) (Ljubljana, Umanotera, 1998) 53.

[23] Commission, 'Agenda 2000 – Commission opinion on Slovenia's application to the European Union', DOC/97/19 [1997], 81–82.

[24] Commission, 'Comprehensive monitoring report on Slovenia's progress in preparing for membership', SEC [2003] 1208 final, 39.

[25] Official Gazette of the RS, Nos 39/06 et seq. The law was in force until the Environmental Protection Act-2 was adopted (on 16 March 2022; it entered into force on 13 April 2022 – Official Gazette of the RS, Nos 44/22 et seq, EPA-2), but it is still partly in force.

[26] Official Gazette of the RS, No 56/99.

[27] Official Gazette of the RS, No 30/93.

[28] Official Gazette of the RS, No 67/02.

[29] Official Gazette of the RS, Nos 51/06 et seq.

[30] For more on this, see S Pličanič, 'Pravo okolja in EU' (Environmental law and the EU) in J Potočnik et al, *Evropsko pravo: zbirka gradiv šole evropskega prava* (*European Law: The Collection of the European Law School Materials*) (Ljubljana, Založniška hiša Primath, 2004) 629, 635–39.

requirements established in the accession process and became a full EU Member State on 1 May 2004.

Slovenia's EU membership therefore made an important contribution to establishing its environmental policy and to regulating some critical environmental areas. However, the legal profession points out that the legislation is often poorly implemented due to its breadth, complexity, inconsistencies between regulations, and ineffective supervision, creating an 'implementation deficit'.[31] This is also reflected in the Commission's warnings and the actions brought by the Commission against Slovenia before the Court of Justice of the European Union (CJEU) for breach of EU law (especially on air quality and waste management).[32]

III. The Implementation of Article 9 of the Aarhus Convention

A. The Legal Framework for Environmental Protection

The legal framework for environmental protection at the national level consists of the Constitution, laws and implementing regulations of the state and municipalities. At the constitutional level, the environment is (directly or indirectly) protected under the following provisions: Article 5 (preserving natural wealth and cultural heritage), Article 72 (the right to a healthy living environment), Article 70 (public good and natural resources), Article 70a (the right to drinking water), Article 71 (the protection of land), Article 73 (the protection of natural and cultural heritage), Article 67 (permissibility of restrictions on property to ensure ecological function) and Article 69 (expropriation). Also relevant, in the context of the Aarhus Convention, are Article 8 (direct application of ratified and published international treaties), Article 20 (the right to justice), Article 25 (the right to a remedy), Article 39(2) (access to information of a public nature)[33] and Article 44 (the right to participate in the management of public affairs).

At the statutory level, the most important are the EPA-2, the Nature Conservation Act (NCA),[34] the Spatial Management Act (SMA-3)[35] and the

[31] Umanotera, Slovenian Sustainable Development Foundation, 'Mirror to Government 2010: The NGO Green Monitor', www.umanotera.org/publikacija/ogledalo-vladi-2010-zeleni-nevladni-monitor.

[32] The government's report shows that Slovenia was the subject of 13 (formal) proceedings in the field of the environment and nature in 2023. See http://vrs-3.vlada.si/MANDAT22/vladnagradiva.nsf/71d4985ffda5de89c12572c3003716c4/5b3d9108b8be2339c1258a6a0039bdd0?OpenDocument.

[33] The Constitution, as opposed to the law, requires a legitimate interest to have access to information of a public nature. The legislation therefore grants a broader range of rights in this respect.

[34] Official Gazette of the RS, Nos 96/04 et seq.

[35] Official Gazette of the RS, Nos 199/21 et seq.

Building Act (BA-1).[36] Additionally, environmental protection provisions are also scattered in many other (sectoral) laws (eg, the Water Act,[37] the Chemicals Act[38] and the Act on the Protection Against Ionising Radiation and Nuclear Safety),[39] and implementing regulations, which makes the legal framework opaque, especially given that it is also characterised by extremely rapid changes in the legal rules.

B. Mechanism(s) Available for Access to Justice in Environmental Matters for the Enforcement of Article 9 of the Aarhus Convention

Slovenia ratified the Aarhus Convention with the Act Ratifying the Convention on Access to Information, Public Participation in Decision Making, and Access to Justice in Environmental Matters[40] on 20 May 2004. The latter entered into force on 22 June 2004 and became internationally binding for Slovenia on 30 October 2004. Slovenia is also a signatory and party to the Protocol to the Convention and the Amendment to the Convention on the deliberate release into the environment and placing on the market of genetically modified organisms.[41]

The Aarhus Convention provisions were implemented in Slovenian legislation mainly through the adoption of the APIA, the EPA-1 – currently, the EPA-2 is in force, as well as through the NCA, the BA-1 and the Spatial Planning Act (SPA),[42] which has later been replaced by the Spatial Management Act (SMA),[43] the Spatial Management Act-1 (SMA-1),[44] the Spatial Management Act-2 (SMA-2)[45] and the Spatial Management Act-3 (SMA-3), which is currently in force.[46] From the perspective of legal protection, the General Administrative Procedure Act (GAPA),[47] the Information Commissioner Act (ICA),[48] the ADA-1 and the CCA are also relevant.

[36] ibid.
[37] Official Gazette of the RS, Nos 67/02 et seq.
[38] Official Gazette of the RS, Nos 110/03 et seq.
[39] Official Gazette of the RS, Nos 76/17 et seq.
[40] Official Gazette of the RS – International Treaties, No 17/04.
[41] Act ratifying the amendment to the Convention on Access to Information, Public Participation in Decision-Making and Access to Justice in Environmental Matters, Official Gazette of the RS – International Treaties, No 11/10.
[42] Official Gazette of the RS, Nos 33/07 et seq.
[43] Official Gazette of the RS, Nos 71/1993, 23/2002 and 110/2002.
[44] Official Gazette of the RS, Nos 110/02, 8/03, 58/03, 33/07, 108/09, 80/10 and 61/17.
[45] Official Gazette of the RS, Nos 61/17, 199/21 and 20/22.
[46] The SPA is still applicable to unfinished procedures (art 338 of the SMA-3).
[47] Official Gazette of the RS, Nos 24/06 et seq.
[48] Official Gazette of the RS, Nos 113/05 et seq.

i. Implementation of Article 9(1) of the Aarhus Convention

a. Access to Environmental Information

Pursuant to Article 15 of the EPA-2, environmental information is public.[49] Publicity of this information is achieved both by making it publicly available (eg, information on ongoing environmentally relevant procedures published on the eGovernment portal) and/or by providing it to individuals and organisations on request,[50] following the law. Access to information of a public nature (including environmental data) is generally governed by the APIA, which establishes a statutory presumption of access to all public information unless there is an exception (Article 5 of the APIA). However, some information is absolutely accessible, meaning that exceptions to free access cannot be invoked, including information on emissions to the environment, waste, hazardous substances at the plant, and information from the safety report (Article 6(3)(2) of the APIA and Article 160(3) of the EPA-2), and, according to the Information Commissioner's practice, also data from the procedures for issuing individual legal acts related to spatial planning interventions.[51] The right of access to public information therefore belongs to everyone, including the concerned public (NGOs), without the need to demonstrate a legal interest.

Providing access to public information is the responsibility of public sector bodies: state authorities, local authorities, public agencies, public funds, other public law entities, holders of public authority and public service providers (Article 1 of the APIA, hereinafter also referred to as 'authority').[52] In addition to these, economic operators under the dominant influence of public law entities are also bound by the law (Article 1a of the APIA). This means, on the other hand, that private entities that pollute the environment are not obliged to provide access to information on pollution (emissions data). These can only be obtained through the competent authorities that collect them, such as the Environment Agency and the competent inspectorate. However, if such information is held by an entity that is obliged to provide access to information of a public nature, the entity is obliged to make it available to the public if it has obtained it from third persons (of a private sector) voluntarily and without a legal obligation. As regards other data (other than emissions data), environmental data obtained voluntarily from third persons can only be made public with the written consent of the person who provided the data (Article 160(5) of the EPA-2).[53]

Access to information of a public nature can be requested by submitting a written (formal) or oral (informal) request, but legal protection is only guaranteed

[49] On what is environmental information, see arts 15(1) and 160(2) of the EPA-2.

[50] U Prepeluh, *Pravica dostopa do informacij javnega značaja* (*Right of Access to Information of a Public Nature*) (Ljubljana, Littera Scripta Manet, Univerza v Ljubljani, Pravna fakulteta, 2005), 413.

[51] Information Commissioner's Decision 090-46/2015/5 of 20 April 2015.

[52] Articles 1 and 1a of the APIA.

[53] *cf* N Pirc Musar et al (eds), *Zakon o dostopu do informacij javnega značaja (ZDIJZ): s komentarjem* (*Access to Public Information Act (APIA): With Commentary*) (Ljubljana, Uradni list RS, 2017), 206.

when a formal request is submitted (Article 13 of the APIA).[54] In a procedure for access to information of a public nature, only the applicant is a party to the procedure if the subject matter of the decision is access to information that is required by law to be public, meaning that is absolutely accessible (eg, certain environmental data). There are therefore no accessory participants in such a procedure. In terms of legal protection, this also means that the appellant can only be the applicant (or, exceptionally, the public interest advocate). Outside these cases, the general rules of the GAPA (Article 44), which allow such participation (under conditions laid down by law), apply.[55]

The liable entity for access to information of a public nature shall decide on the applicant's request without delay and at the latest within 20 working days from the date of receipt of the complete request (Article 23 of the APIA). Exceptionally, it may extend this time limit by a further 30 working days (Article 24 of the APIA). If the authority grants the access request, it shall simply provide the applicant with the information and make an official record thereof (Article 22(1) of the APIA); otherwise, if it dismisses the request in whole or in part, it issues a negative decision (Article 22(2) of the APIA). However, if the authority does not decide on the request at all, after the expiry of the statutory time for taking a decision, the fiction of a negative decision is established because of the administrative silence (Article 22(8) of the APIA) and the applicant has the right to appeal.

b. Legal Protection

Appeals Procedure

The appeal shall be lodged within 15 days of serving the act or after the expiry of the time limit for deciding on the access request in the case of administrative silence and is suspensive (Article 236 of the GAPA). It may be lodged on the grounds of fundamental breaches of procedural rules, misapplication of substantive law, and incomplete or incorrect factual findings (Article 237 of the GAPA).[56]

In certain cases, the first instance authority also has the power to issue a substitute decision (Articles 242–44 of the GAPA). If such a decision is not taken and the appeal fulfils all the procedural requirements, it is forwarded to the Information Commissioner as the appellate body. The latter may dismiss the appeal, annul or modify the decision in whole or in part, or declare it null and void (Article 246(3) of the GAPA). The decision on the appeal must be issued and served on the party as soon as possible, but no later than two months after receipt of a complete appeal (Article 256 of the GAPA). According to the report on the work of the Information Commissioner, the average time taken by the Information Commissioner to resolve an appeal in 2022 was 30 days, meaning that the statutory time limit is

[54] Article 14 of the APIA.
[55] *cf* Administrative Court of the RS Judgment IV U 108/2021-19 of 15 February 2022.
[56] Pirc Musar et al (n 53) 343.

usually respected in practice.[57] There is no administrative fee for the appeal and no special procedural costs.[58]

The APIA confers the power of enforcement on the Information Commissioner, and it shall be carried out on request by the applicant, based on an enforceable decision and a decision authorising enforcement, using coercive measures (imposing a fine) against the authority or economic operators which must comply with the obligation (Article 27a of the APIA). If it fails to comply with its obligation even within the additional deadline, the Information Commissioner shall collect the fine and set a new deadline, together with a higher fine, which will be imposed if the obligation is again not complied with.[59]

Administrative Dispute

The decision of the Information Commissioner is not appealable, but may be the subject of an administrative dispute. A decision may be challenged on the grounds of an incorrect application of the substantive law, a fundamental infringement of the procedural rules, or an incorrect or incomplete finding of the facts (Article 27 of the ADA-1). An action may also be lodged in cases of silence of the first instance authority and/or the Information Commissioner (Article 28(2-4) of the ADA-1). In an administrative dispute, the court examines the legality of the Information Commissioner's decision and, indirectly, the decision of the entity owning a duty to allow access to information of a public nature.

The plaintiff in an administrative dispute is a person who was a party (the applicant) or an accessory participant (a person whose legal interest may be affected by disclosure of the requested information) in the proceedings under the APIA, and also the liable entity for access to information of a public nature,[60] which is an exception to the general rule under the ADA-1, according to which 'the plaintiff may not be the authority which has decided on the completed (administrative) procedure'. A representative of the public interest may also act as a plaintiff.

The action must be lodged within 30 days of the Information Commissioner's decision being served on the addressee. Even though the action does not normally suspend the execution of the contested act in an administrative dispute (Article 32(1) of the ADA-1), according to the provision of Article 10 of the ICA, the liable entity for access to information of a public nature shall not send the requested information to the applicant if the latter lodges an action against the decision of the Information Commissioner, meaning that an action against the decision of the Information Commissioner has a suspensive effect.[61] However, an

[57] Information Commissioner, Annual Report, 2022, 35, www.ip-rs.si/fileadmin/user_upload/Pdf/porocila/LP2022.pdf.

[58] This is the practice of the Information Commissioner. See, eg, Decisions 090-1/2024 of 17 January 2024; 090-83/2024 of 19 March 2024; and 090-50/2024 of 29 February 2024.

[59] Pirc Musar et al (n 53) 347–48.

[60] ibid 350–51. See also Administrative Court of the RS Judgment U 211/2008 of 2 July 2010.

[61] *cf* Supreme Court Decision I Up 72/2016 of 30 March 2016 and the Administrative Court Decision I U 1183/2015 of 12 October 2016.

action brought by an accessory participant in an administrative dispute has no such effect. Nevertheless, the court may, at the request of the accessory participant, grant an interim injunction to suspend the decision (Article 32(2) of the ADA-1). In practice, such motions are usually granted.[62] Namely, once access is granted, it is by its very nature impossible to restore the legal situation as it was before the disclosure of the requested information.[63]

The Administrative Court has jurisdiction to annul the contested decision and refer it back to the Information Commissioner for reconsideration (dispute on the legality of the administrative act), to amend it, and to rule on the administrative matter itself (dispute of full jurisdiction), or only to declare the decision unlawful or void. In practice, it mostly rules on the legality of final administrative acts,[64] which is the basic type of administrative dispute in Slovenia. However, the literature points out that such an approach – at least as far as the procedure for access to information of a public nature is concerned – is ineffective as it prolongs access to the requested information.[65]

If the plaintiff succeeds and obtains the annulment of the administrative act or a declaration that it is unlawful, the court awards the plaintiff a lump sum for costs. These costs are to be borne by the Information Commissioner as the defendant. Otherwise, if the court rejects or dismisses the action, or if the proceedings are stayed,[66] each party shall bear its own costs. In any event, the party shall bear the costs of its own fault and the costs which are attributable to it (Article 25 of the ADA-1). Although the ICA provides that administrative dispute proceedings against a decision or order issued by the Information Commissioner are urgent and should be prioritised, in practice the Administrative Court needs more than one year to decide on actions (the average time to resolve a case in 2022 was 16.8 months).[67]

Both the Information Commissioner's and the Administrative Court's decisions are published online, thus ensuring the transparency and publicity of these proceedings.

ii. Implementation of Article 9(2) and 9(3) of the Aarhus Convention

Article 9(2) and 9(3) of the Aarhus Convention has been implemented in various environmental-related laws. Among the most important are the EPA-2, the

[62] Administrative Court Decisions II U 222/2023-17 of 12 September 2023 and II U 306/2021-25 of 4 September 2023. See also Supreme Court Decision I Up 88/2020 of 5 August 2020.

[63] Administrative Court Decision I U 1777/2014 of 18 November 2014; Administrative Court Judgment II U 412/2016 of 3 November 2016; Supreme Court Decision I Up 72/2016 of 30 March 2014; and Supreme Court Decision X Ips 312/2015 of 9 March 2016.

[64] For example, Administrative Court Judgments I U 1870/2020-24 of 21 August 2023; I U 67/2020-27 of 8 August 2023; and I U 239/2020-19 of 18 January 2023.

[65] Prepeluh, *Pravica dostopa do informacij javnega značaja*, above n 50 at 500.

[66] Article 39 of the ADA-1 provides for exceptions.

[67] Supreme Court of the RS, 'Annual Report on the Efficiency and Effectiveness of the Courts: 2022', 35–36, www.sodisce.si/mma_bin.php?static_id=2023051510484242.

SPA-3, the BA-1 and the NCA. The environmentally relevant decisions against which members of the (concerned) public must have legal protection take the form of both general legal acts (eg, spatial planning acts) and individual legal acts (eg, environmental permits or building permits). The type of legal act in which such a decision is adopted also determines the legal protection, as will be presented below.

a. Legal Protection against Spatial Implementing Acts

Until the entry into force of the EPA-2, legal protection against spatial implementing acts as general legal acts, corresponding to the acts referred to in Article 7 of the Aarhus Convention, was guaranteed before the Constitutional Court. However, the above-mentioned law (in Article 58) established judicial review before the Administrative Court (in an administrative dispute), but in the case U-I-327/20 of 20 January 2022, the Constitutional Court ruled that such regulation is unconstitutional, as the latter is the only court competent to review the constitutionality and legality of regulations. Before this decision was taken, the (practically identical) administrative dispute regulation was transposed into the EPA-3 (Article 61), which has not yet been assessed by the Constitutional Court (the procedure is still pending). However, since the regulation in the EPA-3 is analogous to the regulation in the EPA-2, it is possible to expect the same decision, meaning that until the Constitution is amended, legal protection against spatial implementing acts can only be guaranteed before the Constitutional Court. For this reason, only this form of judicial procedure will be presented below.

To initiate proceedings for the review of the constitutionality or legality of a regulation or general act based on a petition, the petitioner must demonstrate a legal interest, ie, that the provisions of the regulation whose review the petitioner seeks directly affect its rights, legal interests or legal position (Article 24 of the CCA). According to the Constitutional Court's case law,[68] legal interest in challenging a general legal act by a constitutional petition is established if the petitioner has exhausted all (ordinary and extraordinary) legal remedies, including a constitutional appeal against an individual act based on a general legal act, in which it has invoked the alleged unconstitutionality or unlawfulness of the general legal act. However, the Constitutional Court has formulated an exception to this requirement precisely concerning spatial implementing acts, which must, as a rule,[69] be considered to directly interfere with the legal position of the owners of the land to which the spatial implementing act relates.[70] Therefore, these persons

[68] Constitutional Court Decision U-I-275/07 of 22 November 2007. See also Constitutional Court Decisions U-I-330/05, U-I-331/05, U-I-337/05 of 18 October 2007.

[69] Pucelj Vidović (n 14) 135 ff.

[70] Constitutional Court Decisions U-I-6/17 of 20 June 2016; U-I-139/15 of 23 April 2020; and U-I-151/15 of 4 June 2020.

have, in principle, a legal interest in submitting a constitutional petition against a spatial implementing act. Conversely, for members of the concerned public within the meaning of the Aarhus Convention who are not the owners of the land, it is considered that the mere activity of an NGO in the public interest is not sufficient to demonstrate a legal interest in a constitutional petition.[71] Yet, it is not clear whether a different position would apply if the NGO also argued that the contested provision directly affected its legal interest or an interest that the organisation represented under the law.[72] However, the so-called eligible petitioners (including, for example, the Ombudsman, who is particularly important for the protection of the environment) do not have to demonstrate a legal interest (Article 23a of the CCA). Therefore, the Constitution distinguishes between a petition and a request for the review of constitutionality and legality.

On the other hand, the Constitutional Court's case law considers a violation of the prescribed procedure for public participation (in the adoption of spatial planning acts) as a direct contravention of the constitutionally protected right in the management of public affairs under Article 44 of the Constitution, and consequently recognises the existence of legal interest to any legal and natural persons, including NGOs, alleging a violation of the statutory provisions on public participation.[73]

The existence of a legal interest is only one of the formal obstacles to accessing the review of a spatial implementing act. Namely, the Constitutional Court also has the discretion to dismiss a petition if it considers that it does not raise an important legal issue or dismiss it as clearly unfounded without further reasoning (Article 26(2) of the CCA). Therefore, even if a legal interest in the constitutional petition is demonstrated, the petition (and a spatial implementing act) will not necessarily be examined on its merits.

A petition against a regulation may be lodged within one year of its entry into force or within one year of the date on which the petitioner became aware of the occurrence of harmful consequences (Article 24(3) of the CCA). Lodging of a constitutional petition (even if the Constitutional Court accepts it) does not affect the implementation of the contested regulation. However, the Constitutional Court may, *ex officio* or at the petitioner's request, suspend the execution or implementation of a regulation, in whole or in part, pending a final decision, if its execution could lead to consequences that are difficult to remedy (Article 39 of the CCA).[74]

[71] Constitutional Court Decisions U-I-386/06 of 13 March 2018; U-I-316/12 of 21 February 2013; and U-I-107/16 of 1 March 2018.

[72] Constitutional Court Decision U-I-214/12 of 18 September 2014.

[73] Pucelj Vidović (n 14) 141.

[74] For more information on the temporary suspension of the enforcement of a (implementing) regulation, see S Nerad, 'Commentary on Art. 161 of the Constitution' in L Šturm et al (eds), *Komentar Ustave Republike Slovenije* (*Commentary on the Constitution of the Republic of Slovenia*) (Kranj, Fakulteta za državne in evropske študije, 2011) 445.

The Constitutional Court may assess the contested spatial implementing act both concerning procedural (Article 21(3) of the CCA) and substantive constitutional (and legal) compliance (Article 21(1) of the CCA). However, the Constitutional Court is rather reticent when it comes to assessing technical (expert) issues (eg, technical (expert) grounds justifying the change of land use).[75] As a rule, the Constitutional Court examines a constitutional petition in a closed session, but on the motion of the parties to the proceedings (or on the initiative of the President of the Constitutional Court or on the motion of three judges), it may hold a public hearing, while it always adopts a decision in a closed session (Articles 35 and 40 of the CCA).

The Constitutional Court may either abrogate (with immediate effect or deferred) or annul the spatial implementing act and may also simply issue a declaratory decision. An act that is abrogated shall not apply to relationships that arose before the date on which the abrogation took effect if these relationships have not been finally decided by that date. On the other hand, the annulment of a planning act has a retroactive effect: it is considered as if it had never existed (Article 45 of the CCA).

As with other regulations, where a spatial implementing act has been annulled, anyone who has suffered from adverse effects as a result of the act may claim that those effects be remedied. If less than one year has elapsed between the service of the individual act and the filing of the petition or request against the spatial implementing act, the person who has suffered adverse consequences as a result of the individual act has the right to request the amendment or annulment of the individual act from the authority that decided on first instance within three months of the date of publication of the decision of the Constitutional Court. Therefore, the law (at least theoretically) allows an application for the annulment of a building permit, an expropriation or an inspection decision. However, if the consequences have arisen directly from a regulation (a spatial implementing act) annulled by the Constitutional Court, the body that issued that regulation is required to remedy the consequences. Nevertheless, if this is not possible (eg, because the building permit was not even required for the construction), the person is entitled (only) to compensation (Article 46 of the CCA).[76]

In proceedings before the Constitutional Court, as a rule, each participant in the proceedings bears their own costs, unless the Constitutional Court decides otherwise (Article 32 of the CCA). The decisions of the Constitutional Court are published in the Official Journal of the Republic of Slovenia and are thus publicly available. The average time to resolve constitutional petitions and requests in 2021 was 491 days.[77]

[75] See, for example, the following Constitutional Court Decisions: U-I-123/01 of 18 September 2003; U-I-56/01 of 16 October 2003; and U-I-35/94 of 16 June 1994.

[76] For more on this, see Pucelj Vidović (n 14) 157–59.

[77] Constitutional Court of the Republic of Slovenia, 'Work Report 2021', 75, www.us-rs.si/predsednik-ustavnega-sodisca-dr-matej-accetto-predstavil-porocilo-o-delu-za-leto-2021.

b. Legal Protection against Environmentally Relevant Decisions which are Individual Legal Acts: Appeal Procedure and Administrative Dispute

The appeal procedure against an individual environmental act, issued by the constituent bodies within the competent ministry or administrative unit, with the ministry itself deciding on the appeal (or, in some cases, as the first instance authority), is conducted following the provisions of the GAPA and specific laws.

According to the GAPA, in addition to the main party to the administrative procedure, the person who participated as an accessory participant in the proceedings at the first instance also has the right to appeal. To obtain the status of an accessory participant, a person must demonstrate legal interest (Article 43 of the GAPA). A legal interest is defined as a direct personal benefit based on a law or regulation. The authority deciding on the matter must invite these persons to participate in the procedure *ex officio* (Article 143 of the GAPA) and must, throughout the procedure, ensure that everyone whose rights or legal interests may be affected by the decision is involved in the procedure (Article 44 of the GAPA). According to Article 235 of the GAPA, an accessory participant may appeal against an individual act, even if it did not participate in the first instance (however, if it was correctly invited to the procedure but did not participate, it cannot rely on certain grounds of appeal).[78] It may lodge an appeal within the time limit applicable to the main party (15 days) or request service of the decision within that time limit and then appeal (Article 229 of the GAPA).

It is accepted in the administrative case law that the pursuit of a general or public interest is not recognised as a legal interest giving a right to intervene in a procedure as an accessory participant.[79] However, there are exceptions to this rule in the field of environmental law, as NGOs acting in the public interest and citizens' initiatives have a recognised *ipso lege*[80] legal interest in participating in certain administrative proceedings (and administrative disputes).

NGOs representing public interest – 'nature conservation' – have the right to represent nature conservation interests (be a party and use legal remedies) in all administrative procedures and all administrative disputes. On the other hand, the right of NGOs acting in the public interest of environmental protection to participate in the procedure (and access to justice) is only guaranteed in the following procedures: the preliminary environmental impact assessment procedure (preliminary procedure) and the environmental impact assessment procedure, the procedure for issuing an environmental permit and the procedure for identifying and remediating environmental damage. However, administrative case law[81] has also recognised their right to participate in SEA procedures (for the National Energy Climate Plan), including the right to lodge a legal remedy, namely

[78] Kerševan and Androjna (n 8) 139–41.

[79] Supreme Court Decision X Ips 329/2010 of 18 May 2011.

[80] See Supreme Court Decision I Up 15/2018 of 21 March 2018; Administrative Court Judgment I U 1307/2013 of 5 December 2013; and Administrative Court Judgment I U 710/2014 of 5 June 2014.

[81] Administrative Court Judgment II U 145/2016 of 18 January 2017.

an appeal to the government (if the authority preparing the plan is at the national level) or an action in administrative dispute (if the authority preparing the plan is at the local level). Both NGOs (acting in the field of environmental protection and/or nature conservation) also have the right to participate in the integral process of granting the building permit, including the right to pursue legal remedies. This right also belongs to citizens' initiatives (a group of 200 inhabitants residing in the municipality where the construction is planned or in an adjacent municipality). The citizens' initiative can also participate (as an accessory participant with *ipso lege* legal interest) in the (preliminary) environmental impact assessment procedure and environmental permit procedure.

Moreover, the BA-1 also grants the status of an accessory participant to the (ordinary or integrated) building permit proceedings to the owner of the immovable property and the holder of other rights *in rem* in the immovable property which is the subject of the building permit; to the owner of the land adjacent to the immovable property on which the construction is to be carried out, unless the authority establishes that it is affected by the construction, and to any other person if that person establishes that their rights and legal interests are likely to be affected by the construction, both in the course of and after the construction, as a result of its impact on the immovable property concerned by the proposed construction (Article 48 of the BA-1). In addition, any other person may also participate as an accessory participant, but must demonstrate a legal interest (although this does not clearly derive from sectoral laws),[82] ie, according to the general GAPA rules.[83] On the other hand, environmental authorities (eg, the Ombudsman) do not have a specific role in these proceedings. The only exception could be the provision of Article 118 of the NCA, according to which the Institute for Nature Protection has 'the right and duty to represent the interests of biodiversity conservation and protection of natural values in all administrative and judicial proceedings involving components of biodiversity, natural values or protected areas', but the practice on this issue has not yet been developed.[84]

Entities who (may) have the status of an accessory participant in an administrative procedure in environmental matters under special rules are usually informed of the opening of the procedure by public notice (on the eGovernment portal) or by the administrative authority (depending on the type of procedure).[85] They must notify their participation within the prescribed framework (usually 30 days) of the notification, whereby the request for entry into the procedure must include the secure electronic mailbox details (in the case of NGOs and citizens' initiatives); any subsequent request to intervene shall be rejected. The preclusion to intervene in a procedure is therefore regulated differently (more strictly) in the

[82] For more on this, see Pucelj Vidović (n 14) 222–23.
[83] *cf* Supreme Court Judgment X Ips 335/2011 of 29 November 2011. See also Administrative Court Judgment I U 1417/2019-10 of 28 July 2020.
[84] Pucelj Vidović (n 14) 211.
[85] See, for example, arts 97, 113, 127, and 133 of the EPA-2; and art 68(1) of BA-1.

environmental legislation than in the GAPA. This also means that they cannot appeal against a decision and cannot initiate an administrative dispute if they have not participated in the procedure for issuing the administrative act, except in the cases provided for by law. However, these exceptions apply (only) to members of the concerned public (NGOs and citizens' initiatives), who can bring an administrative dispute against certain environmental decisions, such as environmental consent (Article 103(2) of the EPA-2), environmental permits (Article 133(8) of the EPA-2) and integrated building permit procedures (Article 71(2) of the BA-1), even if they did not participate in the prior administrative procedure.

The action does not suspend the execution of the contested act. However, since the specific laws do not expressly exclude the possibility of granting interim injunction, it must be deemed to be admissible under the conditions of the ADA-1, ie, if the plaintiff proves the occurrence of irreparable damage (to it). However, the latter is difficult to prove in the case of NGOs representing the public interest.[86] The decision may be challenged in an administrative dispute on both substantive and procedural grounds (and also nullity), and the court usually rules on disputes concerning the legality of the administrative acts, which (can) significantly prolong the whole procedure. However, the plea of substantial breaches of procedural rules is (at least in certain procedures) broader than in the ADA-1: it covers all breaches of procedural rules, both the general procedural provisions of GAPA and the specific procedural requirements laid down in sectoral laws (eg, the EPA-2 and the BA-1). But this usually applies only where the plaintiff is an NGO acting in the public interest or a citizens' initiative (Article 72(6) of the BA-1 and Article 103 of the EPA-2). Otherwise, some specific laws impose a limitation on the invocation of certain substantive law infringements (eg, Article 71(7) of the BA-1 and Article 103(7) of the EPA-2), making such regulation more restrictive than under the general rules in the ADA-1. In addition, under specific laws (eg, Article 71 of the BA-1), the Administrative Court also has the power to reject an action if it finds that the action brought by an NGO or a citizens' initiative clearly has no consequences for the public interest of environmental and nature protection, or that such consequences are negligible, unless the action involves the resolution of an important legal question. Therefore, the status of NGOs in the public interest or citizens' initiatives does not automatically give them an absolute right to access justice.

Representation by proxy in an administrative dispute is not compulsory, except in the case of extraordinary legal remedies, where the proxy does not have to be a lawyer, but can be another person who has passed the state bar exam (Article 86 of the CPA). However, a plaintiff may also apply for free legal aid: for natural persons, the granting of such an application depends on their financial situation, while NGOs acting in the public interest are eligible regardless of their financial situation, provided that the dispute relates to an activity in the public interest or to

[86] Administrative Court Judgment I U 2541/2018 of 27 December 2018.

the purpose for which they were established (Article 10 of the Free Legal Aid Act (FLAA)).[87] In addition to representation, free legal aid may also include an exemption from the costs of legal proceedings (Article 26 of the FLAA).[88]

IV. The Main Problems Hampering Access to Justice in Environmental Matters and Some *de Lege Ferenda* Proposals

Based on the above, it can be concluded that accession to the EU and ratification of the Aarhus Convention have contributed significantly to environmental protection in the Republic of Slovenia. However, Slovenian legislation still does not provide all the required standards of legal protection as established by the Aarhus Convention, especially for members of the concerned public (NGOs acting in the public interest) against spatial implementing acts and individual decisions on environmental interventions (Article 9(2) and 9(3) of the Aarhus Convention), while, on the other hand, the right to legal protection to access environmental information (Article 9(1) of the Aarhus Convention) is effectively implemented. This position is also accepted by the NGOs acting in the public interest.[89]

The judicial protection before the Constitutional Court in the procedure for reviewing the constitutionality and legality of spatial implementing acts (representing acts under Article 7 of the Aarhus Convention) is significantly restricted, as the petitioner must demonstrate a legal interest, which, according to the established constitutional case law, is interpreted very restrictively and makes it almost impossible in practice for NGOs to access it. Moreover, the Constitutional Court has the power to dismiss a case without a substantive examination as clearly unfounded or because it does not raise an important legal question, which is not in line with the minimum requirements of Article 9(3) and 9(4) of the Aarhus Convention. The procedure is also not adapted to certain other procedural requirements of the Aarhus Convention: it is not aimed at the adversarial nature of the procedure (the main hearing is held only in exceptional cases), the court is restrained in its substantive assessment of the contested act, and the procedure for resolving the constitutional petition is lengthy. Given the above, in the future, it would be more appropriate to (re)provide legal protection against spatial implementing acts before the Administrative Court as a specific administrative dispute, but it is

[87] Official Gazette of the RS, Nos 96/04 et seq.

[88] Vrbica and Videtič (n 16) 9–10.

[89] Plan B for Slovenia: NGO Network for Sustainable Development, 'Aarhus Convention, Human Rights and Climate Change'. https://planbzaslovenijo.si/aarhuska-konvencija-in-podnebje-v-casu-predsedovanja-vabilo-na-posvet-7-9-2021. See also Spatial Planning Network, 'Judicial Protection in Spatial Planning Decisions in the Light of the Requirements of the Aarhus Convention', www.mrezaprostor.si/aktualno/clanki/sodno-varstvo-pri-odlocanju-o-posegih-v-prostor-v-luci-zahtev-aarhuske-konvencije.

necessary to first amend the constitutional provisions on the competence of the Constitutional Court.[90] However, according to NGOs acting in the public interest, there is currently no will of the competent ministry to remedy these shortcomings and there is also a lack of professional debate on the subject matter.

More adequately but still insufficiently, the Aarhus Convention's requirements on legal protection have been implemented for individual acts. This refers in particular to the *ipso lege* recognition of the legal interest of NGOs and citizens' initiatives to participate in the procedures for issuing such an act. However, a position as an accessory participant is specifically granted to them only in enumerated environmentally relevant proceedings, and not in all proceedings (eg, not in the procedure for granting water consent). According to the case law of the CJEU, such a restriction is not compatible with EU law or the Convention.[91] This is also the position of NGOs acting in the public interest in the field of environmental/nature/spatial protection. They therefore suggest that legal protection, as regulated by the NCA, should also be established in other environmental matters, and thus in all administrative in judicial procedures. Moreover, in their view, there is no reason to allow accessory participants to intervene in an administrative procedure only within a certain timeframe after being informed of the procedure (30 days), especially given that in some cases, NGOs are not even aware of the proceedings. In addition, unnecessary (other) barriers to NGOs' entry into the administrative process and consequent access to justice (eg, the requirement for an email inbox) should be removed. NGOs' entry into the administrative procedure should in their opinion be subject to the (general) GAPA regime, which is more favourable, and all information on ongoing (environmental) procedures should be publicly available. Namely, they perceive that the right to information about and participation in (potentially controversial) proceedings is not being fully and effectively exercised under the current regime.[92]

[90] *cf* Pucelj Vidović (n 14) 129 ff.

[91] Case C-664/15 *Protect Natur-, Arten- und Landschaftsschutz Umweltorganisation v Bezirkshauptmannschaft Gmünd* ECLI:EU:C:2017:987, para 45.

[92] NGOs' views on the effectiveness of access to justice in environmental matters were obtained through an online questionnaire (1 July 2024). The questionnaire contained the following questions: 'Is the position of NGOs adequately protected in decision-making procedures on environmental matters? What do you consider to be the main legislative, practical and/or other obstacles that hinder access to justice in environmental matters? How could current regulation/practice on access to justice in environmental matters be improved?'

PART III

Comparative Assessment

10

Administrative Review as an Instrument to Enforce Article 9 of the Aarhus Convention

GIACOMO GATTINARA

I. Introduction

In the following paragraphs the administrative review contemplated in the Aarhus Convention will be presented, with a focus on its interactions with the pillar of access to justice in environmental matters. It will then be possible to understand to what extent the existing administrative remedies for infringements of environmental law, which are available in the national legal systems considered as well as – to achieve a more complete European view – with regard to the activity of the EU institutions and bodies, match the requirements provided for in the Aarhus Convention, as clarified in the case law of the Aarhus Convention Compliance Committee (ACCC), which reviews compliance of the contracting parties with the Convention.[1] Once the existing rules established at the national and EU level are clarified, it will be possible to illustrate the positive consequences administrative review has for access to justice in environmental matters. The time will then be ripe to draw some conclusions.

II. Judicial, Quasi-judicial and Administrative Review in the Aarhus Convention

Administrative review is mentioned in Article 9 of the Aarhus Convention both as an alternative and as a complement to judicial review. A clear reference to administrative review in the Aarhus Convention as an alternative to judicial review is

[1] See recently F Zeitner, *Das Aarhus Convention Compliance Committee (ACCC): Institution, Legitimation, Rezeption* (Berlin, Duncker & Humblot, 2022) 51 and ff.

provided for in the Convention as regards, first, decisions on access to environmental information under Article 9(1) of the Convention, second, the legality control of 'any decision, act or omission subject to the provisions of article 6' on public participation and, third, the more general infringements to environmental law mentioned in Article 9(3), according to which:

> In addition and without prejudice to the review procedures referred to in paragraphs 1 and 2 above, each Party shall ensure that, where they meet the criteria, if any, laid down in its national law, members of the public have access to administrative or judicial procedures to challenge acts and omissions by private persons and public authorities which contravene provisions of its national law relating to the environment.

These instances of review are supposed to be 'independent and impartial', as indicated in Article 9(1) and (2). The Aarhus Convention Secretariat provided a definition in the Implementation Guide (hereinafter 'the Guide') of these requirements as regards Article 9(1) of the Convention, which can however also be extended to Article 9(2). The Guide states as follows:

> 'Independent and impartial' bodies do not have to be courts, but must be at least quasi-judicial, with safeguards to guarantee due process, independent of influence by any branch of government and unconnected to any private entity.[2]

It is then only at these conditions that a review body can be considered as being an alternative to judicial review and then as an independent and impartial body within the meaning of Article 9(1) and (2) of the Aarhus Convention.

The Convention requires a reinforced administrative review, ie, a review that is equivalent, as to its procedure and effects,[3] to judicial review, only for two categories of measures, which, according to the Guide, correspond to, first, refusals and inadequate handling by public authorities of requests for environmental information and, second, to decisions, acts and omissions by public authorities concerning permits, permit procedures and decision-making for specific activities. Conversely, as regards all other kinds of acts and omissions by private persons and public authorities that may have contravened national law relating to the environment, the contracting parties 'may ensure access to justice either by administrative or judicial procedures'.[4]

It follows that the word 'administrative' as an alternative to 'judicial' review in Article 9(3) of the Aarhus Convention does not have the same meaning as

[2] J Ebbesson et al, *The Aarhus Convention: An Implementation Guide*, 2nd edn (New York, United Nations Economic Commission for Europe, 2014) 191.

[3] For instance, as regards access to environmental information under art 9(1) of the Aarhus Convention, the Aarhus Compliance Committee (ACCC) has clarified that this provision 'implies that the final decisions of a court of law or other independent and impartial body established by law are binding upon and must thus be complied with by public authorities' (Moldova ACCC/C/2008/30; ECE/MP.PP/C.1/2009/6/Add.3, 8 February 2011, para 35).

[4] Ebbesson et al (n 2) 188.

'independent and impartial' review, as provided for, on the other hand, under Article 9(1) (2) of the Convention.

However, the Guide also clarified that in order to be compliant with the Aarhus Convention, administrative review procedures that do not guarantee a review by an 'independent and impartial' body also have to respect certain basic requirements:

> While making the distinction between judicial and administrative procedures, certain general requirements are imposed on all reviewing instances and procedures within the scope of the Convention. First, they must be fair, equitable, timely and not prohibitively expensive. Second, they must provide adequate and effective remedies. Third, information on administrative and judicial review procedures must be disseminated to the public, and the Parties are encouraged to establish appropriate assistance mechanisms to remove or reduce financial and other barriers.[5]

In turn, the concept that administrative review may work as a procedural complement to judicial review can be found more explicitly in Article 9(2) as regards access to justice, which has to be granted to challenge 'the substantive and procedural legality of any decision, act or omission subject to the provisions of Article 6' on public participation and the breach, 'where so provided for under national law and without prejudice to paragraph 3 below, of other relevant provisions of this Convention'.

The last subparagraph of Article 9(2) of the Convention provides in this regard that the obligation to allow for judicial review:

> [S]hall not exclude the possibility of a preliminary review procedure before an administrative authority and shall not affect the requirement of exhaustion of administrative review procedures prior to recourse to judicial review procedures, where such a requirement exists under national law.

This complementarity can also exist as regards access to justice under Article 9(3), which explicitly provides for the possibility for the applicant to have access to courts 'where they meet the criteria, if any, laid down in its national law'.

The studies into the different legal systems mentioned in the previous chapters of this book illustrate very good the added value of this review to strengthen access to justice under the Aarhus Convention, which is a cross-cutting pillar, concerning not only review of acts or omissions in breach of environmental law under Article 9(3) of the Aarhus Convention, but also review of measures or omissions adopted in breach of the rules on access to environmental information under Article 9(1) of the Convention, and of those on public participation under Article 9(2) thereof.

[5] ibid.

III. Forms of Administrative Review in Environmental Matters in the Balkans and in the EU: Europeanisation of Access to Justice?

A. Administrative Review as an Alternative to Judicial Review in Order to Ensure Access to Justice in Environmental Matters

i. North Macedonia

Under Article 144 of the Law on Environment, the commission for dispute resolution is competent on the operation of installations before the issuance of integrated environmental permits. While the latter are almost entirely expired, the commission can still be asked to intervene as regards large combustion plants (over 50 MW).[6]

B. Administrative Review as a Complement to Judicial Review

i. Reinforced or Quasi-judicial Administrative Review

a. Albania

A 'reinforced' administrative review, within the meaning explained in section II above, exists as regards the right of access to environmental information, which was introduced precisely to implement the first pillar of the Aarhus Convention. If the public body that receives the request does not meet the 10-day deadline, the concerned party may appeal to the Commissioner for the Right of Information and Data Protection, who has the authority to compel the public institution to provide the requested information and may impose an administrative penalty for non-compliance. A court can decide to suspend the effects of the decisions of the Commissioner, which is an independent public entity appointed by the Parliament.[7]

b. Croatia

Access to environmental information is also the remit of an independent and impartial Information Commissioner, who is appointed by the Parliament and, if the request for information has been wrongfully refused or ignored, can adjudicate on the appeal. The decisions of the Commissioner are binding for the

[6] See Antonovska Joskoska and Bitrakov, ch 6 in this volume, section III.B.vi.
[7] See Terihati, ch 4 in this volume, section IV.A.

public authority concerned and enforceable and can be reviewed in court. The Commissioner can also impose sanctions to ensure compliance.[8]

c. Serbia

The Commissioner for Information of Public Importance is an appellate authority in the procedure for exercising the right of access to environmental information. It has the power to instruct the relevant departments of the administration to take certain decisions and grant access to the appellant. It has developed an extensive body of case law.[9]

d. Slovenia

Appeals against administrative decisions concerning requests for access to environmental information can be filed with the Information Commissioner, who can adopt enforceable decisions as well as coercive measures in order to ensure compliance, such as the imposition of a fine. Decisions of the Information Commissioner are subject only to judicial review and cannot be further reviewed with an administrative appeal.[10]

ii. Ordinary Administrative Review

a. Albania

Administrative appeals (or 'complaints')[11] can be filed, according to the specific area of environmental law concerned, at the local and national levels. For instance, appeals to the Minister for the Environment are provided for as regards the development of public notification and consultation procedures. In other cases where an administrative decision can harm the environment or threat the interests of the community, all concerned entities can appeal to the superior administrative body to control the decision-making process. The decisions taken by these instances of review can be further challenged in court. The interest in seeking judicial redress is that in the event that the administrative appeal is founded, the review body can annul, revoke or amend the contested act, or even issue the act requested by the appellant in case of a refusal to act by the administration. When it is provided for and the relevant rules contain the indication of the competent administrative review body, recourse to administrative appeal to settle administrative disputes before resorting to court is compulsory.[12]

[8] Ofak and Turudić, ch 5 in this volume, section III.
[9] Drenovak-Ivanović, ch 8 in this volume, section III.B.i.
[10] Štemberger Brizani, ch 9 in this volume, section III.B.i.
[11] On the difference between the two legal remedies, see Terihati, ch 4 in this volume, n 1.
[12] ibid section V.A.

b. Croatia

A first administrative appeal can be made against decisions of 'inspectors', ie, public officials carrying out an expert examination in specific areas. The party requesting the inspection is not a party to the procedure, but can seek an appeal against the decision of the inspector, to be filed with a different office of the same service inspectorate. A second appeal is provided for in the Constitution in Article 18 against an administrative decision or an omission, whenever this is provided for in specific legislation, according to the different area concerned. The applicant can seek redress in court against the decision on the appeal. Whenever this administrative appeal procedure is foreseen, the administrative review has to be exhausted before lodging a judicial application. Appellants shall prove impairment of their rights. A third case is the request of re-examination of decisions, acts or omissions of public authorities as regards environmental issues, which has been introduced to implement Article 9(3) of the Aarhus Convention under quite restrictive conditions, such as the need to prove impairment of rights and the provision of tight time limitations.[13]

c. North Macedonia

Apart from the limited area outlined above, administrative review is possible as a preliminary step before lodging a judicial application. However, the entry into force of as well as the need to implement the Aarhus Convention in the national legal order have reshaped the recourse to administrative remedies. Thus, as regards access to justice in environmental matters against individual administrative acts (such as decisions), it is possible for a member of the public and for a member of the public concerned to file an administrative appeal to the State Commission for administrative proceedings and employment proceedings. Decisions of the State Commission can be directly contested in court. The end of a second instance of review procedure is indeed, for certain areas, a necessary procedural precondition to fulfil in order to validly seek judicial redress against an administrative decision. However, an immediate judicial action against an administrative decision is admissible if that decision affects the rights or legal interests of the applicant.[14]

d. Romania

Administrative appeals against decisions, acts or omissions are not only possible but also necessary to further seek judicial review. They are then compulsory except as regards measures or omissions concerning the right to environmental information. The appeal can be filed either with the administration that adopted the act or failed to do so or with the hierarchically superior body.[15] The rules recently

[13] Ofak and Turudić, ch 5 in this volume, sections III–VI.
[14] Antonovska Joskoska and Bitrakov, ch 6 in this volume, section III.B.
[15] This twofold pattern is also followed in other countries: see W Piątek and M Horvat, 'A Comparative Analysis of Limitations in Administrative Appeals in Europe: The Case of Poland and Slovakia' (2018) 11(2) *Review of European Administrative Law* 5, 11.

adopted to transpose the Aarhus Convention have entailed certain changes, in particular as regards access to environmental information, for which the applicant has to prove that the lack of an appropriate response to the request for environmental information has breached some individual rights.[16]

e. Serbia

Administrative appeals are considered as regular administrative remedies under Article 36(2) of the Serbian Constitution and can be filed against any administrative act unless explicitly excluded by law in certain administrative areas.[17] Thus, the exhaustion of the administrative appeal procedure is a requirement to trigger judicial proceedings. As regards the admissibility of the appeal, while it is necessary to prove that the outcome of the proceedings may have an impact on the interest the appellant represents, recent legislative changes carried out to implement the Aarhus Convention also allow environmental protection to be considered as a value of public interest.[18]

f. Slovenia

Two kinds of administrative appeals are provided for.[19] The first relates to environmentally relevant decisions and it requires the participation of the appellant to the previous administrative procedure whereby the measure against which the appeal is filed was adopted. Still, when the appeal is targeted against such individual decisions, it is also possible to obtain the status of accessory participant, if a person demonstrates legal interest. The second remedy is the constitutional petition against spatial implementing acts. In this case, the admissibility of an action is contingent upon the finding of a legal interest, as is typically the case for the owner of the land to which the spatial act relates.[20]

C. The Example of the EU: The Ordinary Administrative Review in Environmental Matters under the Aarhus Regulation

When analysing the effect of the Aarhus Convention on access to justice in certain domestic legal systems and in particular the possible convergence of those systems

[16] Lodoabă-Cordon, Dragos and Neamtu, ch 7 in this volume, section IV.

[17] V Cucić, Administrative Appeal in Serbian Law' (2011) 32(E) *Transylvanian Review of Administrative Sciences* 50, 53. See also D Vučetić, 'Serbia' in Z Kmieciak (ed), *Administrative Proceedings in the Habsburg Succession Countries* (Warsaw, Kluwer Polska, 2021) 181, 186 f; V Cucić, 'Serbia as Part of the European Administrative Space: ADR Tools Applied to Administrative Law' in DC Dragos and B Neamtu (eds) *Alternative Dispute Resolution in European Administrative Law* (Heidelberg, Springer, 2014) 461.

[18] Drenovak-Ivanović, ch 8 in this volume, section IV.A.

[19] 'Ordinary' appeals are foreseen in the general administrative law act: see B Žuber, 'Slovenia' in Kmieciak (n 17) 215, 221 f.

[20] Štemberger Brizani, ch 9 in this volume, section III.

towards a common European standard as regards administrative review, it is useful to complete the study with a mention of the internal review mechanism, provided for in the 'Aarhus Regulation',[21] which concerns the application of the Aarhus Convention to the EU institutions and bodies,[22] and was not examined in Part I of this book.

Under Article 10 of the Aarhus Regulation, non-governmental organisations (NGOs) and individuals are entitled, under the conditions set out in Article 11 of that Regulation, 'to make a request for internal review to the Union institution or body that adopted the administrative act or, in the case of an alleged administrative omission, should have adopted such an act'.[23] The request has to be substantiated with grounds that 'such an act or omission contravenes environmental law within the meaning of point (f) of Article 2(1)'. Thus, while intended as a specific instrument of ensuring respect of environmental law, the internal review mechanism is clearly not a quasi-judicial system of review, but it follows more the pattern of the ordinary review mechanism, already observed in the previous section, since it is often the same institution or body having adopted the act that carries out the review.

As regards the interplay with judicial review, the internal review mechanism does not work as a preliminary step in a challenge of an act before the EU Courts, given that, once the internal review is concluded, it will be the reply to the request for internal review (or the omission to reply to the request) and not the reviewed measure that will be challenged before the General Court of the EU.[24]

Overall, and following the significant changes introduced in Regulation 2021/1767,[25] the internal review mechanism under the Aarhus Regulation is nowadays conceived in such a way that it can be used to protect a general interest – that is, ensuring environmental protection – which is the major concern expressed in Article 9(3) of the Aarhus Convention. This holds true in particular as regards admissibility requirements and grounds for review.

Both NGOs and individuals, whose rights have been impaired or who show a sufficient public interest, can file a request for internal review within eight weeks

[21] Regulation (EC) No 1367/2006 of the European Parliament and the Council of 6 September 2006 on the application of the provisions of the Aarhus Convention on Access to Information, Public Participation in Decision-making and Access to Justice in Environmental Matters to institutions and bodies (Aarhus Regulation) [2006] OJ L264, 25 September 2006, 13.

[22] On which see recently P Chirulli and L de Lucia, *Non-judicial Remedies and EU Administration: Protection of Rights versus Preservation of Autonomy* (Abingdon, Routledge, 2021) 45–48.

[23] Aarhus Regulation, art 10(1), first subpara.

[24] Aarhus Regulation, art 12.

[25] Regulation (EU) 2021/1767 of the European Parliament and of the Council of 6 October 2021 amending Regulation (EC) No 1367/2006 on the application of the provisions of the Aarhus Convention on Access to Information, Public Participation in Decision-Making and Access to Justice in Environmental Matters to Community institutions and bodies [2021] OJ L356, 8 October 2021, 1. For more on this, see M van Wolferen and M Eliantonio, 'Access to Justice in Environmental Matters in the EU: The EU's Difficult Road towards Non-compliance with the Aarhus Convention' in M Peeters and M Eliantonio (eds), *Research Handbook on EU Environmental Law* (Cheltenham, Edward Elgar, 2020) 148; C Leonelli, 'Access to the EU Courts in Environmental and Public Health Cases and the Reform of the Aarhus Regulation: Systemic Vision, Pragmatism, and a Happy Ending' (2021) 40(1) *Yearbook of European Law* 230.

of the adoption of the act or the date on which it should have been adopted.[26] The reply should be provided to them within the following 16 weeks, which can be extended to 22 weeks.[27] A reading of Article 11 of the Aarhus Regulation confirms that such admissibility requirements can be easily met by both 'members of the public' and 'members of the public concerned'.[28] As to the definition of the reviewable act, Article 2(1)(g) of the Aarhus Regulation states that '"administrative act" means any non-legislative act adopted by a Union institution or body, which has legal and external effects and contains provisions that may contravene environmental law within the meaning of point (f) of Article 2(1)'.

As to the grounds for review, they can be considered as having been stated when they are of such a magnitude as to shed 'serious doubts' on the legality of the adopted measure.[29] While the seriousness of the doubts to raise may, according to the content of the measure contested, mean that the applicant has to show an unreasonable exercise of the discretion by the administration, those doubts always have to relate to the possible or actual contravention of environmental law, which is, in itself, part of the definition of the reviewable act (via the notion of 'administrative act' recalled above) and then a condition of admissibility of the request. The word 'contravene' in Article 2(1)(g) of the Aarhus Regulation has to be construed quite broadly according to recital 10 of Regulation 2021/1767,[30] which serves as a useful reference to the interpretation of the Aarhus Regulation, as well as the word 'law' contained in Article 2(1)(g), which has to be read as also meaning rules not adopted in what the Treaties define as 'legislation'.[31]

The exercise of this control in a single case can then be contested before the General Court, the reply to a request for internal review being a challengeable act under Article 263(4) of the Treaty on the Functioning of the European Union (TFEU) just like the omission to reply under Article 265 TFEU. As regards the admissibility of the application before the General Court, an annulment action cannot be founded on new grounds or on evidence not appearing in the request

[26] As of 29 April 2023, a request for internal review may also be made by individuals, although considered as members of the public and thus different from NGOs, provided that the following conditions are met: they demonstrate impairment of their rights caused by the alleged contravention of EU environmental law and that they are directly affected by such impairment in comparison with the public at large *or* they demonstrate a sufficient public interest and that the request is supported by at least 4,000 members of the public residing or established in at least five Member States, with at least 250 members of the public coming from each of those Member States (see art 11(1a) of the Aarhus Regulation).

[27] Aarhus Regulation, art 10(1) and (3).

[28] See art 2(4) and (5) of the Aarhus Convention.

[29] Recitals 14 and 21 of Regulation 2021/1767; see also Judgment in Case C-82/17 P *TestBioTech eV and Others v Commission* ECLI:EU:C:2019:719, para 69.

[30] 'When assessing whether an administrative act contains provisions which could, because of their effects, contravene environmental law, it is necessary to consider whether such provisions could have an adverse effect on the attainment of the objectives of Union policy on the environment set out in Article 191 TFEU. Where that is the case, the internal review procedure should also cover acts that have been adopted in the implementation of policies other than Union policy on the environment.'

[31] Judgment in Joined Cases C-212/21 P and C-223/21 P *Commission v ClientEarth* and *European Investment Bank v ClientEarth* ECLI:EU:C:2023:546, para 85.

for review.[32] However, this 'rule of concordance' between the request for internal review and the further annulment action against the reply thereto is mitigated by the possibility to amplify previous pleas, put forward in the request for internal review, provided that a sufficiently close connection with those pleas can be established.[33] The ensuing judicial review can only relate to the decision by the EU institution on the review request and does not extend to the merits of the initial act considered in the internal review.[34] Accordingly, applicants cannot put forward arguments directly challenging the lawfulness or merits of that initial act.[35] However, they can put forward a claim that the reply to the request is unlawful, 'based' on the reviewed measure being unlawful.[36] Still, in order to achieve this effect, an applicant should argue that the illegality of the reviewed measure was reiterated in the reply to the request for internal review. This could occur, for instance, if the institution has 'endorsed' that alleged illegality.[37]

Moreover, as to the judicial review of the reply to the request for internal review, the Court has so far been keen to keep the internal review as an instrument of control autonomous from judicial review,[38] even though, as regards the intensity of judicial scrutiny, adjudicating on the reply to a request for internal review is not different from judging on whether a measure challenged under Article 263(4) TFEU is unlawful.[39]

Without the internal review under the Aarhus Regulation, the general interest in ensuring that environmental law is respected would hardly be defendable via an action under Article 263(4) TFEU, given that the interest to have a healthy environment can be hardly confined to the limits of the 'direct and individual concern', which is provided for as a condition of admissibility for private applicants in that provision of the Treaty. However, the purpose of the internal review mechanism is not to ask the institution or body that adopted the act to re-start the procedure again in order to adopt a new administrative act. As Advocate General Szpunar put it:

> That internal review procedure is, as follows from paragraphs 2 and 3 of that provision [Article 10 of the Aarhus Regulation], connected so closely chronologically to the authorisation procedure [in that case the procedure having led to the adoption of the reviewed act] that the purpose of the internal review procedure cannot be that new

[32] Judgment in *TestBioTech eV and Others v Commission* (n 29) para 39.

[33] Judgment in Case T-536/22 *Pesticide Action Network (PAN) Europe v Commission* ECLI:EU:T:2024:98, para 46, under appeal in Case C-316/24 P, OJ C, C/2024/3751, 24 June 2024, pending.

[34] Judgment in Case T-177/13 *TestBioTech Ev and Others v Commission* ECLI:EU:T:2016:736, para 56, upheld by Judgment in *TestBioTech eV and Others v Commission* (n 29).

[35] Judgment in Case T-177/13 *TestBioTech Ev and Others v Commission* (n 34) para 56, penultimate sentence.

[36] ibid last sentence.

[37] See in this vein Judgment in Case T-108/17 *ClientEarth v Commission*, ECLI:EU:T:2019:215, para 54, upheld on appeal in Case C-458/19 P *ClientEarth v Commission* ECLI:EU:C:2021:802.

[38] See Judgment in *Commission v ClientEarth* and *European Investment Bank v ClientEarth* (n 31) paras 52–53.

[39] Judgments in Case T-605/21 *TestBiotech eV v Commission* ECLI:EU:T:2023:648, paras 18–19 and in Case T-606/21 *TestBiotech eV v Commission* ECLI:EU:T:2023:649, paras 17–18.

> scientific and technical knowledge and monitoring data that may have arisen should be taken into consideration. Rather, the internal review procedure exists to establish whether there are elements that could have been overlooked in the course of the authorisation procedure.[40]

Overall, given the tight links between the obligations of the Aarhus Convention and the internal review mechanism laid down in the Aarhus Regulation, it can safely be argued that this administrative control shares with Article 9(3) of the Aarhus Convention the nature of an instrument conceived to ensure 'effective environmental protection', as the Court has recalled.[41]

IV. Administrative Review as an Instrument to Make Access to Justice in Environmental Matters More Effective

The reason why the Aarhus Convention places considerable emphasis on administrative review is the need to find alternatives to sometimes lengthy and costly judicial proceedings following the examples existing in several countries and legal systems considered when the text of the Convention was drafted. More specifically, administrative appeals have been and are a standard feature in some of the Balkan countries that were part of the so-called 'Habsburg Succession'.[42] In Austria, appeals were already codified in 1896, about 30 years before the first general law on administrative procedure was enacted.[43] In turn, the 1925 Austrian codification influenced the Yugoslav law on general administrative procedure, including concerning appeals.[44] As recalled in the Guide:

> Many ECE countries have some kind of general administrative reconsideration or appeals process for governmental decisions. This administrative process often functions more rapidly than an appeal to a court and is often free of charge. Applied to review of requests for information, so long as the body is independent and impartial and established by law, such a process could satisfy the requirements of the Convention.[45]

[40] Case C-82/17 P *TestBiotech eV and Others v Commission* ECLI:EU:C:2018:837, Opinion of AG Szpunar, para 32.

[41] Judgment in Case C-240/09 *Lesoochranárske zoskupenie VLK (Slovak Bears I)* ECLI:EU:C:2011:125, paras 45–46.

[42] A Krawczyk, 'The Legacy of the Austrian Codification Thought: A European Perspective' in Kmieciak (n 17) 233, 241.

[43] T Olechowski, 'The History of the Administrative Procedure in Austria until 1925' in G della Cananea, A Ferrari Zumbini and O Pfersmann (eds), *The Austrian Codification of Administrative Procedure: Diffusion and Oblivion (1920–1970)* (Oxford, Oxford University Press, 2023) 26, 35. However, appeals were abandoned in Austria to the benefit of judicial review in 2012: see F Bundschuh-Rieseneder and A Balthasar, 'Administrative Justice in Austria in the Stage of Transition: From Administrative Appeals to Administrative Courts or the Final Stage of "Tribunalization" of Administrative Disputes' in DC Dragos and B Neamtu (eds), *Alternative Dispute Resolution in European Administrative Law* (Heidelberg, Springer, 2014) 209.

[44] S Lilić and M Milenković, 'Administrative Procedure in Former Yugoslavia and the Austrian Administrative Procedure Act' in della Cananea, Ferrari Zumbini and Pfersmann (n 43) 119, 131.

[45] Ebbesson et al (n 2) 187.

Admittedly, administrative review can also compensate for lack of standing that some applicants,[46] namely members of the public concerned within the meaning of Article 2(5) of the Aarhus Convention such as NGOs, can face when seeking judicial redress. In this regard, administrative review can be used to relax the standing requirements consistently, in particular with Articles 2(5) and 9(2) of the Aarhus Convention, according to which whenever requested under the procedural provisions of the contracting party, the procedural requirement consisting in the impairment of a right or in the sufficiency of an interest is 'deemed' to be automatically met for NGOs.[47] Indeed, if the relaxing of admissibility requirements is an obligation for the contracting parties to the Convention as regards access to courts, it can also be easily fulfilled at the stage of the administrative review, then allowing the requester to further seek redress either against the same measure, reviewed by the administration, as occurs in many instances of ordinary administrative review recalled above, or against the position taken by the reviewing body on that measure, as is the case for the EU institutions and bodies under the Aarhus Regulation, even though in that case it is procedurally possible for the applicant to provoke a control from the General Court also on the reviewed measure.[48]

However, more importantly, following the recollection of the main elements observed above in the different legal systems analysed in the book, administrative review can contribute to improving the effectiveness of judicial review in three different ways.

First, administrative review can operate like a 'filter' for judicial review, meaning that it can allow the judge, once the case arrives at the court, to have a better understanding of the case and the parties to better define the subject matter of the case. This can prove particularly helpful in systems, like Romania, where the judge is allowed to reconsider the facts assessed in the decision that was the subject matter of an administrative appeal.

Second, besides the alternative dispute resolution mechanism in North Macedonia, while even a quasi-judicial administrative review never replaces access to courts, it nevertheless lets the court focus only on the respect of certain constitutional guarantees and fundamental principles. This is quite evident for countries like Albania, Croatia and Slovenia (and to some extent Serbia),[49] which have a quasi-judicial body to adjudicate on specific appeals, like those concerning access to environmental information, handled by an ad hoc Commissioner who adopts decisions that are challengeable in court. In those instances of administrative review, judicial review is of key relevance, since it ensures respect of the rule of law, given the quite extensive enforcement powers those Commissioners

[46] ACCC/C/2005/11 (Belgium) (ECE/MP.PP/C.1/2006/4/Add.2, para 40.

[47] On the interplay between access to justice and public participation in particular, see G Gattinara and M Noll Ehlers, 'The Scope and Requirements of Public Participation in EU Environmental Law' in B Peters and EJ Lohse (eds), *Sustainability through Participation?* (Leiden, Brill, 2023) 139, 167.

[48] See section III.C above.

[49] The Serbian Commissioner for access to information can – in certain respects such as independence – also be considered a quasi-judicial body: see D Milovanović, M Davinić and V Cucić, 'Free Access to Information in Serbia', in DC Dragos, P Kovac and AT Marseille (eds), *The Laws of Transparency in Action: A European Perspective* (Cham, Springer, 2019) 501, 502 and 526.

are vested with. In turn, judicial review is also essential in ensuring respect of procedural provisions, which can be of essence when, like in Slovenia, the work of the Information Commissioner can entail the need to ensure a coordination with the Minister of Public Administration.

Third, the Aarhus Convention has further reinforced the assumption that administrative review means an expeditious procedure with limited costs. This proves to be particularly true as regards the administrative appeals before the Commissioners for Information in Albania, Croatia and Slovenia, which have to be decided in particularly short timeframes that in practice do not go beyond 30 days, and in which, like in Albania, the first request for environmental information has to be dealt with within 10 days. This also holds true for the Aarhus Regulation, where a request for internal review can be filed within eight weeks of the adoption of the act or the date on which the act should have been adopted and the institution or body having adopted the act has the obligation to reply within 16 or a maximum of 22 weeks.[50]

V. Concluding Remarks

The Aarhus Convention has certainly provided a new perspective to apply the different rules on administrative review already existing in the contracting parties. Still, when employed in environmental law, and when they become subject to the principles and guarantees set forth in the Aarhus Convention, administrative appeals show their limits. Moreover, the idea that an administrative review system, as sophisticated as it may be, can replace the courts entirely does not seem to be acceptable, given the general principle, also observed in those countries that are not (yet) EU Member States, according to which all measures having legal effects have to be subject to judicial review, including then also decisions taken to uphold or reject an administrative appeal.[51] An example in this regard is offered by the internal review mechanism under the Aarhus Regulation, which is admittedly based on a quite specific system of administrative review, conceived as an element to ensure the respect for environmental legislation, which, however, has, as a last step, an application for annulment against the reply to the request for review according to Article 12 of that Regulation. This is why the most promising perspective of administrative appeals lies in the definition of its interplay with judicial review. Undisputedly, many legislative changes are possible in this regard, in particular as regards the conditions of admissibility of the administrative appeal, which should be shaped on the basis of the principle that access to justice in environmental matters has to be construed widely.

[50] Aarhus Regulation, art 10(2) and (3).

[51] As regards judicial protection in the EU, see the seminal judgment of the Court of Justice in Case C-294/83 *Les Verts v Parliament*, ECLI:EU:C:1986:166, [1986] ECR 1986-01339, para 27.

11

A Comparative Perspective on Environmental Access to Justice in the Balkans

The Role of Europeanisation and the Rising Importance of Rights

ROBERTO CARANTA AND BOJANA TODOROVIĆ

I. Introduction

As the EU is party to the Aarhus Convention, access to justice in environmental matters presents a peculiar amphibious character in the EU. On the one hand, the Convention applies to the EU institutions and bodies. Therefore, the Aarhus Regulation was adopted, and later amended, to implement the Aarhus Convention in the procedures and actions managed by the EU institutions themselves.[1] On the other hand, under Article 4(2)(e) of the Treaty on the Functioning of the European Union (TFEU), the EU shares with the Member States the competence on the 'environment'. Article 192 TFEU further provides the legal basis to adopt harmonisation measures concerning the environment. However, access to justice refers to procedural matters, such as remedies, which are by default left to the procedural autonomy of the Member State,[2] provided that the principles of equivalence and effective judicial protection are complied with.[3] Still, in many areas of EU law, procedural rules – including rules concerning remedies – have been adopted in the past two decades.[4] However, up until today, the EU has failed to

[1] See now Regulation (EU) 2021/1767 of the European Parliament and of the Council of 6 October 2021 amending Regulation (EC) No 1367/2006 on the application of the provisions of the Aarhus Convention on Access to Information, Public Participation in Decision-Making and Access to Justice in Environmental Matters to Community institutions and bodies [2021] OJ L356. See also Gattinara ch 10 in this volume.

[2] Case C-752/18 *Deutsche Umwelthilfe* ECLI:EU:C:2019:1114, para 38.

[3] Case C-71/14 *East Sussex County Council v Information Commissioner* ECLI:EU:C:2015:656, para 52.

[4] M Scholten (ed), *Research Handbook on the Enforcement of EU Law* (Cheltenham, Edward Elgar, 2023).

adopt a directive on access to justice in environmental matters in the Member States, having to content itself with adopting successive communications[5] and with streamlining access to justice provisions in sectoral legislation.[6]

This tepid approach to the codification or even harmonisation of access to justice rights across the EU leaves room for different and divergent solutions in the EU Member State in the Balkans and a fortiori in those states still working their way towards accession to the EU.[7] Most of the states parties to the Aarhus Convention that have been analysed in this book have adopted general rules on access to justice, normally in their general environmental protection legislation. An exception is Slovenia, which has adopted different access to justice rules in different pieces of legislation implementing specific EU directives.[8]

In this chapter, we will compare the different approaches chosen in the various states covered in this book to the different relevant aspects of access to justice, assessing whether some of them might be inconsistent with the Aarhus Convention and more specifically with the interpretation given by the Court of Justice of the European Union (CJEU) to the EU provisions implementing the Convention.

II. Court Systems

The judicial architecture in the jurisdictions covered in this book varies considerably. Still, environmental litigation against public administration generally belongs to courts having competence in administrative law – but not specifically in environmental law – even if their separation from the ordinary courts may be differently modulated, especially concerning the last instance courts. Occasionally, criminal and civil courts may be involved in environmental cases.[9] Romania has a monist judicial system with specialised chambers for disputes against the administration. What is special is that for disputes against the state, the courts of appeal are competent in the first instance.[10] Albania and North Macedonia instead have specialised administrative courts at first instance and for appeals, but one Supreme Court only.[11] Serbia has an Administrative Court judging in first and normally last instance, as the Supreme Court can be seized on by way of an extraordinary

[5] Commission, 'Notice on access to justice in environmental matters' C/2017/2616 [2017] OJ C275/1. Communication from the Commission to the European Parliament, the Council, the European Economic and Social Committee and the Committee of the Regions, 'Improving access to justice in environmental matters in the EU and its Member States' COM (2020) 643 final.

[6] For example, art 23 of Directive 2012/18/EU of the European Parliament and of the Council of 4 July 2012 on the control of major-accident hazards involving dangerous substances, amending and subsequently repealing Council Directive 96/82/EC Text with EEA relevance (the Seveso III Directive). For a detailed analysis, see Eliantonio and Richelle, ch 1 in this volume, sections III.B.i and III.C.i.

[7] See also Todorović, ch 3 in this volume, section II.B.

[8] Štemberger Brizani, ch 9 in this volume, section III.B.

[9] This is, for example, the case for civil actions to avoid harm to an unspecified number of people: see Drenovak-Ivanović, ch 8 in this volume, sections I.B and IV.B.

[10] Lodoabă-Cordon, Dragos and Neamtu, ch 7 in this volume, section I.

[11] Terihati, ch 4 in this volume, section II; Antonovska Joskoska and Bitrakov, ch 6 in this volume, section I.A (here the Supreme Court has functions of cassation only).

remedy.[12] In Slovenia the Constitutional Court has exclusive competence in judging the legality of regulations and other general acts, including planning measures, while the Administrative Court decides in first and normally last instance disputes with the administration concerning individual decisions.[13]

III. Justiciability and Prior Exhaustion of Administrative Remedies

Both positive decisions and other measures taken by public administrations and their inaction or silence are generally amenable to judicial review.[14] However, changes in the North Macedonian legislation and the consequent case law have deleted the possibility to challenge regulations and other general legal acts – or the omission to adopt them.[15]

In many jurisdictions in the Balkans, recourse to appeals is a precondition to judicial review. In Serbia only final administrative acts may be challenged in courts, and therefore unless a decision is non-appealable, appeals are to be exhausted before launching judicial review procedures.[16] When they are available under the applicable legislation, recourse to appeals is a condition precedent to judicial review in Croatia as well.[17] A request for reconsideration or an administrative appeal is also a precondition to judicial review in Romania, but not in the event that the right of access to information is denied. To avoid dilatory inaction, a deadline is set for the public administration to answer the request or appeal. Moreover, administrative remedies do not limit the scope of the judicial procedure, and the claimant may bring new grounds of review before the courts.[18] In Albania, administrative appeals are foreseen only under specific legislation.[19]

IV. Standing

Different public and private interests may be involved in decisions concerning the environment. That state organs prioritise environmental interests over economic

[12] Drenovak-Ivanović, ch 8 in this volume, section I.A.

[13] Štemberger Brizani, ch 9 in this volume, section I.A; similarly, see Antonovska Joskoska and Bitrakov, ch 6 in this volume, section III.B.iii; V Cucić, 'Serbia as a Part of the European Administrative Space: ADR Tools Applied to Administrative Law' in DC Dragos and B Neamtu (eds), *Alternative Dispute Resolution in European Administrative Law* (Berlin, Springer-Verlag, 2014) 461–62.

[14] See, eg, Terihati, ch 4 in this volume, section IV.B; Antonovska Joskoska and Bitrakov, ch 6 in this volume, section I.B.

[15] Antonovska Joskoska and Bitrakov, ch 6 in this volume, section III.B.iii; the only option open, but of dubious relevance in environmental matters, is a direct action in front of the Constitutional Court.

[16] Drenovak-Ivanović, ch 8 in this volume, section I.B; see also V Cucić, Administrative Appeal in Serbian Law' (2011) 32(E) *Transylvanian Review of Administrative Sciences* 50.

[17] Ofak and Turudić, ch 5 in this volume, section IV.

[18] Lodoabă-Cordon, Dragos and Neamtu, ch 7 in this volume, after n 21.

[19] Terihati, ch 4 in this volume, sections II and, for some instances, V.A.

ones cannot be taken for granted, and this is why the idea of 'environmental democracy' finds its roots in participative democracy directly involving different stakeholders normally rooting for different interests. Environmental litigation is therefore highly polycentric, the decision on who can launch or be part of the judicial process is actually a decision on which interest and rights holders will be able to defend their position as to how environmental law must be applied to any given case – and to identical or similar future cases.[20]

A first distinction concerning standing depends on whether a case concerns the right of access to information rather than a challenge to an official measure or to the inaction of a decision-maker. Under Article 4 of the Aarhus Convention, the right of access can be exercised 'without an interest having to be stated'. Correspondingly, under Article 9(1), anyone having been somehow denied access has the right to challenge the breach of her or his rights.[21] Under Article 9(2), instead, access to courts to challenge other breaches of the Convention, and notably of participation rights, is conditioned either on having a 'sufficient interest' or by maintaining 'impairment of a right'. These alternative and different requirements allow some restrictions to standing, which, however, must be consistent 'with the objective of giving the public concerned wide access to justice within the scope of this Convention'.[22] In this context, a special position is given to environmental non-governmental organisations (ENGOs) as the natural defenders of the environment. The same approach applies to challenges against breaches of domestic environmental rules under Article 9(3) of the Convention.[23] The Aarhus Convention Compliance Committee (ACCC) has indeed clarified that the criteria for standing may not be so strict 'that they effectively bar all or almost all environmental organizations or other members of the public from challenging acts or omissions that contravene national law relating to the environment'.[24] According to the case law of the CJEU, this refers specifically – and somewhat narrowly – to NGOs having as their statutory mission the protection of the environment or of some of its parts.[25] The Albanian courts are among those well aware of the special role played by NGOs in the protection of our natural world and require them to show, based on their acts of incorporation, that they are active in some area connected with the environment while individual claimants have to show some

[20] On the polycentric nature of disputes relating to climate litigation, see A Shams, 'Tempering Great Expectations: The Legitimacy Constraints and the Conflict Function of International Courts in International Climate Litigation' (2023) 32(2) *Review of European Comparative and International Environmental Law* 193.

[21] See further Eliantonio and Richelle, ch 1 in this volume, section II.B.

[22] See ibid section II.C.

[23] For analysis and wider references, see ibid; in Case C-252/22 *Societatea Civilă Profesională de Avocați AB & CD v Consiliul Județean Suceava and Others* ECLI:EU:C:2024:13, the CJEU held that national law has wider discretion in limiting access of the 'public' in cases under art 9(3) of the Aarhus Convention.

[24] See also Communication ACCC/C/2006/18 (Denmark) ECE/MP.PP/2008/5/Add.4, para 29.

[25] Case C-263/08 *Djurgården-Lilla Värtans Miljöskyddsförening v Stockholms kommun genom dess marknämnd* ECLI:EU:C:2009:631, 2009 I-09967; according to the Commission, 'Notice on access to

form of connection with the case, such as the ownership of some land affected by the proposed development.[26]

A. Access to Information Cases

In the EU Member States, standing in cases concerning access to environmental information is specifically regulated under Article 6 of Directive 2003/4/EC.[27] As such, it does not raise major issues in Slovenia[28] or in Croatia, the latter having enshrined the right of access in its Constitution.[29] Even among the Balkan states on the path towards accession, access to information is organised in a way to overcome the usual resistance from public administrations. The Serbian Commissioner for Information of Public Importance is an example of good practice actually reducing the need for recourse to the courts.[30]

However, in Romania the presumption of standing of NGOs has not been properly transposed in the law and parties are required to show actual prejudice even to challenge a refusal of access.[31]

B. Judicial Review Cases

As already recalled, Article 9(2) of the Aarhus Convention allows the parties to choose between a 'sufficient interest' or a 'right'-based standing, while allowing a wider access for non-governmental organisations (NGOs).

In Germany, standing is rights-based and restrictive.[32] Many of the judgments from the CJEU concerned the approach to standing in Germany. The right-based approach is followed in substance if not in name in Slovenia concerning the judicial review of individual decisions. Standing is based on a legal interest, ie, a direct personal benefit based on law or regulation. The pursuit of a general or public interest is not recognised as a legal interest.[33] The situation is different with ENGOs, which are allowed to bring cases in the general or public interest based on

justice' (n 5) para 79, 'it appears permissible for a Member State to require that the protection of the environment constitutes a dominant or substantial objective of an NGO'.

[26] Terihati, ch 4 in this volume, section V.B and the cases covered in section V.D.

[27] Directive 2003/4/EC of the European Parliament and of the Council of 28 January 2003 on public access to environmental information and repealing Council Directive 90/313/EEC; see Eliantonio and Richelle, ch 1 in this volume, section III.A.

[28] Štemberger Brizani, ch 9 in this volume, section IV.

[29] Ofak and Turudić, ch 5 in this volume, section III.

[30] Drenovak-Ivanović, ch 8 in this volume, section III.B.i.

[31] Lodoabă-Cordon, Dragos and Neamtu, ch 7 in this volume, n 29.

[32] See B Müller, 'The Aarhus Convention, the Legal Cultural Picture: Country Report for Germany' in R Caranta, A Gerbrandy and B Müller (eds), *The Making of a New European Legal Culture: The Aarhus Convention. At the Crossroads of Comparative Law and EU Law* (Groningen, Europa Law, 2017) 103.

[33] Štemberger Brizani, ch 9 in this volume, section III.B.ii.b.

specific sectoral provisions and – arguably – on a general basis to avoid a breach of EU law.[34] Based on special provisions, standing to challenge building permissions is also granted to citizens' initiatives (a group of 200 inhabitants residing in the municipality where the construction is planned, or in an adjacent municipality).[35]

The exclusive competence of the Slovenian Constitutional Court to hear challenges against normative and general measures, including planning decisions, instead raises numerous issues of consistency with the Aarhus Convention insofar as the Court does not recognise the *ex lege* standing of NGOs and requires a legal interest to bring the petition.[36] Some of these concerns are somewhat mitigated by the fact that the Court treats violation of:

> [T]he prescribed procedure for public participation (in the adoption of spatial planning acts) as a direct contravention of the constitutionally protected right in the management of public affairs under Art 44 of the Constitution, and consequently recognises the existence of legal interest to any legal and natural persons, including NGOs, alleging a violation of the statutory provisions on public participation.[37]

The stricter right-based approach may in principle be relaxed when a right to a healthy environment is enshrined in the Constitution or can be deduced from the highest law of the land.[38] An interesting example is Croatia. In 2001 the mentioning of the environment was deleted from the 'right to a healthy life and environment' recognised in Article 69 of the Constitution. However, a fundamental 2023 judgment of the Constitutional Court held that the right to a healthy environment is to be considered to be implied under the constitutional provision just mentioned.[39] Still, this has yet to be translated into a more generous standing in environmental matters. Instead, the Environmental Protection Act is more restrictive than the general rules on locus standi and requires prior participation to the administrative procedure, including possible appeals, and proof of impairment of a right due to the location or nature of the authorised development.[40] The criteria for NGOs (ie, associations) for initiating the administrative dispute are prescribed by Article 167(2) of the Environmental Protection Act, which requires that: (a) they have the protection of human health and the environment as a goal in their statute; and (b) have been registered in accordance with special regulations governing

[34] Case C-664/15 *Protect Natur-, Arten- und Landschaftsschutz Umweltorganisation v Bezirkshauptmannschaft Gmünd*, ECLI:EU:C:2017:987, para 45.

[35] Štemberger Brizani, ch 9 in this volume, section III.B.ii.b.

[36] ibid sections III.B.ii.a and IV.

[37] ibid.

[38] In the future, this highest law framework might be provided by the ECHR: C Plaza, 'The Impact of the Right of Access to Justice under the Aarhus Convention on the Greening of the European Court of Human Rights' (Chapter 2) in this volume, section 2.

[39] Ofak and Turudić, ch 5 in this volume, section I.

[40] ibid, section IV, rightly arguing that the requirement of prior participation to the administrative phase is inconsistent with Case C-826/18 *Stichting Varkens in Nood and Others v College van burgemeester en wethouders van de gemeente Echt-Susteren* ECLI:EU:C:2021:7. Similarly, see Drenovak-Ivanović, ch 8 in this volume, section IV.

associations for at least two years, during which they actively participated in environment related activities.[41] The choice to limit standing to NGOs specifically focused on the protection of the environment has been recently upheld by the Court of Justice in *Societatea Civilă Profesională de Avocaţi AB & CD*.[42]

The right to a healthy environment is also protected in Article 43 of the Constitution of North Macedonia.[43] However, in North Macedonia a more generous approach to standing, including for NGOs, is deduced from the legislative rules implementing the Aarhus Convention rather than from the Constitution. Therefore, unlike what is provided generally for association, ENGOs do not need to prove that a right or interest of their members has been breached to be granted standing.[44] In Romania too, the right of every individual to a healthy and ecologically balanced environment is spelt out in the legislation.[45] Moreover, the sole requirement in the legislation for an NGO to obtain standing is to explicitly state in its charter that environmental protection is its core mission, as NGOs act to represent natural persons' rights and legitimate interests.[46] However, the equally generous general rules on standing are often interpreted in a restrictive way in Romania, most courts not being forthcoming with NGOs acting in the general interest and instead requiring proof that the challenged measures affected some private interest.[47] This approach runs directly counter to the case law of the CJEU having clarified that Member States may confine to individual public law rights the rights whose infringement may be relied upon by an individual, but such a limitation cannot be applied to environmental protection organisations without disregarding the objectives of wide access to justice set by the law with reference to ENGOs.[48]

Unfortunately, it seems that enshrining a right to a healthy environment in the Constitution does not advance the readiness of the concerned national courts to relax their approach on standing. Apparently, the aversion against *action popularis* is so ingrained in the their *mentalité* that judges remain unmoved without normative pressure from outside. The 'weak' formulation of Article 37 of the European Charter of Fundamental Rights means that EU law can hardly be enlisted to increase the binding force of the national provisions discussed above.[49]

[41] Ofak and Turudić, ch 5 in this volume, section IV.

[42] *Societatea Civilă Profesională de Avocaţi AB & CD v Consiliul Judeţean Suceava and Others* (n 23); the CJEU found it acceptable that the applicants in the domestic case, a law firm without legal personality and no direct interest in the measures challenged, were denied standing.

[43] Antonovska Joskoska and Bitrakov, ch 6 in this volume, section III.A.

[44] ibid section III.B.iv.

[45] See, with reference to art 5 of GEO No 195/2005, Lodoabă-Cordon, Dragos and Neamtu, ch 7 in this volume, start of section IV.D.

[46] ibid.

[47] ibid last part of section IV.D.

[48] Case C-115/09 *Bund für Umwelt und Naturschutz Deutschland, Landesverband Nordrhein-Westfalen eV v Bezirksregierung Arnsberg* ECLI:EU:C:2011:289, 2011 I-03673.

[49] Article 37 of the Charter does not explicitly spell out a right to the clean or healthy environment, betraying a compromise among the Member States aimed at avoiding granting any substantive right

Finally, Serbia is simply requiring an interest and is ready to award standing to 'representatives of collective interests' and to 'representatives of wider interests of the public authorised by a special law'.[50] The obstacles instead lie in the possibility to participate in administrative proceedings as a number of special statutes do not provide for this possibility and – inconsistently with the case law of the CJEU[51] – participation is a condition precedent to the possibility of challenging the measure taken.[52]

V. Intensity of Review (and Expertise)

Article 9(2) of the Aarhus Convention provides for 'substantive and procedural legality'. The big issue is what is the standard of review required by the reference to 'substantive legality'?[53] It is hoped that a very clear answer to this question will come from the ACCC following a communication concerning the intensity of review in England and Wales, Scotland, and Northern Ireland.[54]

For its part, the CJEU has held that national review procedures must allow the competent court or tribunal 'to apply effectively the relevant principles and rules of EU law'.[55] In an infringement procedure, it confirmed that judicial review cannot be limited to the case of total absence of a required environmental impact assessment (EIA).[56] On the contrary, it must be possible to challenge the 'irregularity' of the EIA.[57]

Folk concerned the compatibility of an authorisation for the operation of the hydroelectric power plan with Directive 2000/60/EC (the Water Framework Directive). The CJEU held that a national court is to:

> [R]eview whether the authority which issued the authorisation complied with the conditions laid down in Article 4(7)(a) to (d) of that directive, by determining, first, whether all practicable steps were taken to mitigate the adverse impact of the activities on the status of the body of water concerned; second, whether the reasons behind those activities were specifically set out and explained; third, whether those activities serve an overriding general interest and/or the benefits to the environment and society linked to

in this area: see E Morgera and G Marín Durán, 'Article 37 – Environmental Protection' in S Peers, T Hervey, J Kenner and A Ward (eds), *The EU Charter of Fundamental Rights: A Commentary*, 2nd edn (Oxford, Hart Publishing/Beck, 2021) 1048.

[50] Drenovak-Ivanović, ch 8 in this volume, sections I.B and IV.A.

[51] Case C-826/18 *Stichting Varkens in Nood and Others v College van burgemeester en wethouders van de gemeente Echt-Susteren* ECLI:EU:C:2021:7, [2021].

[52] Drenovak-Ivanović, ch 8 in this volume, section IV.A.

[53] Eliantonio and Richelle, ch 1 in this volume, section III.B.iii.

[54] https://unece.org/env/pp/cc/accc.c.2017.156_united-kingdom, pending since 2017.

[55] *East Sussex* (n 3) para 58; see also Commission, 'Notice on access to justice' (n 5) s 3.3.1.

[56] Case C-137/14 *Commission v Germany* ECLI:EU:C:2015:683; the CJEU refers to Case C-72/12 *Gemeinde Altrip* ECLI:EU:C:2013:712, para 36, and *Bund für Umwelt und Naturschutz Deutschland* (n 48) para 37.

[57] *East Sussex* (n 3) para 47.

> the achievement of the objectives set out in Article 4(1) are outweighed by the benefits to human health, the maintenance of human safety or the sustainable development resulting from those activities; and, fourth, whether the beneficial objectives pursued by that project cannot, for reasons of technical feasibility or disproportionate cost, be achieved by other means which are a significantly better environmental option.[58]

While this seems to stop short of requiring a merits or de novo review, it clearly obliges national courts to go beyond procedural and formal grounds of illegality to address the substance of the legality issues raised by applicants. This is confirmed in *Craeyenest*, where the CJEU held that a national court must be able to verify whether the sampling points to control air quality have been established in accordance with the criteria laid down in the relevant EU law provisions.[59]

Some of the jurisdictions covered in this book fall short of this standard. This is the case in Romania, where the courts seldom look into the facts of the case and refrain from going into the technical aspects of environmental conflicts.[60] The same conclusion is applicable to Slovenia, where the grounds of review may be limited by some specific legislative instruments.[61]

Some jurisdictions where the standard of review appears to be sufficiently intense, like Croatia, might instead be in conflict with the requirements of the Aarhus Convention for a tendency – consistent with the Austrian and German traditional approach embedded in § 39(2) of the Algemeines Verwaltunsverfahrensgesetz[62] and § 46 of the Verwaltungsverfahrensgestetz[63] respectively – to downplay procedural and formal breaches.[64] The CJEU indeed limited this possibility, holding that allowing procedural review only to cases in which the contested decision would have been different without the procedural defect invoked would not be consistent with EU law when:

> [T]he shifting of the burden of proof onto the person bringing the action, in accordance with national law, for the application of the condition of causality, is capable of making the exercise of the rights conferred on that person by that directive excessively difficult, especially having regard to the complexity of the procedures in question and the technical nature of environmental impact assessments.[65]

[58] Case C-529/15 *Folk* ECLI:EU:C:2017:419, para 37; the Court refers to Case C-43/10 *Nomarchiaki Aftodioikisi Aitoloakarnanias and Others* ECLI:EU:C:2012:560, para 67.

[59] Case C-723/17 *Lies Craeynest and Others v Brussels Hoofdstedelijk Gewest and Brussels Instituut voor Milieubeheer* ECLI:EU:C:2019:533.

[60] Lodoabă-Cordon, Dragos and Neamtu, ch 7 in this volume, beginning of section V.

[61] Štemberger Brizani, ch 9 in this volume, section III.B.ii.b.

[62] See S Storr, 'Administrative Procedure and Judicial Review in Austria' in G della Cananea and M Andenas (eds), *Judicial Review of Administration in Europe. Procedural Fairness and Propriety* (Oxford, Oxford University Press, 2021) 38 f; this is combined with – and justified by – judicial review at first instance being extended to cover the merits of the challenged administrative decision.

[63] L Weidemann, 'Administrative Procedure and Judicial Review in Germany' in G della Cananea and M Andenas (eds), *Judicial Review of Administration in Europe: Procedural Fairness and Propriety* (Oxford, Oxford University Press, 2021) 55 ff.

[64] See, eg, the Orljava River case as analysed in Ofak and Turudić, ch 5 in this volume, section VI.

[65] Case C-72/12 *Gemeinde Altrip and Others* ECLI:EU:C:2013:712, para 52; see also *Commission v Germany* (n 56) para 59.

Moreover, the more recent judgment in *IL* indicated that judicial review cannot be excluded if the 'irregularity at issue has denied the claimant his or her right, guaranteed to participate in the environmental decision-making process'.[66]

Clearly, the strong cultural influence of the Austrian – and German – legal tradition in many Balkan countries is leading their courts to fall into the same traps that have already been met with disapproval by the CJEU.

Another issue is that review on the substance of environmental decisions requires technical expertise.[67] However, some courts in the Balkans are reluctant to rely on experts.[68] In North Macedonia expertise is considered to be incompatible with the short deadlines set to Administrative Courts for deciding their cases, including those concerning the environment.[69] This means that the courts rely on the expertise of the administration, which in many cases is actually the expertise of the private developer of the project.[70] Moreover, in Romania there is limited expertise, normally hired by developers, and this raises the spectre of a conflict of interest.[71] Albania stands out as an exception, as a number of cases have been reported in which the parties or the court itself could rely on expertise.[72]

While the CJEU has not yet had the occasion to clarify what roles experts should play, this is an area in which judges and ENGOs clearly need both guidance and support.[73]

VI. Remedies

Interim relief in the form of the suspension of the challenged measure is generally available. This is the case, for instance, in Romania[74] and Slovenia.[75] In Albania, an application for interim relief must be based on written evidence of irreparable harm – a requirement possibly derived from commercial disputes and ill-suited to

[66] Case C-535/18 *IL and Others v Land Nordrhein-Westfalen* ECLI:EU:C:2020:391.

[67] See the contributions collected by M Eliantonio, E Lees and T Palonitty (eds), *EU Environmental Principles and Scientific Uncertainty before National Courts: The Case of the Habitats Directive* (Oxford, Hart Publishing, 2023).

[68] Štemberger Brizani, ch 9 in this volume, section III.B.ii.a.

[69] Antonovska Joskoska and Bitrakov, ch 6 in this volume, section III.B.iii.

[70] D Dragos and B Neamtu, 'The Habitats Directive in the Romanian Courts: Procedure vs Substance' in Eliantonio, Lees and Paloniitty (n 67).

[71] Lodoabă-Cordon, Dragos and Neamtu, ch 7 in this volume, sections VI and VII.

[72] Terihati, ch 4 in this volume, sections V.B, V.D.v ff.

[73] It does not help that the EU courts themselves are very shy on relying on experts and have yet to clarify which tools they want to use to address the review of complex scientific decisions and measures: M Eliantonio and M Krajewski, 'Scientific Uncertainty before the Court of Justice and the General Court: Is the Judicial Toolbox Sufficient?' in Eliantonio, Lees and Paloniitty (n 67) 327.

[74] Lodoabă-Cordon, Dragos and Neamtu, ch 7 in this volume, section V.

[75] Štemberger Brizani, ch 9 in this volume, section III.B.ii.b. *cf* Serbian law: Z Tomić, *Komentar Zakona o upravnim sporovima sa sudskom praksom* (*Commentary of the Law on Administrative Disputes with Case Law*) (Belgrade, Official Journal of the Republic of Serbia, 2012) 450–78.

environmental litigation – and needs to show that the public interest is not harmed by the granting of interim relief. In addition, the court has the discretion to impose a cross-undertaking for damages.[76]

In Romania, besides annulment, courts are empowered to issue orders to the public administration to the effect that a specific action is undertaken.[77] In Slovenia the Administrative Court may order the release of information, but it tends to simply annul the unlawful refusal and to refer the applicant back to the public administration.[78]

A most interesting approach is the one of North Macedonia. Administrative courts are under the duty to decide on the merits of the case unless the facts need to be ascertained or the decision-maker enjoys some measure of discretion.[79] This is normally the case with environmental disputes.[80] Croatia fully follows the German tradition of primary *Rechtsschutz* by providing not just for annulment but also for substitutive remedies allowing the administrative court to take decisions and to perform actions in lieu of the public administration insofar as no discretion was granted to the responsible authority.[81]

The latter approach is arguably required by the case law of the CJEU in *Lies Craeynest*, a case concerning sampling points under Directive 2008/50/EC on air quality. The Court held that the national court also has to have 'jurisdiction to take all necessary measures in respect of the national authority concerned, such as an order, to ensure that such points are sited in accordance with the criteria laid down in that directive'.[82]

Concerning damages, these are normally not available to NGOs bringing cases in the public interest. This is the case, for instance, in Romania.[83]

Finally, in Romania fines against public officials, including fines of a criminal nature, are foreseen to prod compliance with court decisions.[84]

VII. Times and Costs

Delays in deciding about environmental cases are widespread and are normally part of a wider problem of judicial timeliness.[85] In Romania, delays also affect

[76] Terihati, ch 4 in this volume, sections V.B and V.C.
[77] Lodoabă-Cordon, Dragos and Neamtu, ch 7 in this volume, section V.
[78] Štemberger Brizani, ch 9 in this volume, section III.B.i.b.
[79] Antonovska Joskoska and Bitrakov, ch 6 in this volume, section I.B. A similar legislative solution exists in Serbia: V Cucić, *Upravni spor pune jurisdikcije: Modeli i vrste* (*Administrative Dispute of Full Jurisdiction: Models and Types*) (Belgrade, University of Belgrade Faculty of Law, 2016) 245–301.
[80] Antonovska Joskoska and Bitrakov, ch 6 in this volume, section III.B.iii.
[81] Ofak and Turudić, ch 5 in this volume, section IV.
[82] See Case C-723/17 *Lies Craeynest* ECLI:EU:C:2019:533, para 53.
[83] Lodoabă-Cordon, Dragos and Neamtu, ch 7 in this volume, section V.
[84] ibid section VI.
[85] See, eg, Terihati, ch 4 in this volume, section V.C.

interim relief and discourage environmental litigants, including ENGOs.[86] North Macedonia seems to be an exception as a term of a maximum of nine months is set for administrative courts to dispose of their cases, but this discourages courts to go deep into the substance of the case.[87] Reciprocally, in Slovenia, extending the review to procedural and formal breaches leads to longer times in adjudicating environmental disputes.[88]

In Romania, litigation about the right of access to information is free of court fees and must be dealt with expeditiously.[89] Generally fees and local costs are not very high in the Balkans, especially compared with Western Europe (not to talk of England and Wales).[90] Still, the practice of the Romanian courts not to use their discretion to mitigate cost orders against NGOs, thus discouraging litigation, is questionable in the light of Article 9(4) of the Aarhus Convention.[91] Indeed, in the recent *Societatea Civilă Profesională de Avocaţi AB & CD* case, originating from a preliminary reference from Romania, the CJEU held that:

> [I]n order to ensure compliance with the requirement that judicial proceedings not be prohibitively expensive, a court called upon to make an order for costs against an unsuccessful party in an environmental dispute must take into account all the circumstances of the case, including that party's interest and the public interest in the protection of the environment.[92]

Legal aid is not normally available to NGOs, but this is not so in Slovenia.[93] In Serbia it is the Environmental Law Clinic at the University of Belgrade Faculty of Law that provides free legal support, including general legal information (ie, educating ENGOs).[94]

Costs for technical expertise are an issue in Albania[95] and in Romania, where high costs are not compensated by the limited legal aid available to individuals, which is not even available to ENGOs.[96] This is not consistent with the CJEU case law, including the costs of evidence and experts' fees under the requirements of 'not prohibitively expensive' spelt out in Article 9(4) of the Aarhus Convention.[97] The reluctance of courts to rely on experts cannot be considered an appropriate solution.[98]

[86] Lodoabă-Cordon, Dragos and Neamtu, ch 7 in this volume, section V.
[87] Antonovska Joskoska and Bitrakov, ch 6 in this volume, section I.B.
[88] Štemberger Brizani, ch 9 in this volume, section III.b.ii.b.
[89] Lodoabă-Cordon, Dragos and Neamtu, ch 7 in this volume, section IV.A.
[90] See, eg, Terihati, ch 4 in this volume, section VII; Antonovska Joskoska and Bitrakov, ch 6 in this volume, section III.B.iv.
[91] Lodoabă-Cordon, Dragos and Neamtu, ch 7 in this volume, section IV.E.
[92] *Societatea Civilă Profesională de Avocaţi AB & CD* (n 23) para 83.
[93] Štemberger Brizani, ch 9 in this volume, section III.b.ii.b.
[94] Drenovak-Ivanović, ch 8 in this volume, section III.B.iii.
[95] Terihati, ch 4 in this volume, section VII.
[96] Lodoabă-Cordon, Dragos and Neamtu, ch 7 in this volume, section IV.E.
[97] Case C-427/07 *Commission v Ireland* ECLI:EU:C:2009:457, 2009 I-06277, para 92.
[98] Štemberger Brizani, ch 9 in this volume, section III.B.ii.a.

VIII. Conclusions

The picture presented in the country analyses collected in this book is one of both light and shadows. Still, in drawing conclusions regarding the success (or the lack thereof) of the observed countries in the implementation of the third pillar of the Aarhus Convention, we should be mindful of the fact that it is precisely this provision of the Convention that 'results in increasing number of legal disputes concerning the way this pillar is implemented both at the national and at the EU level'.[99] Moreover, one should bear in mind the contextual framework in which this provision is being operationalised, as well as the different status observed countries have vis-a-vis the EU.

Situations in which the approach of some national courts is inconsistent with both the Aarhus Convention and the case law of the CJEU have already been pointed out in the preceding pages. It was also noted that the Austrian tradition shared by many Balkan countries is not helping compliance with the rules on standing and on the standard of review (the assessment is different concerning transparency).[100]

It is now the time to criticise what to us seems a widespread – but not general – tendency of the many courts in the Balkans to pile up obstacles to judicial review of environmental decisions. Courts in the Balkans often do not engage directly with the Aarhus Convention[101] – or with the EU law sources implementing it – being instead focused on possibly unlawful domestic sources.[102] This is especially daunting given that all of the observed countries ratified the Aarhus Convention and in the majority of cases, national institutions (including courts) are obliged to directly apply its provisions as per the principle of monism governing the relationship between national and international law.[103] It is difficult to say whether this is a pattern of a wider tendency to protect official decision-making or of an uneasiness to deal with polycentric disputes that go beyond traditional litigation involving two parties and include conflicts between the 'ostensible' standard bearer of the general interest and ENGOs that care about the environment more than the state authorities. Considering various plausible explanations for this phenomenon, Ofak raises the question of whether the provisions of the Convention itself might

[99] J Jendrośka, 'Access to Justice in the Aarhus Convention: Genesis, Legislative History and Overview of the Main Interpretation Dilemmas' (2020) 17(4) *Journal for European Environmental & Planning Law* 372, 373.

[100] Lodoabă-Cordon, Dragos and Neamtu, ch 7 in this volume, section V.

[101] But see L Ofak, 'Application of the Aarhus Convention in Southeast Europe' in S Rodin and T Perišin (eds), *Judicial Application of International Law in Southeast Europe* (Berlin, Springer, 2015) 43, 53–54, 57–59 and 60–61; See also Terihati, ch 4 in this volume, sections IV and V.D; Lodoabă-Cordon, Dragos and Neamtu, ch 7 in this volume, section IV.C and Todorović, ch 3 in this volume, section III.B.

[102] Ofak and Turudić, ch 5 in this volume, sections VI and VII.

[103] Ofak (n 101) 49.

be overly 'vague' and do not offer enough 'clarity' for the national courts to apply them directly.[104] She also notices that:

> [T]he Parties [to the Aarhus Convention] have the duty to adopt detailed provisions in their legislation to allow the implementation of the Convention. Therefore, direct application of the Convention by the national authorities may not be enough to fulfil the obligations that the Parties have undertaken.[105]

Moreover, for the countries on the EU accession path, the same author reminds us that 'implementation of the Aarhus Convention was part of … a process of harmonisation with EU law', which means that 'in situations where the provisions of the Aarhus Convention are relevant to the merits of the case, the courts will apply the corresponding norms of domestic legislation rather than the provisions of an international treaty'.[106]

Whatever the reason, and while the EU's failure to pass an access to justice directive implementing Article 9(2) and (3) of the Aarhus Convention does not help, that attitude is clearly inconsistent with the principle and right to effective judicial protection now enshrined in Article 47 of the Charter of Fundamental Rights,[107] which is featuring more and more frequently in the environmental case law of the CJEU.[108]

The already recalled *Lies Craeynest* case provides a good illustration of what is required from national courts both in terms of the standard of judicial review and concerning the remedies that must be available.[109] The CJEU held that while the choice of the location of sampling points under the Air Quality Directive 'requires technical and complex assessments, the discretion of the competent national authorities is limited by the purpose and objectives pursued by the relevant rules in this respect'.[110] Moreover, as already indicated, the CJEU held that national courts need to have 'the jurisdiction to take all necessary measures in respect of the national authority concerned, such as an order, to ensure that such points are sited in accordance with the criteria laid down in that directive'.[111] What is specifically relevant here is that, while recalling the national procedural autonomy of the Member State, the CJEU stressed that the national rules 'must not be less favourable

[104] ibid 50–51. See also ch 1 in this volume, section I.
[105] Ofak (n 101) 50.
[106] ibid 52.
[107] And in some case also with the principle of equivalence: see Ofak and Turudić, ch 5 in this volume, section IV.
[108] See the discussion in ch 1 in this book; see also M. Eliantonio 'The Relationship between EU Secondary Rules and the Principles of Effectiveness and Effective Judicial Protection in Environmental Matters: Towards a New Dawn for the "Language of Rights"?' 12(2) 2019 *Review of European Administrative Law* 95; I Hadjiyianni, 'Judicial Protection and the Environment in the EU Legal Order: Missing Pieces for a Complete Puzzle of Legal Remedies' (2021) 58 *Common Market Law Review* 1; I Hadjiyianni, 'Multi-level Governance in Action: Access to Justice in Light of the Aarhus Convention and its Implementation in the EU Legal Order' (2020) 26(4) *European Public Law* 889.
[109] *Lies Craeynest* (n 82).
[110] ibid para 52.
[111] ibid para 53.

than those governing similar domestic situations (principle of equivalence) and must not make it impossible in practice or excessively difficult to exercise rights conferred by EU law (principle of effectiveness)'. Concerning the latter, the Court recalled that 'the right to an effective remedy and to a fair trial is enshrined in Article 47 of the Charter of Fundamental Rights of the European Union, which constitutes a reaffirmation of the principle of effective judicial protection'.[112]

The low level of engagement of many of the courts in the Balkans with the Aarhus Convention compares unfavourably with the much wider openness of specialised institutions, such as the Serbian Commissioner for Information of Public Importance, who often refers to the case law of the European Court of Human Rights.[113] In a similar vein and through engaging in various forms of action – not least through litigation – environmental activists in the region not only exert pressure on national authorities to comply with national and EU law, but also with the procedural requirements stemming from the Aarhus Convention. Additionally, they frequently criticise the EU institutions for their inconsistencies in the enlargement process, as well as for turning a blind eye to instances in which its own environmental access to justice standards are being violated and/or downplayed in practice, thereby further demonstrating that civil society actors are an important piece of the implementation puzzle.[114]

It the end, we return to the main research question that has prompted writing this book – namely, whether, despite all of the national differences both at the normative and practical levels, it is possible to talk about the Europeanisation of environmental access to justice in the observed countries and what role it plays in enabling environmental democracy in the Balkans.

Relying on the insights from both the national and the transversal chapters, it is possible to not only answer in the affirmative, but also safely say that this role is substantial. However, it is necessary to be mindful of the differences between the impact of the various 'faces' of that Europeanisation.[115] The EU – through its legislative and policy instruments and CJEU case law – has traditionally played an immense role in shaping the legislative frameworks and practice of both Member States and candidate countries. This is well illustrated by the Romanian example, where, despite the fact that this country was among the early signatories of the Aarhus Convention, it 'came to life' only with a credible outlook of membership in the EU and the requirement to ensure full alignment with the environmental *acquis*.[116] This corresponds to the observation made by Eliantonio and Richelle in Chapter 1:

> [T]he package of EU (hard and soft) measures designed to implement the Aarhus requirements in EU law insofar as the law of the Member States is concerned have

[112] ibid para 54.
[113] Drenovak-Ivanović, ch 8 in this volume, section III.B.i.
[114] Todorović, ch 3 in this volume, sections II.A and III.
[115] Todorović and Caranta, Introduction in this volume, n 64.
[116] Lodoabă-Cordon, Dragos and Neamtu, ch 7 in this volume, sections II and III. *cf* Štemberger Brizani, ch 9 in this volume, sections III and IV.

> doubtlessly made, together with the case law of the CJEU interpreting the Convention and these EU measures, a significant contribution towards guaranteeing access to justice before Member States' courts.[117]

Likewise, the process of embedding Aarhus standards in national legislative frameworks in the candidate countries has been inextricably enmeshed with the accession process via EU conditionality instruments.[118] The intensity of the 'EU factor' in candidate countries is mirrored in, for instance, the fact that one of the determining factors for the '[f]urther development of Serbian environmental law was the … harmonisation of Serbian legislation with EU legal standards in the field of environmental protection'.[119] While this observation merits further research, it is possible that the painfully slow pace of development of the North Macedonian accession negotiations diluted the effect of the 'EU factor', since '[t]he impacts of [the] EU's action, such as the … aid provided to CSOs for their efforts to bring the Convention closer to the citizens, are limited'.[120]

Thus, the EU has been the defining factor in the (at least formal) implementation of the Aarhus Convention access to justice standards in both Member States and the candidate countries. This holds true despite the lack of uniformity at the EU level and the fact that standards arising out of Article 9 of the Aarhus Convention leave 'room for manoeuvre' (and, by default, 'inconsistencies with EU law') to Member States, especially given that the third limb of this provision did not materialise in a self-standing EU legislative act. The CJEU's 'purposive interpretation of the Convention'[121] and the Commission's watchdog role create a 'protective layer' which provides a guarantee to citizens and their organisations that potential flawed transposition, ie, implementation of the requirements stemming from the Aarhus Convention, will be corrected – even if that takes time. This is where we see a considerable difference between the 'EU effect' on the Member States and the candidate countries, where such a 'protective layer' is not available.[122] What is more, the lack of political consensus for surpassing the status quo with respect to the transposition of Article 9(3) of the Aarhus Convention along with the 'layered' system of protection and a differentiated (and potentially stricter but also more confusing) set of obligations for the legal systems belonging to the EU[123] act as a cautionary tale to prospective members to prioritise the clarity and coherence of available legal pathways over their cumulation in the process of (further) harmonisation with EU law.[124]

[117] Eliantonio and Richelle, ch 1 in this volume, section IV.
[118] Todorović, ch 3 in this volume, section II.B.
[119] Drenovak-Ivanović, ch 8 in this volume, section III.A.
[120] Todorović and Caranta, Introduction in this volume, section III; Antonovska Joskoska and Bitrakov, ch 6 in this volume, section IV.
[121] Eliantonio and Richelle, ch 1 in this volume, section IV.
[122] Todorović, ch 3 in this volume, section II.A.
[123] Eliantonio and Richelle, ch 1 in this volume, section IV.
[124] *cf* Ofak and Turudić, ch 5 in this volume, sections V and VII; Lodoabă-Cordon, Dragos and Neamtu, ch 7 in this volume, section IV; and Štemberger Brizani, ch 9 in this volume, section IV.

Behind the curtain of the debate on (in)consistent, (in)complete and (in) adequate legislative alignment with the stringent access to justice requirements lies a more serious problem that relates to their implementation in practice, which, as we have seen in the national chapters, is far from stellar. This brings us to another aspect in which two different Europeanisation limbs interact and exert influence, albeit in different 'directions' – the EU, as a *top-down* impetus, and the growing environmental activism of civil society actors, exerting *bottom-up* pressure. As was shown in Chapter 3, the role of the EU in this realm is complex and even somewhat controversial. On the one hand, not only is it 'thanks to EU law and policy instruments that environmental issues have been placed higher up on the agenda in both current Member States and candidate countries', but it also enabled the development of a more vigorous civil society in the region.[125] On the other hand, the *top-down* and *bottom-up* Europeanisation 'forces' collide on the terrain of conflicting (environmental and economic) interests. In such cases, civil society actors appear to be a Europeanisation 'force to be reckoned with', especially with respect to the proven ability of cross-border mobilisation for the realisation of regional and/or international activities, making 'top-down Europeanisation appear rather modest, meagre or only superfluous'.[126]

Finally, the influence of the CoE system in the explored realm is less prominent than that of the EU, which is understandable given the boundaries of the competences of the ECtHR and the disparity in the logics behind the Aarhus Convention and the ECHR.[127] Still, the Strasbourg Europeanisation framework paves the way towards not only strengthening procedural environmental rights even for countries that are not signatories to the Aarhus Convention[128] – and a fortiori to an even greater extent in the ones that are – but also for the progressive creation of a substantive, self-standing right to a 'clean, healthy and sustainable environment'. While the path to the materialisation of such a right in a legally binding act at the international level is as much a political/diplomatic tug of war as it is a matter of international (environmental) *law* and the road ahead is long and unpredictable, even the small steps taken in that direction are significant – all the more so given the negative European trends of 'repression and criminalization' of environmental defenders and their activities highlighted in the Position Paper of the UN Special Rapporteur on Environmental Defenders under the Aarhus Convention.[129] National courts have also been recognised as 'significantly contributing' to that trend.[130] Seeing how the judiciary plays a 'crucial role in upholding justice and

[125] Todorović, ch 3 in this volume, sections I.A and III.A.
[126] ibid section IV.
[127] Plaza, ch 2 in this volume, sections II and III.C.
[128] Which the cases against Turkey have shown us – see ibid, section I.
[129] M Frost, UN Special Rapporteur on Environmental Defenders, 'State Repression of Environmental Protest and Civil Disobedience: A Major Threat to Human Rights and Democracy' (2024), https://unece.org/climate-change/press/un-special-rapporteur-environmental-defenders-under-aarhus-convention-releases.
[130] ibid 16.

the rule of law',[131] it is important to consider the ways in which it can be further encouraged to engage more frequently and directly with the Aarhus Convention and the standards it promotes. It appears that national experts in this book speak in a unison voice when they highlight further *education* and *specialisation* in the environmental realm as key factors that would contribute to that end. The positive and, to a certain extent, pioneering examples flagged in the national chapters provide a good (role) model.

[131] ibid.

INDEX

www.ingramcontent.com/pod-product-compliance
Ingram Content Group UK Ltd.
Pitfield, Milton Keynes, MK11 3LW, UK
UKHW020249290926
15470UKWH00002B/820